D0721951

# Reproducing Sectarianism

# Reproducing Sectarianism

*Advocacy Networks and the*
*Politics of Civil Society in Postwar Lebanon*

Paul W. T. Kingston

Published by State University of New York Press, Albany

For information, contact State University of New York Press, Albany, NY
www.sunypress.edu

Production by Eileen Nizer
Marketing by Anne M. Valentine

**Library of Congress Cataloging-in-Publication Data**

Kingston, Paul W. T.
    Reproducing sectarianism : advocacy networks and the politics of civil society in postwar Lebanon / Paul W. T. Kingston.
        p. cm.
    Includes bibliographical references and index.
    ISBN 978-1-4384-4711-7 (alk. paper)
    1. Political participation—Lebanon. 2. Non-governmental organizations—Lebanon. 3. Pressure groups—Lebanon. I. Title.

    JQ1828.A91K56 2013
    322.4095692—dc23                                    2012027406

10 9 8 7 6 5 4 3 2 1

# Contents

# Preface and Acknowledgements

My fascination with Lebanon and its politics has lasted a long time. It was the subject of my first attempt at writing an essay on the Middle East as an undergraduate at the University of Toronto. Later, I had my first opportunity to visit Lebanon in early 1992—just one year after the Syrians coercively brought an end to the Lebanese civil war—as part of my professional duties with the Damascus office of the United Nations Development Programme (UNDP) in Syria, a visit during which I spent much of my spare time traveling around and soaking in the ravaged sights of this war-torn but beautiful country. It was only after I began teaching at the University of Toronto Scarborough (UTSC) that I finally decided to explore more deeply the dynamics of Lebanon's complex political economy. This decision was sparked by my participation in a workshop in the early 1990s sponsored by the Ottawa-based International Development Research Center (IDRC) in which representatives from "civil society" in the Middle East were brought together to meet and network with representatives from "civil society" in Canada. Each Middle East country was represented by spokespeople from a single national NGO coordinating committee—save for the Lebanese delegation that was represented by spokespeople from *two*. While relations between these two Lebanese delegations were cordial and cooperative, clearly there was something there that demanded further examination. My curiosity was peaked, and I have not looked back for over a decade.

I have an infinite number of people and institutions that I need to thank—more than is possible in this short acknowledgement section—but I will do my best to remember those that were of particular importance to me. In Canada, my first word of thanks must go to the Social Sciences and Humanities Research Council of Canada for sponsoring this research in the first place. While completing the book took much longer than they probably would have expected or wanted, this project would never have come to fruition without their crucial support. I would also like to thank my students and colleagues in the Department of Social Sciences at UTSC, the Department of Political Science on the St. George campus, the Near and Middle East Civilization Department (especially Jens Hanssen and Jim Reilly), and those in the International Development Studies program at UTSC—with special thanks to Ken Macdonald for those stimulating conversations, especially with respect to the environmental side of my research, and to Judith Teichman for her academic and moral support in my times of struggle with this project. I am also grateful for the help of a number of research and editorial assistants along the way, including Attiya Ahmad, Ionna Bala, Salwa Maalouf, Caroline Kingston, and more recently Lama Mourad, Begum Uzun, and Carolyn Ursabia, and I would like to devote a special word of thanks to Elinor Bray Collins, who was my original research assistant way back in the mid-1990s and who has been a highly valued and fun companion on my Lebanese journey ever since. There are also several colleagues and friends in Canada who deserve special mention—Minelle Mahtani, Marie Joelle Zahar, Janine Clark, who was kind enough to labor over some of my chapters in their early stages and whose insights have always been invaluable, and Ian Spears, whose conversations (over a beer and a burger!) I always value.

But this was really a project made possible by the help and cooperation of so many within Lebanon itself. Among the most important institutional affiliations to which I owe a debt of gratitude are the Department of Political Science at the American University of Beirut (AUB), where I was based during my sabbatical in 1999; the Near East School of Theology, where I lived during that same sabbatical—a wonderfully hospitable environment for that year; the Center for Arab and Middle East Studies at AUB, with which I was affiliated in 2008 and where I made some terrific contacts—especially Karim Makdisi, Nadia as-Sheikh, Hannes Baumann, and Karin Seyfort; and the Institut francais du Proche-Orient in Beirut, whose library and staff were extremely helpful. I would especially like to thank Elizabeth Picard, whose path I was fortunate enough to cross on several occasions; Karam Karam, whose groundbreaking work on associational politics in postwar Lebanon, in addition to his friendly collegiality and advice, was invaluable; Catherine Le Thomas for her stimulating and enjoyable company; and Myriam Catusse, whose friendly, empathetic, and supportive advice and companionship I greatly appreciated. I would also like to thank Cyclamen Tours for making it possible to regularly escape the confines of Beirut and discover the joys of hiking across Lebanon's beautiful mountains; and the AUB tennis team for keeping me fit, sane, and humbled during my research sabbatical leave in 2008!

To all those activists who gave me lots of their time and put up with my continuous questions as I grappled with the complexities of Lebanese associational and political life, my deepest thanks—especially to Lina Abou

Habib, the late Wadad Chakhtoura, Iqbal Dughan, Mona Khawli, Fadia Kiwan, Linda Matar, Lamia Osseiran, Zoya Rouhana, and Mona Yakan in the field of women's advocacy; Salmon Abbas, Mirvat Abu Khalil, Hala Ashur, Ali Darwish, the late Ricardo Haber, Berj Hatjian, Faisel Izzeddine, Fifi Kallab, Pierre Mouawad, Chris Naylor, Michel Skaff, Clement Zakia, Abdullah Zakia, and Rami Zurayk in the field of environmental advocacy; Nabil Abed, Jahda Abou Khalil, Mohammad Barakat, Mousa Charafeddine, Hyam Fakhoury, Abdullah Ibrahim, Pierre Issa, Nawaf Kabbara, Sylvana Lakkis, Amer Makarem, Adib Nemeh, the team at IRAP, and the team at SESOBEL in the field of disability advocacy; and Leyla Zacharia and Mayla Bahkash for their more general insights into the early postwar dynamics of Lebanese associational life. My biggest hope is that what I have produced here may be of use to their ongoing efforts.

I have too many words of personal thanks than is possible to give. Those whom I cannot forget are Judith Harik, who probably does not remember me, but whose initial facilitation and assistance when I first came to Beirut as a researcher in the summer of 1995 I have not forgotten; the al-Azar family, and especially Rima and Diana, who introduced me to the best of Lebanese hospitality; Lina Abou Habib and Omar Traboulsi, who patiently guided me along the way from the moment I first met them at their Oxfam-UK office in Lebanon to the final stages of my research—their help has been immeasurable; Mirvat Abu Khalil— where do I begin!—without whose assistance this research project would never have gotten off the ground; Youssef Chaitani and his lovely family, whose friendship, open-ended hospitality, and stimulating commentaries on Lebanese political life always enrich my stays in Beirut; Jocelyn Dejong, Tareq Tell, and their two daughters, Tamara and Mariam, whose hospitality and friendship always provided me with an escape from the craziness of life in Beirut—it was certainly my good fortune that these long-standing friends of mine from St. Antony's, Oxford, had made the American University of Beirut their home; Joe and the Helou family for their warm hospitality; Nabil and Sarah Shehadi for their spiritual nourishment; and a special word of thanks and appreciation for two I hold very dear in Beirut: Salma Kojok, for her friendship and companionship; and Denise Badawi, my favorite Arabic instructor, sometime translator, and valued friend. For me, Lebanon will always include Salma and Denise.

Finally, I would like to give special mention to several sets of individuals. I am very grateful for the support of SUNY Press, and in particular, I have greatly appreciated the accommodating approach of their senior editor, Michael Rinella. For their moral support in what has been a long and sometimes difficult journey for me, my thanks as always to all the members of my extended family, especially to Mom, Fred, Liz, and Bex. Finally and most of all, I would like to thank Amal Ghazal. From her hospitality when I stayed with her family in the Beqa, to her fun and insightful companionship while on the interview trail there, to her boundless generosity in reading over countless draft chapters of this book-in-the-making—indeed, for resurrecting this book-in-the-making, I am extremely grateful. Amal may need to work on her ping-pong (!), but she has been an amazing friend and a brilliant analyst of things Lebanese and Middle Eastern. Whatever the faults of this book, its completion and hopefully its contributions would never have seen the light of day without Amal's help. A thousand and one thank-you(s) to her and to all.

# 1

# Advocacy Politics within Weak and Fragmented States

## A Framework for Analysis

Can active and dynamic civil societies make contributions to the strengthening of democratic policies and practices in weak and fragmented states? This is the guiding question in this book on the politics of civil society in postwar Lebanon. After a long fifteen-year period of civil conflict, Lebanon's sectarian democracy—based on a (now) formal power-sharing agreement between its many religious communities and/or confessions—was reestablished in 1991, albeit on the foundations of a precarious state, powerful elite-dominated yet factionalized political networks, and a hegemonic Syrian presence that compromised its sovereignty.[1] Paralleling this reemerging Lebanese state, however, was a resurgent civil society, historically one of the most dynamic within the Middle East region. Among its most active postwar components were several modest but vocal networks of rights-based advocacy associations that maneuvered to make their voices heard in emerging policy debates on socioeconomic and political reconstruction. They critiqued the hegemonic resilience of sectarian political practices, underpinned as they were by the country's confessional, clan, and clientelist political heritages, and called instead for strengthening the country's democratic political heritage through the protection of civil liberties and their promotion within the numerous social policy domains of the state.

This book takes up the analysis of three of these associational advocacy networks within the fields of gender, the environment, and disability. Initially, the efforts of all of these advocacy networks produced significant, if preliminary, institutional reforms and policy successes. These included the introduction of new norms and discourses, the formulation of new laws, the creation of more broadly based policy deliberation institutions that have included within them the participation of civil society actors, and, in some instances, the implementation of new policies and programs, especially within the lower levels or "trenches" of the bureaucracy. Over time, however, it became apparent that these preliminary successes at the policy level have been difficult to sustain and have failed to translate into fundamental changes in institutional practice, let alone shifts in the dominant patterns of state–society relations in postwar Lebanon. Why have opportunities for sustained institutional and policy reform—for which several associational networks within Lebanon's civil society have strongly pushed—been so limited within Lebanon's postwar sectarian democracy? And, in the context of these powerful constraints, where do political opportunities for advocacy lie?

In order to answer these questions, this book uses insights from three distinct conceptual frameworks. The first revolves around the application of "historical institutionalism" with its focus on questions of path-dependency and the challenges of institutional change. The premise here is that Lebanon's sectarian democracy exhibits strong "path-dependent" qualities that create powerful obstacles—both structural and agential—for those within civil and political society interested in strengthening the democratic orientation of its political institutions and policies. Particularly important here is the concept of "feedback"—referring to the political dynamics that emerge to reproduce and reinforce a particular institutional configuration and legacy. It is the thesis of this book that, in the context of Lebanese politics, the broader dynamics of civil society networking—both within and between it and political networks at the elite level—produce powerful system-reproducing mechanisms of feedback.

The second component of the book's conceptual apparatus focuses on the debates that surround the dynamics of "civil society." While accepting the premise that civil society is the realm of associational life separate from the state and the market, this book moves away from theories of civil society that endow it with some kind of coherent, autonomous, and normative importance and move toward defining civil society as an open-ended and disaggregated concept whose coherence and autonomy are highly compromised by the interpenetrations of the market and the state. As a result, the normative significance of civil society is contingent on the socioeconomic and political context within which it exists. In deeply divided societies and polities such as that of Lebanon, not only is civil society likely to be affected by and to reflect these deep sociopolitical divisions, but elements within civil society also are likely to both benefit from and, as a result, work to sustain and reinforce these divisions. In short, belying the assumptions in the democracy and development literature that posit civil society as an agent of democratic reform, I argue that certain actors within Lebanon's civil society are not only privileged by the sectarian social and political order within which they exist but also work to reproduce it over time.

From these two discussions emerges a third—how can one understand the nature of political opportunities for sustained institutional and policy advocacy in the context of such path-dependent dynamics to which elements of civil society also contribute? In the language of historical institutionalism from which the concept of path dependency emerged, how can one unpack the dynamics of "restricted agency"? Complementing the use of civil society as a tool of analysis, this study also adopts the concept of an "associational network"—one that reflects the internal divisions, power asymmetries, and interpenetrations with political society that characterize all civil societies. In short, it is through an analysis of the structure and dynamics of associational advocacy networks in the fields of gender relations, the environment, and disability that we arrive at a more nuanced understanding of restricted agency in deeply divided polities such as that of Lebanon.

But why Lebanon, and why these three case studies? My motivation emanated, first and foremost, from my longstanding (and often bewildered) fascination with its complex politics (see Preface). In that sense, Lebanon selected me. I was also normatively interested in understanding the opportunities and constraints that civil society actors faced when trying to promote an inclusive socioeconomic policy-making process in Lebanon's postwar period. After some preliminary research trips in the mid-1990s, it became clear that some of the most interesting and active subjects of research would be those associational activists within the fields of gender, the environment, and disability. In that sense, my selection of case studies was normatively and empirically driven (rather than "theory driven"). It was also only in the course of the research that *common* patterns, dynamics, and outcomes began to emerge—ones generated by the disadvantaged position of these associational activists vis à vis parallel actors embedded within the country's sectarian political structures.

How this personal history of the selection of case studies and the overall research for this book evolved has important implications for the significance of its findings. Certainly, this book makes some useful empirical contributions to several bodies of academic literature. In the literature on Lebanon, for starters, there are few significant English language studies of its civil society.[2] Nor have comparative studies of civil society in the Middle East region, for the most part, included work on Lebanon.[3] Neither have case studies on Lebanon been incorporated into the broader academic work on civil society politics in post-conflict situations despite Lebanon's paradigmatic status as a post-conflict, deeply divided polity.[4] At the same time, the theoretical contributions and claims of this book are of an important but more modest nature. Because this book focuses on a single country within which are found case studies with similar outcomes, it is difficult to make strong generalizable, middle-range, causal equations that are *directly* applicable to other weak, deeply divided, post-conflict polities. Instead, its main contribution will revolve around its ability to construct what Robert Bates has described as an "analytical narrative" about Lebanon itself. This is defined as a historically informed case study that pays close attention "to stories, accounts, and context" while also maintaining a "close dialogue" with theory.[5] In order to operationalize this approach, I have made two main methodological decisions. The first was to situate the research within Lebanon's rich and complex history—especially as regards the transformation of its state–society relations and the effects this had on associational life over time. The second, motivated by the desire to examine the dynamics of advocacy politics over a longer period, was to stretch the fieldwork out over a ten-year time frame that included numerous short research trips, two year-long sabbatical leaves in 1999 and 2008, and hundreds of open-ended, semi-structured interviews. This opened up the possibility of engaging in hypothesis-guided "process tracing," through which underlying trends in associative action rather than momentary snapshots were revealed.[6] In short, through the construction of an "analytical narrative" by way of "process tracing," it is hoped that this book has produced some "defensible propositions"[7] and "contingent generalizations"[8] that will prove useful when applied to future studies of advocacy politics, not only in Lebanon but also in other deeply divided polities.

What follows in this Introduction is the laying out of the conceptual apparatus within which the subsequent analytical narrative of association-al life and advocacy politics in postwar Lebanon is placed. This threefold conceptual framework begins with a brief examination of the relevant debates in historical institutionalist analysis—especially those revolving around path dependency, feedback mechanisms, and restricted agency. It then examines in more detail the contentious debates surrounding the concept of civil society—ones that problematize its use in this study. The third section brings in the complementary concept of associational net-works, actors on which this study will ultimately focus. Having set forth the conceptual apparatus, the rest of the book turns to the construction of its analytical narrative, beginning with a historical institutionalist account of the emergence, consolidation, and reproduction of sectarian democracy in Lebanon, one that sets the scene for the subsequent examination of the postwar politics of advocacy networks, associational life, and civil society in the rest of the book.

## Critical Junctures, Feedback Mechanisms, and Restrictive Agency: Examining the Path-Dependent Nature of Political Life

There is a consensus among those who examine questions of institutional change that political life has a tendency to be path dependent—a concept that points to the difficulty of reversing a particular institutional trajectory once it has been launched.[9] Histories of state formation, for example, are often discontinuous, consisting of "critical junctures"—defined as periods of significant contingency during which particular state forms may emerge[10]—followed by long stretches of institutional continuity. Atul Kohli has written, for example, that "the process of state formation in the developing world has proceeded in a series of "big bangs" with formative moments few and far between."[11] These critical junctures are important because they produce "basic" changes in the nature of political institutions and rules.[12] However, equally important are the "feedback mechanisms" that consolidate and transform these basic changes into institutional legacies that persist over time—ones that are distinct from those factors that produced the critical juncture in the first place. Indeed, Paul Pierson has argued that identifying feedback mechanisms is the key to uncovering the dynamics of path dependency.[13]

A second emerging consensus among scholars of path dependency is the particularly intensity of institutional "stickiness" within political systems where informal political dynamics are powerful and often hegemonic—precisely the features possessed by many of the power-sharing political regimes in the developing world such as that of Lebanon. Jack Knight, for example, describes informal rule dynamics as being tenaciously resilient, even in the face of formal institutional developments.[14] At the root of this resilience are unequal distributions of power that often underpin the political realm, providing the basic resources for processes of reproduction. Informal institutional orders are further strengthened by dynamics of *self*-reinforcement that emerge through the cultivation of a set of "ingrained" expectations among those who must comply with the rules, not unlike the consensual but inequitable dynamics that underlie clientelism.[15] Finally, those benefiting from these informal dynamics also will seek to strengthen them by instrumentalizing the state for their own particularist purposes, transforming it into a de facto "third party enforcer" of informal rules.[16] Indeed, in order to prevent the state from acting as a focal point for collective action or as an ally to those who seek to challenge the institutional status quo,[17] power holders within the prevailing informal institutional order often perform a careful balancing act, capturing the state in order to use it for their purposes while hindering the development of the state by limiting its overall power and scope.[18]

A third general consensus among those who study issues of path dependency within the political realm revolves around the idea that while political systems—particularly those infused with powerful informal dynamics, as is the case with Lebanon—are characterized by a remarkable degree of stability, this institutional "stickiness" is not static but gives rise to possibilities and processes of gradual institutional change. Kohli, for example, suggests that "incremental changes have certainly altered power configurations," even if the process is "rare and tends to be drawn out and complex";[19] Ira Katznelson argues that institutional legacies are "durable but not immutable";[20] and Paul Pierson stresses that "nothing in path-dependent analysis implies that a particular alternative is permanently "locked in" following the move into a self-reinforcing path." Rather, "change continues, but it is bounded change—until something erodes or swamps the mechanisms of reproduction that generate continuity."[21]

So what promotes institutional change within path-dependent institutional environments? While some focus on the possibility of "learning," this study focuses on power struggles. Knight argues, for example, that because many institutional orders are built on significant asymmetries of power, they give rise to considerable contestation over the institutional rules of the game.[22] James Mahoney has similarly written that where political institutions are supported by a small elite, they are susceptible to mass challenges or what he calls "reactive processes" that, over time, can have a transformative, as opposed to a self-reinforcing, effect on institutional arrangements.[23] Ruth and David Collier add a temporal dimension to this debate, suggesting that contestation may be most pronounced at the early stages of a critical juncture where institutions have not yet been consolidated, an idea that dovetails with the interesting hypothesis of Pierson that it is "the first mover" in the aftermath of a critical juncture that can most influence subsequent institutional development.[24] In short, whether the result of processes of institutional contestation or the emergence of an effective "first mover" in an early post-critical juncture stage, path-dependent institutional contexts are dynamic—not hermetically sealed—and give rise to opportunities for the emergence of what Katznelson has called "restricted agency."[25] It is to an analysis of one potential "restricted agent" of institutional change—associational networks that arise out of various segments of civil society—that we turn now.

## Toward a Political Economy Analysis of Civil Society

Civil society is generally defined as the realm that exists between the state, the market, and the individual. This realm is made up of associations and the relationships between them, some of which are formal, others of which are more informal. As a result of the interaction both within and between these associations, norms promoting mutual trust, reciprocity, and a commitment to social and political engagement—what Adam Seligman describes as adding up to "some sense of a shared public"[26]—will begin to strengthen and spread and, if practiced over time, result in the emergence of associative and/or social capital. This social capital, in turn, provides civil society with some degree of collective, autonomous, organizational, and normative influence when interacting with the broader social and political systems.

But what does this associative capital emanating from civil society actually do? The general assumption is that it will promote "the stability and effectiveness of democracy."[27] Indeed, in the latter part of the twentieth and early twenty-first centuries, the belief in the democratic potential of civil society has reached new heights, spawning all sorts of national and international development programs aimed at its "strengthening" and "deepening." Liberal and neoliberal theorists and policy makers alike, for example, have supported the promotion of civil society on the basis of the "neo-Tocquevillian" belief that associations can help revive communities, train effective citizens, reinvigorate the public sphere, limit intrusive bureaucracies, and, hence, promote the consolidation of liberal democracy.[28] Others on the left have articulated an even more expansive set of goals for civil society, transforming it into the foundation "of a new strategic vision" and/or "utopian social project" for a new left that was searching for a transformative project in the face of the collapse of old paradigms. In these versions, civil society became a haven for the growth of counter-hegemonic popular movements that were independent from discredited political parties and separate from the state.[29] Describing the former notion of civil society as being aimed at contributing to effective democratic governance and the latter being aimed at curbing authoritarianism, Michael Edwards and Bob Foley argue that both versions treat civil society as "an autonomous sphere of social power."[30]

Do these expectations concerning the role and potential of civil society correspond on a consistent basis to political reality? John Ehrenburg is skeptical that civil society necessarily possesses either of these capacities. Based on his assessment of civil society in the West, he argues that civil society is often a "minor player" when it comes to the politics of development and democracy, "too weak to seriously contest the effects of inequality." Neither is it clear that civil society necessarily promotes freedom, participation, pluralism, and/or equality, suggesting instead that it may actually do the opposite in certain circumstances. The result, concludes Ehrenburg, is that "civil society cannot automatically be theorized as a democratic sphere."[31] Geoffrey Hawthorn is similarly pessimistic about the importance of civil society in the Global South, arguing that it is "simply mistaken" and "unrealistic to suppose that . . . associations can act to extend the scope and power of public policies to improve the well-being of the majority of the population."[32] Adding to this chorus of skeptics has been Joel Migdal, who is critical of the "lingering assumptions" that surround the concept of civil society, particularly its presumed tendency to generate an integrating normative and/or moral consensus that works to pull all of its diverse associations and interests "in a single direction."[33] Writes Migdal, rather than transcending the social realities in the developing world, ones characterized by social hierarchies, social exclusions, and sharp differences in interests and solidarities, civil societies tend to simply reflect them.[34]

In response to these criticisms, scholars have been hard at work reexamining and re-theorizing their understanding of civil society. Sunil Khilnani, for example, advocates abandoning civil society as a "substantive" and "self-sufficient" category with a determinate set of institutions that throw up "inputs" and "outputs," recommending instead that discussions about civil society and its impact be conditioned by the socioeconomic and political structures that surround it.[35] Omar Encarnacion, in his comparison of the dynamics and influence of civil society in Spain and Brazil, similarly concludes that civil society is a "neutral" actor, constituent of the political context within which its associational actors operate.[36] Finally, describing civil society as the social relations and structures that not only lie between but also are "determined by" the state and the market, Ehrenburg stresses that civil society "can only be grasped by looking at what its constituent structures do, how they are organized, and what political and economic forces are at work—no matter how strenuous some theorists try and describe it as an autonomous sphere of democratic activity."[37]

What follows, therefore, is a general discussion of the ways in which these structural contexts revolving around markets and states can impact the makeup and orientation of civil societies in the developing world. I argue, for example, that the development of civil society is directly linked to processes of social transformation and the penetration of capitalist markets. In the developing world, these processes have been uneven, leading to complex, fluid, and fragmented social structures that combine emerging but weakly delineated class formations with resilient social formations linked to kinship, ethnicity, and religion—what Hawthorne has called "vertical heterogeneities" and "horizontal inequalities."[38] I further argue that processes of state and regime formation have been equally important in structuring dynamics within civil society—heavily influencing the ways in which civil society actors access the resources of the state. A paradoxical feature of weak states, for example, is their tendency to provide elite-based actors with political opportunities to establish and entrench strong and resilient regimes. These, in turn, structure access to the institutions and/or resources of the state in partisan and particularist ways, empowering allies of state power within civil society while disadvantaging opponents. Hence, as a result of the uneven structuring effects of markets, states, and regimes, civil societies are not open playing fields in which all associational actors have universal and institutionalized opportunities. Rather, they consist of structurally advantaged actors that are empowered and act to reproduce the prevailing sociopolitical system as well as structurally disadvantaged actors—"restricted agents" in the words of historical institutionalist theory—that seek to challenge it. Before delving into a discussion of how these structurally disadvantaged actors within civil society attempt to overcome these entrenched constraints on their activities, it is to a more in-depth analysis of the structural context within which they operate that we turn first.

*Community, Class, and Civil Society: Uneven Development and the Fragmentation of Associational Life*

The makeup and dynamics of any given civil society are directly linked to the penetration of capitalist markets and the resultant processes of class formation that these processes unleash. Dietrich Rueschemeyer, Evelyne Stephens, and John Stephens, for example, describe class as the "master key" to understanding the social structuring of interests and power in society.[39] They argue that classes exhibit "central political tendencies"[40] and that class coalitions are "particularly revealing" of how societal complexities work themselves out, particularly with respect to civil society.[41] Paralleling Migdal's critique of the overly optimistic tone of the bulk of civil society literature, they argue that "the political effect of the growth of civil society can only be understood in connection with its articulation with the structure of class power."[42] Laurence Whitehead, likewise, argues that civil society derives many of its special characteristics from "the deeper socio-economic structure and the distribution of interests, social norms and power resources which society embodies."[43] To understand the "variable political functions of civil society," argues Whitehead, we must link them to "a basic theory of socioeconomic transformation."[44]

The nature of class formation within the developing world, however, is uneven and weak, leading to class formations and identities that are porous and fluid rather than rigid and clearly defined. Reuschemeyer and colleagues argue, for example, that the working classes have for the most part been subject to "a whole array of partly contradictory interests,"[45] a problem that they argue is key to explaining "the infrequency of full democracy and in its instability where it did emerge."[46] Neither has the bourgeoisie, which they describe in terms of its "great internal heterogeneity,"[47] been able to fulfill its "historic" role as a primary agent of democratization. Rather, it has acted in more ambiguous ways and has proven to be very susceptible to the hegemonic power of the upper classes.[48] Finally, Rueschemeyer and colleagues argue that ethnic and religious social actors and divisions can hinder the emergence of "counter-hegemonic" class coalitions. On the one hand, they can capture and instrumentalize market forces in such a way as to strengthen rather than weaken their structural position within any given society. At the same time, these same divisions can be used as a "conduit" for upper class hegemony that can penetrate deep into civil society.[49]

What is the impact of these uneven processes of class formation on the development of associational forces within civil society? On the one hand, it must be stressed that there is no exact equation here, there being degrees of "associational slippage," defined as the disjuncture between the level of associational development and the social power that underpins it.[50] Moreover, although linked in general to structural forces in society, the creation of associations within civil society cannot be seen merely as a function of socioeconomic forces alone. Rather, through effective strategies of resource mobilization and collective action, some associational actors may be able to transcend the limitations of their structural position, allowing their associational activities to establish "a dynamic of [their] own . . . outside of the imperatives of economic structures."[51] This helps to explain, for example, the influence of "uncivil" associational actors, those willing to use extortion and violence as a way of promoting their interests.[52] At the same time, there will be other associational actors who will prove unable to take advantage of their structural position within society—some pointing to the educated middle classes within the Middle East region as a prime example.[53]

Nonetheless, understanding processes of social change and class formation in any given national context remains a necessary starting point for any analysis of associational life, one that has several important implications. First, if uneven capitalist penetration produces social structures that are characterized by "vertical heterogeneities" and "horizontal inequalities,"[54] one should expect the formation of civil societies with similar diverse associational characteristics. Second, depending on the degree of inequality and conflict of interest that lies beneath the surface of this diversity, one should also expect relations between civil society's different components to be characterized by significant degrees of associational contestation. This leads to a third important implication for the study of civil societies in the developing world—that they will find it difficult to regulate and/or integrate themselves, leading to situations whereby associational actors within civil society will not only be vulnerable and susceptible to the penetration of social and political forces "from without,"[55] but *they will often call these same external forces into play as a way of bolstering their own associational competitiveness*, a key argument of this book.

Hence, social structures play a crucial role in generating the "varieties of social capital" being promoted by the various components of a given civil society. At the same time, they cannot by themselves explain the overall influence of each of these associational components, let alone how each would choose to use that power. In that sense, they are necessary but insufficient components of the complex civil society equation, leaving unanswered the question of how the social-structural foundations of civil society translate into influence in the political realm. For this, we need to extend our analytical equation to include, first, the structuring effect that states and regimes have on civil societies—one that generates political opportunities for some associational actors while denying them for others—and, second, the ways in which associational actors within civil society take advantage of, or overcome, these differential political opportunity structures through strategic collective action. Before turning to an examination of these latter debates about civil society agency, it is to an examination of the political context that structures this strategic action that we turn now.

*Strong Regimes, Weak States, and Political Opportunity Structures for Civil Society*

States and regime structures have a crucial effect on civil society, influencing the relative strength and influence of its different components. Peter Evans has argued that where effective state institutions exist, they create favorable environments within which more civic-oriented associations can thrive as well as enhance the developmental capacities of states.[56] Similar arguments have been made by Jack Knight and Henry Farrell in their discussion of "an institutional account of trust." Critiquing Robert Putnam's assertion that social capital is the key factor in explaining economic and political success, they argue instead that it is institutions (and the power relations that underpin them) that are the driving forces behind the production of social capital, rather than the other way around.[57] Indeed, in an earlier work, Knight goes further by arguing that the existence of an institutionalized and unified political realm was crucial to the formation

of civic-oriented movements of collective action both by acting as a target for their activities as well as by emerging as a "third-party enforcer,"
directly supporting their campaigns for change.[58]

However, in much of the developing world, strongly institutionalized
and autonomous states are hard to find. Migdal, in his extensive writings
on the state, has highlighted the absence of institutionalized and/or normative frameworks within which states of the developing world operate
today. Rather than being dominant, for example, the state acts more like a
"confused conglomerate of people and agencies,"[59] "a crippled giant,"[60] and
a series of "fragments" that often work at cross-purposes to themselves.[61]
It rarely operates according to unified set of rules, nor is it necessarily
the preeminent rule maker in society. Moreover, rather than being distinct and autonomous from society, it is often penetrated by a variety of
competing social forces, all vying for hegemonic power, that appropriate
parts of the state and end up producing a political order characterized
by "multiple sets of practices," "alternative sets of rules," and, ultimately,
the absence of integrating frameworks of authority.[62]

Weak states, however, do not necessarily produce weak regimes. On
the contrary, regime structures within weak states—usually of a highly
informal nature—are often powerful, resistant to change, and, hence,
highly resilient. Indeed, it is precisely the weakness of the state apparatus
that allows powerful social actors to structure politics in ways that serve
to entrench and reproduce their power. Hence, politics in weak states is
not only about penetrating the state in order to pillage it; it is also about
penetrating the state in order to structure politics in ways that maximize
the access of certain elites to the state while minimizing that of others.
In this sense, Midgal's path-breaking analysis of the relationship between
strong societies and weak states is an incomplete one, missing the crucial
discussion of regime structures that emerge between them.

Understanding this contrast between weak states and strong regimes
is crucial for our ensuing discussion of civil society, for it is regimes rather
than states that structure state–society relations, determine the ways in
which citizens can access the political system, and, hence, heavily influence the evolution of associational life and its access to those with political
power. In regimes underpinned by strongly institutionalized states, for
example, political rules structuring relations between state and society
are predominantly formal in nature, embodied within constitutions and
electoral laws. It is in this political context, as in the argument by Evans
discussed previously, that high levels of "civic" associationalism, profiting
from their institutionalized, universal access to the state, can often flourish, especially if the regime is a democratic one. On the other hand, in
weakly institutionalized states where formal rules are not the only game

in town, regimes tend to be hybrid in nature, characterized by a complex intertwining of the formal with the informal, of the universal with the more particularistic. In these situations, the access of associational life to the state and its resources is likely to be less universalist and more reflective of the particularistic political dynamics generated by the regime's hybridity, thus providing enduring advantages to some segments of associational life while disadvantaging others.

Several features of hybrid regime types emerge as being particularly disadvantageous for those advocating for universal citizenship and social rights, many of which are associated with the deleterious effects of clientelism. Jonathan Fox, for example, in the context of Latin America, and in particular Mexico, looks on clientelism as being inimical to the achievement of full citizenship rights.[63] Douglas Chalmers argues further that when clientelism is expanded "to incorporate the 'whole' system of political relationships between citizen and the state, [it] becomes a rationale for the excessive concentration of power in the hands of a 'few' patrons."[64] And, in their comparison of several forms of "representational regimes," Elizabeth Friedman and Kathryn Hochstetler argue that rights-based advocacy politics are particularly difficult within hybrid regimes that are fragmented into competing and adversarial clientelist networks—essentially because the state is effectively neutralized as a mediator and/or "third party enforcer." Not only does this make it difficult for civil society associations to come together in the form of stable and cross-cutting advocacy networks, but it also significantly complicates their efforts to establish, let alone sustain, access to the policy-making apparatus of the state.[65] The result is often advocacy efforts that are fleeting and that give rise to at best "temporary formulations of understandings around particular issues."[66]

Hence, states and their regimes have important structuring effects on civil society, influencing its makeup, dynamics, and political influence. Using the terminology of social movement theory, states and regimes help to determine the "political opportunity structures" within which the myriad of civil society associations operate. As we have seen above, however, the weak and uninstitutionalized nature of many states in the developing world has led to the emergence of hybrid regimes whose particularist informal dynamics often overpower the more formal rules of the game, providing differential rather than universal access to state resources. As we have just argued, this can be a particularly enduring feature of political systems dominated by fragmented, adversarial, and competing forms of clientelist networks. With respect to civil society actors, this facilitates the empowerment of a regime's associational allies within civil society while marginalizing its associational challengers, potentially leaving them "marooned on embattled islands" with little to no significant access to the political arena at all.[67] With respect to incumbent elites, it not only provides them with greater room for maneuver, but it also transforms components of civil society into useful actors in the broader game of reproducing their power. In short, empowered by unequal and asymmetrical systems of regime access, favored components of civil society emerge as feedback mechanisms, contributing to the path-dependent quality of hybrid political systems in weak and fragmented states.

Yet there remains a paradox with respect to the path-dependent dynamics of such hybrid political systems, with their mix of the formal with the informal. For, however unequal and entrenched power relations may be within any given polity, they are "rarely if ever 'one way.'"[68] Indeed, the very informal nature of these mechanisms of political access and the often-shifting nature of political alliances and power relations that characterizes them—particularly apparent within power-sharing regimes such as that of Lebanon—also creates opportunities for more open-ended processes of political bargaining. Fox uses the term "semi-clientelism" to describe the spaces that can emerge, that allow for greater associational autonomy and "other kinds of unequal exchanges,"[69] and Chalmers argues in similar fashion that the political spaces that emerge within hybrid regime structures can have "democratic potential."[70] It is here that possibilities for the exercise of restricted agency emerge. Through intelligent and strategic action, for example, structurally disadvantaged civil society actors may nonetheless find ways, if only of a fleeting nature, to transcend the entrenched power asymmetries that constrain them and exert political and/or policy influence. It is the assertion of this study that manifestations of restricted agency are best captured through an analysis, not of civil society politics per se, but of the attempt by select civil society actors to access the political arena through the construction of and participation within cross-cutting policy networks. It is to the analysis of the advocacy potential of policy networks—the final building block of this study's theoretical framework—that we now turn.

## Restricted Agency, Associational Networks, and the Politics of Advocacy

There are numerous definitions of policy networks. Joseph Wong describes them as the "patterned interaction . . . of state and society actors who have a stake in a particular policy area";[71] Steven Heydemann, in his work on "networks of privilege" in the Middle East, has defined them as "a regular set of contacts of similar social connections among individuals and groups";[72] and Margaret Keck and Kathryn Sikkink, in their work on transnational advocacy networks, have described them as being "voluntary, reciprocal, and horizontal patterns of communication and exchange" made up of "webs" of personal relationships that are "lighter on their feet than hierarchy."[73] While rigor varies with respect to how networks analysis has been used, with Gould arguing that many of its applications are more "metaphorical" than "analytical,"[74] all agree that networks provide a useful tool for understanding advocacy politics in highly fluid and weakly institutionalized political arenas that are underpinned by significant power asymmetries.

Networks operate within policy domains and/or policy arenas; indeed, their activities help to create them.[75] While they are not legally recognized entities and, as such, are to be differentiated from state ministries, they are sometimes looked upon as "new governing structures" that are "neither state nor society . . . but hybrid structures that carry out their own functions."[76] Whereas in the context of the developed world, policy domains are "relatively autonomous,"[77] in the context of weakly institutionalized regimes within the developing world, this assertion of autonomy is more problematic. Heydemann argues, for example, "that policy domains are far more interconnected . . . reflecting the density of elites, their concentration in positions of power, and their interlocking relationships that bind them to one another."[78] This porous nature of policy arenas and their linkage to broader struggles for hegemony also means that ensuing political battles often transcend policy debates and reach right to the heart of political contestation between state actors and different social forces. As Migdal recognizes, "these are not simply policy arenas in which various groups attempt to shape public policy . . . [S]truggles and accommodation also take place over the basic moral order and the very structure within which rights and wrongs of everyday social behavior should be determined."[79]

The outcome of these political battles being waged within policy domains is determined by two basic factors: the structure and, hence, power of the various competing policy networks at play and the strategic resources—including cognitive ones—each brings to bear on its struggles. While network structures can vary enormously, for example, there are two, lying at the polar ends of the continuum, that are most relevant to our analysis: policy communities and issue and/or associative networks. While no network is "entirely closed," the most exclusive is called a policy community and is characterized as small, highly restricted, insulated, and dominated by elites who share strong personal relations of trust and loyalty.[80] While some scholars suggest that they can foster incremental policy changes, most argue that these types of networks represent "a clear structural inequality in the access to, and influence over, government policy making" and, as a result, act as "a major source of inertia" in the policy-making process.[81] In short, policy communities can be conceptualized as a feedback mechanism that contributes to the path-dependent nature of political life.

At the opposite end of the policy network continuum lie issue and/or associative networks.[82] Rather than being small, homogeneous and tightly knit, these networks are characterized as large, holding a diversity of interests and resource endowments within them, and possessing a structure that tends to be unintegrated. Whereas policy communities are seen as being fairly stable, issue, and/or associative networks are characterized by a great deal of instability and discontinuity[83] and often emerge out of an "unexpected coalition of actors."[84] They also are usually "non–hierarchical" in structure, and it is this, according to Chalmers, that gives them the potential to represent the interests of the popular classes in the policy-making arena.[85] Rising out of research into the policy-making process in the United States, the notion of issue/associative networks challenged the characterization of the policy-making process being dominated by "subgovernments" and "iron triangles,"[86] promoting instead the notion that policy-making processes could be "fairly open" and more inclusive than was previously conceived.[87]

What facilitates the success of an issue/associative network? Keck and Sikkink, for example, stress that the strength of a network is not determined merely by the sum of the network components but rather by the sum of the "interaction of voices," in short, by its structural effect. Write Keck and Sikkink, "[T]he network-as-actor derives a great deal of its effectiveness from the network-as-structure."[88] They highlight two particular features of a network structure that facilitate the success of network advocacy: network density and network access. Density on the want hand can be determined by the number of actors within the network, the regularity and intensity of exchanges, the degree of internal consensus, and the internal distribution of resources and, hence, power. These determine the relationship, for example, between network "peripheries" and "cores." Access to the network, on the other hand, is facilitated by the number of "nodes" or points of contact it possesses within the policy domain as well as by the nature of those "nodes." Kekk and Sikkink stress, for example, that effective networks are not only made up of idea-generating actors, there also must be powerful elite actors located at the "core" of the policy domain itself "who are vulnerable to persuasion and leverage" and who would be willing to take costly action to promote issues either because "they care about [them] deeply" or because they have "other incentives to act."[89]

The success of issue/associative networks, however, is not determined only by their structure; it also is heavily influenced by the nature of the issues and policy ideas being promoted. The most important function of associative networks is "cognitive," writes Chalmers, determined by their ability to promote debate, transmit, and reshape competing claims over policy in ways that, if successful, can lead to "the redefinition of interests."[90] In this sense, associative networks perform a "deliberative as much as a bargaining function."[91] Indeed, Chalmers argues it is really only through deliberation that less powerful actors can overcome the structural inequalities inherent in the policy-making process and, hence, make their presence felt.[92] Other scholars make similar assertions about the prior importance of the cognitive impact of advocacy networks. Keck and Sikkink, for example, have described advocacy networks as "communicative structures" and write of their importance in formulating and/or framing "causal claims" that are "short and clear."[93]

Even here, however, the cognitive dynamics of advocacy networks are limited by the prevailing political and/or cognitive structures that surround them. Wong writes that notions of justice and equity are "grounded in empirical reality" and, as a result, efforts to promote such policies as a reduction in poverty may depend on "the degree to which society is willing to tolerate such a distribution."[94] Keck and Sikkink are even clearer on this essentially path-dependent argument, emphasizing that issues need to be framed in such a way that they can "fit into institutional venues." Add Keck and Sikkink, "new ideas are more likely to be influential if they fit well into existing ideas . . . in a particular historical setting." Hence, a principle challenge for associative networks is being creative—framing new policy issues and ideas in ways that address "some elements of structural problems" without attacking them directly.[96] In short, new policy ideas are more likely to promote incremental—rather than path-breaking—institutional change within the confines of an existing political legacy.

## Conclusion

Political institutions—and policy-making processes—are generally resistant to change. As we have argued, this resistance can be particularly acute within weak states because they provide opportunities for political elites to build informal and clientelist-based regime structures that have proven to be extremely effective in preserving factional power. Depending on the degree to which they buttress the power and maneuverability of elite cartels, communal power-sharing agreements can be especially prone to path-dependent dynamics. Underpinning this regime resilience are numerous feedback mechanisms, and it is a major argument of this study that certain actors within civil society emerge as some of these mechanisms of reproduction. Taking advantage of their informal and factional links to, and alliances with, elites within the regime, these civil society actors both can act as a conduit for the penetration of regime elite interests into civil society and/or represent, promote, and protect the interests of regime actors within civil society itself, all the while strengthening their ability to do so due to their privileged access to the state, its resources, and its power.

However effective these civil society feedback mechanisms may be in promoting regime resilience, the informal and fragmented institutional climate within which they operate also can open up opportunities for restricted agency by counter-hegemonic civil society actors. Extrapolating from the literature on policy networks, a useful concept for analyzing such restricted forms of agency are associative networks. Unlike popular sector social networks or more homogeneous elite-oriented policy communities at the highest level of a polity, associative networks usually combine a diverse range of actors who include—in an unstable, informal, yet salient network structure—both selected elites at the commanding heights of the state along with key actors in civil society. Depending on the internal network structure and the strategic calculations that take place within them, especially as regards the framing of advocacy campaigns, associative networks have the potential to promote incrementally more universalist-oriented policy change within the context of highly resilient and often exclusionary institutional contexts.

What follows in the rest of this book is an examination of the dynamics of associative policy networks in the context of postwar Lebanon. In Chapter 2, we examine the practice of sectarian democracy over the course of Lebanon's modern history—from its emergence in the late Ottoman period, to its consolidation and reproduction during the colonial and post-colonial periods, to its reconsolidation and reinforcement during the periods of the civil war and Syrian hegemony. Particular emphasis is placed on highlighting feedback mechanisms—from the exogenous shocks of the French and, subsequently, Syrian presence, to endogenous elite networking at the national, regional, and subnational levels of Lebanon's political field—that have served to reinforce the path-dependent hegemony of sectarian political practices over the weakly institutionalized democratic ones. In Chapter 3, we turn our attention to the effects that this reconsolidation of sectarian democracy in Lebanon has had on the emerging postwar associative sector, focusing in some detail on the efforts of national-oriented associative and popular networks to challenge the returning hegemony of postwar sectarian practices.

It is at this point that we turn our attention to a detailed examination of the three case studies of associational advocacy in the fields of gender, environment, and disability. All feature the postwar rise of several dynamic associative networks seeking to take advantage of perceived opportunities in the immediate post–civil war period to promote the mainstreaming of rights-based social policies into the institutional heart of the postwar Lebanese state. Chapter 4 examines the efforts of women's associations pushing for gender equality; Chapter 5 examines the campaigns of environmental associations to establish a rule-bound environmental policy domain founded on the principles of sustainable development; and Chapter 6 examines the tenacious advocacy work of disability associations pushing for the development of a disability policy domain founded on the principles of "rights" rather than "belonging." In a concluding chapter, we compare the challenges faced by these three advocacy networks, ones that revolved around the resistance of powerful sectarian elite networks and the reinforcing support of their sectarian associational allies within Lebanese civil society. While these associative networks achieved some notable successes in institutionalizing their presence within the country's civil society, their efforts to promote new rights-based directions in postwar Lebanese state formation have ultimately been stymied by the institutions and political forces that combine to entrench and reproduce over time the country's sectarian political system.

## 2

# Sectarian Democracy in Modern Lebanon

*Its Emergence, Consolidation, and Reproduction*

What is sectarian democracy, why was it adopted as a way of governing Lebanese society, and why has it been so resilient, returning even after fifteen years of debilitating civil conflict? These are the questions that are discussed in this chapter. First, providing a precise definition of sectarian democracy is difficult outside of the context within which it operates. Certainly, it refers to a type of political regime—one that establishes a set of rules of both a formal and an informal nature that combines democratic and sectarian elements. On the democratic side of the equation, it also points to the ways in which power is organized around basic democratic principles—namely formal respect for the rights of individuals combined with a system of protecting those rights through the establishment of representative institutions and the holding of elections. It further suggests, on the sectarian side of the ledger, that while the procedural rules of politics are democratic, substantive political dynamics are often hegemonically sectarian. But what about "sectarianism" itself, a concept that has been described as "slippery,"[1] unable to be "positioned as a solitary explanatory devise"[2] and, hence, one that defies "formulaic generalizations"?[3] Given its crucial importance for this study, the concept of sectarianism must be unpacked, first, by examining the mainstream theoretical debates that surround the concept, and, second, by examining how they apply historically to the Lebanese political context.

Ussama Makdisi defines sectarianism as being the product of a series of processes "through which a kind of religious identity is politicized, even secularized, as part of an obvious struggle for power."[4] Lying behind this useful starting point is a myriad of debates that surround the concept and inform Makdisi's subsequent analysis. Foremost among these are the theoretical debates about the origins and dynamics of "sectarianism." Much of the popular, though less scholarly, literature on sectarianism, for example, implicitly follows an Orientalist paradigm. This is based on the notion that sectarianism's origins are rooted in some cultural essence and, hence, linked to primordialist and/or ethnoconfessional models of analysis.[5] This study rejects these notions and assumes that sectarianism has been "constructed" and "produced" by various socioeconomic and political factors (and, hence, also can be "unmade").[6] A second paradigm explains the salience and dynamics of sectarianism with reference to the instrumentalist machinations of political entrepreneurs. While this study accepts this approach, it also argues that it provides at best a partial explanation for the rise (and fall) of sectarian political dynamics. A more comprehensive paradigm for the rise and reproduction of sectarianism—the approach that this study adopts—explains sectarian dynamics as emanating from the complex and contingent interplay of a variety of socioeconomic and political forces—some structural, some agential. Among the most underlying of these forces in the Middle East and Lebanon have been capitalist penetration and the launching of processes of state formation—both of which have had uneven and destabilizing effects on preexisting power relations and which continue in the present era of globalization to spark competitions for wealth and power. In the context of the notable dominated and multicommunal society of Mount Lebanon in the nineteenth century, for example, Makdisi argues that the interplay of these processes produced "a reconfiguration of both religion and power in Lebanese society" that led to a "a far-reaching crisis of co-existence" out of which sectarian forms of identity emerged and became increasingly dominant as a way of organizing social and political life and defining identity.[7]

A second factor complicating easy and formulaic definitions of sectarianism revolves around its historical variability. Sectarian politics take multiple forms, operate at multiple levels of a political system, and, as a result, have multiple histories. For example, political systems organized on a sectarian basis—which, in the Lebanese context, is referred to as confessionalism and, in the broader political science field, consociationalism[8]—refer to regime types that revolve around the formal sharing of political power between different religious (and in consociationalisms, perhaps also ethnic) communities. This "macro-oriented" focus—which is a crucial starting point of this study—has been described as representing "sectarianism from above."[9] Sectarian dynamics, however, can simultaneously flow from a series of sociopolitical processes, some informal, others institutionalized, that operate within civil and political society. This "meso-oriented" focus—this study's point of reference, which also can include informal sectarian dynamics of a transnational nature—has been described as representing "sectarianism from below."[10] Finally, one also can think about sectarianism as referring to more "micro-oriented" questions of identity formation, an approach that this study does not directly address.[11]

A final complicating factor when defining sectarianism is that its dynamics—when restricted to the communal and/or religious—fail to encompass "the web of conflicting and contradictory relationships" that makes up a sectarian political field.[12] Rather, there are a myriad of coexisting, overlapping, and sometimes competing interests and identities that complicate relations within communally oriented societies and that contribute to the varying degree of salience of sectarian dynamics. Many power-sharing political systems, for example, incorporate both religious and nonreligious communities—the case of the participation of the Kurds in the broader, if implicit and "liberal," consociational power-sharing formulas of Iraq being a prime example.[13] A similar analytical conundrum revolves around the incorporation of other "subterranean actors" into broader sectarian dynamics[14]—especially those relating to kinship and tribe. Including these in the broader sectarian political equation, for example, can help to explain why some of the most intense political conflicts and competitions within sectarian systems occur *within* rather than *between* religious communities. Further questions about the conceptual inclusiveness of sectarianism revolve around the degree to which class dynamics fuel and/or complicate sectarian dynamics. In the Lebanese context, for example, this has led to the formulation of concepts such as "sect-classes," the building blocks of what Donald Horowitz calls "ranked ethnic systems."[15] Indeed, all communal power-sharing systems are built around agreements and pacts among communal elites whose power is dialectically generated as much by their class as by their communal status. All of this suggests that there is a broader set of factional dynamics within sectarian systems than those relating to religious communalism—the primary ones among them relating to ethnicity, kinship, and class.

In short, this study accepts a "slippery" definition of sectarianism. It privileges a contextualized and historicized understanding of the concept, rather than an essentialized one, with an emphasis on sectarianism as being produced—and reproduced—by forces of both a structural and an agential nature; it utilizes an inclusive understanding of the elements that comprise sectarian dynamics—accepting communal/religious variables as a starting point (rather than an end point) of analysis yet recognizing that the factionalism that typifies sectarian polities is generated by the complex interaction of a variety of factional dynamics relating not only to religious communalism but also to ethnicity, kinship, and class; and it assumes that the processes that produce and reproduce sectarianism have a multidimensional character—taking different forms and operating at a variety of different levels of analysis, the most important from the perspective of this book being the recursive interaction in postwar Lebanon between processes of sectarianism "from above" with those "from below."

What follows in this chapter is an analytical narrative focusing on the emergence, consolidation, and reproduction of sectarian dynamics within modern Lebanon. It begins with an analysis of how Lebanon's sectarian political field emerged during a critical juncture in the late Ottoman period. It then focuses on three stages of state formation within modern Lebanon—the colonial stage in which Lebanon's sectarian critical juncture was consolidated, the post-colonial stage during which several forces emerged to challenge the sectarian political legacy forged during the late Ottoman and colonial periods, and the civil war and early postwar stages in which the dynamics of conflict and Syria's hegemonic presence within Lebanon combined to produce reversals in processes of political development that not only reentrenched sectarian political dynamics but also reinforced the path-dependent sectarian nature of Lebanese political life. It is this deepening of the processes of sectarian reproduction in the country—both institutional and extra-institutional—that sets the scene for the subsequent analysis of the challenges that advocacy networks faced within postwar Lebanon.

## Creating the Preconditions for the Rise of Political Sectarianism: The Emergence of Lebanon's Modern "Political Field"

A fundamental prerequisite for modern social and political life—including the rise of civil society—is the emergence of a unified "political field." This is defined in broader terms than simply the state to include patterns of "organization, mobilization, agitation and struggle" that develop alongside it.[16] In the case of Lebanon, the historical roots of what became its modern political field run quite deep. Indeed, its starting point can be traced back to the late sixteenth century with the emergence of an autonomous principality that created the first united and overarching "secular authority" in the area over a number of hitherto separate lordships.[17] Though the territorial foundations of Lebanon's modern political field were less certain until 1920,[18] this uncertainty did not prevent the growth of social, economic, and political ties throughout the area, especially within Mount Lebanon. In the early to mid–nineteenth century, for example, Georges Corm wrote of the emergence of a "socio-economic symbiosis" between the leaders of the principal religious communities of the mountain (Maronite, Druze, and Shi'a).[19] With the intensification of commercial links between the mountain and the coastal cities throughout the nineteenth and early twentieth centuries, these habits and customs of socioeconomic interaction further developed. Hence, despite the territorial discontinuities in the history of the Lebanese entity and the ebb and flow of conflict between its diverse communities, one can nonetheless write of the emergence of a Lebanese "political field" by the time the French colonized the Levant in 1920 and created the territorially expanded modern state of Lebanon.

The story of how this emerging modern "political field" came to develop its sectarian democratic character, however, is a complex one determined by the contingent interaction of a number of actors, social processes, and political forces. A good starting point for understanding the democratic roots of Lebanon's political field is the *tanzimat* era—a period of Ottoman state building in the nineteenth century influenced by republican intellectual currents with their emphasis on equality, liberty, and fraternity. This republican thrust of the *tanzimat* reforms culminated in the 1876 adoption of an Ottoman constitution that established an indirectly elected parliamentary regime, confirmed the empire's commitment to guaranteeing the liberty and equality of all of its subjects, and officially transformed the Ottoman Empire into a constitutional monarchy. Republican principles—revolving around electoral representation—also were embedded within the institutional workings of governance in Mount Lebanon with the inauguration of indirect two-stage elections to the twelve-member Administrative Council of the *mutasarifiyya* that was established in 1861. This institutionalization of republican principles into Ottoman governance institutions also spawned numerous social and political movements infused by these same principles. In the Mount Lebanon region, this encompassed anything from peasant revolts in the Mount Lebanon region in the mid-nineteenth century,[20] to protesting workers in the ports of Beirut during the late nineteenth century,[21] to shifting currents in cultural and intellectual life in the late nineteenth century associated with *an-nahda* (renaissance) that arose within the Levant region and were particularly centered in the urban areas of Lebanon. These republican principals also were increasingly reflected in the activism of the administrative council of the *mutasarifiyya*, especially with respect to its demands after the First World War for Lebanese independence and the establishment of a parliamentary democracy based on the principles of liberty, equality, and fraternity, including the protection of minority rights and religious freedom.[22] Describing the administrative council as becoming an embryonic national assembly, Engin Akarli argues that its institutionalization helped to explain why Lebanese politicians adapted so easily to a parliamentary system during the mandate period. In short, remarked Akarli, the democratic-participatory orientation of Lebanon's polity was "more deeply rooted in history than is often presumed to be the case."[23]

Complicating this story of democratic development in Mount Lebanon, however, were a variety of socioeconomic, political, and institutional processes that led to the strengthening of a parallel sectarianism, one that, as Makdisi argues, led to the emergence of a "pure communal actor" that had not existed before.[24] Uneven processes of capitalist penetration and development in the nineteenth century, for example, had ambiguous effects on processes of class formation within the Lebanese "political field." On the one hand, they promoted social differentiation both within and outside feudally organized communities that opened up the potential for the emergence of cross-cutting class ties at an embryonic national level. On the other hand, their uneven and dislocated nature generated alternative forms of grievance and identity that began to resemble what have been called "sect-classes."[25] If Corm is correct in referring to the emergence of a "socio-economic symbiosis" between the communities of Mount Lebanon during the days of the autonomous principality, the uneven communal impact of capitalist penetration in the mid- to late nineteenth century weakened these cross-cutting dynamics, creating in their wake heightened senses of communal identity and suspicion.

Further contributing to the emerging hybrid nature of Lebanon's modern political field in the nineteenth century was the instrumentalization of communal principals and sentiment by an array of political entrepreneurs—be they political elites, religious clerics, foreign consuls, or subaltern classes.[26] European powers cultivated communal partners, for example, in order to strengthen their influence in the area—especially successful in the case of French cultivation of connections with the increasingly hegemonic Maronite community. Ottoman officials, Egyptian occupiers, and representatives of the old feudal order also exploited communal divisions as a way of bolstering their decaying or challenged authority. As the local political apparatus began to grow, especially after the establishment of the *mutasarifiyya*, local notables also joined the ranks of sectarian entrepreneurs, exploiting communal identities as a way of strengthening their access to increased patronage opportunities that were vital in resuscitating their clientelistic hold over local populations.[27] And subaltern groups, who had initially showed signs of mobilizing on the basis of a nascent class solidarity, experienced processes of unravelling at the hands of communal entrepreneurs—most noticeably seen in the descent of peasant protests in mid-nineteenth century Mount Lebanon into widespread communal rioting and massacres that spread well beyond the region of Mount Lebanon into the urban areas of Greater Syria in 1860.[28]

It was the progressive incorporation of communal principals into the area's governance mechanisms during the nineteenth century, however, that arguably was the crucial factor in forging the sectarian democratic path along which Lebanon's subsequent political development would travel. This process began with the initial short-lived creation of separate Maronite/Druze governance arrangements in 1841 (the *qa'immaqamiyyah*); it was shortly thereafter transformed with the establishment of communally mixed councils in these separate districts—councils that were described as Lebanon's first formal communal power-sharing institutions;[29] and, with the emergence of the *mutasarifiyya* in 1861, it culminated in the establishment of a unified and indirectly elected administrative council whose seats were distributed proportionately on the basis of communal demographic weight. It was as a result of these institutional developments, argued Akarli, that confessionalism emerged as "a fundamental principle of governmental organization" in the area during the period of the *mutasarifiyya*.[30]

Hence, the confluence of socioeconomic and political processes that came together in the mid- to late nineteenth century in Lebanon created the conditions for profound transformations in the area's political field in which democratic and sectarian governance principals came to be cojoined. While the political dynamics associated with emerging sectarian practice grew in salience over the course of the *mutasarifiyya*—underpinned as they were by elite-driven political power associated with newly emerging and factionalized forms of political clientelism—they remained unconsolidated, leaving the future path of Lebanese state and regime formation an open one. Tipping the balance decisively toward the sectarian side of Lebanon's hybrid political equation, however, were the political dynamics unleashed by the destruction of the Ottoman Empire and the imposition of French mandatory rule in Lebanon at the end of the First World War, and it is to an examination of these dynamics that we turn now.

## Consolidating Sectarian Democracy:
## The Political Legacies of French Colonial Rule

There are two levels of analysis with respect to the consolidation of Lebanon's sectarian democratic path of state and regime formation during the French mandate period. The first focuses on the ways in which the French reestablished this regime type within the expanded state of Greater Lebanon—choosing to build the foundations of its colonial hegemony on the political legacy of the late Ottoman period. Encompassing both formal institution building and informal modes of colonial statecraft, it is the reimposition of sectarian democracy that represents the promotion of "sectarianism from above." The second focuses on the mechanisms unleashed by French colonial policy within Lebanese civil and political society that reproduced this regime type—mechanisms that represent the promotion of "sectarianism from below." It was the interweaving dynamics of these two sectarianizing processes that led to the consolidation of Lebanon's system of sectarian democracy, one that has proven to be remarkably path dependent and, as we shall see, resilient in the face of the socioeconomic and political challenges of the post-independence era.

Upon assuming their power over the Lebanese and Syrian territories, French colonial officials reinstated the institutional foundations of Mount Lebanon's late Ottoman political legacy. As an interim measure, they immediately reestablished the communally based administrative council that had been in operation under the *mutasarifiyya*, and, after a prolonged period of delay, they eventually promulgated Lebanon's first constitution in 1926, one whose underlying principals reflected the hybrid democratic/sectarian tradition of the previous era. On the democratic side, it guaranteed personal liberties, broadened the (male) electorate by abolishing property requirements,[31] reduced the minimum voting age, and, after amendments in the late 1920s, enhanced the powers of the presidency so that it could act in a more autonomous, nonsectarian, and unifying manner. On the sectarian side, the constitution maintained the Ottoman practice of proportional religious representation in the assembly, cabinet, and civil service; safeguarded the independence of communal educational institutions; and guaranteed the autonomy of each community in matters of personal status law—stipulations that also had been laid out in the charter of the French mandate.[32] In short, the new Lebanese constitution represented that late Ottoman compromise between "centralist Jacobin ideas and pragmatic acceptance of the political reality of a number of independent communities."[33]

The most powerful sectarian impact of France's presence, however, was released by its colonial statecraft. First and foremost, despite operating under the rubric of a republican constitution, French colonial officials remained, for the most part, "detached" when it came to supporting its republican precepts.[34] On the contrary, French statecraft was decidedly authoritarian—involving such activities as the rigging of elections in support of collaborative elites, the suspension of the constitution and the imposition of direct colonial rule when parliamentary debate became too destabilizing, and the general use of coercion to suppress activities within civil society, be it by quelling urban protest movements, arbitrarily detaining protestors, or placing restrictions on the flow of information in the press and the broader public sphere. Finally, French colonial statecraft contributed to processes of "ethnicizing" Lebanon's political field through efforts to cultivate an intercommunal collaborative elite beyond the Maronite community in the context of an overall colonial strategy of divide and rule.[35]

The French decision to promote the establishment of separate communal councils and courts in the realm of personal status law, for example, launched a formal process of institutionalizing communal religious power. This formally began with a decree requiring the Shi'a communities to establish their own religious court system in 1926, one that gradually led to its transformation from "a sect-in-itself" to a "sect-for-itself."[36] This was paralleled by French encouragement to the Sunni community to rebuild its own millet-like institutions in the wake of the withdrawal of the Ottoman state to which it had been previously intimately attached—encouragement that was part of a larger strategy of organizing separate millet-like institutions within all of the Muslim communities and, with a subsequent decree in 1936, within all religious communities, Muslim and Christian alike.[37] Further institutionalizing the autonomy of Lebanon's religious communities was the intensified use by French colonial officials of religious social welfare and educational institutions to fulfill colonial state social policy. The consequences of both sets of policies for processes of state formation in colonial Lebanon were serious and long-lasting, establishing the foundations of what Elizabeth Thompson called "a parallel regime of power" in the country that in the long term would serve to weaken the basic authority and legitimacy of the Lebanese state itself.[38]

An additional thrust of French mandate policy was to cultivate the support of regionally based elite families, especially in the outlying areas of the country such as the North, the Biqa Valley to the East, and the South, all of which had initially seen resistance to the imposition of French rule.[39] Land tenure and agricultural development practices were promoted, for example, that facilitated the ability of these regionally based families to consolidate large *latifundias* in ways that would buttress their regional political standing.[40] In order to harness this landowning elite to the state, the French also crafted electoral laws in 1926—ones in which constituencies were local and within which were multiple seats distributed on a communal basis—that deliberately privileged candidates of the leading local families. Further entrenching the electoral power of leading local families was the stipulation that all Lebanese must vote within their birthplace and/or village of origin. In theory, this electoral system—most of whose features remain in place to this day—was designed to promote cross-communal political alliances within each of its multi-communal, multiple-seat constituencies. But, as Elizabeth Picard has noted, the mélange of electoral alliances (called lists) that ultimately emerged was in reality constructed, not on the basis of which set of candidates could establish the most cooperative relations but, rather, on the basis of which

set of candidates could generate the greatest local clientelist power.[41] Buttressing the clientelist power of landed elites still further was their access
to the resources of the mandate state that elections and a seat in parliament gave them. Given that landlords held considerable sway in Lebanon's mandate assembly, the result was the penetration of factionalized
elite power deep into the Lebanese state—power whose dynamics were
informal as much as formal, factional rather than national, and whose
entrenchment made it extremely difficult to develop alternative, broad-
based forms of political organization and representation.

The final component of French colonial policy was the cultivation of
a growing, if Maronite-dominated, commercial and financial bourgeoisie.
There were several actions that proved crucial to the success of these latter
collaborative arrangements, foremost among them being French commitment to maintain Lebanon's laissez-faire economic status that had taken
root during the late Ottoman period and that had begun to pay dividends
in terms of Beirut's development as a commercial relay station for the rest
of the Arab interior. Equally important were French decisions to promote
significant infrastructural development throughout the country, most of
which benefited Beirut itself and which was, in part, designed to be a
showcase for French accomplishments in the Levant.[42] Many of Beirut's
growing merchant/financier class also used their wealth and connections
with the French to acquire large tracks of land in Mount Lebanon and the
Beqa' Valley, facilitating their entry into the ranks of the large landowners
and, thereby, integrating them more deeply into the dynamics of the mandate state, despite their relatively limited representation within the mandate Lebanese parliament.[43] Indeed, all components of Lebanon's emerging
political elite were "quick to embrace" the opportunities provided by the
burgeoning service-oriented political economy of the mandate period
and the politics that surrounded and sustained it.[44] This pointed to "the
blending of the sources of political power and economic wealth," power
and wealth that were used to support political campaigns, enter into joint
ventures with members of the political class, as well as buy favors with
the French high commissioner.[45] While, on the one hand, the growing
power of this bourgeoisie contributed to the consolidation of the power
of a small, "closely intertwined" political elite[46]—traditionally referred to
as the *zuama*,[47] on the other hand, the wealth of this emerging bourgeois
class, operating as it did within the hegemonic sectarian framework of
political life, energized factionalized networking and sectarian competition within colonial Lebanon in ways that undermined "the political and
administrative fabric of the state."[48]

The key to understanding the longer-term impact of French colonial
policy, however, was to examine the ways in which political opportunities

for factionalized mobilization unleashed by the French "from above" were taken advantage of by the emerging coterie of collaborating Lebanese elites "from below." It was the agency—and, in particular, the networking dynamics—of the *zuama*, for example, that proved crucial in routinizing sectarian politicking in Lebanon, routinization that Firro refers to as "the Lebanese system."[49] This networking operated at several dimensions—some at the national level within and between members of the Lebanese elite themselves, others of a supranational nature that connected with supportive elements at the regional and global levels, and still others at a subnational level that linked up with allies within civil and political society. It is the argument here that these networking dynamics acted as feedback mechanisms reinforcing sectarianism "from below."

*Inter-elite Networking as a Feedback Mechanism*

Inter-elite political networks during mandate Lebanon were powerful mechanisms reinforcing the sectarian dynamics of Lebanon's political field. Their underlying logic was often factional and clientelist (rather than strictly communal), their purpose being to secure access to the patronage resources of the state and, hence, to protect one's position within the political order vis à vis rival elites. A crucial resource in this competition for factional political advantage, however, was the communal system itself, which provided political elites with an institutionalized set of principals on which to base their political claims.[50] Indeed, fueled by the uncertain parameters surrounding the communal power equation during the mandate period, struggles between Lebanon's factional elites over communal access to state resources quickly came to dominate political debates. Be it with respect to the communal share of executive power (which until 1943 remained unfixed), appointments to the bureaucracy, and/or budget allocations, Lebanon's elite strata became intensively involved in "an all out competition . . . to get a hold of as great a stake as they [could] in the distribution of power within the Lebanese system."[51]

Crucial to success in this "all-out competition" was the ability to construct, enter into, and maneuver between crosscutting alliances and networks, especially at certain critical moments. During the mandate period, for example, the onset of treaty negotiations in 1936 between the Syrian and Lebanese governments and the French that were designed to bring about the de jure independence of both countries provided one of those critical political moments, sparking an intense period of factionalized communal networking. Realizing, if reluctantly, pragmatically, and gradually, that their futures now lay within Lebanon itself, political elites from all religious communities refocused their efforts toward aggrandizing their own communal share of political power within Lebanon itself, precipitating a "wave of confessionalism" across the country.[52] The confessional race was truly on, one that began to deepen its hold over Lebanese political life and transform it into "the only game in town."[53] Even the emergence of the National Pact in 1943—ostensibly a show of nationalist, cross-communal solidarity in the face of French colonial power—was equally driven by intensifying and shifting factionalism that opened up new opportunities for cross-cutting alliances, affirming Max Weiss's analytical conclusions that "national unity was forged through the making of sectarian difference."[54] Indeed, it was out of the 1943 National Pact that Lebanon's more rigid system of power-sharing arrangements emerged—adopting not only the preexisting six-to-five Christian–Muslim ratio of representation in the Lebanese parliament but also (informally) fixing in stone the communal distribution of the executive offices of the Lebanese state, with the president being reserved for a Maronite Christian, the prime minister for a Sunni Muslim, and the Speaker of the parliament to a Shi'a Muslim. In short, despite its often cross-communal nature that led to occasional if fleeting moments of national unity, Lebanon's constantly shifting system of elite networking—both within and between communities—served over time to continually reinforce factional divides in the country. It is for this reason that they are being highlighted as classic examples of "feedback mechanisms"—set in motion by the political legacies of Ottoman and French rule—that have served to reproduce the asymmetrical power of the communal over the democratic within Lebanon's fledgling republic.

*Supranational Networking as a Feedback Mechanism*

Further reinforcing the factionalism of Lebanon's political field were the external dimensions of elite networking. In the constant search for political leverage vis à vis rival political networks, for example, the calculations of Lebanese political elites were not confined to the national arena but extended into the regional and global political arenas. Maronite politicians, for example, had long relied on their strong ties with France and, as the future independence of the Lebanese polity began to loom on the horizon in the 1930s, even began to dabble in potential alliances with their Zionist neighbors to the south.[55] This tendency to cultivate regional networks of support was equally pronounced within Lebanon's Muslim political elites—tied as many of them were to Syrian and wider pan-Arab political networks. In times of acute intercommunal tension during the mandate period, for example, it was not unusual for Lebanese Sunni politicians to send urgent appeals to their fellow Sunni leaders in Syria and the surrounding Arab world.[56] Regional tension also filtered back into

Lebanon's receptive communal political equation in ways that energized and strengthened the communal logic of politics—often with potentially destabilizing implications when such support was channeled in an unmediated manner onto Lebanon's communal street. Finally, there was a recursive dimension to transborder political networking, with external actors often playing on Lebanon's internal divisions to their own advantage—a dynamic that was clearly and decisively at work in the negotiations surrounding the National Pact, with Britain being described as "the real power broker[s] behind this great national achievement."[57] In short, in the competition for political advantage between political factions within Lebanon, regional and international factors provided decisive sources of leverage. At certain moments, as in 1943, external factors worked to facilitate communal consensus; at other times, they exacerbated communal discord. At all times, however, their dialectical interactions with the Lebanese political field contributed to the reinforcement of factionalism itself.

*Subnational Networking as a Feedback Mechanism*

Civil and political society also emerged as a fertile terrain within which factional political elites sought to mobilize networks of support, especially with the onset of the mandate period, which sparked a growth in associational life that Thompson described as "frenzied."[58] Some of these new associational actors sought to challenge the sectarian dynamics that were gathering steam and encroaching onto the emerging civic order, though, as Zamir argued, these associations "either had no influence or were forced out of the system altogether."[59] Far more numerous and influential within Lebanon's emerging civic order, were those associations, movements, and parties linked to the country's familial and communal heritage—from the increasing array of family associations that have always been the most numerous in Lebanon,[6] to the growing number of confessional social welfare organizations,[61] to more popularly rooted sectarian movements and political parties, which, as Traboulsi pointed out, suggested that the dynamics of Lebanon's democratic sectarianism were starting to be absorbed by the country's "new social forces."[62] Foremost among the organizations representing this growing communalization of Lebanese civil and political society were the political movements and parties called the *Kataib*, the *Najjada*, and the *Talai* associated with the Maronite, Sunni, and Shi'a communities, respectively.[63] Emanating from an emerging middle class linked to, yet "deeply dissatisfied" with, the exclusionary and corrupt machinations of Lebanon's elite political class, these organizations, with their mix of populist sectarian rhetoric and propensity for violence, catapulted themselves into the forefront of Lebanon's late-mandate public sphere, engaging in the ongoing battles for sectarian privilege through their menacing presence in the streets at politically critical moments and influencing the factionalized alliance making and networking that surrounded them.[64]

Particularly revealing of the ways in which Lebanon's factionalized political field began to be constantly reproduced over time, however, has been the capacity of Lebanon's elite political elements to repeatedly mobilize—indeed, instrumentalize—these popular sectors within civil and political society in ways that protected and buttressed their own bases of power and enhanced their access to the resources of the state. In order to bolster their negotiating positions in advance of the impending 1936 Franco-Lebanese Treaty negotiations, for example, Sunni political leaders were described as having instigated "a well orchestrated campaign" of demonstrations in Tripoli and Beirut, ones that subsequently escalated into large-scale riots in which many were killed and hundreds injured.[65] Equally revealing of this instrumentalization of civil and political society by the country's sectarian elites were the reactions of the leaders of the Muslim communities to attempts by French officials to establish a secular personal status legal code in the late 1930s[66]—a successful instrumentalization that consisted of the Sunni establishment organizing widespread countermobilizations among their constituencies and clients that ranged from the closing of markets, to the organization of mass meetings in mosques, to the mobilization of thousands in mass street demonstrations in Tripoli, Beirut, and Sidon.[67] While it is important to stress that these popular and associational sectors were more than just passive actors at these moments, it is nonetheless true that the routinization of competitive elite networking within the country's associational and popular sectors had the overall effect, as Picard astutely notes, of keeping them "under the thumb of Lebanon's political class," making it difficult for them to break away from communal and factional political channels of access to the state that the political elites controlled and constantly nurtured.[68]

Hence, emerging political practices of factional networking during the mandate period—at the national, regional, and subnational levels—represented powerful mechanisms of "feedback" within the Lebanese political system, ones that contributed to the consolidation and reproduction of Lebanon's system of sectarian democracy after it was reinstitutionalized by the French. Yet, because no political situation is static and because institutional configurations are not "locked in,"[69] we need to understand how forces of change can affect path-dependent institutional contexts. The post-independence period of Lebanon provides a fascinating series of case studies of precisely these dynamics.

## Sectarian Democracy Under Siege:
## Challenges and "Veto Points" in Post-Independence Lebanon

Of the various forces for institutional change that emerged within post-independence Lebanon, we highlight three. The first were "slow-moving" processes that emanated from significant demographic growth and uneven transformations in the country's class structure in the post-independence period. These led to the emergence of vibrant and reformist-oriented associational networks within civil society, especially among the Lebanese working classes.[70] The second source of institutional change in post-independence Lebanon emerged from efforts by reformist elites to bypass the institutional constraints of the existing political system through a strategy of "institutional layering." Defined as "the partial renegotiation of some elements of a given set of institutions while leaving others in place,"[71] this change emerged in the wake of the destabilizing civil violence of 1958 through efforts by the reformist administration of the new Lebanese president, Fuad Chehab, to create parallel institutions that, it was hoped, would assume "more and more prominence" and successfully challenge the institutional status quo.[72] The final source of institutional change emerged from the numerous cracks in Lebanon's disaggregated institutional realm with its "multiple and contradictory logics"—ones whose openings had the potential to provide marginalized groups with leverage "well beyond their apparent meager power resources."[73] In Lebanon, it was these contradictory dynamics at the commanding heights of the Lebanese state that provided Kamal Jumblat—simultaneously the traditional *zaim* of the Druze community and the populist leader of the Progressive Socialist Party (PSP) and the Lebanese National Movement (LNM)—with contingent political openings through which to promote secular, political reforms. Paralleling all of these processes, however, were the forces of sectarian reproduction that coalesced around a series of "veto points" and that worked to thwart efforts at political reform and reinforce the stickiness of Lebanon's institutions.[74] This led to a situation whereby the forces for institutional change in post-independence Lebanon emerged, clashed, yet ultimately failed to transcend the self-reinforcing dynamics of Lebanon's sectarian democracy.

*Slow-Moving Causal Processes of Institutional Change*

Lebanon experienced tremendous and destabilizing socioeconomic transformations in its post-independence period, ones linked to its seemingly laissez-faire neomercantilist capitalist system. Fueled by an economic boom both during and after the Second World War, by the increasing inflows of Arab oil revenues, Arab émigré capital, Lebanese remittances, and later by the development of a vibrant export-oriented industrial sector in the late 1960s and 1970s,[75] Lebanon, and in particular its capital Beirut, experienced unprecedented economic expansion in the post-independence era.[76] Yet, as powerful as these post-independence forces of economic transformation were, they continued to have a highly uneven and iniquitous impact on processes of socioeconomic development and class formation in Lebanon, leaving entire regions of the country and groups of people excluded from its narrowly distributed benefits. Growth, for example, was by and large concentrated within the commercial and financial service sectors of Beirut, which contributed an unprecedented 70 percent to the country's gross national product (GNP) in 1970.[77] Benefiting the most from these accumulations were two groups—a powerful coterie of foreign capital interests that came to dominate the Lebanese banking industry before the civil war;[78] and Lebanon's small group of merchants and bankers consisting of approximately thirty families whose wealth and power were used to secure monopolistic control over numerous sectors of the country's import–export economy.[79] Not only did this lead to the factionalization of Lebanon's economic field, paralleling if not fueling the factionalization of its polity, but it also led (as I argue below) to the entrenchment of built-in political obstacles—"veto points"—to the development of the country's productive and employment-generating agrarian and industrial sectors. As a result, Lebanon's economic development path was "lopsided," more equipped to serve the interests of foreign capital and its small allied Lebanese elite than those of the majority of the local population.[80]

Left out of the benefits of these transformations was Lebanon's class of agricultural, industrial, and informal-sector laborers. While Lebanon's population almost doubled in the twenty years after independence, the rural sectors where most people lived experienced a process of "decomposition and permanent crisis," with the overall share of agriculture in Lebanon's GNP decreasing from 20 percent in 1948 to 9 percent by 1974.[81] This led to precipitous growth in the numbers of rural landless and led to "swift and jarring" rates of rural-urban migration between 1965 and 1980.[82] Despite significant industrial growth in the 1960s and 1970s, the industrial sector—stunted by the hegemonic "veto" power of Lebanon's trade-oriented merchant and financial classes—employed (and at low wages) only 20 percent of these rural migrants flooding into Beirut, leaving the remaining migrants—often described as the "menu people"—to survive within the informal sectors in extremely precarious conditions.[83] In short, a significant majority of Lebanese society in the post-independence period experienced processes of socioeconomic dislocation and impoverishment that were both rapid and intense. Pushed from the country's periphery, they increasingly congregated within suburban areas of the major cities, mostly Beirut, where they threatened to become a collective counterforce challenging the asymmetrical power relations that were denying them a better life.

How would this collective counterforce be manifested? Initially, Lebanon's working classes intensified their presence within the country's civil society through the establishment of workers' associations and unions. In the post-independence period, labor activism experienced an impressive rebirth, especially in the period after the June 1967 war, which was symbolized by a "nearly uninterrupted series of strikes and protest movements."[84] By the 1970s, this frenetic pace of labor activism showed signs of more sophisticated coordination and institutionalization, culminating in the expansion of the General Confederation of Lebanese Trade Unions (CGTL) in 1970 and the establishment in 1973 of the National Union of Agricultural Workers. The former created a unified trade union movement in the country for the first time, and, through repeated threats of a general strike in the 1970s, it used this newly consolidated national status to demand improvements in the conditions of all workers in the country, formal and informal, industrial and rural alike.[85]

There were numerous factors, however, working against the ability of workers in Lebanon to establish collective power with respect to their various employers, let alone structural power with respect to the Lebanese state—in short, the kind of power that had proved so crucial in promoting more equitable incorporations of labor into the political economies of several Latin America states.[86] The power of individual unions, for example, was constrained by the fact that commerce and industry in Lebanon continued to be dominated by the family firm.[87] This meant that unions formed after independence were numerous,[88] small, and firm oriented.[89] Moreover, the generally restrictive nature of Lebanon's labor laws provided channels through which Lebanon's political class could disrupt, thwart, and co-opt labor power.[90] A further impediment to factory-level worker activism was the state's willingness to crush labor action with the robust use of force.[91] At the national (as opposed to the firm) level, the CGTL was further hampered by its relatively small representation of the labor force as a whole, membership adding up to at best 14 percent of the entire Lebanese workforce by the mid-1970s.[92] Moreover, the fragmented and localized union structures made efforts at mobilization at the national level highly vulnerable to the factionalizing dynamics of clientelism and confessionalism, especially when placed in the larger context of the entirety of Lebanon's working classes—most of whom remained outside formalized union structures and, hence, particularly susceptible to the competing clientelist penetrations.[93]

Hence, while remaining a powerful source of popular power for those who could successfully mobilize these groups, Lebanon's broad array of pre–civil war working classes remained largely unconsolidated—emerging as a class "in themselves" but highly vulnerable to becoming a class "for someone else." In that sense, they stood on the precipice of being an agent for political change in the country—having as much potential to act in ways that would reinforce Lebanon's clientelist and confessional political legacies as they did to act in ways that would challenge them. Crucial to the direction this popular-based activism would take were the political channels used to extend their influence. What we turn to now is an analysis of attempts to create new and alternative representative channels to the Lebanese state—one by way of creating a parallel and rational-legal administrative apparatus within the state itself, the other by way of establishing reformist-oriented elite political networks working to drive a wedge through the cracks of the clientelist and confessional regime structures of the country through which these new political forces could extend their influence.

### Institutional Layering as Political Reform: The Case of Chehabism in Post-Independence Lebanon

Chehabism provides a classic case of reform via the strategy of "institutional layering"—with all of its dynamics and its weaknesses. It was initiated by the administration of Fuad Chehab, who became president of the Lebanese Republic in the wake of destabilizing sectarian violence in 1958. Reluctant and self-effacing, Chehab nonetheless was determined to use the power of his presidency to reform the Lebanese political system and prevent the kind of sectarian breakdown and immobilism that had precipitated the civil conflict of 1958. There were several facets to the Chehabist project. The first was to reestablish political balance in the system, the absence of which had precipitated the intense factional power struggles. The second—and most celebrated—was to neutralize the power of Lebanon's factionalized elite by using the powers of the presidency to build up a parallel and more efficient state. This is what we have called a strategy of "institutional layering." The third component of Chehab's strategy was to use the coercive power of the state both to protect this state-in-the-making and to prevent local and/or regional political actors from challenging it through the mobilization of popular dissent—a dynamic that had contributed in powerful ways to the breakdown of the state in 1958. After analyzing these components of what became known as "Chehabism," we turn our attention to examining why its successes were so fleeting.

Chehab's first priority after assuming executive power was to restore the political balance between the various Christian and Muslim factions; el-Khazen writes of him wanting "to restore a collective direction for the nation."[94] Externally, he established a more neutral, if not pro-Arab, stance on foreign policy issues, symbolized by the emergence of cordial relations with President Nasser. Internally, Chehab took immediate steps to increase the Muslim share of the administrative pie—passing the Personnel Law in 1959 that guaranteed the distribution of posts on a fifty–fifty Christian–Muslim basis and targeting social and economic development policies (such as road building and electricity provision) to the country's remote and underdeveloped regions, many of which had large Muslim populations. The third of Chehab's initial steps was to restore the old political game to a semblance of its earlier "health."[95] This was accomplished by expanding the number of deputies in the Lebanese parliament, a measure designed to reintegrate political elites previously excluded from power by the previous administration (such as Kamal Jumblat). Cabinets, on the other hand, while adhering to strict sectarian proportionality, were kept small, with the hope of insulating them from the factional politics that dominated the parliament. In order to give his rule some kind of social base, Chehab also relied for much of his time in office on alliances with the two most institutionalized and popular sectarian parties in the country—the *Kataib* led by Pierre Gemeyal and the Progressive Socialist Party (PSP) led by Kamal Jumblat. It is argued that these alliances provided Chehab with some "relative autonomy" from the factional infighting of the elites.[96]

Having resuscitated the old confessional political game and, hence, avoided any immediate backlash on the part of Lebanon's political classes,[97] Chehab got down to the business of trying to build up his parallel state designed to bypass the immobilizing dynamics of the *zuama*. Using the considerable powers endowed in the Office of the President,[98] Chehab effected a significant expansion in the state's size—the number of employees increasing from 5,421 in 1947 to more than 26,000 in 1966, the size of the ordinary budget of the state increasing from about 60 million Lebanese pounds in 1947 to 585 million Lebanese pounds in 1966, and the size of the Lebanese Army increasing from 6,000 in 1952 to more than 15,000 by the end of 1964.[99] Among the new recruits to the state was a group of young technocrats unconnected to the traditional political class who shared the Chehabist reformist vision and who would act as a crucial network of support for Chehab within the Lebanese bureaucracy. Hudson described them as owing their loyalty "entirely to the President" and, hence, of facilitating direct presidential control over the new administrative apparatus.[100] With his team in place, Chehab worked to establish the foundations of a robust administrative apparatus that could extend its power more deeply into the socioeconomic and political affairs of the country. This included the sponsoring of the first extensive survey of the country's development problems by the IRFED[101] under the auspices of the newly invigorated Ministry of Planning, the overhauling of virtually every branch of the bureaucracy, the creation of a Civil Service Council to rationalize (and hopefully de-clientelize) the recruitment process, the establishment of the country's first social security institution in the form of the National Social Security Fund (NSSF), the development of the publicly funded Lebanese University, and the creation of seventy independent authorities, all of which were placed effectively under the authority of the President's Office.[102]

The third prong of Chehabism was an illiberal one, revolving around the establishment of a powerful security branch of the Lebanese Army called the Deuxième Bureau. It was Chehab's political—as opposed to technocratic—watchdog, intervening at various levels of the political process to ensure the hegemony of the Chehabist project and its officials. Of primary concern to the Deuxième Bureau were political forces threatening Lebanon's "internal sovereignty."[103] The bulk of Deuxième Bureau activities, however, were directed at the domestic political arena—interfering regularly in elections in favor of Chehabist candidates, penetrating *zuama* clientelist networks as a way of buying the support of their followers, interfering in the trade union activities in order to prevent destabilizing labor action, and contributing more generally to an increase in the suppression of political liberties in the country, especially with regard to the censorship of the press.[104] Indeed, as the Chehabist state extended its influence into the heartland of *zuama* territory, so too did the Deuxième Bureau—violating what Hudson described as the convention of "sovereign equality" and noninterference in their local affairs.[105] This brought the Deuxième Bureau into direct competition with the *zuama* in its efforts to control political developments on the ground, often employing the same violent and corrupt tactics used by their traditional clientelist middlemen or *qabadays*.[106]

Chehab's initiatives had some success, especially in terms of sectarian rebalancing at the administrative level and social redistribution at the national level. These were not insignificant accomplishments for Chehab's short tenure as president, followed as they were by a much reduced reformist drive under his successor, Charles Helou. Yet, as a program of institutional and political reform, Chehabism had several fatal flaws—all of which revolved around its inability to dislodge the mechanisms through which factional and sectarian power was reproduced within the country. First, whatever political space Chehab had also was linked to "the relative lull in inter-Arab relations" that emerged in the post-1958 era,[107] a situation that was clearly transitory and would begin to change dramatically in the face of emerging polarization within the region as the 1960s progressed, symbolized by the creation of the Palestine Liberation Organization (PLO) in 1964 at the end of Chehab's term in office. As we shall see, the Palestinian issue would burrow deeply into the Lebanese "political field," lead to the increasing polarization and bifurcation of elite networking in the country, and destroy whatever neutral political space the Chehabist state had benefited from and had managed to sustain.

Second, Chehabism never had any real popular support, leaving the Lebanese masses free to be mobilized along factional lines. Indeed, el-Khazen described the country's popular sectors as being completely unmoved by Chehabism; it was "a bourgeois current representing the interests of the bourgeois state."[108] Instead of encouraging the growth of industry, something that could have alleviated Beirut's growing unemployment problem, for example, Johnson criticized Chehabism's approach to Lebanon's popular sectors as essentially being confined to "us[ing] the Deuxième Bureau to control *qabadays* and criminal networks amongst the sub-proletariat."[109] Neither did Chehab show any interest in organizing the country's popular sectors into some kind of political movement—something that could have challenged one of the key bases of *zuama* power. Not only was he disdainful of the political life more generally, but he also was acutely aware of the sectarian contradictions that might have been unleashed had a more populist version of Chehabism been promoted. As Kamal Salibi astutely noted, it was quite likely that a populist version of Chehabism would have been both too radical for the Christian "street" while not radical enough for the Muslim "masses."[110]

Finally, Chehab left the underlying sectarian and factional political components of the country's regime intact. Indeed, Chehab has been described as promoting a "strict application" of the dictates of the National Pact, further strengthening the system he sought to undermine.[111] As the regime increasingly competed with and alienated the various clientelist networks of the country, it gradually began to lose its temporary autonomy as *zuama* politicians joined forces and fought back to defend "the Lebanese system." Indeed, with the dramatic expansion in the size of the state under Chehab, the clientelistic incentives for penetrating and appropriating state resources had grown enormously. In short, Chehab, and his strategy of "institutional layering," failed to change the basic underpinnings of the Lebanese state and its regime—built as they both were on the fragile and shifting array of alliances between its factional components. Indeed, as a result of the alliances struck with both the *Kataib* and the PSP, ones that ushered in a period of their "state-protected institutional growth,"[112] Chehab's policies, in the end, were accused of reinforcing "almost every single feature of the old superstructure."[113]

As a result, the Chehabist strategy of "institutional layering" as a gradual driver of political change proved to be extremely short-lived in the reform-resistant Lebanese polity. Paradoxically, with the demise of Chehabism and the subsequent dismantling of the repressive features of the Chehabist state—especially the Deuxième Bureau—new opportunities for reformist politics began to emerge within the growing political cracks, not only within the state apparatus itself but also within the realms of civil and political society, where shifting pockets of unoccupied political space opened up.[114] We now turn to an analysis of the (ultimately unsuccessful) efforts to take advantage of these emerging spaces by the counternetworking and political mobilization activities of Kamal Jumblat and the Lebanese left.

*Challenging Lebanon's Sectarian Political Legacy—*
*Jumblat's Push for Political Reform:*

In his definitive study of Lebanese politics published in the late 1960s, Michael Hudson argued that Lebanon's system of factionalized politics—facilitated by a consensus over the importance of confessional proportionality that Chehab had reaffirmed—had begun to show signs of creating conditions amendable to accommodation and the "widespread sharing of power";[115] it was what Hudson called a "narrow" if "precarious" flexibility that emanated from the disaggregated nature of the Lebanese political system and the shifting nature of the political alliance making within it.[116] Hudson also found evidence at this time that Lebanon's electoral system was becoming more accessible to a greater diversity of actors and opinions, arguing that, in the two decades after independence, "more and more" Lebanese were participating in the political system and that electoral contests were becoming "steadily more competitive."[117] He also found signs of a growing rate of turnover among deputies that allowed new elements (professionals instead of landowners) to enter the system.[118] To Hudson, all this suggested that the Lebanese political order was "not entirely stagnant in the face of demographic and social change."[119] While its factionalizing dynamic posed "formidable obstacles" to the emergence of broad-based political movements and parties,[120] the system did show signs of being remarkably adaptive, "more liberal, more open to citizen participation, more legitimate, and more capable of executive action."[121]

Hudson's guarded optimism with regard to dynamics at the center of political power points to the possibility for gradual institutional change in Lebanon's post-independence confessional democratic system, however powerful were the array of factors that worked to buttress factionalized elite power. It was this sense of possibility that motivated various reformist oriented politicians in the post-independence period, foremost among them being the Druze *zaim* and leader of the Popular Socialist Party (PSP), Kamal Jumblat, who, after some success in elections in 1960, decided to adopt an approach of "constructive engagement" with the Lebanese state, not only with Chehab's administration but also with the much more circumscribed ones of Presidents Helou and Franjieh.[122] He did so knowing, however, that his power as a *zaim* alone would be limited—both given his status as a Druze politician that shut him out of access to the executive offices of power as well as due to the entrenched hold of communal and class power within the state itself. While it was clear that maintaining a foothold inside the state would be of crucial importance—if only to ensure the delivery of patronage to his political base of supporters, especially in his Chouf constituency, where he continued to face intra-sectarian competition from the rival Druze Arslan family—it also was clear that without a broader, cross-sectarian basis of support, it would be difficult for reformist agendas to have much political traction. Jumblat's strategy, therefore, became to increase his political leverage inside the state by linking it to the burgeoning processes of sociopolitical mobilization outside it,[123] ultimately tying his fate to an alliance with the regional network of power linked to the increasingly Lebanese-based PLO. In essence, Jumblat's strategy came to mirror the national, supranational, and subnational networking dynamics of the country's factional political elite—but this time in order to challenge rather than reproduce the sectarian status quo. As Nazih Richani concluded with respect to the reformist approach, Jumblat, at least until the outbreak of the civil war itself, always viewed the crisis in "political terms," and, while he never ruled out the use of force, he never called for "revolutionary action."[124]

Jumblat's mobilizational campaign developed in stages. After an initial period of supporting the autonomous activities of the labor and student movements prior to 1967, for example, Jumblat's strategy shifted toward supporting the organization of a broader political movement. This shift coincided with the growing regionalization of political conflict in Lebanon, characterized by, among other developments, the growing "on the ground" presence of the PLO in Lebanese affairs. Jumblat was described as being "indefatigable" in his efforts to organize fronts and coalitions among the Lebanese left, efforts that led ultimately led to the formation in 1975 of the LNM. Energizing these efforts was the surge in popular support for the Palestinian resistance—symbolized by the massive demonstrations on their behalf that regularly broke out on Lebanon's streets. Indeed, the Palestinian issue accelerated the mobilization process further by providing both a unifying discursive focus and energy to leftist campaigns and access to the resources of the PLO's growing organizational infrastructure in the country, especially after the signing of the Cairo Accords in 1969.[125] In order to capitalize on the mobilizational opportunities provided by the PLO's presence, Jumblat was described as working to forge "close political links with virtually every organization, radical and conservative alike, that was identified or linked to the PLO,"[126] part of a broader strategy that included the striking of regionalized alliances with Arab states among all Lebanese political factions. For Jumblat, this strengthening alliance with the PLO was designed to enhance his ability to strike a bargain with Lebanon's ruling classes; he repeatedly offered to act as a moderating influence on the PLO in exchange for the granting of greater political power to the Muslim communities of the country and the implementation of moderate socioeconomic reforms.[127]

The final and fateful phase of Jumblat's odyssey was his slide into armed conflict. Analyzing why this happened is crucial for understanding the array of constraints on institutional reform in Lebanon. Much of this revolves around what Hudson also argued was the overall "structural rigidity" of the Lebanese system, despite the incremental signs to the contrary.[128] This rigidity emanated from the ability of various components of the post-independence political elite to coalesce in defense of their factional power—creating what the historical institutionalist school would call "veto power" and "veto points." Three such "veto points" have proven particularly effective in thwarting reformist efforts within the Lebanese political system—those inhibiting the emergence of cross-sectarian national political parties, those preventing significant social and economic reform, and, most fatefully, those blocking changes to the communal power-sharing arrangements.

Lebanon's electoral system, for example, established during the mandate period, has traditionally worked to the advantage of local factionalized political elites. While there are political parties in Lebanon, most revolve around powerful notable families and have "not yet [been] the agencies through which and by means of which Lebanese voters are integrated and represented." As Labib Yamak argued in the 1960s with resilient relevance to this day, Lebanon had plenty of political parties but lacked a party system.[129] Even ideologically oriented parties have been distinctly molded by the system, unable to garner significant cross-sectarian electoral support and, hence, remaining strongly rooted within sectarian communities.[130] In short, regardless of their ideological inclinations, the Lebanese political system has forced political parties—if they wanted to achieve electoral success—to organize themselves along the same lines as the broader factionalized struggle for political power and resources in the country.[131]

Lebanon's political system also has facilitated the emergence of "veto points" over questions of social and economic reform. Even during Helou's administration (when the Deuxième Bureau was still strong), the power of "big capital" strongly exerted itself through efforts to dismantle the Chehabist state after his departure.[132] In 1970, this veto power became even more apparent when a technocratic cabinet under the prime ministership of the leading Beirut *zaim*, Saeb Salem, tried to promote what it termed "a revolution from above" in order to forestall what threatened to become "a revolution from below"—one that posed a particular threat to his own clientelist networks. Be they efforts to formulate policies to promote the national development of industry or those to construct a more equitable pharmaceutical regime with the hope of reducing the price of essential medications, all proposals for reform were systematically blocked by the intertwining networks of "parasitic capitalism and political feudalism."[133] Indeed, it was the country's merchant associations—representative of the power of this commercial/financial oligarchy within Lebanon's civil society[134]—that led these protests with their threats of strike action or through brazenly unjust efforts to reduce the supply of essential medications on the open market in the case of proposals to reform the pharmaceutical sector.[135] Even with growing rifts between the Christian and Muslim sections of the country's bourgeoisie over questions of political reform, their intersectarian elite networks remained cohesive enough to veto even minor reforms to the country's economic structure,[136] and this was coupled with an increasing willingness to use state coercive power to repress the rising swell of popular demonstrations.[137] Hence, despite the fractious and increasingly bitter nature of their political relationships in the late 1960s and early 1970s, Lebanon's "power bloc" still managed to reach enough consensus to use the seemingly immobilized state to maintain a powerful class-based hegemony.

The final and perhaps most resilient "veto point" revolved around the ability of confessional elites to prevent changes to the country's confessional power-sharing arrangements. While contained for much of the 1960s,[138] confessional tensions increased accordingly as the issue of Palestine began to intrude more forcefully into the Lebanese political arena, manifested by the more persistent demands on the part of the country's Sunni Muslim leaders to alter the political and economic terms of "the unequal partnership."[139] Resistance within the ranks of the Maronite community, however, became increasingly intransigent and backed by a variety of countermobilizational efforts. Loose political alliances within

the Maronite community, for example, were tightened in the form of the
*Hilf*,[140] and, parallel to the state's suppression of worker protests, Maronite
political elites increasingly proved able to instrumentalize the coercive
arms of the state to suppress the activities of the Palestinian resistance,
who, by the early 1970s, were described as "provocatively appearing on
Beirut's streets brandishing arms and wearing full battle dress."[141] The real
force behind the Maronite communal veto, however, was the emerging
hegemony of the *Kataib*, a party whose existence was described as under-
mining "whatever possibility existed for an institutional restructuring of
the Lebanese political system."[142] Backed as this was by the escalating
development of its military apparatus prior to the outbreak of the civil
war in 1975—characterized by the increased importation of weapons, the
increasing coordination with the Lebanese Army in its assaults on Palestinian commandos, and the development of an extensive paramilitary
infrastructure—the *Kataib*'s power became hegemonic, able to mobilize,
if not force the virtual closure of, Maronite political ranks.[143]

In effect, therefore, the increased mobilization and infrastructural
power of both the *Kataib*, on the one hand, and the PSP/LNM, on the
other—each strengthened by networking at the national, regional, and
local levels—eliminated what little room for maneuver existed between
the cracks of the factionalized Lebanese political system, polarized the
political field along communal lines, and froze the Lebanese system in
its tracks. Already prone to extra-state violence as a result of the inability of the state to maintain a monopoly over its use, Lebanon's political
field now descended into violent confrontation between these two poles.
While the LNM (and its military wing, the Joint Forces) was an extremely
heterogeneous entity that struggled to impose civil order in areas that
it controlled,[144] at the national level, it came very close to achieving a
military victory over the *Kataib*-led forces of the predominantly Christian
right in 1976, a victory that could have led to the emergence of a new
critical juncture in Lebanese history and might have opened the door to
significant socioeconomic and political reform in the country. The possibility was thwarted, however, by the military intervention of the Syrians, who coercively returned Lebanon to its confessional political roots,
ones that the Ba'thist regime in Damascus could more easily manipulate
and control for its own political and geostrategic purposes. As we shall
see in the final section of this chapter, not only did this bring to an end
the most ambitious attempt at promoting structurally oriented political
reform in Lebanon, but Syria's intervention and the establishment of its
political hegemony over Lebanon also ended up reversing patterns of
state and regime formation in the country, erasing whatever incremental
reformist gains had been made in the pre–civil war period and returning

the country's political system back to its factionalized, sectarian political foundations.

### Reconsolidating Political Sectarianism: Civil War, Pax Syriana, and Reversals in Lebanese State Formation

The main legacy of the civil war period between 1975 and 1990 was the consolidation of new sectarian political networks that superseded those of the traditional *zu'ama* through the institutionalization of militia entities. It was these entities that precipitated the destruction of public space in the country and the infliction of what Corm calls "unspeakable violence on civilian populations" though sniping, kidnapping, blind shelling, and the sectarian cleansing of mixed communal villages in order to establish strict demarcation lines between newly established urban sectarian enclaves.[145] Whether the "corporatist entity" established by the Lebanese Forces,[146] the diaspora-funded neopatrimonial networks of the AMAL Movement,[147] the emerging, externally funded "Islamic Welfare State" of Hezbollah, or the nascent networks revolving around the Sunni businessman and philan-thropists Rafiq Hariri that would be transformed in the postwar period into the Sunni-oriented Future Movement,[148] most (with the exception of the less institutionalized and less-coercively oriented Hariri political networks) worked to combine coercive power, often subsidized by foreign patrons, with consolidated political control over defined pieces of terri-tory, control that eventually developed, to varying degrees, into institu-tionalized sectarian "quasi-states" and cantons.[149]

Buttressing the power of these new sectarian elite networks was the profitable nature of the war itself, whose dynamics increasingly came to resemble those of a "war economy." Picard writes, for example, that the "need and creed" that were at the root of the outbreak of civil war in the country were "progressively superseded by the crude and growing greed of the antagonistic parties."[150] In order to finance the initial costs of war, the various militias embarked on a variety of predatory activities—principal among them being the looting of state property such as ports; the cre-ation of protection rackets through extortionist taxation of maritime trade, commerce, and citizens; and increasing militia involvement in illicit black market activities relating to trade in such commodities as drugs, arms, and toxic wastes. Further contributing to this growing economic war chest was the paradoxical tendency among the various militias to cooperate in the division of war spoils, Picard writing of "forms of interaction—and even of interdependence and cooperation—that seemed almost out of place given the intensity of violence between the highly polarized communities."[151]

Not surprisingly, the profitable nature of these predatory activities facilitated the intertwining of these militia enterprises with preexisting social and economic networks. The Syrians, for example, increasingly began to insinuate themselves into the predatory economic networks of the war, something that completely transformed the scale of the militia economy as a whole, with strong implications for the postwar period.[152] Moreover, symbolized by the increasing tendency on the part of the militias to reinvest/launder black market profits back into formal economic activities, militia networks also engaged with the more long-standing economic networks of the prewar Lebanese bourgeoisie. "One should not underestimate," argues Picard, "the discreet but continuous participation of the largest fortunes from the prewar era in these new profitable ventures, nor the complex financial ties that formed between nonmilitary economic elites and the new entrepreneurs who prospered in the shadow of the militia system."[153] This included an especially strong inclination to invest in property development, Picard writing of a powerful "craving for land."[154] All of this helped to consolidate the power and influence of a new class of wartime entrepreneurs, labeled by Samir Makdisi as the war's "nouveaux riches" and by Picard as "the militia lumpen-elite."[155] It was this new social group, part of a now-transformed—though a much more fractious and antagonistic—political class in the country, that would carry over the wartime patterns, practices, and projects of accumulation into the postwar period.

However, at the same time that various sectarian networks of power were being enriched, the structural conditions produced by the civil war were creating "slow-moving" causal processes that moved in the opposite direction. In addition to the significant demographic changes brought about by the violence and ethnic cleansing of the civil war,[156] the structural power underlying nascent movements of civil resistance that began to emerge in the latter years of the civil war was impeded by the significant levels of out-migration that numbered almost 1 million Lebanese, almost one-third of the prewar population. As Salim Nasr remarked, this deprived the country of its "economic backbone" given that most were from the middle classes.[157] Samir Makdisi further estimated that the civil war resulted in a precipitous 33 percent fall in real per capita income between 1974 and 1990, with wage earners and fixed income groups being particularly hard-hit by the declining wages, rising inflations rates, and currency devaluations of the mid- to late 1980s.[158] Most indicative of this regressive structural trend, however, was the deterioration in income distribution in the country. This was starkly revealed by a study of household income conducted in the early postwar period (1998) that showed income inequalities to be comparable to those of the late 1950s, significantly worse than their levels in the early 1970s, leading to the emergence of "a striking dualism" within Lebanese society and the persistence of stubbornly high rates of poverty, with the most abject poor being hidden in the remote rural areas of the Beqa and Akkar.[159]

Hence, Lebanon's civil war produced an array of sociopolitical transformations that would significantly alter the dynamics of Lebanon's postwar political economy and shift the sociostructural conditions underlying the country's civil society. It produced new powerful, sectarian political networks that were more fragmented and antagonistic and that superseded those of the country's traditional elites. It also spawned unruly and predatory forms of capital accumulation that led to the widening of socioeconomic gaps between these new elite political networks and Lebanon's middle and lower classes, reversing more favorable socioeconomic transformations in the 1960s and 1970s. In short, the socioeconomic conditions underlying the Lebanese polity at the civil war's end were less conducive to the reestablishment, let alone consolidation, of the democratic political life and the empowerment of secular-oriented, nonsectarian networks within the country's postwar civil society. Hence, rather than opening up possibilities for new directions in Lebanese political life, the civil war set the stage for reversals in processes of state formation that would reinforce the path-dependent nature of its factionalized political trajectory.

It was the period of Syria's "protectorate" over Lebanon at the civil war's end (between 1990 to 2005), however, that reconsolidated the system of sectarian democracy on the backs of these wartime sociopolitical legacies.[160] This reconsolidation was represented, in part, by the Syrian-sponsored constitutional reforms agreed to at the Taif Conference in 1989 by remnants of the Lebanese parliament, which, despite the parliament's call for deconfessionalization,[161] ended up amending and, most importantly, formalizing Lebanon's sectarian power-sharing formula.[162] Backing up the effects of these constitutional amendments were the political processes unleashed by Syrian statecraft that reinforced the fragmenting and inequality-generating dynamics of the country's political system while weakening its democratic ones. These reinforcing dynamics revolved around the consolidation of Syria's coercive power, its instrumentalization of formal state institutions, and its development of hegemonic collaborative political networks.

The basis for Syria's hegemony in Lebanon was coercive, epitomized by its robust military (and Western-sanctioned) intervention in Lebanon at the end of 1991 that brought the civil war to an end. A process was immediately started of deploying the Syrian and Lebanese armies across the country in the form of military bases, security offices, and checkpoints, and this was paralleled by the disarmament of the Lebanese

militias themselves—with the significant exceptions of Hezballah's and
that of the Israeli-backed South Lebanese Army. This was followed by an
extensive program of military reconstruction that resulted in the expansion of the Lebanese Army from a prewar level of 15,000 to a postwar
level of more than 60,000 (in 2002)—a process that Nicholas Blanford
referred to as its "Syrianization." This also transformed it into one of the
most important employers in the country that provided a livelihood for
more than 500,000 people and that consumed in excess of 15 percent of
government revenues by the early 2000s.[163] Combined with the de facto
integration of Lebanese and Syrian security forces, the result was the consolidation by Syria of a "near monopoly of force" in the country.[164]

Syria used this coercive power to dominate the Lebanese political
economy.[165] It did so by constructing a complex system of political control that "effectively neutered genuine Lebanese politics."[166] This revolved
around a twofold strategy of weakening the democratic institutions of
the state—namely its parliament, cabinet, and executive offices—while
constructing a variety of dispersed and collaborative political networks
beneath them. Through its manipulation of electoral laws and alliances, for example, Syria effectively promoted the "depoliticization" of the
Lebanese parliament.[167] Standing in stark contrast to the prewar period
between 1962 and 1976, which had been characterized by a stable set
of election rules, the first three postwar elections were all organized
around distinct electoral regulations.[168] Paralleling this gerrymandering
activity was Syrian interference in the formation of electoral lists and
alliances to ensure the election of pro-Syrian candidates and prevent
the election of noncompliant deputies, particularly within the Christian
and Sunni communities. Bassel Salloukh described the Syrians as being
"intimately" involved in these processes, vetoing the inclusion of anti-
Syrian candidates in certain electoral lists and forcing the inclusion of
pro-Syrian candidates in others.[169] As a result, the Lebanese parliament
suffered a serious loss in popular legitimacy, symbolized by the boycott
of Christian voters in the parliamentary elections of 1992 and the low
voter turnout in the ones that followed—especially among the younger
"wartime generation."[170] Indeed, in comparing elections in the pre- and
postwar periods, Farid el-Khazen noted that "whatever the imperfections
of Lebanon's prewar democratic system, [prewar] Lebanon was one of the
few developing countries where opposition politics made a difference and
had a decisive impact on the political process." In the postwar period,
concluded el-Khazen in 1998, "none of the vigour and assertiveness of
prewar opposition politics are present."[171]

Equally important for securing and perpetuating Syrian hegemony
in postwar Lebanon was its instrumentalization of executive power. Here,

Syria's main point of entry came about as a result of the dispersal of sectarian power at the executive level between the president, prime minister, and Speaker of the assembly—the "troika," as they have been called. The resultant blurred lines of authority led to numerous procedural disputes[172] accentuating a political process that was already characterized by extra-institutional forms of bargaining and "a continuous mode of ad hoc decision making."[173] In order to get around these immobilizing sectarian dynamics, each of "the presidents" carved out his own independent sphere of influence within (as well as outside) the state. Prime Minister Rafiq Hariri proved particularly adept at developing mechanisms to enhance his overall bargaining power—creating an "inner cabinet" of loyal ministers as well as an influential network of support within the private sector referred to as "the bureau";[174] building up the Office of the Prime Minister and the Council for Reconstruction and Development (CDR) into what Leenders called "a substitute government," accountable to no one except the prime minister;[175] and continuing to cultivate strong ties with his political and financial networks outside Lebanon, both in the Gulf region as well as in the West. Yet, however successful Hariri's efforts were in developing his own informal networks of power in and beyond Lebanon, the factional dynamics of Lebanese politics—accentuated by Syrian statecraft—ensured that they remained paralleled by the political networks of his "presidential" rivals as well as by the overarching veto power of Syria's security agents in the country. When taken together, the result of Syrian statecraft was the emergence of immobilizing dynamics at all levels of the postwar Lebanese state—from the executive to the cabinet to the parliament—that weakened the salience of democratic institutions and strengthening informal political dynamics emanating from the factionalized and sectarianized political life of the postwar period.

Indeed, Syria selectively used and cultivated these networks "to penetrate into the far reaches of Lebanese society."[176] The most central and powerful were those cultivated during the war years with the militia enterprises, especially those within the Shi'a community. Syria also was able to take advantage of long-standing alliances with certain traditional Lebanese political elite families, from the Karamis of Tripoli, to the Franjiehs of Zghorta, to the more variable support of the Jumblats of the Chouf region. Finally, in order to back up these local networks of "extended collusion,"[177] the Syrians co-opted—indeed, manufactured "from scratch" through various forms of electoral interference—an entirely new coterie of dependent political elites that had little to no sociopolitical base in the country, transforming them into what el-Khazen described as politicians and parties "without partisans."[178] It was these that allowed Syria to insinuate itself into a series of local, regional, and national networks of power, a process described by el-Khazen as a new modality of authoritarianism "by diffusion."[179]

What is crucial to understanding the overall impact of the "Syrian variable" in Lebanon's postwar political equation, however, is that rather than dramatically altering the underlying factional and sectarian political dynamics of the country, the Syrian presence merely accentuated them. While the Syrian presence did work to stabilize political order in the country, its use of coercive power and its direct and indirect interference with the institutions of Lebanese political life weakened the possibilities for the development of Lebanon's democratic heritage in the immediate postwar period. At the same time, its cultivation and manipulation of numerous informal networks of clients and collaborators deepened the various forms of factionalism within the postwar political arena, effectively destroying hopes of deconfessionalization as called for by the Taif Accord. In essence, therefore, the Syrian presence—paralleling some of the dynamics of French mandate statecraft before it—acted as a powerful feedback mechanism, weakening the institutional foundations of democratic life in the country while strengthening the many parallel, informal, and sectarianized regimes of power revolving around religion, kinship, and class. Given that the prewar period had seen piecemeal signs of greater political openness, even if weak and partial, these early postwar developments—ones that reinforced the structural trends of the civil war itself—set the stage for intensified processes of sectarianization in postwar Lebanese state–society relations, including its civil society.

## Conclusions

Lebanese political life exhibits powerful path-dependent qualities. Emanating from the long, drawn-out critical juncture of the late nineteenth century, when sectarianism first emerged as a principle of governance, sectarian dynamics have maintained a hegemonic hold over Lebanon's political field, resisting the myriad challenges to its dominance—whether those of a gradual and slow-moving nature or those more combative attempts that ultimately culminated in the use of coercive force. The resultant resilience of this "Lebanese system," however, rather than being a product of a particular and enduring political culture, is the result of the continual and recursive interaction between its confessional institutional order and its reinforcement by external actors that have contributed to processes of sectarianism from above, and the multilevel networking of political elites who, in their efforts to preserve their own factionalized bases of power, have contributed to the reinforcement of sectarianism from below. Indeed, these dynamics of sectarian reinforcement and reproduction have proven to be particularly powerful in Lebanon's civil war and postwar periods, precipitating reversals in state and regime formation. It is to an analysis of the effects of these reversals on Lebanese political life itself—focusing on the relations between Lebanon's postwar political elites and its emerging community of secular-oriented civil associations—that we turn now.

3

# Struggling for Civic Space

*Associational Politics within*
*Lebanon's Postwar Sectarian Democracy*

One of the fascinating developments in Lebanon's early postwar period—
precipitated by the return of the Lebanese state—was the dramatic growth
in civil society. Despite Syria's growing presence, heightened sectarian
tensions, and a lingering sense of uncertainty, the number of associations increased steadily in the 1990s at an annual rate of 250, creating
by the end of the decade a sector that ranged between 4,000 and 6,000
organizations.[1] Overall expenditure in the associational sector also was
large, estimated at $300 million annually throughout the 1990s, with large
associations handling annual budgets in excess of $5 million.[2] Of further
note is the fact that more than 60 percent of associational funding was
derived from sources internal to the country (e.g., services fees, donations,
and so forth), indicating that the sector had a "good sustainability basis"
or, in other words, was firmly rooted in the country's political economy.[3]
This rootedness of associations also was exemplified by the number of
Lebanese involved with associations, with more than 50,000 estimated
to have been members and an additional 50,000 estimated to have acted
as volunteers—more than 50 percent of whom were said to be women.
In short, as a 2001 World Bank report surmised, the associational sector
in postwar Lebanon had the capacity to mobilize in excess of 100,000
people, "a very substantial figure for a country of a small population of
4 million inhabitants only."[4]

This chapter seeks to unpack these seemingly impressive but politically ambiguous trends. First, in order to understand their potential
political significance, these numbers need to be placed in the context of
both the Syrian presence (examined in the previous chapter) as well as
the postwar maneuverings of Lebanese political elites (examined below)
who had to operate within these restrictive, though for some empower-

ing, parameters. It is this latter context—one that revolves around the flourishing of systems of unruly capitalism that had been carried over from the civil war, the intensification of various forms of clientelism, and the invigoration of the (often openly coercive) politics of exclusion aimed at challenges from oppositional social forces below—that we will examine to shed light on the opportunities and challenges facing advocacy associations as the country moved into its postwar period. The rest of the chapter examines the struggles of these associations and of the "civil movements" that they helped to spawn to establish a counter-hegemonic, nonsectarian presence within Lebanon's postwar civil and political society. Three case studies are taken up—one linked to efforts to build national nongovernmental organization (NGO) coalitions, another linked to the development of "civil movements" for political reform, and a third linked to the Independence Intifada—the national cross-sectarian mobilizations that occurred in the wake of the assassination of Rafiq Hariri and that precipitated the withdrawal of Syrian troops from the country in the spring of 2005. It is from these case studies that general insights are developed that can be applied to the more specific case studies of associative action examined in the rest of the book—ones that point to, first, the types of relative openings and shifting space that can emerge within Lebanon's fragmented postwar political environment; and, second, the challenges that the "shifting" nature of political opportunities posed for agents of change.

### Unruly Capitalism, Clientelism, and Coercion: State–Society Relations in Postwar Lebanon and the Reinforcement of Sectarian Democracy

One of the most important underlying dynamics contributing to the retrenchment of Lebanon's postwar sectarian democracy was the continuation of the wartime system of unruly capitalism. Initially, the Lebanese population had hoped for better, especially with the appointment of the Hariri government after the elections of 1992. According to Guillain Denoeux and Robert Springborg, for example, Hariri was looked upon as "the merchant prince" who offered "the desperate Lebanese . . . the ideal combination of pride in his country, selfless commitment to its rehabilitation, and the deep pockets necessary to bring it about."[5] Within the first year of his premiership, he had formulated an ambitious program of reconstruction called Horizon 2000 designed to reestablish Lebanon's historic role as a laissez-faire regional banking and commercial center.[6] While successful in promoting a tremendous recapitalization of the country in the early postwar period that resulted in initial growth rates of 8 percent, however, Hariri's reconstruction agenda also provided Lebanon's postwar elite with enormous opportunities for the continuation of what Debie has called *le capitalisme de guerre*.[7] This was clear from the sheer size—let alone design—of state investment in the first years of the reconstruction program, which was staggering and risky for a country of Lebanon's size; indeed, Denoeux and Springborg describe it as a "Faustian bargain" that played right into the hands of Lebanon's war and postwar elites.[8] Symbolic of this "Faustian bargain" were the perceptions and wealth of anecdotal evidence pointing to ubiquitous and large-scale corruption. While always present in the Lebanese political system, Hudson describing it as "the inevitable price for political cooperation,"[9] the scale of corruption in Lebanon's postwar period has been described as unprecedented.[10] Asked to comment on the postwar problem of corruption, George Corm, the former minister of economy under the Hoss government (1998 and 2000), remarked that, in effect, corruption had ended up robbing the country twice—once during the war and again during the postwar period.[11]

Yet, with corruption being as much a symptom as a cause, its flourishing was made possible by the various structural and institutional changes in Lebanon's postwar political economy.[12] A key factor facilitating grandiose corrupt practices was the changing nature of Lebanon's competing and powerful oligarchic socioeconomic elite networks. In the prewar period, these were described as having a greater tendency to work *with* rather than *against* the state, a dynamic that kept levels of corruption at "sustainable" levels.[13] In the postwar period, however, these signs of complementary dynamics largely disappeared, creating governance conditions described as unpredictable, erratic, and extremely volatile.[14] Neither did the more inclusive but unclear and immobilizing political formula of the post-Taif era offer much promise that the Lebanese state would be able to transcend "the volatile and competitive game" being played out between these different economic networks.[15] Indeed, instead of attempting to agree on basic reforms to the state apparatus that might have contributed to the emergence of a minimal public sector, Lebanon's most powerful postwar elites simply competed for the right to control and instrumentalize different pieces of the state apparatus. This not only facilitated the continuation of the state's neopatrimonial role as the distributor of confessional patronage, but it also resulted in the Lebanese state becoming one of the principle agents enforcing and protecting unruly capitalistic accumulations, particularly apparent (as we shall see) in its continuous and deliberate failure to regulate lucrative but environmentally destructive practices in the quarrying industry and the de facto commercial development of the ostensibly state-owned coastal region. Hence, despite increased fractiousness, Lebanon's competing postwar elites were able to instrumentalize the latent power of the postwar Lebanese state in two paradoxical ways. By taking advantage of its weakness, they were able to transform corruption into the rule rather than the exception in the post-war period, extracting considerable amounts of rent from the state in the process; by taking advantage of its authoritarian potential, they were also able to use their negotiated access to distinct parts of the state to protect and promote their more particularistic accumulations—creating what, in effect, was a classic example of "dispersed domination."

One of the consequences of the flourishing of unruly capitalism in postwar Lebanon, unchecked by the disciplining forces of either the state or the market, has been the further increase in levels of socioeconomic deprivation that had taken root during the war—conditions under which postwar clientelist dynamics have thrived. These clientelist dynamics man-ifested in several ways—through bureaucratic processes at the command-ing heights of the state, during elections as a result of the intensification of electoral forms of political clientelism, and through the growing insti-tutionalization and autonomy of sectarian social welfare sectors, the most spectacular being the consolidation of the social welfare institutions of Hezbollah in the postwar period. Opportunities for bureaucratic clien-telism, for example, increased exponentially in the postwar period with the expansion of the postwar state itself.[16] The number of people employed by the state continued to rise in the early postwar period, the product of the politicking around issues of militia demobilization and reemployment. The result was that, by 1998, the state became the largest single employer in the country, employing between 26 and 35 percent of the working population.[17] Moreover, given the ability of most employees to call upon a higher-level political protection, it became virtually impossible to alter the situation, as Hariri discovered during his efforts to "purge" the bureaucracy in 1993.[18] Further exacerbating this bureaucratic morass was the prolifera-tion of ministries and specialized agencies. In 1993, for example, the first Hariri government created eight new ministries, a public policy initiative clearly designed to stave off immobilizing intra-elite conflict in a large and fractious cabinet by spreading more widely the patronage opportuni-ties of ministerial office. Neither were any of the already existing mecha-nisms of bureaucratic oversight and accountability—such as the Conseil de la Fonction Publique created during the Chehabist era—allowed to operate in an autonomous manner. This debilitation of an already weak rationalizing dynamic within the postwar Lebanese state exacerbated pre-existing tendencies for bureaucratic units to become personalized and politically autonomous zones of influence. The CDR, for example, has been described as being accountable to no one but then–Prime Minister

Hariri;[19] similar judgments were passed with regard to Berri's control over the Council of the South and the newly created Ministry of Expatriates;[20] and a glaring example of the neopatrimonial instrumentalization of the postwar Lebanese state was associated with Walid Jumblat's control over the Ministry of the Displaced.[21] While a dominating dynamic throughout the entire postwar Lebanese state, bureaucratic forms of clientelism were particularly intense with respect to the relations between the "three presidents," so much so that Leenders wrote of it as being routinized in the postwar period.[22]

Paralleling the postwar routinization of patronage politics at the executive level of the state was the intensification of various forms of sect- and clan-based political clientelism associated more directly with electoral politics. Already touted in the prewar period as being the highest in the world on a per capita basis, postwar electoral expenditures reached unprecedented levels even by Lebanese standards, especially during the elections of 2000 in which Rafiq Hariri competed fiercely with the partisans of the Syrian-backed President Lahoud.[23] Research by a Lebanese social worker, Ghada Jabbour, on "the price of giving" in the Beirut quarter of Karm el-Zaytoun prior to the parliamentary elections of 2000 revealed a sudden burst of activity at the newly opened office of the Hariri Foundation—intensity that was clearly the product of changes in the electoral boundaries of the city that had transformed the area into "a strategic region."[24] Reflecting on the subtle but powerful influence of clientelist electoral practices, Jabbour remarked that while the newly opened office of the Hariri Foundation was not used directly in the electoral campaign, it nonetheless represented a timely "symbolic investment" that generated among the beneficiaries of its services a powerful sense of obligation to vote for Hariri in the election.[25] This intensive descent of Hariri into the world of electoral clientelism—mimicking *zu'ama* practices among the Sunni elite of the prewar period—testified to the powerful mechanisms of reproduction at work within Lebanon's sectarian democracy as a whole.[26]

Finally, in addition to bureaucratic and electoral clientelism, postwar Lebanon also saw the intensified development of institutionalized forms of clan- and communally based clientelism—evidenced by the wartime and postwar growth in the number of religious and clan-based civil institutions.[27] Indeed, one early postwar study of their expansion describes the phenomenon as "a contagion," especially in Beirut, where it exceeded "anything that . . . had been known before."[28] This development was particularly of note within the Shi'a communities of the country, and especially within the "resistance society" of Hezbollah, where there has emerged a complex and dense network of socioeconomic associations.[29] These have ranged from numerous social welfare institutions;[30] to a large, decentered network of educational institutions and schools designed to renew Hezbollah's social base;[31] to a variety of socioeconomic, cultural, and religious institutions that includes the Mahdi Scouts, whose membership reached numbers in excess of 45,000 youth.[32] These have been paralleled by an increase in the number of sectarian institutions within the Sunni communities of Beirut, sparked by the growth and penetration of *salafi* networks and the counter networking of Dar al-Fatwa.[33] While it is difficult to unpack the exact influence of these institutional developments on the growing hegemony of sectarian movements and parties, it is clear, as Judith Harik concluded with respect to those offered by Hezbollah, that their political impact has been "profound."[34]

The enrichment, intensification, and institutionalization of various clientelist networks in postwar Lebanon have had a powerful impact on state–society relations, contributing to the deepening of sectarian identities in postwar Lebanon. This has, in part, been epitomized by the increase in expressions of individual religiosity within each community;[35] the increased penetration of sectarian logic into universities, the media, publishing houses, charitable networks, and sport; as well as the increased expression of political grievances and rights in sectarian terms. Indeed, in contrast to the prewar period, when expressions of confessional sentiment were described as being "nuanced, subtle, and furtive," Khalaf described such expressions as being "much more invasive," penetrating "virtually every national discourse and public issue," and sparking "confessional hostility and anxiety" in the postwar period.[36] Further evidence of an increase in sectarian sentiments has been the noted postwar increase in communal volunteerism, of crucial underlying importance for understanding postwar developments within Lebanese civil society. Lara Deeb, for example, has written of an unprecedented growth in the number of women volunteering in *jamaiyyas* (associations) in the southern suburbs of Beirut in the postwar period.[37] This is, in fact, a phenomenon that has affected all of the various sectarian communities and political parties— whether Hezbollah's Mahdi scouts, or those of Berri's AMAL Movement, or the partisans of Hariri's Future Movement, or the activities of youth in Michel Aoun's Free Patriotic Movement.[38] Noting this increase in what he calls "voluntary servitude" on behalf of communal leaders and parties, Ahmad Beydoun lamented the fact that active citizens in postwar Lebanon have tended to limit their ambitions "to the confines of their community." Added Beydoun pessimistically, "[W]hat we are living does not lack followers."[39]

The final system-reinforcing dimension of postwar state–society relations in Lebanon revolves around the continued ability of the country's elite political classes to veto reformist efforts, at times resorting to coercion against actors within civil and political society. Consistent with prewar practice, for example, Lebanon's postwar political class, now bolstered by its intertwining relationships with Syrian economic and political networks, consistently ignored calls to formulate economic development policies aimed at promoting the development of the country's industrial and agricultural sectors.[40] Neither have postwar political elites allowed for the formulation, let alone implementation, of social policies that could compensate for these "market" deficiencies, a situation that stands in contrast to the Chehabist period following the country's civil unrest in 1958 when institutions such as the NSSF were formed. Indeed, given the worsening socioeconomic situation in the postwar period caused by high and growing levels of postwar debt[41] and increasingly austere and regressive taxation policies,[42] the country's already inadequate prewar system of social assistance has become even less able to nibble away at the widening socioeconomic gaps that have emerged. Despite the Lebanese spending up to 20 percent of their gross national product (GNP) on social services and welfare—a figure higher than in many industrialized countries[43]—Kochuyt estimated that only 45 percent of Lebanese in the postwar period have access to medical insurance, with less than 35 percent having access to any social insurance at all. Neither has the Ministry of Social Affairs (MSA) (as discussed below) been able to compensate for these growing deficiencies, given that it apportions less than 20 percent of its stagnant budget to the provision of its own direct social services, a reality that effectively blocks its ability to make significant public policy initiatives in the social service sector, let alone formulate "an energetic social policy."[44]

However, it has been the active use of the latent coercive state power by postwar political elites—designed to infiltrate, divide, intimidate, and, if need be, repress opposition groups within civil and political society—that represents a distinct shift from the prewar period. The Ministry of the Interior, for example, under the direction of the Syrian-allied Michel Murr for much of the 1990s, took a much more interventionist approach to the activities of civil associations in postwar Lebanon. According to the law, civil society associations are merely required to "inform" the Ministry of the Interior of their establishment through the delivery of their bylaws (*ilm wa khabar*). Throughout the 1990s, however, the ministry abrogated for itself the role of licenser, dissolving 138 associations and political parties in 1992 and, in a celebrated case, refusing to accept the legality of an important postwar advocacy association called the Lebanese Association for Democratic Elections (LADE), at one point issuing veiled threats to its executive in response to its attempts to monitor postwar elections.[45] The ministry under Murr also tried to take a more active role in monitoring the internal governance of associations by declaring its right to supervise associative internal elections. While this practice was repudiated as "an abuse of power" by the Constitutional Court in 2003, in the early postwar period it contributed to the emergence of an uncertain and confused legal environment within which the associational realm operated.[46]

The highest-profile example of postwar interference and infiltration into the internal workings of associations, however, concerned the General Confederation of Lebanese Trade Unions (CGTL), interference that precipitated the most intense period of state–labor conflict in Lebanon's history.[47] As we have seen, the labor movement in prewar Lebanon, after struggling through periods of weakness and division, finally achieved some degree of unity with the amalgamation of all federations under the banner of the CGTL in 1970, success that allowed it to act as the principal interlocutor in negotiations with the state.[48] The CGTL also was able to sustain this tacit unity during both the latter years of the war in the form of broad-based antiwar demonstrations of 1987 as well as in the early years of the postwar period, symbolized by the holding of numerous strikes and demonstrations that included those that brought down the first postwar government of Omar Karame.[49] The subsequent government of Rafiq Hariri also was forced to negotiate with the CGTL, reaching agreements with respect to general annual wage increases between 1994 and 1996. By the end of 1996, however, heightened labor militancy sparked a shift in the Hariri government's approach. Buoyed by the emergence of a momentary cross-sectarian elite alliance that was backed by Syrian acquiescence, Hariri turned to the Lebanese Army to quell growing labor unrest and enforce a comprehensive ban on strikes and public demonstrations. He paralleled this with the intensification of the long-standing elite practice of interfering in and/or fragmenting the CGTL's executive, effected through the co-optation of existing federation leaders, the creation of new compliant federations, and the direct interference in executive committee elections. As Joseph Bahout wrote as early as 1994, "[T]he present difficulties encountered by the CGLT and its efforts to maintain its autonomy are undoubtedly a part of the difficult struggle being carried out by all independent associational networks against the appetite of the State. One should not forget, after all, that the Lebanese state is being rebuilt, in part, by the same forces which tried, throughout the war, to fragment and smother civil society."[50] In short, through the combination of coercive and confessionally manipulative statecraft, the Hariri government, backed by a momentary cross-political elite consensus, used the latent and normally circumscribed power of the state to fragment, and in effect destroy, the CGTL's collective associational power, dynamics that have continued to thwart the subsequent reemergence of labor power in postwar Lebanon.

Hence, associational activists in Lebanon, already constrained by the coercive presence of the Syrians and their political allies, would have to contend with an enriched/enriching political elite involved in a fierce competition among themselves for the spoils of the returning state and the compliance of clients within Lebanese society. These dynamics set the context for the three case studies that follow on the efforts by associational networks and civil activists at the national level to both work within and challenge these restrictive sectarian dynamics—creating and cultivating space from which they can launch reformist discourses and policy agendas and, in the case of a few more ambitious associational leaders, using what shifting civil space they managed to create as a platform on which to expand their influence within Lebanese political society. Starting with the case of the politics of NGO coalition building in early postwar Lebanon, it was clear that these dynamics linked to the various processes of sectarianization—from above and from below—forced associational and civic activists to adopt preemptive advocacy strategies that could best be described as "self-limiting."

## Competitive NGO Coalition Building and the "Reconstruction" of Lebanese Civil Society

The politics of NGO coalition building in the postwar period must be placed in the historical context of the country's "first NGO boom" in the 1960s and 1970s.[51] It was out of this that a robust sector of nonsectarian and development-oriented associations arose. While continuing to be dwarfed by the parallel increase in the number of family and religiously based associations,[52] these new voluntary-based associations—fueled by the supportive framework provided by the Chehabist state, by the growing numbers and influence of students, and by the increase in the size and wealth of the country's middle classes—established themselves as prominent players in Lebanon's pre–civil war public sphere. Perhaps the most symbolically important of these was le Mouvement Social Libanais (MSL), founded in 1956 by Gregoire Haddad, a Greek Catholic bishop with a long-standing interest in promoting the social gospel well before Vatican II. Motivated by a vision of promoting "comprehensive secularism" within Lebanon,[5] the MSL's main activities revolved around the promotion of social development within the remote, often Muslim, areas of the country through the establishment of medical clinics, social development centers, and the recruitment of volunteers from all of the various regions and communities of the country. The rise of new associations like MSL had impor-

tant impacts on the country's postwar associational sector as a whole. It
not only turned the structure of the country's pre–civil war associative
sector "upside down," but it also left a legacy in terms of the people who
would go on to establish new associations and become active associative
leaders in both the civil war and postwar periods.[54] One network of these
associations—most of which were involved in larger-scale social welfare
and relief activities—attempted to become "prime movers" in the country's
postwar civil society, ready to assert its influence in the event of the end
of the country's civil war, by forming a national coordinating mechanism.

Efforts to create coordinating mechanisms among associations had
a longer history in Lebanon. One of the first during the civil war was
initiated by a network of "solidarity-oriented NGOs" (including the MSL)
that established the National Forum for Social Development (NFSD). The
initial motivation for getting together was fear of an impending humanitarian crisis in the country, brought about by the intensification of the
war and the resultant flight of donor agencies from the country. At its
first meeting in the headquarters of Oxfam-Lebanon in late 1986, it was
clear that NFSD also had a broader purpose in mind—to challenge the
sectarianization of donor relief in the country during the civil war, to create more open channels of information and communication between the
regions and communities of the country, and to emphasize the importance
of relief work being intimately connected with the promotion of development and solidarity.[55] It "strongly challenged" the dominant modes of
relief that worked through channels connected to the state, the militias,
and/or the sectarian social welfare networks—arguing that these channels
reinforced the segmented, fragmented, and dependent nature of Lebanese society. It stressed that if relief was going to be successful, it had
to be connected to awareness-raising efforts designed to uncover "the
underlying causes of the emergency situation and encourage individuals
to take collective steps toward self-reliance." In short, relief work had to
be motivated by a sense of self-reliance rather than charity; it could not
favor one group over another; and it must be geared to the needs of the
local population. Translated into practical terms, it stressed the need to
focus on such areas as primary health care rather than the distribution
of medicines, on income generation rather than on welfare provision, and
on training programs for local communities.[56]

However, defining some central concerns was one thing; determining how to effect changes in the prevailing system was another. On the
one hand, at it initial meetings in Cyprus in 1987 and 1988, its members
expressed their belief that NGOs could play an influential role in the
postwar period, arguing that they had become "a present reality that the
powers that be cannot discard."[57] Indeed, some in the group went so far

as to describe NGOs as being in the "vanguard of efforts to reconstruct a new secularized Lebanese state and society."[58] On the other hand, others recognized that this kind of statement had an air of unreality in a country in the midst of civil war. As one member of the core group remarked, it indicated a general tendency on the part of NGOs "to take themselves too seriously."[59] One of the issues that the founding network found particularly challenging was that of membership. It recognized, for example, that the success of any coordination initiative would be highly dependent on the existence of a minimum degree of a "shared philosophy" among the participants—which for this NGO network meant bringing together those NGOs willing to work "across regional and confessional lines, for a secular and unified Lebanon, and towards empowering the poorest of the poor" and excluding those embedded within "the prevailing power structures" of the country.[60] Because it also recognized, however, that its influence would depend on the existence of a critical mass of NGOs, it decided to adopt as broad and inclusive an approach to the question of membership as possible within these ideological parameters, agreeing, as a way of safeguarding its own associational autonomy, to keep the initiative an informal one, based on the model of "a forum" for the exchange of information rather than that of "a cartel" controlled by a small group of local and international NGOs. As the preparatory committee for the first NGO meeting in Cyprus concluded, "the endeavor is all about . . . establishing a consultative network . . . on the basis that the NGOs involved do not represent all the work being done in Lebanon [and] not even all the partners which share a certain homogeneity of approach and practice."[61]

However, the NFSD did not last long. It held several meetings in Lebanon throughout the last half of 1988, but by the middle of 1989, its European partners were describing the initiative as a dead one. In part, this was because the NFSD virtually imploded, caught in a myriad of personal and agency rivalries. Despite the desire not to become a type of cartel, it was apparent that the initiative was being dominated by a few of the larger NGOs. This helped to explain the decision of the Middle East Council of Churches not to join in the first place—led by Gabi Habib, who previously had been an influential pre–civil war leader within the Movement of Orthodox Youth—and it also led other NGOs such as the MSL to subsequently withdraw their membership. All of this impeded the NFSD from formulating a program of collaborative action, preoccupied as it was with its own internal bickering.[62]

This marginalization of the NFSD became readily apparent with the announcement in January 1989 of an impending mission of the International Committee for Voluntary Agencies (ICVA), a Geneva-based global umbrella organization for NGOs, to Lebanon. The NFSD was cautious but initially encouraged by the announcement, coming as it did in the midst of the most brutal and demoralizing period of the Lebanese civil war, but it also was concerned about what the mission's terms of reference were—who had invited it, what were its goals, and with whom it would meet. It was particularly worried that the ICVA mission would be closely linked to a new and rival coordinating network called the Lebanese NGO Forum (LNF) that had emerged that year and whose membership was closely allied to the country's leading sectarian communities. In a public statement, the NFSD offered to help organize and facilitate the visit, stressing that it hoped the ICVA mission would meet with NGOs that worked in all regions of the country and not with those organizations linked to the sectarian communities.[63] One of the sponsors of the NFSD initiative, Oxfam-Lebanon-UK, also was strongly concerned about the motivations of the ICVA mission. It criticized ICVA's naïve thinking that "getting people around a table" is "a good thing" regardless of who is doing it,[64] and it subsequently described ICVA officials as being "blithely oblivious of the minefields [they had] walked across—not only political and confessional divides but divides within confessions, and more relevantly in this context, tensions between Lebanese NGOs, which reflect[ed] both local ambitions but also world view."[65] In order to minimize the damage, it made some concerted lobbying efforts to convince ICVA to back away from the mission—or at least move beyond its proposed partnership with the LNF—efforts that in the end proved unsuccessful.

This brings us to the LNF itself—the second and more sustained effort to formalize an NGO network with the hope of establishing for itself a dominant national role in the postwar period. The driving force behind the creation of the LNF was two individuals: Ghassan Sayegh, the longtime head of the YMCA, and Mohammad Barakat, the longtime head of the Social Welfare Institute/Islamic Orphanages (SWI). While both had long discussed the usefulness of creating a national NGO coordination mechanism, if only to facilitate the capture and distribution of foreign humanitarian and development assistance, their strategy was diametrically opposed to that of the NFSD. Rather than eschew confessionalism, Sayegh and Barakat preferred to build upon the confessional realities of the country by bringing together a number of the leading social welfare organizations within the various communities.[66] In short, by design, the initiative was meant to be both powerful and exclusive.[67] Sayegh was never apologetic about the sectarian roots and logic of the initiative—arguing that it brought several advantages. It created a truly national coordinating mechanism, particularly because each member agency was connected to a whole host of smaller, communally based associations at the local levels. Indeed, the YMCA had grown to become one of the largest NGOs in the country by the war's end, possessing a nationwide network of 124 licensed dispensaries, 23 regional hospitals, and a relief program reaching 120 smaller NGOs.[68] Second, by bringing together all of the confessional organizations under one roof, Sayegh argued that the LNF could facilitate the process of aid disbursement because it eliminated the unpalatable task of choosing between confessional partners and, hence, broadened the options of local partners beyond the few nonsectarian associations such as those that had tried to congregate within the NFSD. Sayegh also challenged the normative arguments of Lebanon's nonsectarian NGO community by arguing that, because the LNF initiative encouraged the religious communities to think more in terms of the common good, it was a fundamentally progressive one.[69] Finally, characteristic of Sayegh's hard-nosed, realist approach to politics within Lebanon's NGO sector, he argued that because the institutions of the LNF were all big enough "to terrorize each other . . . they [also were] big enough to know that cooperation is important."[70] No doubt, these arguments were all put forth to ICVA and helped the LNF to gain its recognition as the country's lead NGO coordinating committee.

In one of the first articles on NGO politics in Lebanon's postwar period, Jon Bennett argues that the LNF contributed to a significant reconstruction of the country's civil society, describing it as "breaking down confessional barriers in the country and, hence, of laying the foundations for national reconciliation."[71] Certainly, the LNF went on to play an active role in the immediate postwar world of Lebanese NGOs. It organized several national conferences on such issues as social needs, children and development, and NGO–state cooperation; it established the Migration Unit Project, designed to push the Lebanese government to become more interested in issues of the internally displaced; it made efforts to outreach to the wider NGO community through the establishment of management training programs as a way of increasing the professional capacity of the sector; and it agreed to act as a channel through which humanitarian aid could be provided to the largely neglected Palestinian community in the country. Of particular interest were the LNF's efforts in the early postwar years to lobby on behalf of the rights of associations in the country. In conjunction with Ghassan Moukheiber, the LNF's lawyer in its early years and a staunch and vocal human rights advocate in the postwar period more generally, the LNF launched several court cases challenging the right of the state to interfere in the internal governance of NGOs.[72] It also took the lead role in establishing a parliamentary center designed to facilitate civil society networking as well as create a channel through which associations could liaise more easily and directly with parliamentary committees.[73] All of this led Sayegh to stress the important role played by the LNF in the early postwar period in Lebanon with respect to the promotion of development and democratization.[74]

In reality, however, the dynamics underlying the initiative of the LNF were less ambitious, the most tangible purpose that emerged being to maintain the national stature of the YMCA in the postwar world. The YMCA under Sayegh's leadership emerged as a major NGO during the war, acting through its Emergency Relief Program as a node through which large flows of wartime relief were channeled into the country. Indeed, it was here that the YMCA was able to establish its extensive ties with the numerous confessionally based social welfare and medical institutions in the country, especially with regard to its wartime program of distributing essential medicines. In essence, the LNF was an attempt to keep these useful networks—and the YMCA's central place within them— alive into the postwar period. Hence, while Sayegh always insisted that the LNF was "more than the YMCA," it was nonetheless clear that, under his aggressive leadership, the YMCA was the driving force behind and chief beneficiary of the initiative. However, not only was the LNF designed as a mechanism to attract postwar aid flows into the YMCA, flows that in the end proved minor in relation to the YMCA's more significant direct relationship with U.S. Agency for International Development (USAID), but it also was designed to act—through the network of ties cultivated with the leading sectarian social welfare institutions in the country—as a latent mechanism of protection in the uncertain postwar world. Discussions with Sayegh about his approach to political advocacy, for example, revealed his acute awareness of the constraining political environment within which he worked, arguing that "if you want to compete with them, they will cut you off." He subsequently asked, "Why take to the streets?," suggesting instead that it would be better to find "civilized means and ways to influence policy" by both "knowing the system" and working from "inside" it.[75] In short, while Sayegh was a very aggressive and competitive participant within the realm of "civil society," especially with the less-protected sector of non–sectarian-affiliated NGOs, his political acumen led him to be more circumspect when it came to his approach to "political society." Sayegh's approach, in fact, worked remarkably well, the YMCA transforming itself into a major service-delivery NGO in postwar Lebanon, benefiting in particular from its strong ties with USAID, whose "apolitical" approach to advocacy proved similar.[76] Given the instrumentalized nature of the LNF, it was not surprising that its membership— never active in a collective sense and focused primarily on cultivating opportunities for financial development within its respective confessional communities—quickly fell away. Indeed, by 1995, even its co-founder, Mohammad Barakat left, describing the LNF as being "in a coma."[77]

A third attempt to create a national NGO coordinating committee also emerged in the late civil war years called *le Collectif*. Its establishment was the work of Gregoire Haddad, the founder of the MSL, who had never given up on his pre–civil war efforts to promote coordination among non-confessional NGOs.[78] Joining Haddad were many of the NGOs that had been involved with the NFSD initiative—the MECC, Secours Populaire (affiliated with the LCP), Amel, and Najdeh (working with Palestinians in Lebanon). However, associations with strong confessional and family affiliations—such as Caritas (affiliated with the country's Catholic communities), the Sadr Foundation (run by the Rabab al-Sadr, the sister of prominent pre–civil war Shi'a leader Musa al-Sadr), Maqassid (affiliated with the prominent Beirut Sunni Salam family), and the Hariri Foundation—all joined *le Collectif*, transforming it into Lebanon's second national NGO body. Whereas the LNF initiative was squarely rooted within Lebanon's sectarian framework and focused primarily on attracting postwar aid flows into the country, that of *le Collectif* had loftier if ill-defined goals that revolved around both harnessing the expertise of the country's NGO community in the postwar reconstruction phase in cooperation with the emerging state as well as establishing a cross-regional and cross-confessional "civil society" platform on which the voices of some of its prominent members could be heard. In short, many associations within *le Collectif* had reformist political ambitions, Karam writing of them in Chehabist terms as wanting to stimulate "a third system."[79] As a way of affirming its civic credentials, for example, Joseph Farah, a former coordinator of *le Collectif* and the executive director of Caritas-Lebanon, made a point of distinguishing between the "administrative system" of the LNF—which he described as a "mask" hiding membership made up of primarily "patronage NGOs"—with that of *le Collectif*, whose membership relied more extensively on an active volunteer base.[80]

However, while *le Collectif* embarked on some collaborative programs, especially in the context of relief operations during the Qana massacre in 1996, it had difficulty establishing an institutionalized platform on which to promote cooperative systems of governance on social policy with the reemerging state, let alone a more forceful and unified "civil society" voice into the country's postwar reconstruction debates. At the center of these difficulties were concerns to prevent the internal decision-making process of *le Collectif* from being penetrated by broader political interests. These concerns were reflected in ongoing debates surrounding three issues: membership criteria, internal governance, and the receipt of foreign aid. There was recognition, for example, that the membership base would have to expand beyond Haddad's small network of nonconfessional NGOs, focusing instead on NGOs that can work in more than one region and sector. While this led to the decision to include organizations with strong roots in the country's sectarian system, it also brought tensions into the internal deliberations of le *Collectif*, with Mayla Bakhash, executive director of the MSL for much of the early postwar period, remarking, "I don't know how associations as different as Maqassid and Secours Populaire and Mouvement Social . . . [can] put together a position paper on at least one or two issues in this country, [let alone] a follow-up position paper to put it in practice."[81] Further immobilizing le *Collectif* in the postwar years were the ambitions of the Hariri Foundation to take over the coordinator's position, ones that were strongly resisted by the core network within; "if the Hariri Foundation [becomes] the coordinator of le *Collectif*," noted Bakhash, "there is no more *Collectif*."[82] Indeed, in order to prevent le *Collectif* from being driven apart internally, the group avoided holding elections for executive positions, preferring to reach these decisions by consensus. There also were divisions over whether to accept donor finance—le *Collectif*'s core group being extremely wary of the consequences of its agenda being donor driven and, instead, wanting its activities to be based solely on the contributions of its membership;[83] "le *Collectif* is not strong enough to avoid being fund-driven," argued Bakhash, adding that, given the politicized nature of donor finance, funding issues had the potential to "break down le *Collectif*."[84]

The result was a national NGO coordinating body that was effectively immobilized throughout the 1990s, especially as a "civil society" platform on which some of the prominent voices within Lebanon's NGO community could be heard. Be it the CGTL strike against the decision of the Hariri government to raise the price of gasoline in 1995, the campaign of civil associations demanding the holding of municipal elections in 1997, or the question of Lebanon's membership in the World Trade Organization (WTO), the voice of le *Collectif* was mute, its membership being unable or unwilling to reach any consensus on what its advocacy position should be. Karam, in fact, described both the LNF and le *Collectif* as being "the silent and neutral partners" of the state.[85] While Bakhash was disappointed by le *Collectif*'s failure to strengthen its advocacy voice, arguing forcefully that "we do not have to ask permission to do anything in this country; we must promote our own position regardless of what Hariri thinks or Jumblat thinks," she recognized that most NGOs were deeply implicated in the political system and, as a result, felt compelled to make "all the regular Lebanese calculations." "In our society," added Bakhash, "no one wants to make enemies."[86] The result was the emergence of a "civil society" platform whose achievements were mainly deliberative and relational, getting prominent NGOs in Lebanon's early postwar era of diverse sociopolitical backgrounds to commit themselves to sitting at the same table. Hemmed in by the penetrating and fragmenting dynamics of Lebanon's political society, however, the practical achievements of *le Collectif* were more elusive. This was recognized by several leading participants in *le Collectif* initiative, Bakhash describing it in a positive light as representing "the potential" of civil society,[87] and Farah looking on it somewhat more fatalistically by arguing that it embraced a "minimalist definition of civil society," adding that "it is better than nothing and we're willing to keep it."[88]

## Civil Associationalism and the Rise of Lebanon's Postwar "Civil Movements"

Away from the limelight of Lebanon's large and service-oriented NGO community, however, was a significant development revolving around the emergence of a small number of advocacy associations and "civil movements." These associations largely escaped the eye of the donor community in the early postwar era, preoccupied as they were with more grandiose development and reconstruction programs being carried out by the Lebanese state and with their own more abstract programs of civil society development that targeted the larger and professionalized service-driven NGOs in the country, such as those represented within the LNF and *le Collectif*. Nonetheless, building on the experiences and expertise of Lebanon's pre–civil war and wartime nonconfessionally-oriented NGOs, this group acted as a catalyst to wider civil society politics in the 1990s, spawning the emergence of a number of "civil movements" and providing expertise to a number of policy-oriented associative networks, including those relating to women, the environment, and disability. What follows is an analysis of the rise of this small but effective network of advocacy associations, focusing in particular on their goals, their *modus operandi*, and their effects on Lebanon's postwar political field.[89]

The main goals of these associations revolved around redefining the meaning of citizenship within the new postwar Taif regime—moving away from one mediated by the increasingly entrenched structures of confessionalism and clientelism toward one grounded in Lebanon's republican constitutional principles. In a political context where the boundaries between the civil, the communal, and the political were "confused" and "permeable,"[90] these associations worked to clarify them using the instrument of the law. Their tools for carving out more defined space for democratic citizenship was the constitutional infrastructure already in place—one that included the 1909 Ottoman Law of Associations, the republican principles carved into the 1926 Lebanese Constitution, as

well as the modifications found within the Taif Accord that included its
enshrining of the International Declaration of Human Rights, its recommendations promoting decentralization and deconfessionalisation, and its
commitments to establish new institutions aimed at promoting socioeconomic and political rights in the country, such as the Constitutional
Council and the Economic and Social Council. With respect to the issues
in which this core group of civil associations became involved, almost
all were concerned directly with questions of human rights, associations
rights, and electoral laws—in short, the essential legal infrastructure on
which a more vibrant civil associational sector would ultimately depend.[91]

Several facets underpinned the approach of these core advocacy
associations. The first was their use of professional expertise—especially
legal expertise—to gain legitimacy and access to the system. Indeed, lawyers and jurists were described as having a "primordial" place within
this group of advocacy associations.[92] Second, many of these associations
placed a strong emphasis on establishing democratic norms of internal
governance—Karam writing of this as "an obsession" within certain advocacy associations.[93] There also was a strong determination to prevent the
penetration of clientelist influences into their associations, symbolized
by their reliance on independently based (and predominantly foreign)
sources of financial support.[94] Of further interest is Karam's claim that
many of these associations succeeded in "depersonalizing" their collective
action, with associational elections resulting in a significant turnover of
personnel within executive positions. Karam also writes of the existence
of an implicit "associative contract" within the advocacy sector, based on
openness, dialogue, and an acceptance of the diversity of opinion within,
an ethos that has been contrasted with the emphasis within leftist circles
in the pre–civil war days on unity and solidarity.[95] While this may have
facilitated the intrusion of wider political struggles—whether between
families, factions, and/or parties—into the internal deliberations of many
of these associations, these struggles rarely resulted in the dissolution of a
particular association, and even when irreconcilable splits occurred, those
who left often redeployed their associative expertise elsewhere, leading
Karam to comment on the existence of a "striking commitment" to the
institutionalization of the advocacy field.[96] Further helping to strengthen
the advocacy sector was the relative homogeneity of its social base. It
was made up for the most part of middle- and upper-class elements that
included in its ranks students, young professionals, and academics; it was
intergenerational—consisting of overlapping networks that spanned the
pre–civil war, the wartime, and the postwar periods; it was interconfessional in nature; and at its center was a strong and Beirut-based core.[97]
Finally, the members of these associations were characterized by their

"multipositionality"—acting as reservoirs of expertise and experience for the civil associational sector as a whole as well as holding multiple associational memberships themselves. In short, as a result of their developing institutional strength and the associational interconnectedness of their membership, this core group of advocacy associations emerged as nodal actors within the postwar network of civil associations, ones that were central to the rise of a number of "civil movements" in the mid- to late 1990s.[98]

The most significant "civil movement" was the first one. It emerged in 1997 and was called the "Gathering for the Holding of Municipal Elections." At its core was the Lebanese Association for Democratic Elections (LADE), which had hosted a meeting with a wider group of activists after the parliament had decided to postpone the municipal elections scheduled to be held in 1998 for a year. Already viewing the upcoming municipal elections—not held since 1963—as an opportunity to deepen democratic practice within postwar Lebanon, this group now raised the question of whether their postponement opened up political opportunities for a campaign of civil contestation. On the one hand, the Ministry of the Interior, under the direction of Michel Murr and closely allied with the Syrians, had been active and purposeful in restricting the activities of certain civil associations—violating their rights of association, interfering in their internal affairs, and, with the banning of all civil demonstrations in the wake of labor unrest in 1995, severely restricting their access to public space. Underpinned by the coercive presence of the Syrians, there was a large measure of uncertainty as to what the limits of civil action were and fear of what could happen if those uncertain boundaries were crossed. On the other hand, the factionalism that characterized Lebanon's postwar political elite, reflected in debates over the timing of the municipal elections, seemed to suggest that some opportunity for a civil campaign might exist. The activists, therefore, decided to go ahead, launching a civil campaign that had a number of distinct attributes. In order to avoid the need for formal registration, for example, the decision was taken to organize themselves as a "gathering" (liqa). This quickly translated into a loose network of more than 150 different associations, private institutions, and political parties held together by several layers of organization that revolved around a central committee within Beirut that met weekly and was open to all. These were, in turn, supported by meetings at the regional and issue levels, giving the "gathering" a national scope. In order to protest within the confines of the law, the activists also decided to launch a petition (in which they garnered more than 60,000 signatures). They also effectively used their connections in the media to promote their message, supported a (successful) legal appeal of fourteen deputies to the Constitutional Court, and organized a sit-in in front of the Lebanese parliament. When the parliament eventually backed down and decided to go ahead with the elections after all, the "gathering" then decided to continue its campaign, adjusting its focus toward raising public awareness about the broader democratic importance of participation in the municipal elections.[99] Despite the fact that many associated with the "gathering" had decided to throw their hats into the electoral ring, they decided not to support any candidates running in the elections for fear of crossing that line from the "civic" to the "political" and, hence, opening up possibilities of state interference. In short, the "gathering" avoided challenging the structural foundations of Lebanon's state, working instead both within the law and within the "islands" of civic space offered by Lebanon's system of limited pluralism.

The greatest success of the campaign was not so much with the holding of municipal elections themselves—indeed, only a few of the candidates affiliated with the "gathering" actually won seats, with most results being determined by the prevailing communal and clientelist political dynamics in the country.[100] Rather, the campaign had implications for the nature of Lebanon's postwar civil society. First, it affirmed the possibility of creating civic space in postwar Lebanon that was relatively free from communal and clientelist influences, thereby reinjecting civic activism back into the prevailing rules of the game in the postwar era. Second, through the creation of new actors and the formulation of new modes of contestation, the "gathering" helped to produce new civic forms of associative capital—in fact, it had proved more successful in this regard than the larger NGOs in the country, symbolized by the failure of those NGOs within *le Collectif* to lend their collective support to the campaign of the "gathering." Third, the "gathering" contributed to an expansion in public space in the postwar era, creating opportunities for the civic mobilization by others. Indeed, Karam wrote of the "gathering" as having "detonated" new cycles of civic contestation in the late 1990s—sparking campaigns on a number of issues, from the promotion of civil marriage (which we examine in the next chapter), to the campaign to gain the vote for persons aged eighteen and older, to the campaign on behalf of the disappeared.[101]

The question remained, however, as to whether this fledgling associative capital could be translated into political capital. There were two main ways that associational activists jumped into the political arena—through running for electoral office or through involvement in the formation of political movements and parties. The municipal elections of 1998 proved to be the first real test of the political salience of associative capital—there being numerous associational activists, especially within the field of the environment, who had decided to run for office. By 2000, associational activists began to think more seriously about running for parliament—Karam highlighting the campaigns of four leading activists within various civic associations.[102] Sparking this rising interest in bridging the divide between the civil and the political was the perceived opening of political opportunities in the late 1990s—brought about, in particular, by the election of Emile Lahoud to the presidency in 1998 with his call for an end to corruption, the promotion of the rule of law, and the protection of public liberties. Even as the bloom faded from Lahoud's presidency, other factors emerged to shake up the political realm, especially at the regional and global levels with the withdrawal of the Israelis from the South in 2000, the death of the Syrian President Assad in that same year, and the events of September 11, 2001, with their implications for a more aggressive anti-Syrian and pro-democracy American foreign policy in the Middle East. All of this led to a gradual intensification of political life in the country, energized by the perceived opportunities to poke holes in the Syrian-dominated postwar political order.

Yet the exigencies and challenges faced by associational activists in the political realm were daunting. The first revolved around the continued manipulation and oversight of elections by the Syrians; a second revolved around the absence of limitations and accountability on electoral spending.[103] In the face of these two factors alone, argued Karam, the political and financial resources available to new associative actors seeking electoral office were grossly insufficient.[104] Perhaps the most deep-rooted problem for associative actors wanting to enter into Lebanon's political field, however, was the dominant role played by the country's other forms of social capital—mainly familial and confessional—which Karam described as being "much weightier" in comparison with the "embryonic" social capital produced within civic associational life.[105] In his evaluation of associational actors in the electoral system, it was those that spurned connection with more traditional forms of sociopolitical capital that fared the worst. Hani Abu Fadil, for example, an activist in the field of the environment whom we shall encounter again later, lost badly in his attempt to gain a municipal seat in the Matn in 1998, in part due to his refusal to "enter into the game of partisan and familial alliances" that dominated village life, a reality that Karam argued indicated the difficulty of translating associative capital into political capital, especially when the former set itself up in competition with the latter.[106] In fact, all of the associational actors who tried to run in the 2000 parliamentary elections (and, subsequently, the 2002 by-election) were able to call upon preexisting familial political capital, though, as a result of their unwillingness or inability to play the game of electoral clientelism, all were effectively shut out.[107] Moreover, despite numerous debates around

establishing new political movements and/or parties, no unified associative project emerged. Instead, activists dispersed, putting their associative
expertise at the service of different members of the country's preexisting,
albeit reformist, political class. While this may have helped to modernize
political discourse and practice in the country, it is doubtful how much
it served to transform it.

Hence, Lebanon's new postwar civic advocacy associations challenged, expanded, but were ultimately blocked by the prevailing dynamics of Lebanon's postwar political arena. They challenged the prevailing
political order by their demands to safeguard existing civil and political
liberties embedded within the constitution and its affiliated documents—
thereby rearticulating norms of citizenship lost during the long civil war
period. They expanded the civil and political arena through their ability
to mobilize a new generation of civic activists, by their insistence on
depersonalizing and institutionalizing their internal procedures, and by
their ability to organize and mobilize new "civic movements" in the early
postwar years, when the boundaries of civic space within which they
operated were highly uncertain and often coercively penetrated. However,
while expanding the size and scope of the country's public space, they
remained unable to forge their own autonomous linkages with the state
itself, relying for the most part on traditional channels of access within
political society revolving around confession and clan. Even here, their
presence remained on the margins of political life, failing to gain much
traction within the electoral system and being forced instead to use their
accumulated civic and political experience in the service of preexisting,
if reformist-oriented, political elites in the country. While having contributed to the reconstruction of postwar Lebanese civil society, therefore,
they remained of limited influence when it came to the reconstruction of
Lebanon's political society, especially with regard to the implementation
of democratizing and de-confessionalizing reforms advocated by the Taif
Accord of 1989. What we turn to now is an examination of whether the
departure of the Syrians in 2005—the effect of which was to remove a
powerful mechanism of feedback that had served to reinforce the existing political order—would make any difference by opening up genuine
political opportunities for civic associations within the postwar period
in Lebanon.

## The "Independence Intifada" and the Limitations of
## Civic Mobilization in Postwar Lebanon

By far, the most significant popular mobilizations in postwar Lebanon
occurred in the aftermath of the assassination of Rafiq Hariri on February

14, 2005. Dubbed the "Independence Intifada" for its demands of "Liberation, Sovereignty, Independence" from the thirty-year Syrian presence in
the country, it was characterized by an escalating cycle of protests over a
one-month period that culminated in demonstrations in Beirut's Martyr's
Square on March 14 in which more than 1 million people participated. At
the forefront of these demonstrations was an eclectic multigenerational,
multiconfessional, and multiclass mix of activists linked to both civil and
political society—a mix that ranged from students who played a major
role throughout, to independent civic activists, to associational activists, to
journalists, to businessmen, to various individuals associated with political movements and parties in the country, particularly the Democratic
Left, many of whose founders had come from Lebanon's postwar network
of civic advocacy associations. Particularly important was a small core of
these civic activists. They immediately established a tent city in Martyr's
Square near the Muhammad al-Amin mosque, beside which Hariri's body
lay, that would help to anchor the protest movement; they coined innovative and fun text message slogans such as "If you want the truth, call
1559!" (which referred to the United Nations Security Council (UNSC)
Resolution calling for, among other things, the withdrawal of Syria from
Lebanon); they organized a petition that grew to almost 200 meters long;
and they acted as crucial mediators, both logistically and strategically,
between the various eclectic factions that had come to be involved.[108]
Buoyed by various successes in the midst of their escalating campaign—
the resignation of the Karami government, the decision of the UNSC to
investigate the Hariri assassination, and the subsequent announcement by
the Syrians that they would begin the process of pulling their troops out
of the country (though not yet commit to full withdrawal)—some began
to speak of the growing protest movement as representing not only the
push for Lebanese sovereignty and independence but also the push for the
deepening of Lebanese democracy. Samir Kassir, for example, a prominent
journalist with the influential *al-Nahar* newspaper who would be assassinated later in the same year, expressed hope that the Independence
Intifada might help to reestablish Lebanon as "the democratic model of
the region."[109]

But did this really represent "a budding civil society movement,"
as one analyst claimed?[110] On the one hand, Rayan Majed argued in her
study of student activism during the Independence Intifada, that many
of the protestors had indeed acted on a voluntary basis, "free from any
particular political loyalties," let alone "primary ties and solidarities."[111]
Melhem Chaoul has written of the protest's dynamics in similar fashion,
describing the networks that underpinned them as being characterized
by "egalitarian relations" and "horizontal connections." In contrast to
the political mobilizations of the late 1960s and early 1970s, which were

organized "from above" by "specialized militants," Chaoul argued that the spirit of the March 14 protests was very different, unfolding on a daily basis rather than being centrally planned, and organized by "volunteer militants" who "opposed a unifying tendency and instead proposed a strategy for the management of plurality." In short, concluded Chaoul, the March 14 protests were underpinned by "new practices and new rituals" whose underlying individualism ran "completely contrary to the spirit of the previous century."[112]

It would be a mistake, however, to ignore the deep-rooted sectarian political dynamics at work before, during, and after the March 14 demonstrations, ones that, while providing a temporary opportunity for the emergence of protests, also contributed to their unraveling. On the one hand, the civic actions that, in part, characterized the March 14 demonstrations were made possible by the coming together, prior to the assassination of Rafiq Hariri, of a relatively unified political opposition that was linked to powerful transnational forces. For example, while students had been active on campuses in the late 1990s and early 2000s, sometimes in advance of the politicians, their activities had remained relatively restrained, characterized by a refusal to cross an imaginary "red line."[113] It was only with the emergence of an emboldened political opposition—this coming in reaction to the transformation of Syria's security regime in Lebanon under the new Syrian president, Bashar al-Assad, into one that was both "cruder" and more corrupt[114]—that things began to change. By the time Hariri was assassinated in February 2005, for example, the various factions that made up the opposition to Syria—from the Council of Maronite bishops; to the Qornet Shehwan grouping of Christian politicians; to the Democratic Forum under the leadership of Nassib Lahoud; to Aoun, Jumblat, and (unofficially) Hariri himself—consolidated themselves into a loose alliance called the Bristol Gathering. Backing this alliance was the growing support of the United States for democratization efforts in the Middle East in the wake of its invasion of Iraq, support symbolized by the passage of the Syrian Accountability Act by the U.S. Congress in the fall of 2003, and, in response to Syria's decision to extend the mandate of its Lebanese ally President Lahoud, by its subsequent support for UNSC Resolution 1559 in the fall of 2004. It was at this point, argued Majed, that students became more openly defiant, organizing across many of the factional lines that existed on campuses and setting the stage for the reemergence, at least on a temporary basis, of a student movement that had played such a vital role in oppositional politics in the pre–civil war days.[115] In short, the political space that had emerged and been appropriated by Lebanon's array of civic activists during the heady days following the assassination of Rafiq Hariri was in large part the product of (and, hence, was ultimately dependent on) the externally supported political unity generated by Lebanon's factionalized opposition.

The fragility of this political space in the face of Lebanon's factionalized political realities, however, was readily apparent, even at the height of the Independence Intifada during the demonstrations of March 14. Coming as they did in the wake of Hezbollah's own mass rally on March 8, for example, Michael Young argued that the March 14 demonstrations have to be understood in part as being connected to the competitive processes of sectarian mobilization—a sectarian "payback," as he called it—which were a reflection more of "Lebanon's pluralist cacophony than [of] its unity."[116] Attesting to this fact was the active role played by the network of sectarian-affiliated social welfare NGOs in mobilizing demonstrators—an interesting example of the "Janus-faced" nature of Lebanon's broader civil society, supporting demonstrations on behalf of a "Lebanese" cause while simultaneously representing factionalized power.[117] Student protestors on March 14 also were subject to these same contradictory dynamics, Majed describing many of them as bringing along not only Lebanese flags to the protests but also an array of posters, pictures, and flags representing their own political movement and leaders—actions that foreshadowed the "illusory" unity that underlay the demonstrations.[118] It was therefore not a surprise, added Majed, that in the aftermath of the March 14 demonstrations, the student movement experienced "a significant regression" and sense of defeatism as a result of the deepening sectarian divisions within its ranks.[119] However, it was "the resurgent sectarianism" during the parliamentary elections in May and June 2005—with the leaders of the March 14 coalition competing and maneuvering among themselves for particularist advantage—that truly revealed the resilient factionalism at work, overriding whatever fleeting commitment had existed for the creation of a "new" Lebanon. Not only did this leave many of Lebanon's civic-minded feeling "jaded, disillusioned, and bitter" at the turn of events,[120] but it also revealed the remarkable ability of the country's postwar political elite—using the institutional arrangements deeply entrenched within Lebanon's political system—to rechannel widespread popular sentiment in the country in sectarian directions. Majed, for example, wrote of the reemergence of le suivisme within student ranks after the March 14 protests, characterized by their repeating "like parrots the discourse of their leaders, without any sense of critique or rebellion."[121] The end result, as Hirst caustically remarked, was that the "people power" so evident in the Beirut spring of 2005 ended up being delivered "back into the arms of the self-same elite of sectarian "strongmen" that the system had always favored."[122]

The most debilitating political dynamics for civic activists in the wake of the March 14 demonstrations, however, revolved around the deepening rift between the March 14 and March 8 factions, a rift sustained by emerging geostrategic rivalries at the regional and global levels. Anchoring this rift were the rules of Lebanon's communal power-sharing system itself—ones that gave an effective veto to each of the country's main political confessions; in this case, the Shi'a represented by both Hezbollah and AMAL, who made up the core of the March 8 alliance. Threatened by the departure of the Syrians, whose support had been crucial in consolidating its communal power in the postwar period, especially with respect to the growing socioeconomic and military infrastructure of Hezbollah, the March 8 alliance not only used its veto power to preserve its influence and thwart the March 14 alliance's pretensions of political hegemony, but it also worked aggressively to back up its institutional power through the mobilization of extrainstitutional "feedback" support—nationally through the cultivation of an alliance with the dissident Maronite leader, Michel Aoun; supranationally through the strengthening of ties with its regional allies, Iran and Syria; and subnationally through its continued mobilization of popular support within Lebanese society. Further reinforcing these political divisions was the growing geostrategic competition at the regional and global levels, symbolized by Sunni fears of an emerging "Shi'a Crescent," on the one hand, and the growing confrontation between the United States, Israel, and Iran (especially after the election of President Ahmadinajad in 2005), on the other. Indeed, Blanford describes the degree of these regional and global influences in post-2005 Lebanon as being "unprecedented." While this statement overlooks the intrinsic nature of these polarizing external dynamics within Lebanese politics, Blanford was nonetheless correct to emphasize the degree to which "the tussle for control of the Middle East [was being] played out in Lebanon, its inherent weaknesses and confessional cleavages seemingly forever fating it to be a pawn of broader, more powerful interests."[123]

In short, driven by the growing extrainstitutional political competition between Lebanon's political factions, be it at the political, regional, or popular level, the post–Independence Intifada era has been characterized by the deepening and institutionalization of sectarian factionalism, creating divisions "as profound as any the country had ever experienced."[124] While the Syrian protectorate may have reinforced these factional dynamics within the Lebanese polity, the post-Independence Intifada also made clear that these sectarian dynamics had deep roots within the Lebanese political field, roots that were constantly reinforced by the networking activities of Lebanese political elites themselves and of the political system that they continually protected and reproduced. As one critique starkly remarked in the bitter aftermath of Beirut's short-lived "spring" of 2005, "with or without Syria . . . [Lebanon's] was a sick regime."[125]

## Conclusions: The Shifting Constraints on Associative Action in Postwar Lebanon

Lebanon's political system allows for numerous islands of undominated, if unprotected, public space. It is within these spaces that a variety of civic-oriented (as well as non–civic-oriented) associational initiatives can emerge, even during periods of extreme political polarization.[126] Clearly, these initiatives have had a strong self-limiting character—le Collectif proving unable to take positions on pressing postwar issues seen to be political, and Lebanon's active network of advocacy associations using civil law as a form of protection in its public action campaigns. Also enhancing the ability of associational activists to carve out public space has been those rare moments within Lebanon when a significant proportion of the country's ruling elite have been able to forge some kind of overarching political consensus—as seems to have been the case in the period leading up the March 14 demonstrations of 2005. As Johnson wrote, there have been many moments within Lebanon's political history when "liberal society"—including its associational components—has been able to assert itself.[127]

Yet also clear from this examination of selected associational developments during Lebanon's postwar period is that the political opportunities for civic associational activism are shifting and fleeting, hemmed in by the frenzied competition between the country's political factions that penetrate deep into Lebanese society. The contingencies of history can certainly exacerbate these tendencies—note the crucial impact of 9/11 on changes in U.S. foreign policy in the Middle East, with all that this has entailed for the intensification of regional—and, hence, Lebanese—political tension. Yet this factionalism also is deeply institutionalized within Lebanon's political system itself, with communal, clan, and clientelist networks competing every four years for access to the patronage that electoral office provides. Moreover, while regional and global tensions have often penetrated into Lebanese politics and exacerbated its divisive tendencies, it also is the case that Lebanese political actors have actively cultivated these transnational connections as a way of enhancing their domestic political leverage.

The consequences of these factional dynamics for Lebanese associational life are profound. On the one hand, there is a clear dynamic within

Lebanon's sectarian democracy that intrinsically favors the expansion of
associational life linked to the country's communal and clan-based heritage. Not only do these associational types flow easily from the country's social structure, but they also have benefited from a preferential
and deeply embedded historical relationship with the state. As a result,
communal and clan-based political space in the country—enriched by the
processes of unruly capitalism and by the clientelist processes that these
practices nourish—has achieved a significant degree of institutionalized
sociopolitical protection, and it is from within this protected space that
a corresponding associational life has been able to flourish. On the other
hand, civic-oriented associational life—while empowered by the liberal
norms embedded within Lebanon's constitution and by the "slow-moving" dynamics of socioeconomic transformation that have, at times within
Lebanon's history, led to the growth of the country's educated middle
classes—has been highly constrained. Unable to rely on institutionalized
access to the Lebanese state, these associational elements within Lebanon
have had little option but to work within the more contingent political space that emerges by default as a result of the inability of any one
political faction in the country to establish hegemonic political control.
Though giving rise to Lebanon's unprotected sociopolitical space, however,
the institutionalized competitive dynamic within Lebanese politics also
militates against the translation of these opportunities for civic-oriented
action into sustained and institutionalized success at the national level.
Indeed, the more polarized the Lebanese political arena becomes, the
more constricted is the political space within which civic-oriented associational elements can operate. Indeed, the political polarization in the
wake of the 2005 Beirut spring ended up penetrating deep into the heart
of many civil society associations in the country, tearing the internal institutional fabric of some of them apart.[128]

What follows is an examination of the precarious nature of these
contingent spaces, seen through the lens of three social policy–oriented
case studies of civic associational activism. Each case study—dealing with
activism around gender relations, environmental rights, and disability
rights—is organized according to a common narrative. First, because they
all deal with questions of policy deliberation and implementation, each
chapter begins by outlining the nature of its particular "policy domain,"
providing historical explanations as to how this domain has been structured and why its particular structure has been reinforced over time.
Second, each case study examines the emergence of associational activism
in the early postwar period, focusing in particular on attempts by each
of these associational networks to promote institutionalized platforms—

within civil society if not within the state itself—on which their advocacy politics can be promoted and sustained. The third and final section of these case studies turns toward explanations as to why these efforts at institutionalizing associational access to the state, let alone reforming policies at the national level, have been so unsuccessful.

Campaign poster for Rafik Hariri, the caption reading "Father of the Poor."

Lebanese Army patrols Beirut streets as part of crackdown on labor demonstrations, summer, 1996.

Beirut demonstration in support of Women's Nationality Campaign (courtesy of CRTD-A).

Head office of the League of Islamic Women's Charitable Organizations, Beirut.

Headquarters for National Commission for Lebanese Women, Beirut.

The late Wadad Chakhtoura (left), founder and president of the Rassemblement Democratique des Femmes Libanaises, Beirut Office, 2008.

Mayla Bahkash, former Executive Director of Le Mouvement Social Libanais.

Zoya Rouhana, founder of KAFA, at their Beirut office, spring 2008.

Meeting between the Lebanese Environmental Forum (LEF) and
Lebanese Prime Minister, Salim al-Hoss, 1999.

Environmental legal activist Abdullah Zakia with Mirvat Abu Khalil,
founding member of Green Line, spring 2008.

Michel Skaff (left) with Druze leader Walid Jumblat, spring 2008.

Paul Abi Rashed, environmental activist and founder of the
environmental NGO, Terre-Liban, in 2008.

Ricardo Haber with forest guard at
Horsh Eddin Nature Reserve, spring 1999.

Youssef Touk (right), environmental activist in the Becharre region, with a representative from the Canada Fund, 1999.

Salmon Abbas, founding member of Green Line, at environmental fair, Hamra, Beirut, 2004.

Sign for the Ministry of the Environment (Antelias office).

Ali Mushamish, founding member of the Philanthropic Association
for the Disabled (PADC), with author at their Nabatiyya office, 1996.

Employment program for people with disabilities, Beqaa office of the
Lebanese Physically Handicapped Union (LPHU).

Sylvanna Lakkis, with members of the
Lebanese Physically Handicapped Union, Beirut Office, 1999.

Hyam Fakhoury and Piere Issa, Beirut offices of Arc en Ciel, 1999.

Nada Ismail, founding member of Philanthropic Association
for the Disabled (PADC), Nabatiyya office, fall 2008.

# 4

# Confronting Sectarian "Veto Points"

## *Women's Advocacy Politics in Postwar Lebanon*

> It is often said that women find participation in civil society easier
> to negotiate than . . . at the level of the state. . . . [Yet], in the con-
> text of the contemporary Middle East (as elsewhere), both state and
> civil society are complex terrains—fractured, conflictual, threatening
> spaces that are as much a source of oppression as they are spaces of
> opportunity for struggle and negotiation.[1]

Lebanon provides an interesting and paradoxical example of gendered
citizenship. On the one hand, it is one of the more advanced societies in
the Middle East region with respect to women's literacy rates, women's
health indicators such as life expectancy at birth, and the percentage of
women in higher education. On the other hand, statistics with respect
to women's participation in the formal private and public sector workforce combined with the broader array of legal and institutional restrictions on their freedom that surrounds them—particularly in the case of
married women—points to the existence of powerful systems of gendered discrimination in the country. This has created a situation where
reforms promoting the equal status of women in Lebanon have lagged
behind those in other Middle East states. Indeed, a recent report by a
leading feminist nongovernmental organization (NGO) in Lebanon with
region-wide experience remarked that while legal and institutional change
remains within the realm of possibility in most Middle East countries, in
Lebanon, "it is difficult to imagine even minor changes . . . being made
in the near future."[2]

This chapter, through an examination of gender equality advocacy
in the postwar period, seeks to understand the source of this institutional
resistance to reform. Its particular focus is on the ways in which actors
within civil society, broadly defined to include those associations affiliated

with families and sects, have contributed to the perpetuation of systems of gender inequality in the country and prevented the emergence of a women's policy domain within the state built upon the principles of gender equality. The chapter begins by examining the historical entrenchment of systems of gender inequality in the country—those that find their roots in the critical period of state formation during the mandate era. It was during this period that the potential of the state to act as an autonomous actor with respect to gender issues was effectively eliminated, transforming it instead into a defender of the power of the patriarchally oriented religious clerical class in the country. The second section of this chapter examines postwar efforts by an array of civil associations and networks to challenge the deeply embedded power—constitutional, institutional, and political—of these state–clerical alliances with the aim of constructing a more equality-oriented women's policy domain. The third section examines the mechanisms that contributed to the overall failure of these efforts, focusing in particular on the dynamics of various feedback mechanisms that served to reinforce preexisting systems of gender inequality and prevent the emergence of a more autonomous, institutionalized, and equality-oriented women's policy domain. One of the main contributions of this chapter is to highlight the ways in which Lebanon's women's associational sector itself—hegemonically intertwined as many of its component parts are with the country's political and clerical elites—has acted as one of these feedback mechanisms reinforcing the patriarchal status quo.

### The Structuring of Gender Advocacy Politics in Lebanon: The Historical Roots of a Women's Policy Domain

Modern Lebanon has had a long history of women debating their status and demanding their greater inclusion in the country's public sphere. Thompson has documented the rise of a politicized women's movement during the mandate period in Lebanon, which, from its modest beginnings in the 1920s, "steadily widened" the scope of its activism beyond the traditional areas of charity and education to include such concerns as health, labor, and the right to vote. Though women's activism was elitist and lacking in popular roots, Thompson nonetheless argued that, by the 1930s, it had managed to carve out for itself "a significant presence in the civic order."[3] The crowning achievement of this early activism came in 1953, with women gaining full voting rights. Buoyed by the success of their cross-sectarian campaign, a group of Muslim and Christian women's associations subsequently came together to form a unified coalition called the Lebanese Women's Council (LWC), an institution that has more or less—and, as we shall see, problematically—occupied the center of the women's sector from that point on. Hovering around the LWC in the pre–civil war period were a variety of other forms of activism, some more traditional, some aiming to deepen the drive for equal status through legal activism, notably by Laure Moughaizel, to whose work we return later, while others operated from within the growing pre–civil war movements of the left that worked to politicize the fight for equal women's status. Representing the emergence of "second wave feminism" in Lebanon,[4] these latter efforts were symbolized by struggles to institutionalize a distinctive women's voice within movements, parties, and militias through the creation of women's committees and departments.[5] Finally, in the post–civil war period, encouraged by the rise of machinery, funding, and conferences designed to promote the status of women on a global basis, Lebanon has seen the proliferation of an increasing number of autonomous women's associations, NGO networks, and campaigns devoted to improving the status of women. This has been paralleled by a significant mobilization of Islamist women within communal frameworks, especially within the Shi'a communities of the country and, in particular, within Hezbollah.[6] In short, women have become increasingly active and, at certain times and within certain leftist and secular circles, vocal advocates for gender equality within Lebanon's public sphere.

It is on the difficulty that these women's activists have had in transforming their equality-oriented activities and campaigns into policy successes that this chapter is focused. In the past, these difficulties have revolved in part around the absence of institutionalized women's "machinery" within the state devoted to defining the parameters of policy making, insulating policy discussions from wider sociopolitical concerns and providing women with what Anne Marie Goetz calls "a critical point of leverage" within the political system as a whole.[7] Although the National Commission for Lebanese Women (NCLW) was eventually created in 1995, a product of the Fourth United Nations (UN) World Conference on Women in Beijing, it has not succeeded, or even really tried, to consolidate a state role in the women's field, penetrated as it has been by the influence of powerful elite actors. In order to understand why this has been such a difficult process, we need to return to a critical period in the history of state formation in Lebanon during the French mandate period when a series of "gender bargains" was struck between French officials, religious patriarchs, and Lebanese political elites that served to weaken the role of the state with respect to gender issues.[8]

The starting point was the decision by French mandate authorities to leave jurisdiction over family and personal status law to the clerical leadership of the country. This decision eliminated the potential for the state to act as a powerful advocate for—or third party enforcer of—women's personal status rights. The system as it was constructed has never allowed for the existence of a higher civic authority to which men and women can appeal the decisions of these courts. Nor has it allowed the state to create mechanisms to overcome discrepancies and inequality-generating contradictions between the various religious legal codes, thereby preventing Lebanese law from playing an "integrative role" in establishing norms of citizenship regardless of religious affiliation.[9] Hence, on matters relating to personal status—be it with respect to marriage, divorce, child custody, or inheritance—Lebanese citizens are not only forced to pass through the numerous "portals of religion," but they are not allowed to go any further.[10] This had the added effect of accentuating the power of religious officials from all confessions, transforming them into "the nature allies" of the existing political order with whom women activists have to contend,[11] power that was consolidated through the development of communal legal apparatuses in what was a paradigmatic example of "duplicatory sectarianism."[12] Particularly consequential for the promotion of women's equality and rights in Lebanon has been the use of this institutionalized power to police the movement across communal boundaries, especially with respect to cross-communal marriage, and hence freeze Lebanon's sectarian divisions in place. It is in this sense that Suad Joseph argues that this delegation—if not conscious abdication—of responsibility by the Lebanese state for personal status law has served not only to maintain "differentiated realities of citizenship" within the country, but also to "create" and actively construct them.[13]

The most serious consequence of this multiple and heterogeneous legal system for Lebanese women has been its contribution to the strengthening of subordinating informal processes that revolve around kin-based patriarchy—the latter being defined as the privileging of males and seniors and the legitimating of those privileges in the morality and idiom of kinship.[14] Religious courts have played a key role in this process, symbolized by their consistent and across-the-board designation of the male as the head of the household. In Lebanon, children essentially belong to their fathers, who possess both ultimate rights of child custody as well as exclusive rights to the transfer of nationality and citizenship. In matters of divorce, women's interests also have been subordinated to the interests of men, a subordination that has been enforced by religious courts that are male dominated, hierarchically organized, lacking in autonomous civil mechanisms of accountability, and, hence, susceptible to *wasta* and corruption. Described as central to "the reproduction of order" within Lebanon's political system as a whole,[15] kin-based patriarchal norms and practices also are deeply interwoven within its civil society, reducing hopes that it "might have offered alternatives to women."[16]

Further weakening the structural position of challengers to the patriarchal status quo is the role of women and women's associations (as suggested above by Joseph) in reproducing and reinforcing that status quo. In short, while women and women's associations confront patriarchy in every sphere, some also participate in it and develop a stake in its perpetuation. In part, this difficulty points to the active agency of women themselves, who, as a result of strategic necessity, acquiesce to the dictates of patriarchal networks and institutions, especially that of poorer women, given that it is through these networks that the benefits of citizenship flow.[17] It also points to the existence of alternative norms around gender relations, especially within Islamist communities where some women's groups champion norms of gender complimentarity, rather than equality. It is also clear, however, that women not only acquiesce to patriarchal norms and practices on tactical or normative grounds in certain circumstances, but they also actively accept and participate in them.[18] Be it with respect to the apologetic attitudes of some women toward violence against women,[19] the deferring relationship between female patients and their male doctors found by public health researchers,[20] and/or the appalling indifference of upper-class Lebanese women to the exploitation faced by foreign female domestic servants,[21] it is clear that patriarchal norms not only are being propagated by religious and political elites, but they also are being internalized by some women and, as we shall see below, by some women's associations themselves. In other words, there exist not only powerful processes of gender disciplining within Lebanon but also hegemonic processes of self-disciplining. This helps to explain the relatively modest numbers of women being mobilized in support of issues of gender equality, with these activities and campaigns being limited, for the most part, to the networking and "gatherings" of secular-oriented associations that are part of Lebanon's postwar "civil movement."[22]

Hence, women activists working to create a more defined and equality-oriented women's policy domain in Lebanon must confront a formidable array of normative and institutional obstacles. These obstacles not only emanate from political society and the state; they also have been deeply embedded within the recursive dynamics between political and civil society. However, these dynamics are not all encompassing. The embedded nature of patriarchal norms in the country, for example, does not provide an unchanging normative blanket of discrimination against women. Rather, it is clear that patriarchal norms *differ* from place to place depending on the effects and contingencies of state formation processes in particular localities. Thompson has argued, for example, that gender bargains struck between colonial officials and local elites in one country varied from those in others.[23] In her study of the interaction between state formation and women's rights in Tunisia, Algeria, and Morocco, Mounira Charrad likewise argues that gender policies in some Middle Eastern states are "more patriarchal than others."[24] Moreover, systems of patriarchy over time *change*—though in the context of the modern Middle East, many have argued that these changes have not moved in the direction of gender equality. Thompson writes of the "regendering of citizenship" and of the creation of a "new colonial patriarchy"[25] during the French mandate, transforming it into something quite different from what it had been at the fall of the Ottoman Empire. Nonetheless, the overall point here is that patriarchy is a complex concept, subject to significant variation and degrees of contestation over time and space.

The opening up of *normative* possibilities for equality-oriented advocacy with respect to women in Lebanon that patriarchy's complex manifestations offer is paralleled by similar institutional opportunities for advocacy within the fragmented political order. Joseph captures this well when she writes of citizenship and gender rights being determined by relationships. Arguing that the public arena in Lebanon is "teaming" with relationality, Joseph notes that when citizens do gain public goods, they do so not because they have abstract rights but because they successfully create access to them through relationships and networks.[26] While the most "basic" networks in Lebanon are associated with the extended family and religious community that privilege men over women,[27] their informal and fragmented nature leave women some room for "negotiation, mediation, play, and empowerment."[28] As a result, Joseph stresses that they hold within them "webs of possibilities" for women, especially for those who can embed themselves within advantageous social relationships.[29] In short, using the language of historical institutionalism, there remain possibilities for the emergence of restricted forms of agency in the women's policy domain within the range allowed by the institutionally and normatively enforced (and reinforced) critical juncture.[30]

We turn now to an analysis of the emergence and initial success of these "restricted agents" in the context of those women's associations pushing for gender equality in postwar Lebanon. First, we examine transformations in the socioeconomic status of women in Lebanon from the pre- to postwar periods, raising questions about the degree to which these represent "cumulative" and "slow moving" processes of change. We then examine the reemergence of two distinct women's advocacy networks in the postwar period. One revolves around the LWC, resuscitated in the early postwar period as a mechanism for facilitating Lebanon's participation in several global conferences related to women's rights. The other revolves around the revival of legal advocacy networks that focused on issues of strategic importance to the status and well-being of women in the country. It was principally through the determination and dynamism of these women's advocacy networks, assisted by developments within the global women's movement, that sensitive debates and new discourses concerning women's issues were pushed into the postwar public sphere. As we shall subsequently examine in the final section of this chapter, however, it was also this same determination and dynamism that sparked the resuscitation of counter-networks within both civil and political society that worked to neutralize these advocacy efforts and, hence, reinforce the underlying structural foundations of the country's long-standing system of gender inequality.

### Generating a Critical Juncture? The Reemergence of Women's Advocacy Politics in Postwar Lebanon

Certain human development indicators improved significantly for Lebanese women by the early postwar period. The question is: Were these "slow moving" changes enough to forge a critical juncture in Lebanon's budding women's policy domain, generating "threshold effects" that would have the potential to drive reforms on an incremental basis, albeit within the context of Lebanon's patriarchally oriented institutional legacy?[31] Life expectancy at birth, for example, is now among the highest in the Arab world and higher for women (72) than for men (69),[32] and Lebanon has made similar regional achievements in levels of infant mortality. Closely connected with these health gains have been significant advances in educational status for women in Lebanon. Between 1970 and 1997, for example, women's illiteracy rates have declined from 37.8 percent to 5.7 percent, giving Lebanon one of the lowest rates of female illiteracy in the Arab world, though this does vary from region to region in the country.[33] Lebanon also ranks first in the Arab world in terms of the enrollment of girls in primary and secondary education. Moreover, facilitated by the regionalization of the campuses of the Lebanese University during the war that made higher education more accessible to middle- and lower-class families, women now make up more than 50 percent of all students enrolled in universities. In short, women have been the primary beneficiaries of what analysts have called an educational boom in the country.[34] There also have been parallel socioeconomic transformations related to changing patterns of family life and marriage—symbolized by an increase in the proportion of unmarried women between the ages of twenty and thirty-nine, delays in the average age of marriage, as well as increased rates of divorce.[35]

Less encouraging have been human development indicators with regards to women's economic status—with only 21.7 percent of women between the ages of fifteen and sixty-four participating in the formal labor force, a figure that surprisingly lags well behind average levels in the rest of the Arab and developing worlds.[36] In addition, women continue to be excluded from more than 90 percent of all executive positions in the private and public sectors, and the number of women who own businesses has been "abysmally low."[37] As Sofia Saadeh remarked, "a female "boss" still sounds like an anachronism in Lebanon."[38] Women also remain effectively excluded from many of the professions—being pocketed for the most part in such fields as social work and education—though there have been some noted increases in the fields of medicine, law, pharmacy, and, argues one scholar, even in banking.[39] Moreover, women not only have been systematically paid less than men in terms of salaries, bonuses, and promotions, but they also make up the majority of the working poor in the country.[40] Finally, in the public and political sectors, women have been described as being "almost invisible."[41]

Yet embedded if not hidden within these statistics may be some silver linings. First, as a result of the exigencies of the civil war period, there has been an almost 10 percent increase in the number of women active in the formal workforce compared to 1970—50 percent of which are estimated to be single; and there has been a burgeoning increase in the number of women active in the informal workforce—a phenomenon that includes anything from work in domestic service, to running a micro-enterprise, to working on a family farm. Indeed, conservative estimates suggest that the number of women engaged in the informal sector may be roughly equivalent to the number of those employed in the formal sector. Moreover, though predominantly in rural areas, there has also been a noted increase in the number of female-headed households.[42] In short, though more by force of circumstance than by design, more Lebanese women have left the confines of the home and have become integrated into the workforce, albeit often in a clearly subordinate fashion. It is part of a wartime process described as "forced emancipation" that led to "a fundamental modification in social relations" in the country. Indeed, writing in the early postwar period from her position as both an academic and activist, Lamia Shehadeh concluded hopefully that the cumulative effect of the forced entry of women into the public sphere would create a momentum that would be difficult to reverse.[43]

The question is: What direct effect could these underlying structural developments have on the status of women within postwar Lebanon? By themselves, they cannot be creators of political opportunities, challenging the historically entrenched normative and/or institutional context within which women live. Needed are agents of change—individuals, associations, and networks often linked to regional and global actors—willing to pry potential opportunities open. In the context of postwar Lebanon, we examine two agents of women's advocacy. The first was a network of secular feminist activists initially linked to the LWC in the early postwar period. They used the timely series of UN global conferences on women's issues in the early 1990s to rebuild dormant women's advocacy institutions in the country and launch a number of campaigns. The second was an overlapping network of women activists that focused particularly on legal advocacy, linking their local campaigns for gender equality to the UN Convention on the Elimination of All Forms of Discrimination against Women (CEDAW) that the Lebanese government had ratified (with three significant reservations) in 1996.

*The Beijing Process and Gender Advocacy in Postwar Lebanon*

The emergence of women's advocacy networks in Lebanon is directly linked to the mobilization of movements of the left. It was within these movements that women began to make vocal demands for gender equality, demands that resulted in the creation of women's committees and departments within various leftist political parties. For many women, this represented the first time that they had a chance to become more involved in politicized activities as women, separate from the charitable work of the country's female bourgeoisie. Yet it quickly became clear to many of these women activists that the party structures within which they operated—whether nationalist parties of the right or revolutionary parties of the left—were themselves infused with patriarchal ways of working. Wadad Chakhtoura, for example, an activist within the Organization of Communist Action in the prewar period who eventually went on to establish her own women's NGO called Le Rassemblement Democratique des Femmes Libanaises (RDFL) in 1976, described herself and her colleagues as encountering "lots of problems" with their male comrades, who, she argued, were "not ready to cede their place" and only acquiesced reluctantly to the demands of their women colleagues for a women's committee, saying "OK, establish your women's committee . . . and leave us alone."[44] An even more scathing critique of the experience of women within leftist political parties was expressed by Yolla Polity Sharara, who described women's committees as being marginalized within the party, excluded from positions of power, and instrumentalized for the purposes of demonstrations, electoral campaigns, and in the context of civil war, relief work. She added that the women's cause was "effectively abandoned" by leftist political leaders for the sake of their wider "gendered" alliances.[45] Not satisfied with their marginalized positions within the various political parties, therefore, activist leftist women such as Wadad Chakhtoura turned their attention to creating their own associations where they could focus more directly on issues of concern to women. When one of Lebanon's long-standing and leading women activists in both the pre- and postwar periods, Linda Matar, was asked why she devoted her career as a women's activist to an NGO, the League for Women's Rights, rather than to the Lebanese Communist Party (LCP), of which she was a member, she responded that she could both meet and speak about women's issues with a greater number of people and with greater liberty. Noting the strict ideological dogma of the LCP, for example, she remarked that, in the end, "it's not fair; each person is free."[46]

As the long period of relative isolation during the civil war came to an end, this small group of Lebanese women's activists was given a significant boost by its reconnection with the growing international machinery promoting women's equality. Key to this process was the timing of the Fourth World Conference on Women in Beijing, China, in 1995, coming as it did just four years into the postwar period. Indeed, the Beijing conference was part of a rapid sequence of conferences in the 1990s that unleashed "a veritable funding frenzy" for UN-related activities with respect to women.[47] In Lebanon, this gave rise to what has been called "the Beijing Group," a small network of women activists and feminists intent on using the Beijing process as a way to revive the moribund women's movement in the country. Wanting to promote a united women's front, they chose to focus their attention on reviving the LWC, which had effectively been frozen throughout the war, strategically so as to prevent a more formal split between its Christian and Muslim members. As we shall examine in more depth later, the LWC was not an unproblematic institutional choice. It had already begun to lose ground as the representative of the Lebanese women's movement in the 1960s in the face of the new associational actors such as unions and political parties. Its membership was made up primarily of traditional and confessionally based associations that were described as being "more feminine than feminist,"[48] and its immediate postwar circumstances were not promising. As one active member of the LWC in the postwar period described, the first meeting of this small network of women took place in the LWC offices "among dirty boxes full of documents. The organization had no funds, some of the forty organizations still members of the LCW had not communicated with each other for years, and the country was still suffering from a psychological divide between the Christian and

Muslim regions. . . . [T]he picture was not rosy except for the will of these women and their belief in the unifying dynamic that women['s] issues can play."[49] Because the LWC still offered the greatest potential for inclusiveness and unity, however, especially in light of the wartime proliferation of more regionalized and sectarian-oriented women's networks, the decision was made to both revive the LWC and, if possible, politicize it.[50]

With the Beijing process in the background, therefore, the LWC and the small coterie of women activists hovering around it worked hard to recapture the center ground of the women's movement in postwar Lebanon. They amended the administrative structures of the LWC to include regional representation in the executive in order to cope with the decentralized associational legacies of the war; they held new elections, with one of the leading members of "the Beijing Group," Aman Shaarani, being elected president; they launched a recruitment drive to resuscitate its membership—something that clearly generated some excitement, especially among women's groups in outlying areas of the country that had been cut off from Beirut throughout the war;[51] and they embarked on some preliminary studies of the postwar women's sector that resulted in the compilation of a database that, as one women activist optimistically remarked, was "the starting point for the reunification of the Lebanese women's movement."[52] More directly related to the Beijing conference, the LWC, with strategic donor support, created a special NGO Committee to act as the "national" civil society representative—a committee that included both LCW members as well as independent activists.[53] Moreover, it successfully lobbied to create its own mechanism for participation at Beijing—the National Committee for the Preparation of and the Participation in the Fourth World Conference on Women—that included not only representatives from the state but also a significant number of representatives from civil society, including seven members from the newly reconstituted LWC.[54] Together, these committees embarked on a wide range of activities that included the hosting of awareness-raising seminars, workshops, panels, and conferences in different parts of the country. All in all, this frenzied activity instigated by a small network of women within and around the LWC and strategically supported by a few foreign donors represented a promising start to the process of regrouping leading women and women's associations in the country "around a feminist agenda."[55] It also was hoped that this activity would put these women in the position of being "prime movers" in forging a more progressive policy agenda and a more institutionalized women's policy domain in the postwar world on which an improvement in the status of women in the direction of gender equality could be more confidently and substantively pursued.

*"The Moughaizel Effect": CEDAW and Women's Legal Advocacy
in Postwar Lebanon*

Paralleling and overlapping with this postwar reconstitution of the LWC
were renewed efforts to eliminate all forms of legal discrimination against
women. In Lebanon, efforts to achieve comprehensive legal gender equality have been at the core of the women's activism; as one longstanding
women's activist has remarked, it has been "a primordial question for
us."[56] The symbolic head of this legal activism was Laure Moughaizel, a
lawyer, women's activist, and founder of several legal and human rights
advocacy associations, who was present from the beginning of the post-
independence women's advocacy efforts starting with the campaign for
the right to vote in 1953. Described as "a tireless proponent for the rights
of women and those unjustly treated,"[57] Moughaizel worked according to
a modus operandi that became standard operating procedure for legal
activists in the women's field, using Lebanese constitutional and international legal tools to eliminate discriminatory gender laws within the
country. Her method consisted of compiling inventories of various discriminatory laws and regulations, preparing concrete modifications using
examples from reforms in other countries (especially in the Arab world),
targeting laws on a case-by-case basis rather than more comprehensively
so as not to disaffect the political classes,[58] mobilizing public support for
the proposed changes by taking advantage of the backing of associations
and the media,[59] and, perhaps most importantly, cultivating and taking
advantage of connections with those in political society. Reflecting on the
decision by the Lebanese government in 1983, in the midst of the civil
war period, to annul the sections within the criminal code illegalizing the
use of contraceptives, Moughaizel stressed that this had only been made
possible when the president of the Lebanese Family Planning Association
(FPA), who had been campaigning on this issue for years, was appointed
minister of health—"proof, if one needed more," added Moughaizel, "of
the importance of NGOs participating in power."[60]

Moughaizel's pioneering and, by all accounts, dogged legal activism
has left several important legacies. First, she contributed to the emergence of a growing, if loosely connected, network of women lawyers and
jurists whose talents would increasingly be at the disposal of secular feminist and associational activists. Alia Bertie Zein, for example, one of the
country's leading postwar lawyers specializing in women's and human
rights law, remembered Moughaizel having mentored a group of young
women lawyers of which she was one, acting as their "opening" to broader
local, regional, and international human rights networks around them.[61]
Moughaizel's later work with the Lebanese Association for Human Rights

in collaboration with her husband was similarly described as having transformed the association into a veritable "nursery" in terms of its cultivation of new groups of human rights activists.[62] It remains unclear how tight or proactive this legal network of human rights lawyers actually is, divided by generational, ideological, and professional/jurisprudential factors with different lawyers and judges pursuing different strategies for legal reform and aligning themselves—or not—with different associational networks and actors.[63] Moreover, Iqbal Dughan, a lawyer and leading women's activist in the country who has established her own association to provide legal advice and assistance to working women, argues that lawyers in general have a difficult time acting collectively, preoccupied as they are by the demands of running a practice.[64] Nonetheless, however unintegrated this loose network of legal activists may be, they have provided associational actors, when called on, with crucial expertise in the preparation and launching of their various campaigns for legal reform as well as with crucial contacts inside the political realm.

The other major contribution made by Moughaizel and the human rights team that increasingly surrounded her[65] was the reforging of connections with the international human rights arena at the end of the civil war, efforts that ran parallel to those aimed at reestablishing links with the international women's machinery by way of the Beijing process. Effectively using their combined access to the global human rights community and the political process in Lebanon, they convinced the new and fractious array of deputies to amend the Lebanese Constitution in 1990 to include an explicit reference to the UN Charter and the Universal Declaration of Human Rights and, subsequently and most significantly for Lebanon's small community of women activists, to ratify the CEDAW protocol in 1997. Despite the insistence of the Lebanese government on three reservations that denied CEDAW jurisdiction over personal status laws, questions of nationality rights, and the highly patriarchal penal code, the ratification of CEDAW nonetheless represented a significant development for Lebanon's gender equality activists, not because they were able to translate it into immediate legal gains—which they could not—but because it created a legal platform, strengthened by connections to the international human rights community, from which new leverage opportunities could be created. In fact, some of these new leverage opportunities were actually built into the CEDAW process itself, the result of periodic reporting requirements on the part of the Lebanese government and the newly created NCLW to the CEDAW Committee in New York. This latter committee has proven to be very aggressive, providing strong critiques on a wide range of areas of weak or noncompliance.[66] Commenting on the legal and policy leverage that the ratification of CEDAW brought to the women's advocacy field in the country, Linda Matar remarked that it has been "like a weapon for us."[67]

Yet fulfilling the Moughaizel legacy has been a much more difficult achievement. Certainly, a variety of new associations have moved in to fill the void created by her absence after her death in 1997. Some continue to work on a variety of legal issues on a case-by-case basis; others have turned to specializing on one area of legal discrimination against women; and all, to a greater and sometimes lesser extent, have tried to work together to forge common advocacy positions on the key issues at stake. Indeed, activists speak of five different campaigns for the elimination of legal discrimination against women that have targeted personal status laws, the penal code, labor and social security laws, family protection laws, and nationality laws. All have achieved preliminary successes in a number of areas: bringing issues of gender discrimination back into the postwar public sphere by sparking debates, raising awareness, and introducing new secular feminist discourses; broadening the social base of their advocacy networks by attracting a larger group of allies outside the immediate associational sector itself; and, developing quiet working relations with the "trenches" of the Lebanese bureaucracy. However, tangible legal reforms have been few and far between, with the exception of the removal of discriminatory provisions within labor and social security laws in 2000. This was a full thirty years after the campaign had begun, noted Iqbal Dughan, president of the League of Working Women, who had promoted these reforms in the postwar period along with the League of Lebanese Women and a CEDAW-oriented coalition called *al-Liqa' al-Watani*. Added one colleague with respect to Dughan's efforts: "[I]t's the same contribution as Laure Moughaizel . . . a Rottweiller approach. She went on until the end."[68] Various factors have hindered the broader success of these nascent advocacy networks. Some are linked to the challenge of cultivating a critical mass of strategically placed supporters within the state; others are linked to the competitive dynamic within the women's sector itself that has hindered the consolidation of cohesive associational platforms from which advocacy networks can launch their campaigns. While the former is the focus of the third section of this chapter, we examine the second by comparing the relative unity of those working in the field of violence against women with the more challenging reality of those working on the issue of nationality.

A courageous addition to Lebanon's postwar women's sector has been the emerging network of new associations specializing in the area of violence against women. This is a serious problem in Lebanon that affects more than one-third of the female population within the country and includes anything from domestic violence to honor crimes.[69] Despite efforts over the years by women activists to make it otherwise, it has also been a "taboo" issue in the country, relegated to adjudication within the private realm of the family and in which the legal system has been extremely reluctant to intervene on the basis of gender equality. It was a push from the global arena that helped to bring the issue of violence against women back into the public sphere in the early postwar period, the product of preparations for the Beijing conference that included calls for a series of public hearings on the issue throughout regions of the world.[70] It was then that Zoya Rouhana, a longtime activist with Secours Populairs Libanais (SPL), the development arm of the Lebanese Communist Party, became interested and decided to organize the first-ever hearing on the issue in the Arab world in 1995 in Beirut. Attended by representatives from more than thirty countries, the meeting was so successful that it established a permanent regional network that would focus its activities around the periodic holding of an Arab Women's Court—the first being held in Beirut again one year later. Commenting on her subsequent decision to leave SPL and, with a core of dedicated women, set up a separate association in 1997 called the Lebanese Council to Resist Violence Against Women (LCRVAW), Rouhana remarked that there was "a real tragedy taking place [in the country] without anybody noticing it, without anybody talking about it. . . . It was a clear demonstration of the patriarchal system in Lebanon."[71]

The core of LCRVAW's work and subsequently that of KAFA, the association that Rouhana also created and moved to in 2005 after leaving LCRVAW, was the establishment of a support system for women caught in situations of domestic violence.[72] From the inception of its work in the late 1990s, for example, LCRVAW, and subsequently KAFA, have served hundreds of female victims of domestic violence, all having suffered from some kind of "physical, emotional, verbal, sexual, or financial abuse in an intimate adult relationship" that has led to serious psychological damage—if not suicidal tendencies.[73] In addition to the provision of emergency services, the work of LCRVAW and KAFA has subsequently branched out into a variety of activities. These have included training and raising awareness activities among a variety of frontline stakeholders—from social workers working with the Ministry of Social Affairs, to police officers, to religious court judges, to primary and secondary school teachers, to women themselves, in addition to increasing involvement in parallel fields relating to child sexual abuse, violence against women with disabilities, the trafficking of women, promoting the socioeconomic empowerment of women and girl victims of violence, and, with respect to KAFA, a legal reform campaign pushing for a more explicit provision within the criminal code dealing with domestic violence, something that is at present absent. Closely related to this latter campaign of KAFA has been a variety of research and documentary projects aimed at raising awareness of the workings and lack of transparency of the religious and criminal court system with respect to violent crimes against women, projects that have included a two-year study of Sunni and Maronite religious appeals courts, the creation of a computer software program designed to facilitate more systematic documentation of court proceedings, and the publication of an extensive study examining the proceedings of sixty-six court cases on domestic violence against women, a book the author had originally wanted to call "femicide."[74]

Enhancing the work of LCRVAW and KAFA has been the emergence of a nascent but growing network of local, regional, and international allies. At the local level, for example, was a small group of associations quietly working in the field, many before the creation of LCRVAW and KAFA, that included (among others) the YWCA, which was able—indeed, as we shall see, virtually the only one allowed by the Ministry of the Interior—to establish a shelter for "abandoned women and their children" in 2002.[75] LCRVAW and KAFA also cultivated a network of reform-minded representatives of the legal system, including judges in both the religious and civil courts as well as a budding network of lawyers. Of further critical importance to this broadening array of network actors—associational and otherwise—has been the financial and strategic support from international donors. The technical support of the UN Special Rapporteur on Violence Against Women and the moral support of the New York staff of CEDAW, for example, have proven crucial in preparations to launch the draft law inserting domestic violence against women in the criminal code;[76] UNFPA also has provided important strategic assistance by working to establish a regional network of associations working in the area of "gender-based violence"; and a variety of bilateral and independent donors have provided important project and, in the case of KAFA, strategic funding.[77] What have been particularly interesting about the effects of donor financing on this sub-network within the broader women's and gender field, however, are its essentially positive effects. First, most donor-funded programs have fit into the already existing priorities of local actors rather then generated them. Indeed, much of the initial work in this field has been initiated with little donor support at all, only to receive funding later. Laura Sfeir, for example, one of the founders of LCRVAW and subsequently its president, described her initial efforts to open up an office in Tripoli in 1999—helpline and all—with virtually no funding, budget, or support staff at all; and Zoya Rouhana cited the domestic violence draft law project—initially an unfunded initiative—as evidence of the determination of KAFA to remain a donor-supported rather than donor-driven

NGO.[78] Moreover, donors have had to adjust their strategic approach to a variety of social and political environments—there is no "one size fits all" in the field of violence against women in Lebanon.[79] Finally, in part because of the dual focus on legal reform and service delivery in a field where the on-the-ground needs are huge, foreign funding does not seem to have fostered a counterproductive competitive dynamic between the local NGOs in this field, something that, as we shall see below, complicated the efforts of those involved in the nationality campaign.

Finally, emerging women's advocacy networks in the area of violence against women also have tried to bridge the political divide by cultivating contacts within the state apparatus, including selected legislators, representatives of the police and Internal Security Forces (ISF), as well as officials within the Ministry of Social Affairs. Particularly important in this regard was Nayla Mouawad, the Social Affairs minister between 2005 and 2008, who was described as having "opened the space" for collaborative efforts on this issue between NGOs and various levels of the MSA—within the Higher Council of Childhood (on issues of child sexual abuse), within the MSA's Women's Unit itself, as well as with the Social Development Centers (SDCs) that are often located in some of the poorer districts of the country. Indeed, Rouhana described the level of cooperation between MSA social workers and LCRVAW, RDFL, and KAFA as being not only "very successful"; it also was critical to their grassroots work, especially given the spread of SDCs throughout the country. "You cannot take over the role of the state," remarked Rouhana, in reference to those who would belittle its potential contribution. Indeed, not only did social workers from these associations have a lot of direct contact with social workers working for the MSA, but they also were described as being "on call" to the MSA if their assistance was needed. When I asked whether this emerging set of actors in the field of violence against women—which included working contacts with the "trenches" of the state apparatus itself—might represent an emerging "nodal" network within the broader women's field as a whole, Rouhana remarked by saying "maybe . . . they are the only ones working on the ground."[80]

The network around the nationality issue—fighting for the right of women to pass on their nationality and, hence, citizenship, to their children and/or their husbands—was a more recent development within Lebanon's postwar women's associational sector, the product of renewed advocacy efforts that were sparked by a Beirut-based association called Collective for Training, Research, and Development—Action (CRTD-A). Having begun a regional campaign on the issue in 2001, CRTD-A and its founder, Lina Abou-Habib, launched its Lebanese campaign in 2005. It consisted of a number of components: research that has included

comparative legal studies of the nationality issue in the Arab world combined with the collection of both quantitative and qualitative data on
the nature and extent of the problem; public awareness-raising efforts,
facilitated by receptive and sustained "nonstop" media coverage, that have
included sit-ins and promotional events, grassroots work within schools
and universities that has been able to take advantage of some of the local
infrastructure of a number of supporting women's associations, and the
preparation of media materials that has included the establishment of a
Facebook blog; the launching of a pilot project legal support unit using the
Social Development Centers of the MSA within several poorer districts of
Beirut (Sin el-Fil and Bourj Hammoud); and, finally and most recently,
the reinvigoration of political advocacy, last attempted by Laure Moghaizel
in the very early postwar period, that CRTD-A hoped would be backed
up by both a local women's network of associations and a regional one
that had launched a broader CEDAW-oriented campaign called "Equality
without Reservations." While the political advocacy efforts have been peri-
odically hampered by the unstable political equation in the country—a
crucial meeting with parliamentarians having been indefinitely postponed
as a result of the July 2006 war with Israel—the campaign has nonetheless
made progress, especially with respect to the network's ability to reach
and mobilize women who have been adversely affected by discriminatory
nationality laws, something that Abou-Habib describes as "fantastic" and
"a major step forward because when we started, nobody was ready to talk
about herself. . . . They were all scared."[81]

However, the campaign also has been plagued by defections from
within its small network of associations, the result of a competitive
dynamic that has been endemic within Lebanon's small community of
women's associational activists. Having initially established a more formal network of seven associations, for example, CRTD-A, at the launch
of its more vigorous political lobbying campaign at the Beirut Marathon
in 2005, was confronted by the withdrawal of two of its members, the
League for Women's Rights that is affiliated with a broader coalition, *al-
Liqa' al-Watani*, which subsequently launched its own campaign with a
distinct proposal, advocating for the right of the mother to pass on her
nationality to her children but, in contrast to CRTD-A's approach, not
to her husband. Moreover, just as CRTD-A was about to relaunch its
campaign in the wake of the Doha Accord in 2008 after a long period
of dormancy, UNDP-Lebanon awarded financing for its own "nationality
campaign" initiative to an association called the NGO Committee (*al-
Lajna al-Ahliyya*), also a member of CRTD-A's network, that sparked serious internal divisions and spawned accusations that it was also devising
a "counter campaign."[82] All of this has created confusion among both the

women affected by the discriminatory law who are waiting for a successful advocacy campaign to be launched and interested parliamentary deputies waiting for the presentation of amendment proposals.

What has been at the root of this divisiveness? Part of the explanation is linked to competitive quarrels of a more personal and/or institutional nature, it being difficult to distinguish between the two given the degree to which the popular names of many associations are synonymous with those of their leaders. As one observer of women's politics in postwar Lebanon noted, "[S]uspicion runs high in the women's advocacy community."[83] Exacerbating this competition have been the interventions of foreign donors—bringing to the fore an underlying tension within most associative networks as to whether one "grabs" donor funding as a network or as an organization. In the case of the nationality campaign, the size of the UNDP grant on offer ($270,000)—"more money than we've spent since the start of the campaign," noted Abou Habib—heightened these existential tensions considerably and, in the end, left the previously congenial coalition of NGOs "completely divided" over what was, in effect, a "pot of money." Resentful at the demise of its coalition, CRTD-A described it as a classic case of donor intervention "undermining local processes."[84]

Intertwining with these donor-exacerbated petty wars of position, however, were substantive differences in political and strategic approach. CRTD-A, a small, research-oriented association without a strong grassroots membership base, has the institutional liberty to stand on a strictly feminist platform; "fundamentally, it is about equality," noted Abou Habib, "so you cannot be a feminist human rights organization . . . and say that there are differences that I will accept for tactical and/or strategic purposes. It doesn't work, at least not intellectually, it doesn't work." Added Abou Habib, "a statement of principle is never informed by reality. It's a statement in principle . . . they [the political classes] will go to the least common denominator anyway. So, why give it to them easily."[85] To the other side of CRTD-A stands al-Liqa' al-Watani, a diverse coalition of associations—established to pursue the implementation of the CEDAW protocol—that combines strong roots in the political left with a variety of other seemingly contradictory tendencies. Noted one of its chief spokespersons, "we are not just progressive feminists of the left. There are those on the right and the left, there are those who are more religious, those that believe and those that do not. . . . [In short], there is a breadth of social groups within the al-Liqa'."[86] Indeed, despite the challenges that this diversity of opinion creates when formulating more immediate advocacy strategies, it is nonetheless looked upon as a longer-term advantage by the leftist vanguard of al-Liqa' who have little faith in the "quantitative"

changes that legal reform can bring and who are much more interested in
the potential of a broad-based coalition like *al-Liqa'* to spark "qualitative"
change through the mobilization of secular, democratic social movements.
Noted one of its active leftist members, "[T]his is civil society . . . [and]
it is a struggle, not a job. It needs a political project."[87] Restrained by its
deliberate recruitment of a diverse membership base, *al-Liqa'* has ended
up formulating constrained, if seemingly contradictory, advocacy positions[88]—such as that with respect to the nationality campaign—that have
kept its efforts distinct from those of the others within the gender equality
camp.[89] Finally, in the middle of both of these groups sits the NGO Committee—created as a result of the Beijing process—which has focused its
activities around writing a "shadow CEDAW report," conducting research,
particularly in the field of gender-inclusive education, and raising public
awareness.[90] Assisted by a steady, if modest, flow of financial support from
foreign donors and headed from its inception by Aman Shaarani, the first
postwar head of the LWC who has made no secret of her broader political
ambitions, its approach towards women's advocacy has been more flexible and pragmatic, grounded in "Women in Development" (WID)-like
strategies, with their focus on women's inclusion in economic, social, and
political processes. While its project-oriented work has been carried out
with efficiency and competence, it has found itself susceptible to charges
of a co-optive professionalization, what some have referred to as "NGO-
ization," characterized by a preoccupation with "its organization" and "its
projects."[91]

     None of these conflicting orientations—personal, institutional, stra-
tegic—was unbridgeable or permanently debilitating. All fundamentally
live within the same world of gender equality advocacy that employs an
incremental and state-oriented approach initially carved out by Laure
Moghaizel. All work for an end to legal forms of discrimination and a
dramatic improvement in the status of women in the country and, no
matter how their projects may differ, all campaign around the same basic
goals. Moreover, their efforts have certainly contributed to a much higher
profile and greater social awareness of women's issues within Lebanon's
postwar public sphere. The fundamental issue setting these associations
apart is their differing strategic approaches to gender equality advocacy—
all of which take a distinct approach to the challenge of gaining influence within the state through the forging of effective policy networks
that incorporate influential members of Lebanon's political elite. Save for
the cultivation of quiet working relationships with the "trenches" of the
bureaucracy or the establishment of ties with a few individual deputies
and ministers, Lebanon's small community of women's activists, like the

more secular segments of its civil society as a whole, are essentially shut out of the political arena. As one of *al-Liqa*'s male activists, Samir Diab, remarked, "[W]e are out on the streets."[92] It is to an explanation of why this has been the case, why the seemingly political opportunities for advocacy on women's issues in the early post–civil war period have gradually narrowed, that we turn now. As we shall see, while the agency of religious clerics and their backers within the country's political class have been the driving forces behind restricting political opportunities for the creation of a more bounded and insulated women's policy domain geared toward promoting gender equality, political dynamics within the women's associational sector itself have greatly contributed to these narrowing political opportunities as well.

## Confronting "Gender Pacts": Religious Clerics, Politicians, and Women's Advocacy Politics in Postwar Lebanon

Clerical classes have proven powerful forces of resistance to gender reform in Lebanon—a testament to the ways in which women have continued to be "markers of cultural authenticity" and, hence, "objects of social control."[93] If religious clerics were to support gender equality, for example, they not only might leave their religious authority open to criticism, but they also would leave themselves vulnerable to charges of weakening the cohesion of their own communities, a dangerous proposition given the heightened degree of sectarian tension in Lebanon's postwar period. As a result, clerical leaders across the various confessions in Lebanon have colluded and cooperated to preempt efforts to challenge their autonomy in this realm. Further acquiesced to by political elites, the result has been the existence of resilient, inequality-generating "gender pacts."

What follows in this section is an examination of the complex interplay within and between religious communities over the question of equality-oriented gender reform in postwar Lebanon, interplay that was energized by the postwar attempts to promote reform in the field of personal status law. This section begins with an analysis of these dynamics within each of the three major religious communities in the country— Sunni, Maronite, and Shi'a—before examining the reactions of their religious officials to the proposals to establish an optional, unified, and civil personal status code in the country in the mid- to late 1990s. The rest of the chapter examines the ways in which these reactions of the country's clerical establishments reverberated throughout the women's sector as a whole, activating a number of supporting feedback mechanisms within the state (namely the newly created NCLW within the Office of the Prime Minister) as well as within civil society (and the LWC in particular) that served to reinforce the existing parameters of the country's gender political order.

*Enforcing Patriarchy: The Politics of Personal Status Reform in Postwar Lebanon*

The strongest opposition to proposals to establish an optional civil personal status code came from within the religious leadership of Lebanon's Sunni communities, reactions that were, in part, linked to their shifting internal postwar politics. The political strength and cohesion of Lebanon's Sunni communities in the postwar period remained uncertain, hemmed in, on the one side, by the growing demographic weight and increased institutionalization of the Shi'a communities and, on the other hand, by increased contestation within their own community itself, principally by Sunni Islamists, including transnationally backed Salafi movements. Caught in the middle of these contestations was the Beirut-based Dar al-Fatwa, which was struggling to maintain its authority and legitimacy in the postwar period. This had been weakened by the wartime assassination of the popular anti-Syrian Mufti Hassan Khalid in 1989 and by the subsequent extension of Syrian hegemony into the heart of its decision-making process—epitomized by its orchestration in 1996 of the election of Khalid's successor, Mohammad Rashid Qabbani, and by the parallel reforms to the Higher Islamic Council that transferred increasing power over the community's affairs to its civilian leadership.[94] As one official admitted, because Dar al-Fatwa was seen as having become part of the Syrian-dominated postwar state, "it was also seen as part of the problem."[95] Further challenging Dar al-Fatwa's legitimacy was its weak institutional capacity, especially with regard to its ability to regulate religious developments within the Sunni communities.[96] Both contributing to and taking advantage of these weaknesses were new Islamist groups (such as al-Jamaa al-Islamiyya and al-Jamiyat al-Mashari al-Khayriyya al-Islamiyya, known as *al-Ahbash*), Rougier describing them as "gain[ing] great autonomy from an institution that [was] normally responsible for controlling both their religious management at the organizational level, and their interpretation at the doctrinal level."[97] Indeed, combined with the external sources of support from countries such as Qatar, Saudi Arabia, and Syria, the emerging competition between this diverse array of Islamist networks and the Sunni religious establishment contributed to a growing sense of communal insecurity in the postwar period.[98] Hemmed in by its declining political capital and weakening institutional capacities,

Dar al-Fatwa found itself increasingly outflanked and marginalized by the conflicting Sunni postwar political dynamics around it, having little option but to stand aside in the face of the rise of more militant Islamist activities. One official from Dar al-Fatwa lamented rather starkly that "here, it's anarchy."[99]

Contributing to the growing and diverse forms of contestation within the Sunni communities of postwar Lebanon has been the increasing participation of Sunni women within Islamist parties, if not within their own Islamist women's associations, something that is part of a broader trend within the Middle East as a whole.[100] While unable to provide exact numbers, Mona Yakan—wife of the late head of the Lebanese branch of the Muslim Brotherhood, Fathi Yakan, and herself a pioneering leader among Islamist women, having received a doctorate from the Sorbonne, the distinction of being one of the first *da'iyat* (Islamic women preachers) in Tripoli, and who became the president of Al-Jinan University in Tripoli established by her late husband after his death—described this trend as "a healthy phenomenon which denote[d] an awareness and understanding of the measure of the responsibility they have towards their country and their nation."[101] This trend, in fact, finds its roots in the early 1960s "at a time when the field of the feminist Islamic call was void of Islamic 'women participants' "[102] and, hence, mirrors the more general expansion in the number of civil associations during the Chehabist period. Yakan herself wrote about her involvement in founding the Tripoli-based Islamic Women's League—legally recognized in 1972—that has attracted the participation of hundreds of women in numerous charitable activities, and she added that, while Islamist women were particularly active within the Tripoli area, there also were significant women's movements "with an Islamic background" emerging in other areas of the country, especially Beirut and the northern regions of Akkar and Dennieh. There remains a wide diversity of opinions with regard to questions of women's status within these Islamist women's circles, Yakan's criticism of "the social culture of patriarchy which keep[s] women deprived of their rights" and her acceptance of the general idea of equality symbolized by her measured support for the CEDAW protocol[103] being juxtaposed with the conservative approach of other Islamist women, which has, itself, been reigned in by the strong pressure brought to bear on them to maintain solidarity with the broader Islamist cause. What is important for the purposes of this chapter, however, is that the emergence of lively debates within Sunni Islamist women's circles has had the effect of further complicating relations within and between the various factions within Lebanon's Sunni communities. As Omayma Abdullatif and Marina Ottaway concluded with respect to the broader Middle East, Islamist women "want to be seen as potential leaders, not just foot soldiers, and in many countries they are pushing the leadership of their movements for change."[104]

Maronite religious officials also have found themselves on the defensive in the postwar period; indeed, the church and its communities were described as having emerged "battered" from the events of the civil war.[105] Part of this defensiveness stemmed from its historical roots as a minority and rural-based church where most of the priests are locally trained, recruited, and have little higher education—all of which has contributed to a church that has been cloistered, deeply traditional, and resistant to change.[106] Although there were attempts in the prewar period by a movement of Christian leftists to open up the Maronite Church to more progressive ideas, these movements lost out in the civil war process to a highly defensive, conservative, and right-wing Maronite faction, led by the Order of Lebanese Monks, that consolidated its hold over the church, even above that of the traditional church hierarchy. When combined with the disastrous events of the late civil war and early postwar period—including the war between Christian militias in the late 1980s, the signing of the Ta'if Accord signaling the end of Maronite political hegemony in the country, and its subsequent uneven enforcement by a Syrian occupation—there emerged a strong sense of disillusionment (*ihbat*) within Lebanon's Maronite communities that was mirrored by that within the church itself. An extensive survey of grassroots congregational attitudes commissioned by the Vatican in 1993, for example, revealed an alarming degree of resentment, bitterness, and despair on the part of the lay members of the church toward the wealth, privilege, and patriarchal attitudes of the clergy and church hierarchy. Parallel to this were concerns about the growing numbers of women in the church seeking divorce and the growing cynicism among the youth of the church, who were described as being alienated, hardened, and uninterested in questions of either citizenship or belief.[107] There also emerged concern about the growth of more evangelical and "fundamentalist" Christian churches in the country, many with lots of external financing to promote their cause.[108] Hoping to rejuvenate and "purify" the church as a way of preserving its strong presence in the country and in the region, the Vatican embarked on its own forceful program of postwar religious reconstruction, emphasizing the importance of abandoning the instincts for survival that had paralyzed intellectual innovation and social and political initiatives in the past and of promoting processes of spiritual renewal and communal reconciliation—"breaking down the walls," to paraphrase the words of Pope John Paul II—that were not unlike the appeals for increased public piety by certain leading clerical figures within the Shi'a communities of the country.[109] However, while the Maronite Church did experience a "mini-spiritual renewal,"[110] much of this renewed religious social capital was used, in the words of Carol Dagher, to build up rather than break down walls—defending the Maronite and Christian communities in the face of the creeping sectarianism of the postwar period.[111] As Picard notes, social and political trends within Maronite and Christian circles in the postwar Lebanon have been characterized by "a retreat back to community."[112]

Standing in contrast to the postwar sense of insecurity within the Sunni and Maronite religious establishments has been the greater sense of confidence within the Shi'a communities of the country, a confidence inextricably bound up with their growing organizational and political power within postwar Lebanon as well as with the growing regional influence of Iran.[113] Rather than struggling to maintain authority in the face of communal fragmentation, as has been the case with respect to Sunni religious authorities, or "retreating" back into community, as has been the tendency within the Maronite communities, debates within the Shi'a communities have been heavily influenced by their emerging communal strength and have revolved around their "claim to modernity" and how best to project this claim.[114]

Postwar debates on gender relations within the Shi'a communities must be seen within this context. The roots of emerging postwar debates within the Shi'a communities over questions of gender can be found in pre–civil war activities of Musa al-Sadr, who publically lamented the difference between the active role played by women in the early Islamic period and the absence of women from the contemporary public sphere. Instead, he argued that women should move beyond the realm of family life and pursue their own opportunities through education and *ijtihad*. He also backed up these statements with the creation of a variety of new institutions for women and girls, a broader trend within Islamists communities as a whole—Sunni and Shi'a alike.[115] By catering to the needs of women previously untouched by the Lebanese state, al-Sadr was described as having contributed to the creation of a new generation of women activists, especially among poor Shi'a women, as well as sparking a nascent process of "rethinking gender constructs" within the Shi'a communities.[116]

Leading postwar Shi'a intellectuals have continued in this tradition—evidenced by the numerous juridical rulings, books, pamphlets, literary materials, seminars, and public pronouncements that have opened up debates on the status of women. In fact, Mallouk Berry argues that the collective effect of these rulings and publications—significantly influenced by developments within Khomeini and post-Khomeini Iran[117]—has been to shift some of the prevailing gender norms away from those promoting "complementarity" grounded in notions of motherhood toward those promoting "equality," though she adds that this has occurred "gradually" and in a way that "fit[s] the context of Islamic discourse."[118] This included such developments as the 2007 *fatwa* of Mohammad Husayn Fadlallah in support of the International Day for the Elimination of Violence against Women, which a leading Lebanese women's activist described as being "very, very, very developed and open-minded";[119] Mohammad Shams ad-Din's judgments that husbands have an inherent legal obligation to look after their wives' emotional and psychological well-being;[120] and the critique of Mohammad Hasan al-Amin, the Supreme Shari'a judge concerned with personal status laws in Lebanon, that the Shari'a has been used incorrectly as some kind of "magic wand" by the Islamic court systems in ways that have unfairly affected women.[121] Collectively, these writings, rulings, debates, and mobilizations of women have served to break the monopolizing hegemony of the discourse of the pre–civil war Shi'a religious establishment on issues relating to gender relations within Lebanon's Shi'a communities, creating a situation whereby competing discourses now coexisted.[122] Indeed, Berry went so far as to say that the sum total of these developments has sparked "the beginnings of feminist consciousness."[123]

Paralleling this lively debate has been the growing participation of Shi'a women within their communal affairs—most visibly in the southern suburbs of Beirut, where they have become an integral part of the development of the emerging "Islamic sphere" through their volunteer activities in the realm of social welfare—mirroring the growing activism of Islamist women within Lebanon's Sunni communities.[124] Particularly prominent has been Hezbollah's Women's Association (HWA), whose roster of women volunteers has grown tremendously since the end of the civil war. Working through *husseiniyyat* and local networks, volunteers with the HWA have played an active role in encouraging Shi'a women to become more engaged in the community's affairs.[125] There has been a particular emphasis on empowering poor women through the provision of vocational training and, hence, employment opportunities outside the home, and some scholars have noted a marked similarity between the approach taken by many of the new Shi'a social service organizations such as HWA and those adopted by international development organizations.[126] In short, through the mobilization of women into institutionalized social development networks within the Shi'a communities, Shi'a women have found new channels through which to become more actively involved in social and political affairs, legitimating their political engagement "outside of the private sphere."[127]

However, despite the lively debates about gender relations and the increased mobilization of women within pubic piety movements, there has been no indication that a critical mass of women within the Shi'a communities have joined Lebanon's modest wave of "second-generation feminism" or that clerical leadership would countenance such a development. While the HWA is characterized by strong grassroots participation, it also has been described as a "very hierarchical organization," guided by a "pre-set agenda" on women's issues determined by the dictates of the party's religious authorities and the Islamist and resistance-oriented paradigm within which they work.[128] This subordination is even clearer within religious circles, where gender debates remain bounded within patriarchal norms, albeit shifting ones.[129] Finally, AMAL and Hezbollah, along with leading clerical figures from Sadr to Fadlallah, all shared a common belief that, while the Lebanese political system needed to move in the direction of secularization, the Lebanese public sphere needed to be more deeply infused with religious belief. As Sadr was said to have argued, "piety and citizenship go hand in hand in Lebanon."[130] One of the logical consequences of this widespread consensus was that personal status law would have to be kept under the jurisdiction of religiously organized courts. Hence, while women within the Shi'a communities of Lebanon have clearly been entering the public sphere in unprecedented numbers, searching for what Peleikis called "maneuvering spaces" beyond the household,[131] the contours of that public sphere and the role of women within it continue to be defined by Shi'a communal political projects.

Bringing these internal communal dynamics together in the postwar Lebanon was a proposal to reform Lebanon's personal status code—initially proposed by civil society groups and eventually introduced as a draft piece of legislation by President Hrawi in November 1996.[132] Though not as ambitious as many activists would have liked, the draft law was radical enough to wrestle authority over definitions of marriage and divorce away from religious authorities and into the hands of civil courts through the inclusion of such universal provisions as divorce by mutual consent, the banning of polygamy, and the easing of restrictions on intercommunal marriage. Hence, when the draft law was eventually accepted by the cabinet in March 1998, it precipitated one of the biggest sectarian outbursts in the postwar period, one spearheaded by the embattled Dar al-Fatwa that mobilized Sunni clerics around the country. What followed was a remarkable process of "sectarian disciplining" aimed at reaffirming the legitimacy of Dar al-Fatwa as the defender of Sunni Islam in the country as well as defending the autonomy of the religious communities from interference by the state. In effect, it was a successful attempt at reinforcing—by returning to a more strict enforcement of—the political parameters of Lebanon's "critical juncture" with respect to gender relations.

The countercampaign had two dimensions—rhetorical and mobilizational. Rhetorically, the Sunni clerical class was extremely effective in transforming the issue of a unified civil personal status code—strategically framed as "optional" by its advocates—into an existential and apocalyptic threat not only to the authority of the clerical classes in the country, but also to the integrity of the family, the national unity of Lebanon, and the integrity and authenticity of Islam. Reacting with what one observer described as "a rare virulence," the Sunni clerics denounced the "germ of civil marriage" and accused President Hrawi of promoting, among other things, "the utter dissolution of traditional family values"; of "making a mockery" of the clerical leadership; of precipitating "an insult to the Muslims and the shari'ah which was dictated by God and upheld by the constitution"; of opening up the floodgates to widespread secularization in the country; and, in particularly provocative fashion, of leading the country down the dangerous road to "apostasy."[133] Paralleling these vitriolic words was an aggressive mobilizational campaign by Lebanon's Sunni clerics that escalated from sit-ins in mosques to large and widespread "anti-civil" street demonstrations, violating with impunity the Ministry of the Interior's previous all-encompassing ban.[134]

This escalating rhetoric and social mobilization had a powerful and swift disciplinary impact on other members of the religious and political leadership in the country. The Maronite Patriarch, Nasrallah Boutros Sfeir, for example, not only rejected the proposed optional civil personal status law, but he also threatened excommunication to those who submitted themselves to it—a stance that was widely supported by many within both the clerical and lay leadership of the Christian communities who were concerned about the widespread defection of Christians into the "civil" fold. As one commentator wrote in the context of the broader Christian fear about their emerging minority status, "secularism . . . means the triumph of Islam."[135] The Shi'a clerical leadership, who, as we have seen, did not face the same independent radical pressures from below as did the clerical leadership within the Sunni community,[136] and who had been more open to debates about issues relating to personal status and the practical application of the provisions of the shari'ah, initially reacted with "caution and prudence" when the draft law was originally accepted. However, after a meeting at Dar al-Fatwa in late March 1998, they changed their tune, coming out publicly and forcefully by equating civil marriage with the legalization of adultery and threatening, in a provocative fashion, to bring "everyone capable of moving" onto the streets if the proposal went any further.[137] Finally, Lebanon's political class also fell into line, shaken as it was by the extremity of the religious reactions around it.[138] Indeed, Hariri, despite having had a civil marriage, also was closely involved in mobilizing opposition to the draft law, not surprising given his connections to the conservative Saudi regime, his personal political competition with Hrawi, and his own interest in constructing a unified Sunni movement that could provide a firmer foundation for his political ambitions.[139]

This sectarian outburst had three major implications for the future of women's advocacy politics in the country. First, religious officials were able to preserve and reinforce their central, if not decisive, "veto" role within any nascent women's policy domain. This had immediate effects on the activities of several women's associations in the country. Strategic decisions were made, for example, to channel advocacy efforts through religious officials themselves. At the forefront of these efforts was LCRVAW, which had experienced considerable and aggressive "push backs" from religious court officials in reaction to its advocacy efforts on behalf of women suffering from inequitable court rulings. In an effort to (re)build lines of communication, it began a quiet campaign aimed at cultivating networks with reform-minded religious court judges. Similar efforts were made by the Middle East Council of Churches (MECC) with respect to the Christian religious courts, hosting ecumenical dialogues and training sessions for clerics and judges in an attempt to promote greater awareness of a "human rights approach" to the workings of the religious court system, with some of this networking extending into the Sunni and Shi'a communities by way of the officially sanctioned Interfaith Committee on Religious Dialogue.[140] However, while there has been some receptiveness within religious circles to these initiatives, the results have by and large been piecemeal and disappointing. None of the communities has moved away from the core patriarchal principle of the man being the head of the household; the religious court systems themselves have remained both inaccessible—especially for poor women unable to afford the numerous fees for court time, lawyers, and *wasta*—and unaccountable, with none of the initiative's laws or proceedings being published; and the attempt to develop advocacy networks across the secular–religious divide has been severely constrained. Rouhana, for example, remarked that while KAFA has been able to make individual contacts with religious clerics, it has not been able to approach them in an official capacity; in short, it has proved extremely difficult to transform personal networks into policy networks.[141]

The "disciplining" of the women's policy domain did not stop with the reactions of religious officials. Indeed, one of the clear lessons from the debacle surrounding the optional draft personal status law was that, in the face of determined opposition on the part of the religious clerical class, Lebanon's political classes not only fell into line; they also became enforcing agents of restrictive clerical dictates within the broader state apparatus itself, effecting the work of bureaucratic officials dependent on their political patrons. This has forced many women's associations, all of which have had good working relations with the MSA, to tread carefully with respect to the types of programs and projects on which they jointly collaborate. In an effort to generate "a public demand" for personal status law reform, for example, KAFA and the MSA had entered into a project aimed at training MSA social workers on how to inform women about their personal status rights—a project that immediately seemed to spawn a significant thirst for knowledge, especially among lower-class women, who tended to frequent Social Development Centers the most. In order to avoid invoking the ire of religious officials, however, KAFA and the MSA have treaded carefully, emphasizing that this legal advocacy program would not critique the workings of the court system, nor would it provide anything more than "preliminary answers" to women's queries so as not to prejudge the rulings of religious courts themselves.[142] The most telling example of the restrictive climate within which state bureaucrats worked, however, concerned the difficulty of establishing shelters for battered women. While attempting to establish Lebanon's second shelter in the early 2000s, for example, the YWCA's president, Mona Khawli, had to overcome numerous objections from the Ministry of the Interior relating to questions of accountability and scope, objections that emanated from the implicit "veto" power possessed by religious officials with regard to decisions taken by the ministry. Backed by the willingness of the MSA and its director general, Naamat Kanaan, to enter into a joint agreement with the YWCA to establish the shelter, and assisted by the YWCA's own "network of women" within the Ministry of the Interior itself, the YWCA was eventually given permission to establish it—but only after changing its designation from a shelter for "abused women" to one for "abandoned women and their children."[143] Noted Khawli, this discursive distinction was crucial in garnering the acquiescence of religious officials because, whereas the word "abandoned" pointed to the issue being outside the family, "abused" merely suggested the existence of problems within an existing family—problems over which religious courts claimed exclusive jurisdiction.[144]

Finally, it also is clear that the dynamics unleashed by the clerical outburst against the optional unified civil personal status code permeated Lebanese associational life; it is here that processes of disciplining intertwine in a hegemonic fashion with processes of self-disciplining. Symbolic of the intertwining relationships between the civil, religious, and political spheres in Lebanon, for example, has been the ease with which religious authorities, in the wake of the draft law proposal, were able to penetrate Lebanon's associational sector and mobilize a diverse array of organizations—from family leagues to local quarter associations to sporting clubs to social service associations to, most tellingly, traditional women's associations—into a strong "countermovement."[145] Combined with the large-scale mobilization of individual supporters for the various sit-ins and demonstrations, the "vociferous" campaign of the clerical classes was able to completely outmatch the relatively modest, hesitant, and slow-to-respond actions of Lebanon's more secular-minded associations and political parties.[146] Moreover, the hegemonic effect of this dramatic exertion of clerical power extended long past the intensity of the moment. Despite its promising postwar revival, for example, the LWC has never been able to break free from the tentacles of religious and political power and has become an extremely useful channel through which the clerical and political classes regulate the discourse and actions of associational actors in the women's sector, despite attempts to make it otherwise. This disciplining/self-disciplining power—diffuse but debilitatingly effective—has been evident on a number of occasions, from the reversal of the LWC's initial willingness to debate, if not support, the early postwar campaign for a unified, optional civil personal status code[147]; to the LWC's official and last-minute pullout from the International Women's Day demonstrations in March 2000, when it became apparent that the proposal for optional civil marriage would be one of the event's themes[148]; to the increasing tendency of LWC members to vet candidates running for electoral office within the LWC executive based on their opposition to civil personal status reform. Noted one candidate who ran for the LWC executive in 2008, people would not vote for anything "against Islam."[149] While this dynamic is not a new one—it has been a constant refrain of Laure Moghaizel that "the time was not ripe" for challenging the religious court system directly—it does appear to have been particularly hegemonic in the postwar period, especially when compared with the more daring days of the 1970s, when, as many women activists have noted, talk of creating a unified civil personal status code was "everywhere."[150] This suggests that this reaffirmation and reconsolidation of clerical hegemony within the emerging women's policy domain in postwar Lebanon—extending from the state apparatus into a broad range of associations within Lebanese civil society—represent a significant reversal and regression from developments before the civil war.[151]

*Deferring to Patriarchy: Political Elites, Their Wives, and the NCLW*

What kind of space is left for women activists to define a women's agenda and carve out a more salient women's policy domain in the wake of this reconsolidation of the influence of this alliance between clerics and political elites within the field of women's issues? Religious officials, for example, have certainly established virtual "veto" power over the extent and targets of advocacy efforts. They also have made it more difficult, given the institutionalization of their power within the structure of the state, for women to use the bureaucratic apparatus and capacity of the state as a mechanism for promoting their agendas. Yet, however pervasive and hegemonic this clerical influence is, it is not all encompassing, nor could it have been given the fragmented state through which it functioned. This has left some room *within* the state apparatus itself for competing and contradictory initiatives to emerge. In a variety of other countries within which "women's machinery" has been newly created, for example, Anne Marie Goetz has observed that many have acted more like advocacy NGOs than bureaucratic units, trying to provide women with an institutionalized channel through which they can begin the process of challenging patriarchal hegemonies embedded within the state.[152] Recognizing this potential contribution that women's machinery could also make in postwar Lebanon, women's activists associated with "the Beijing group" and foreign donors successfully pushed for the creation of the NCLW—first established by decree in 1996 before being institutionalized into law in 1998. For various reasons linked to the institutional parameters established at its birth, however, the NCLW has made little to no impact as a channel for women's advocacy efforts, let alone as an instrument contributing to the formulation of a more defined public policy agenda for women in the country. Indeed, on a public level, its existence remains virtually unknown. While this obscurity might, paradoxically, provide it with some potential room for maneuver, it is ultimately too entwined with and dependent on the various patriarchal structures of the Lebanese state to serve as a "critical point of leverage" for women activists within the Lebanese state as a whole.

Many of the problems with the NCLW can be traced back to its founding moment in 1998. For starters, the proposal to create the NCLW was never enthusiastically received by the deputies of the parliament. One women's activist described the process of pushing for its establishment as being "laborious and difficult," requiring strategic lobbying at the highest levels of the state and numerous political compromises concerning its power and structure.[153] Rather than creating an autonomous body, let alone a Ministry of Women, which had been the practice in some other Arab countries, the NCLW was eventually established as an advisory body without a separate budget line and linked to the Office of the Prime Minister, where it ironically sits parallel to, and is dwarfed by, the Sunni establishment, whose link to the Lebanese state runs through the same channel. As Laure Moghaizel remarked in response to a previous failed attempt to create more robust national machinery for women, this amounted to "institutionally consecrat[ing] the inferior condition of women."[154] Symbolic of its politically subordinate status was the manner in which appointments were made—the NCLW president being appointed by the president of the Republic and the remaining eighteen to twenty-four members being appointed by the prime minister—all of which left the NCLW with little autonomy from the broader political process. Not surprisingly, appointments have followed the same logic as that of the political system—characterized by sectarian balancing (on a fifty–fifty basis), with leading political figures operating in patrimonial fashion by nominating their own wives. This has had debilitating consequences for the internal dynamics within the NCLW. First, the majority of women on the NCLW have little awareness of, let alone activist experience in promoting, women's issues. Most were described as seeing their appointments as *un droit honorifique* rather than a serious responsibility. One member of the NCLW, in fact, described most of her colleagues as being "sweet" but also "completely passive" if not "antifeminist."[155] The appointment process also has translated into national commissions that are predominantly traditional and elite based with no formal requirements for representation from civil society—a reversal from the informal national committee in the pre-Beijing period. Neither have there been any requirements for representation from the public sector and the lower classes, let alone from the growing Islamist women's sectors. In short, as another former member of the NCLW concluded, "it's an elitist apparatus."[156] Moreover, within the NCLW also can be found "a hidden decision-making process,"[157] the product of petty if politically motivated competition between the wives of the leading political figures that has nothing at all to do with the status of women and that has had, at times, a debilitating effect on its work—even threatening its very creation.[158] The NCLW also has been highly sensitive to the oscillations of the "troika" as well as to the confrontations between the March 8 and March 14 factions leading up to the Doha Accord in May 2008—the latter having left the NCLW virtually frozen. In short, the manner in which the NCLW was created by Lebanon's male political elite has left it both divided by political networks from within and penetrated by political networks from without. Describing the NCLW as "a small baby born out of error," one of its few activist members admitted that, "in the end, we couldn't protect [it] enough to make it grow."[159]

These legacies of its institutional birth have severely hampered the efforts of the NCLW to establish a defined and institutionalized policy-making process for women. To start, its budget is small and, lacking a permanent budget line, is dependent on the yearly whims of the Office of the Prime Minister; indeed, it had no budget at all in 2006 to 2007. As a result, its office has been restricted to a small professional and administrative staff, the goodwill of its volunteer-appointed members, and a very short time line. While a strategic plan was drawn up in the late 1990s, it was a nonbinding document that was not endorsed by cabinet and, hence, had no policy leverage at all.[160] It also has never been revised, evaluated, and accompanied by a work plan. As one NCLW member remarked, "it's just a piece of paper!"[161] Neither has the NCLW officially responded to two critical evaluations of its work by foreign donors,[162] and it was only after a tough, four-hour public meeting with representatives from CEDAW in New York in July 2005 that the NCLW was "shocked" into taking the CEDAW process seriously, eventually hiring a women activist–lawyer as a consultant to rewrite a more serious version of its CEDAW periodic report.[163] In short, hampered by extremely limited and contingent resources, blocked by the implicit red lines drawn up by the country's political class with respect to the scope of the NCLW's work, especially with regard to the issue of personal status, and working as it does on a consensus basis, the NCLW has avoided taking stances on almost anything. "I cannot represent the position of the National Commission," emphasized one of its disheartened activist members, "because there is no such thing. . . . The NCLW, it's a name. It's empty."[164]

Finally, the NCLW has failed to act as a "network node" for other agents of women's activism. No provisions were made in the defining statute of the NCLW for the official representation of civil society actors, and the NCLW has, by and large, taken a back seat to the campaigns and mobilizations of women's NGOs. The NCLW also has failed to extend the range of its activities into the Lebanese bureaucracy—despite the creation of fourteen different bureaucratic gender focal points. Indeed, when the gender focal points were created, their appointments were deliberately not included as part of the official structure of the ministries within which they worked, and, hence, they were not given any formal power or bureaucratic entry point to perform their new roles. Moreover, given that these individuals were already working public servants, they received no extra remuneration for their efforts. As a result, they are not taken seriously, and, as one consultant remarked, "are often not invited to attend meetings or events directly falling within the terms of their appointment." Neither has the NCLW stepped in to offer them support, leaving the relationship between them undefined, irregular, distant, and hierarchical.[165] Finally, the NCLW has made little attempt to network with parliament, with relations between the NCLW and the parliamentary committee on Women and the Family being described as nonexistent. In short, the NCLW is utterly penetrated by political interests that have little concern for issues relating to women's status; it has failed even its minimum test of acting "like an NGO" within the state apparatus, which, as Goetz pointed out, units like it have managed to do in other developing world contexts. When I asked one of the members of the NCLW to explain this lack of interest or effort in cultivating allies and networks that could enhance its lobbying influence within the state, she revealingly responded that "if we want to, we can. Lebanon is a country of 3.5 million; everybody knows everybody. Women in the commission are related somehow in different ways to these deputies. If they want, they can. If they have the motivation, they can. But they don't because they don't see the need. They don't even attempt. We are talking about something which is non-existent."[166]

In comparative terms, none of these challenges is surprising. As Goetz has also written, there continues to exist "profound bureaucratic resistance to gender-equitable integration of women as subjects of public policy," a resistance that has contributed to both the marginalization of gender machinery from the state and its disconnection from civil society.[167] Neither is the situation in Lebanon completely without hope. Certainly, given the lack of autonomy of the NCLW from political forces and networks within the broader state arena, much depends on the existence of a stable political equation. Leadership at the highest levels as well as within the NCLW, given the personalized, informal, and "relational" dynamics of politics, also can make a difference. Moreover, foreign donors continue to view the NCLW as a crucial institution for the promotion of women's status and, hence, have offered capacity-building assistance, particularly as regards the development of its national strategy, a post-strategic work plan, as well as a variety of other ideas and finance for the development of interesting projects on the ground.[168] Finally, even those most critical of the NCLW would admit that there has occurred some kind of learning process. Some of this has come due to the opportunities given to the NCLW's members to participate within the Arab Women's Organization (AWO) of the League of Arab States—where to a certain extent, "they have to work." A similar dynamic existed with respect to the NCLW's responsibility for making regular reports to the CEDAW Commission in New York—work that has raised the consciousness of some women on the NCLW; "you cannot work on the [CEDAW] report," noted one NCLW member, "if you are anti-feminist." Moreover, many associated with the NCLW were starting to recognize that its machinery was inadequate for the tasks and challenges at hand and that a Ministry for Women with a regular budget and more full-time personnel was in order. In short, despite its obvious failures, the NCLW could be seen as a first step. Added one member of the NCLW in recognition of the powerful and resilient political forces within and around the women's sector that militate against more dramatic beginnings, "these are tiny things but this is how we work in this country. We are resigned to this."[169]

*Reproducing Patriarchy: The Politics of the Postwar LWC*

As the oldest and largest umbrella for women's associations, the LWC sits in the associative center of Lebanon's postwar women's policy domain. Its postwar associational membership has regularly exceeded one hundred; it now has more balanced representation from associations from various regions of the country, including the marginalized regions like Akkar and the Beqa; and it has representatives, even if demographically imbalanced, from most of the country's confessions. Its decision-making process is democratic, with elections for the executive office taking place every four years and policy decisions being taken on a consensus basis within the executive, and it alternates access to the presidency between Muslims and Christians. Indeed, it was in order to take advantage of the LWC's basic sectarian inclusiveness that members of the Beijing group decided to revive it at the end of the civil war period, hoping to transform it into a "prime mover" within the emerging postwar women's policy domain. As we have seen, they originally met with some success. The LWC retained its status as the state-recognized women's umbrella; it embarked on a number of capacity-building programs assisted by foreign donors; it succeeded in expanding and diversifying its membership base, recruiting more from the historically underrepresented Shi'a communities, which included a handful of women's associations affiliated with Hezbollah, as well as representatives from women's committees from most of the country's political parties; and it has, for the most part, elected presidents who were leading women's activists in the postwar world who have used their time in office to push for more aggressive programs of women's advocacy, particularly with respect to establishing a system of quotas for women's representation within the national assembly.[170] Indeed, despite the many problems with the LWC that we will see below, it is interesting to note how much of a reference point it continues to be for most women involved in advocacy work. Linda Matar, for example, who experienced tremendous opposition when she was president (1996–2000) to her plans both to remove sectarian power-sharing arrangements from the LWC's constitution and to secure LWC support for the optional civil marriage proposal, nonetheless emphasized that she remains committed to the LWC despite all of its faults.[171]

However, the LWC has not been a "prime mover" within the postwar women's policy domain, at least for gender equality activists. Rather, like the NCLW, it has been plagued by a number of historical legacies that have debilitated the LWC's capacity to focus on women's issues and facilitated

the penetration of clerical and political influence. These institutional legacies revolve around two main factors. The first is the broad and undefined
criteria for membership, which has facilitated the dominance within the
LWC of charity-focused associations, run by elite women, that are representative of a previous associational generation. The second revolves
around the deep-rooted sectarian dynamics within the LWC, the product of formal rules about confessional power sharing as well as informal
processes revolving around internal sectarian networking. These legacies
and the resultant internal dynamics have made it difficult for the LWC to
consolidate within itself its own internal equality-focused women's policy
domain, let alone fight for a more defined and equality-oriented one at
the national level.

First, the membership of the LWC is representative of the pre–civil
war generation of women's activism. The LWC's nickname, for example,
is *al-khityariyya*, meaning a society of old women, not inaccurate given
that (at the time of this writing) there were no women under forty who
participated in the LWC's affairs. One of the youngest members of the
LWC, a Shi'a from the marginalized Beqa' region, for example, who joined
in 2000 as a way of gaining access to women's networks in Beirut, was
shocked in her first meeting by the generational makeup of the LWC,
describing most of women there as being "antiques" and adding that these
were not the kind of women with whom politicians could be convinced
to work.[172] Lamia Osseiran, another young secular Shi'a who ran for the
presidency of the LWC and lost in 2008, also argued (prior to her electoral defeat) that "it is very difficult for ambitious young women activists to find a role to play within an institution where the possibilities
of advancement are blocked by an older generation that refuses to give
up." In trying to explain this generation lag, Osseiran pointed to several
factors: the volunteer nature of the work—harkening back to a previous
generation of "society women"—which has made it extremely difficult
to attract and engage younger professionals; the hidden competitiveness
within the "old guard" itself, which has served to block the ascendance
of others; and, perhaps most damagingly, the existence of hidden rules
revolving around generational hierarchies, ones that contributed (among
other factors) to collective (but unsuccessful) pressure being placed on
Osseiran to withdraw as a candidate for the LWC presidency in 2008 in
favor of an older and more established one.[173] Attempts have been made
to reform and rejuvenate the membership base of the LWC, but these
were vetoed by the politically influenced and motivated Ministry of the
Interior, whose approval was needed to change the LWC's bylaws.[174]

Linked to this issue of generational gaps has been the predominance
of a traditional gender discourse. In her scathing critique of pre–civil war
women's politics in Lebanon, for example, Sharara described the approach

of the LWC as "naïve" and "pathetic," characterized by an eagerness to preserve privilege and status and predisposed to working within the existing patriarchal environment. She was particularly critical of its members' timid attitudes toward gaining the right to vote, mocking them for not wanting to make "too much use of these rights" and for voting instead as their fathers and husbands would.[175] This constrained discourse and practice has kept its grip on the advocacy work of the LWC in the postwar period, frustrating the efforts of women activists to politicize it. Lamented Wadad Chakhtoura, a leading activist in the postwar world who was heavily involved with these initial efforts, "we worked hard . . . but I feel that it is impossible to transform [the LWC's] internal spirit. It's a spirit blocked by a very traditional way of thinking, very traditional," she remarked with a resigned laugh, adding that "even if the women were convinced . . . they are constantly contained by political masters. It is impossible to get past this way of seeing, this way of thinking."[176]

Reflective of this traditional discursive approach to women's politics has been the prevalence of particularist and charitable modes of action on the ground; "charity, charity, and more charity," noted one member of the LWC.[177] An early postwar study of LWC revealed that only 33 percent of its members were directly engaged in work on behalf of women; most were involved in traditional social service provision, a trend that was reinvigorated by the legacies of the civil war period.[178] Commented Laure Moghaizel with respect to the more general effects of the war on women's associations, "women's rights are no longer a priority; the war forced us to shift our struggle to the necessities of mere existence and survival."[179] Moreover, in a revealing set of interviews with a deeply rooted and influential network of women's associations in the Sunni quarters of Beirut called *al-Rabita al-Nisaiyya al-Islamiyya*, its work was described mostly in terms of responding to the falling living standards of Sunni middle-class families who were hit hard by the economic uncertainties of the war and postwar period, who were struggling to meet the costs of educating their children, and who, in a revealing addition, also were finding it hard to compete with the rising wealth of Beiruti Shi'as. Using informal lists derived from personal contacts and networks, for example, the association targeted its assistance for the most part at struggling middle-class Sunni families. "I know some very good families," noted one member, "they are in real need. We help them without being asked." When asked if it had considered being proactive by extending assistance to the growing numbers of poor people in its quarters, many of whom were being drawn into Sunni Islamist networks, one leading member of *al-Rabita* answered by stating that "our policy is not for the poor people of the streets . . . unless they ask." Moreover, when its members spoke of their actual work with women in their quarters, which consisted of computer training, English classes, and public lectures, it was apparent that these programs were not only designed to build the capacities of individual women; they also were part of an implicit strategy to preserve what was left of the prewar fabric of Beiruti society, with its bourgeois emphasis on traditional Islam and interconfessional mingling, especially given the challenges of Islamist "fanatics" emanating from both within and outside their communities.[180] In other words, it was apparent that goals related to women's empowerment were taking a back seat to other imperatives underlying the work of these associations—ones which were related to the preservation of traditional Sunni Beirut family structures, middle-class privilege, orthodox Islam, and elite-level intercommunal family networking.

The LWC's second institutional legacy revolved around the intertwining of women's advocacy with sectarianism, the product of what Wadad Chakhtoura described as "the confessional fiber" that ran through the heart of the women's associational sector.[181] The LWC, for example, had been the product of a union between two separate women's councils in the 1950s, one Christian, the other predominantly Sunni Muslim. As a way to ensure an equal power-sharing agreement between them, it was agreed at its inception that the presidency of the LWC would alternate between these two religious groups—though with no specification as to power sharing within each of the confessions, especially with respect to the Shi'a—transforming the LWC into a gendered replica of the 1943 National Pact, complete with its tensions and dilemmas. In the postwar period, one of the most underlying tensions revolved around questions of membership, ones that emerged as a result of the unchanging "demography" within the LWC that had left it dominated by Beirut networks of Sunni women's associations such as al-Rabita. This implicit Sunni dominance has been accentuated by the falling away from active membership of many Christian associations, symbolized by the difficulty in attracting viable Christian candidates for the LWC presidency. Further complicating the sectarian dynamics within the LWC has been the historical underrepresentation of women's associations from the Shi'a communities, glaring in the postwar period given their growing demographic and political weight at the national level. Finally, included within the membership of the LWC have been the women's committees and other affiliated women's organizations of the country's political parties, which, when combined with the informal political allegiances of seemingly independent women's associations, provided these political parties and zu'ama with multiple informal points of entry into the LWC. Everyone on the LWC is "somehow" connected to these political and religious networks, noted one of the LWC members.[182] In short, as Iqbal Dughan remarked when asked about the political dynamics within the LWC, "it's a photocopy of Lebanon—but without the fighting!"[183]

The inability of the LWC to insulate itself from these sectarian political dynamics was clear during the elections for its presidency in 2008. The politicking was sparked by a decision of Lamia Osseiran, the young Shi'a former vice president of the LWC, to run for the presidency. The timing was of crucial importance, coming as it did during the tense and immobilizing standoff between the March 14 and March 8 political groupings, underlying a powerful sectarian divide in the country (and region) between the Sunni and Shi'a communities. What followed was an LWC election that duplicated many of the dynamics at the national level—the emergence and trading of confessional blocs of votes that led to the compilation of "silent" lists of candidates, competing appeals to political leaders for support that often led to voting directives from outside the LWC, a focus more on personalities and identities than on gender, and, most significantly, the instrumentalization of sectarian fears, particularly by the Beirut-based Sunni networks who wanted to prevent the unprecedented election of a Shi'a, and a young Shi'a at that, to the LWC presidency, whose Muslim "share" had been traditionally controlled by the Sunnis. It was for these reasons that Aman Sharaani, a leading postwar women's activist, was recruited to run for the LWC presidency a second time in the hope of convincing Osseiran to stand down. Though part of the explanation for the fierce electioneering process that followed revolved around a desire to "rescue the council" after a period of acute dormancy,[184] the most underlying explanation revolved around intensifying sectarian fears, ones that became even more acute after the violent conflict in early May 2008. In the end, the strategy worked and Osseiran was defeated—though by a turnaround of only fifteen votes that had sparked a frantic preelection lobbying effort that was reputed to have included appeals to the Mufti himself. Indeed, the 2008 election was described as being "completely confessional," producing an executive council that, for the first time, fell into line with the confessional divides in the country. Shocked by the manner in which the LWC seemed to be reproducing the system, one disaffected member remarked that in comparison with the early postwar years, when efforts had been made to create a nonsectarian structure, the LWC now seemed to be taking "a step backwards," entrenching sectarian dynamics only a decade after having talked about abolishing it.[185] Lamented Linda Matar, who during her presidency had pushed for de-confessionalizing reforms of the LWC, in response to the powerful sectarian dynamics within the LWC electoral process of 2008, "[I]nstead of having a collective discussion with all the women [of the council] . . . what do they do? The Druze meet by themselves, the Shi'ites meet by themselves, the Sunnis and the Christians meet by themselves in order to propose and present their own candidates. But why? Why do this? On the contrary, we must be together and chose women who can work effectively."[186]

In response to the persistent failure of the LWC, most of Lebanon's small coterie of equality-oriented women's activists have tried to create alternative women's networks—from the NGO Committee to *al-Liqa* to the short-lived and donor-generated emergence of the Lebanon Women's Network, these being complemented by the issue- and campaign-oriented networks that also have emerged. While these efforts may have helped to increase the profile and presence of women within Lebanon's postwar public sphere as a whole, however, they have not succeeded in bridging personal, political, and/or strategic divisions that could have led to a more unified women's voice. Some donors have even given up on the women's NGO sector altogether in favor of supporting younger, politically promising, and up-and-coming individual women interested in getting involved in "real politics" at the municipal and national levels.[187] Yet, as we have seen from the abysmal comparative statistics on women's participation rates within the political system as a whole, this particular section of Lebanon's gendered glass ceiling seems to be a glaring one, symbolized by the failure of Lebanon's leading secular feminist activists to come close in their bids for municipal or national election.[188] Amid all of these strategic debates and maneuverings among women activists in Lebanon, however, the LWC continued to sit "like the elephant in the room," obstructing its ability to construct both a unified discourse and an associational base to the postwar women's policy domain. Though the LWC is clearly and willingly penetrated by the cacophony of nonfeminist political voices and agendas in the country, at the same time, it also is historically entrenched and representative of the highly fragmented nature of Lebanon's public sphere as a whole. As such, it appears for the foreseeable future that gender equality activists will have little option but to return to the LWC—as many have tried to do all along—in an attempt to use it, direct it, or reform it, and this will remain one of the many predicaments that will confront Lebanon's energetic coterie of women associational activists for a long time to come.

## Conclusions

There are important sociostructural transformations affecting women in Lebanon that have the potential to destabilize conditions that sustain existing inequalities in gender relations. More and more women are entering the halls of higher education; more and more women are entering the

workforce, albeit often in the informal sector and with limited chances
for promotion; and increasing numbers of Islamist women across the
Sunni and Shi'a communities have become active in charitable networks
and have, hence, taken on public roles outside the household. In short,
there are a variety of "slow-moving" processes at work that are bringing
women increasingly into the public sphere and, hence, bringing issues of
gender relations and the role and rights of women within those relations
into more prominent focus.

Coinciding with these internal sociostructural transformations have
been developments within Lebanon's women's advocacy sector. This chapter has focused on those linked to Lebanon's "second wave of feminism,"
sparked first by the efforts of women's activists within leftist circles before
and during the civil war and, second, by the emergence of several equality-
oriented women's associational networks in the postwar period. Taking
advantage of the rise of global women's networks, with their normative
and financial support for gender equality around the world, these wom-
en's advocacy networks have carved out a more institutionalized presence
within Lebanon's postwar public sphere. Among their greatest successes
have been their continued promotion of discourses and the raising of
awareness around gender equality, the cultivation of a working relationship with the lower levels of the Lebanese bureaucratic apparatus that
work to improve the status of women, and the forging of network connections—albeit more personalized than professionalized—with selected,
like-minded elites within religious and political circles.

Yet neither slow-moving sociostructural processes of change nor the
emergence of active, if restricted, advocacy networks promoting gender
equality have been able to make reformist inroads into the religious and
political networks that work to enforce—and reinforce—systems of gender
inequality in the country. In contrast to advocacy efforts in the fields of
the environment and disability that we examine below, women's advocacy
networks have had difficulty establishing sustained policy linkages with
religious and political actors with influence in the policy-making process.
This has left them politically isolated and disconnected—islands of advocacy for gender equality amid a resistant and resilient patriarchal political
sea. In short, there has been a notable absence of political opportunities
for policy advocacy in the area of gender equality in postwar Lebanon,
despite the various efforts we have noted above to forge them.

This illusive absence of political opportunities for gender reform
in the post–civil war period is the result of several overlapping political
dynamics. Underpinning these are Lebanon's constitutional structures—
forged during the period of the French mandate—that endow religious
communities with exclusive rights over personal status law. This series

of decisions "from above" not only placed personal status law within the hands of religious patriarchs who have used this power to enforce patriarchal understandings of family law, but it also has contributed to the emergence of a highly fragmented and disaggregated women's policy domain that has enormously complicated advocacy efforts on behalf of gender equality within the country. In short, the embedding of the power of religious patriarchs within the constitution itself has institutionalized the fragmented structure of the country's women's policy domain and, hence, has made it particularly resistant to change.

Yet it is the political dynamics that surround these gender inequality–enforcing institutions that are the key to explaining why their power is continually reproduced over time. The activation of networks between the religious and political leaders of the sectarian communities in the face of efforts to promote secularizing reforms has proved an enduring, if latent, resource reinforcing their constitutional power. These networks "from below" have proved extremely effective at preempting reformist efforts, embedding their disciplinary dynamics deep into civil and political society. As we have seen, the autonomy and power of the NCLW—the first body created in the wake of the Beijing process to improve the status of women in Lebanon—has been completely emasculated by its subordinating location within the Office of the Prime Minister, which has all but ensured that the NCLW will remain a compliant body, colonized by elite women who are intimately intertwined with and dependent on the political establishment.

However, it is the penetration of the structural power of Lebanon's religious patriarchs into the heart of the country's civil society—symbolized by the internal political dynamics within the LWC—that has proven to be an effective addition to their political tool kit. Initially a pioneer in the struggle for women's right to vote, the LWC has subsequently been transformed into a guardian of the patriarchal contours of the country's policy domain for women. Not only has the LWC been subject to the influence of religious and political patriarchs, but its membership has participated actively in instrumentalizing these connections in the context of its own internal competitive battles. While there have certainly been efforts to break free of this stultifying historical legacy and transform the LWC into an agent promoting comprehensive gender equality in Lebanon, its internal mechanisms of sectarian reproduction have proven to be extraordinarily powerful and resilient, severely circumscribing opportunities for advocacy in the postwar period that many had initially hoped would be more significant.

# 5

# The "Greening" of Sectarianism

## The Rise and Fall of Environmental Advocacy in Postwar Lebanon

*"Au Liban. . . . c'est l'etat qui encourage les predateurs."*

The "environment" was a new policy issue in postwar Lebanon. It emerged more robustly as a result of developments within the global arena at a time when Lebanon was embroiled in its long civil war. Hence, much of this chapter is about attempts by a variety of actors implicated within this emerging policy domain to define its parameters in the postwar world to their advantage. On the one hand, Lebanon's emerging postwar political elites worked to keep the boundaries of this policy domain porous so as to enhance their own political maneuverability. On the other hand, Lebanon's emerging community of local and national environmental associations/ nongovernmental associations (NGOs), along with a coterie of environmental experts and consultants, worked to institutionalize more clearly its principles and limits, setting in place regulatory policies that would constrain the actions of the country's political elites. Floating between both of these sets of parties were a variety of external actors and donors whose actions often intensified these debates through their own financial and political interventions. In short, the dynamics involved in creating an environmental policy domain in postwar Lebanon were intensely political, involving debate and struggle between a variety of political forces over the nature of "environmental power," defined more generally by Adams as "the control that one party has over the environment of another."[2]

There are two crucial dimensions in this process of negotiation and struggle over the nature of environmental policy. On the one hand, the actors within these struggles are embedded within highly unequal power relationships—ones that are often historically generated—that ensure that the ensuing bargaining process "is not a pluralistic context among equals."[3] These asymmetrical power relations, in turn, translate into an unequal distribution of the cost of environmental degradation, it being "more of a crisis for some actors than for others." On the other hand, while power relations within the field of the environment are unequal, "they are rarely, if ever, 'one way,'" creating a dynamic whereby "alliances, interests, and capacities of actors can shift and mutate."[4] Rather than leading to environmental policy domains characterized by "convergence and stability," therefore, policy domains in the field of the environment are often characterized by "disequilibrium and change" in which "contradictions, competing ideologies, and active agents ensure that the terrain and political contestation is forever unfolding."[5] This shifting nature of power relations, in turn, opens up possibilities for the strategic use of power in which "intelligent agency can sometimes outmaneuver resource-rich adversaries."[6]

This chapter, like that on women before it, divides its analysis of the rise (and subsequent fall) of associational agency in the field of the environment into three sections. The first section outlines the historical and structural parameters of what was to become Lebanon's environmental policy domain in the postwar period. The second section examines the rise of environmental advocacy politics in postwar Lebanon. At debate is the degree to which environment actors—through the generation of collective power and new discourses—were able to begin the process of carving out the parameters and institutionalizing a defined environmental policy domain in the postwar period. The third section analyzes the effective defeat of these efforts, characterized by the realignment of environmental advocacy efforts with the prevailing sociopolitical power structures of the country.

## The Historical Parameters of Lebanon's Emerging Postwar Environmental Policy Domain

The idea of unifying a series of policy issues under the rubric and theme of "the environment" has global origins. It was the result of deliberations and conflicts between scientists, states, business, and global civil society actors over the health and future of the planet. Keck and Sikkink point to the Biosphere Conference in 1968 as the beginning of this process. This was followed in short and quick succession by a host of other developments. This culminated in the 1992 United Nations (UN) Conference on Environment and Development (UNCED)—held just a year after the civil war was brought to an end—which led to the ratification of several global environmental conventions and the creation of robust funding institutions, the most important being the Global Environment Facility (GEF) housed within the World Bank. Adding to the centripetal dynamism of these initiatives was the emergence of vibrant global civil society actors that coalesced into "literally hundreds" of transnational environmental advocacy networks.[7] All of this pushed "the environment" into becoming a new fixture in global policy circles—what some described as the "the third pillar" of world politics alongside security and development[8]—that has provided environmental activists with a useful platform on which to promote more robust systems of environmental protection.

However, despite the normative thrust of the campaigns, conferences, and conventions, the emerging global environmental policy domain remains unconsolidated and subject to a considerable degree of contestation. In comparison to the global field of human rights, for example, Keck and Sikkink have described it as being "less bounded" and "not as clearly principled," resembling more of "a frame" within which a variety of claims and interests are debated.[9] Douglas Torgeson has similarly argued that the green movement faces a problem of identity because it has no "well-defined center" and "lacks a clear oppositional stance"—all of which makes it very difficult to formulate an effective "strategic posture."[10] The main tension has been associated with the inherently political nature of the relationship between environment and development, symbolized by the ambiguous concept of "sustainable development" that essentially leaves the door open to privileging processes of economic accumulation. Corporate interests have been particularly successful in opposing restrictive environmental regulations, laws, and conventions, especially in the lead-up to the Rio Conference in 1992, and this has been paralleled by the ability of elites in developing countries (such as Lebanon) "to hide behind the rubric of development" when confronting environmental problems in their countries.[11] The result, at the global level, has been the emergence of a more open-ended environmental policy domain. On the one hand, it has provided a forum for the embedding of environmental discourses, norms, and laws; on the other hand, its consolidation has been complicated by the structural limitations imposed by powerful interests linked to sovereign states and global capital.

What is important for our purposes is the way in which these complex interactions between agents of environmentalism and its powerful detractors at the global level mirror and have filtered down into local policy arenas such as Lebanon. As it made its transition from civil war to civil peace, for example, Lebanon witnessed a remarkable bubbling up of environmental activism—particularly at the grassroots level. Environmental degradation had been widespread, encompassing everything from the illegal dumping of imported toxic wastes; to the illegal private development and exploitation of public property, particularly along Lebanon's coastal area; to the wanton destruction and exploitation of areas within the Lebanese mountains due to unregulated waste dumping, construction, and quarrying—all of which was estimated to have cost the country approximately $100 million per year.[12] In the absence of the Lebanese state, its ministries, and municipalities during the war and early postwar period, it was Lebanese citizens who responded to the increasing destruction of their local environments—demanding the removal of toxic wastes, an end to the extraction of sands and illegal encroachments onto their public beaches, and the regulation of the wanton proliferation of quarries throughout the country with their little regard for the health, safety, or integrity of the local populations and landscape. Indeed, it was through this emerging *ecologisme du base*, argues Karam, that the environmental field was born in Lebanon itself.[13]

Assisting this local activism was a broadening array of environmental actors and networks at the national level. These were represented by a number of nationally oriented environmental NGOs, NGO networks, and, by the mid-2000s, two "green" political parties—all of which were supported by a small but active coterie of students, scientists, legal experts, and journalists who provided the fledgling environmental movement with the kind of support and epistemic weight that all hoped would "de-localize" environmental issues, legitimating them as a national concern.[14] Assisting this associational activism was support—both financial and political—from a variety of actors and networks within the global arena, the most significant being that of Greenpeace, which established its first regional office in the Eastern Mediterranean region in Beirut in the mid-1990s. Further adding to the growing energy of the emerging environmental sector in the early postwar period was the flooding of the public arena with environmental discourse, symbolized by the emergence of a variety of environmental campaigns; the rapid spread of awareness-raising programs, particularly within the country's public school system; the rise of environmental journalism, which included the publication of weekly columns in many of the country's newspapers; and the emergence of more explicitly environmental academic programs and degrees within the country's universities. All of this awareness-raising activity was crucial in moving away from the prevailing "scattered and limited" conceptions of what "the environment" means—associated in narrow ways with such things as "garbage" and conservation. As one Lebanese environmental activist remarked, "the problem is to unify . . . [and] frame the issue," adding that this needed to be done "in such a way that people can easily and logically make connections between . . . different issues."[15]

Finally, the Lebanese state also began to create its own "green" institutions, beginning with the Ministry of the Environment (MOE) in 1993. This was followed by the creation of a parliamentary committee responsible for environmental questions in 1999, a number of interministerial committees dealing with a variety of environmental issues, and some environmental committees within various municipalities—all of which were undergirded by the ongoing formulation of numerous environmental laws and regulations, such as the National Code for the Environment, ratified (though not implemented) in 2002, and the signing and ratification of international environmental conventions—principally the Convention of Biodiversity (UNCBD), the Framework Convention on Climate Change (UNFCCC), and the Convention on Combating Desertification (UNCCD). Moreover, while the MOE was a small and "second class" ministry within the Lebanese government—it being created by Hariri in 1993 as a mechanism to broaden his government's patronage options and, as Karim Makdisi argued, "to soak up international donor aid"[16]—its presence alongside a fledgling environmental movement created opportunities for enterprising oppositional politicians to strike alliances between the ministry and environmental activists as a way of increasing its—and their—own voice within more central political networks, in effect, transforming the ministry into a platform for NGO policy advocacy. Indeed, as we shall examine later, this was exactly the dynamic in the late 1990s during the ministerial tenure of the Druze and Progressive Socialist Party (PSP) politician Akram Chehayeb. In short, as Lebanon passed into its postwar period, the country quickly developed from scratch some of the necessary conditions needed to promote the emergence of a defined and focused environmental policy domain—a growing coterie of environmental activists, civil society networks, discourses, and national environmental institutions, in addition to external donor support.

Pitted alongside these environmental actors and institutions, however, were powerful political networks, historically rooted in Lebanon's political economy, whose overwhelming interests were to prevent the emergence of a disciplining environmental policy domain. At the core of these networks were Lebanon's political elites, who, as the country entered the postwar period, were desperate to take advantage of the potentially lucrative opportunities emanating from the emerging reconstruction process. Historically, Lebanon's political elites—despite the precarious nature of their political alliances—had been extraordinarily successful and vigilant in preserving Lebanon's status as a laissez-faire "merchant republic" and in preventing the emergence of robust forms of state regulation on external trade and internal commerce. In effect, they exercised in Lebanon's economic realm the kind of "veto power" wielded by religious clerics in the realm of gender. While preserving individual family monopolies over particular import sectors in the internal market, for example, they have collectively sought to prevent the erection of tariff barriers that could inhibit external trade. Equally important has been the ability of these elite coalitions to prevent the institution of any significant form of land use planning in the country—symbolized by the negligible and unenforced rates of land taxation that have encouraged the long-standing practice of land speculation. Further facilitating unfettered processes of accumulation in Lebanon has been the dearth of regulations concerning building construction—epitomized by Article 17 in the 1971 Code of Construction, which virtually removed restrictions on construction in 90 percent of the Lebanese territory not subject to urban planning laws, contributing to an overall planning regime based on the principle of "generalized constructability."[17] The outbreak of war and the virtual collapse of the state further accentuated these dynamics of unfettered development and accumulation. Fueled by the enormous amounts of capital generated by the predatory war economy, land speculation intensified exponentially, symbolized by the often illegal encroachment onto previously regulated urban zones and publically owned areas of the coastal area. It is in this context that Picard has written of the powerful "craving for land" that led to the widespread construction of coastal land reclamation projects, marinas and seaside resorts, luxury hotels, gated communities, and shopping malls.[18] Hence, if environmental activists in Lebanon hoped to stop, if not reverse, the devastating environmental effects of the postwar continuation of this *capitalisme de guerre*, they would have to contend and/or negotiate with these powerful economic networks.

Exacerbating this already enormous challenge, however, was the control exercised by distinct components of these groups over parts of the Lebanese state, using it to protect and facilitate their predatory economic activities. Institutions like the Council for Reconstruction and Development (CDR) were important in helping to facilitate if not organize the postwar processes of accumulation by Lebanon's elite classes, but it was the Ministry of the Interior (MOI)—powerfully reinforced by the support of Syrian officials during the days of their "protectorate" who were deeply implicated in these rent-seeking activities—that was crucial to their protection. The MOI had regulatory power over a wide range of socio-economic activities in the country, from the activities of civil associations, to the activities of the various decentralized levels of government (e.g., mohafazats, cazas, municipalities), to a variety of local commercial activities. Indeed, in the immediate postwar world, the MOI was at the heart of the political center—it was close to the Syrian intelligence agencies, it had control over the Internal Security Forces (ISF), it had a large and growing budget, and, as Makdisi described, "it was greatly feared by the public." Moreover, as was clear with respect to the relationship between the MOI and the quarrying industry, it played a "preeminent" role in blocking threatening environmental initiatives by NGOs and the newly created MOE, at one point trying to institutionally swallow up the latter altogether. As a result, concluded Makdisi, there were clear, if informal and opaque, connections in the 1990s between the powerful MOI and "uncontrolled growth in large development projects" in the country.[19] Indeed, argued Makdisi on a more general basis, the Lebanese elite have "such a degree of control over the state apparatus that, for obvious reasons, environmental constraints serve only as a nuisance for the continued exploitation of the country's natural resources and for 'development.' "[20]

Further challenging civil society actors were the powerful, subordinating, and fragmenting dynamics of clientelism. These dynamics were set to become especially intensive in the early postwar period—characterized by the frantic and competitive drives by new and old elites alike to reconsolidated local political and/or communal bases of power. The subordinating effects of these clientelist dynamics—reinvigorating powerful forms of compliance within Lebanese society as a whole—made it extremely difficult for civil society activists within such fields as the environment to mobilize significant and sustained grassroots national support that could cut across ties of community and class.[21] These same limiting dynamics also affected the volunteer base for emerging environmental activism, the most significant levels of "environmental" volunteerism—or "voluntary servitude," as Beydoun described it—occurring within the various political and sectarian movements of the country, mobilized for such sporadic, superficial public relations campaigns as the cleaning of the country's beaches.[22] As one environmental activist recognized, "it is difficult to mobilize people on issues that don't fit the dominant [political] structure of the country."[23] In short, constrained by the regeneration of powerful clientelist networks, environmental activism in postwar Lebanon would be limited to the organization of "gatherings" and "networks" among a narrow social group of associational leaders and middle-class activists rather than lead to the more widespread mobilization of environmental social movements. If environmental actors and networks hoped to wield policy influence, they would have to move "upward" and strategically engage with political and policy-making elites within Lebanese political society.

Complicating this movement into political society, however, was a further hegemonic dynamic within Lebanon's clientelist system—characterized by the penetration and participation of clientelist elites within civil society and associational life itself. Indeed, as we have examined above, this has been a long-standing dynamic within Lebanese social and political life—represented historically by the vast array of familial, class, and communal institutions that emerged in response to the socioeconomic challenges spewed up by the modernization process. The emerging postwar field of the environment would be no different—with political elites proving adept at creating their own environmental associations in order to monitor, if not benefit from, this new field as well as entering into clientelist alliances with existing environmental associational actors in order to expand their networks of compliance. Providing incentives for this hegemonic penetration into Lebanon's emerging environmental sector was the provision of external donor capital, a dynamic that was particularly powerful within the field of conservation. In short, paralleling the dynamic observed at the global level, Lebanon's political elites have used "hegemonic forms of power"—rooted in an array of competing coalitions with civil society associations—to protect and promote their interests within the emerging environmental policy domain.[24]

One of the environmental sectors in postwar Lebanon where these political dynamics are particularly strong has been solid waste management. The country has faced ever-growing waste flows in the war and postwar periods, a Greenpeace representative in Lebanon at one point describing the country as "drowning in its own waste."[25] Estimates from the CDR, for example, suggest that annual waste flows increased by 30 percent between 1994 and 2001 and will increase by 63 percent by 2030.[26] While caused by high rates of urbanization, population growth, and consumption, the social and environmental impacts of these rising waste flow rates were exacerbated by the wartime collapse of waste management systems and the municipal governments that were supposed to organize and administer them. This has resulted in the proliferation of improvised local solutions often consisting of the widespread, uncontrolled dumping and burning of unsorted waste on hillsides and/or the seaside throughout the country. This has, in turn, contributed to the destruction of fertile land and sensitive ecological areas; the pollution of watersheds, streams, and the coastal area, and the dangerous mixing of a variety of organic, nonorganic, toxic, and hospital wastes. The most egregious example of these practices was the wartime emergence of the huge, unsorted, and untreated urban and coastal-based landfill sites in Beirut, Saida, and Tripoli. While the situation improved marginally in 1997 with the institution of an emergency plan for Beirut and much of Mount Lebanon, solid waste management in the rest of the country has continued to be relegated to dumping and burning. Indeed, at one point, there were more than 700 unregulated and unsanitary dump sites throughout the country, including the "mountain of waste" in Saida that reached more than 50 meters in height and that collapsed on a regular basis into the Mediterranean Sea.

Explaining this degree of policy immobilism—despite the long-standing campaigning of local communities, NGOs, and the provision of assistance from foreign donors—is only possible if we examine the broader political dynamics of the sector, strongly influenced by structurally embedded interests relating to class and clientelism. On the one hand, for example, the politics of solid waste management is all about accumulating resources and profits, one NGO activist describing the solid waste management business in Lebanon, especially that related to collection and dumping, as being a recipe for "money printing."[27] Particularly profitable was the contract awarded to the Hariri-owned company Sukleen by the Hariri government itself for the collection, sorting, and treatment of waste in the Greater Beirut Area in 1997—a contract that paid two to three times more than the international benchmark.[28] One environmental activist went so far as to say that "Sukleen is stealing our money"—both selling its services at exorbitant rates while also making money on the sale of recycled materials.[29] The awarding of the lucrative Sukleen contract, however, awoke others to the possibilities that the sector offered for economic accumulation. With the resignation of the Hariri government and the emergence of the Lahoud-Hoss regime one year later, political pressure intensified to expand the distribution of spoils. Describing 1998 as "a watershed" in the solid waste management sector, the World Bank witnessed the emergence of a multitude of new, opportunistic, and often highly impractical proposals on solid waste management that resulted in the decision-making process within the sector becoming "totally frozen," so much so that the World Bank eventually decided to withdraw its comprehensive loan financing for solid waste management projects altogether.[30] Commenting on the inability of foreign donors to insulate the solid waste sector from Lebanon's wider political game, one Lebanese expert was unsurprised by this dynamic, arguing that because the government "is the driver of the sector" and actually provides the bulk of the financing, it was logical to expect that it would be subject to "the same political divisions as the government."[31]

The consequence of this growing and politicized interest in Lebanon's solid waste management sector, however, was the emergence of protracted and unresolved negotiations over how to organize it—with each new political entry into the debate expanding the scope of discussions in search of ways to benefit financially from the division of its potential spoils. This was evident in the several phases of thinking on the issue in the postwar period revolving around where and how many sites would be chosen for solid waste management facilities. These began with an original Solid Waste Management Master Plan organized on the basis of the four mohafazats, then moved to a World Bank plan designed to create

fifteen landfill sites throughout the country, before expanding further to
a broader-based program embodied in the National Solid Waste Investment Program that was presented to but not passed by the Council of
Ministers in 2004 in which twenty-two areas were designated for various
kinds of facilities. As an expert on solid waste management remarked
with respect to the ever-expanding number of solid waste management
sites, "it's a patronage game all the way through. . . . Of course, everybody
would like to have a share."[32]

Complicating these deliberations further has been the periodic outbreak of local resistance, sparked by hints and rumors that solid waste
management facilities such as landfill sites were being designated for
particular regions and/or communities. This resistance has emerged for
a variety of often overlapping reasons, some ecological, some economic,
some political, and some simply the result of the "not-in-my-backyard"
phenomenon. Complex and underlying socio-sectarian grievances, for
example, have been at play in impeding progress in the solid waste
management sector—the World Bank citing such "ethnic" suspicions
as contributing to what it described as "persistent outbreaks of social
resistance" to proposed solid waste management solutions.[33] In 1997,
for example, violent protests broke out in a southern suburb of Beirut
that led to the closing down of Lebanon's only waste incinerator—events
that were dubbed Lebanon's first "environmental intifada" and that were
motivated in part by a sense of sectarian grievances on the part of its
predominantly poor Shi'a residents. In the Armenian quarter of Bourj
Hammoud in Beirut, parallel protests broke out in that same year over
the continued growth in the size of "the mountain of waste" represented
by its Normandy dump. Indeed, it was in response to these initial violent
protests over the consequences of the complete absence of a solid waste
management plan in the early postwar years that the Hariri government
of the time instituted its emergency solid waste management plan—the
World Bank noting that "the government took this drastic action . . . in
order to avoid a potential civil strife that would have launched the country
into another round of social and militia resistance."[34]

These grievances have been exacerbated by the opaque decision-
making processes about issues that directly affect citizens' well-being.
Abdullah Zakhia, a leading environmental lawyer and activist, spoke
repeatedly of "the lack of trust" between Lebanese citizens and those
making decisions on waste management issues, who were perceived to
be always prioritizing their personal and political interests over public
ones; "if we don't take the waste management dossier out of the hands of
politicians," noted Zakhia, "one will not be able to find solutions," adding,
"how are we to improve the state of our environment when the manage-

ment of these issues is assumed by Ali Baba?"[35] As a way of alleviating this mistrust, the World Bank recommended, in hindsight, the adoption of "a participatory approach" in the waste management sector as a way of building consensus between the communities, municipalities, and the central government.[36] Similar messages have been spread by NGOs such as Greenpeace, whose volunteers at one point imaginatively stood by a large, transparent banner outside the main offices of the CDR calling for "Transparency Now!" with respect to the system of contracting in the solid waste sector.[37]

The key to understanding the prevalence of such sectarian social resistance, however, is to examine the ways in which local grievances not only induced political elites at the center to act, but also were "triggered" by them for broader, non–waste management–related political purposes.[38] In response to the various failed experiences in building sanitary land-fills in localities such as Baalbak, Koura, Jbeil, and Saida, for example, World Bank staff concerned with Lebanon concluded that much of the politicking emanated from "local residents with strong political links."[39] Environmental activists were similarly aware of the complications that their local activism could provoke. On the one hand, the promotion of greater social mobilization was crucial in forcing Lebanon's political elite to be accountable to the public interest—one activist arguing that "the solution lies somewhere in the streets."[40] On the other hand, it could eas-ily be deflected in sectarian directions, resulting in a situation in which "Muslims and Christians refus[ed] to have each other's waste dumped near their homes."[41] One expert in the solid waste sector described this dynamic in recursive terms, arguing that the local and the national levels "feed into each other," creating situations whereby local issues escalated into and were absorbed by larger national ones. Indeed, when asked whether social grievances are used by political elites to promote other political causes and battles, this expert remarked "absolutely," adding that it was the classic way in which elites created political leverage when negotiating with other elites. It was "a tit for tat" dynamic, he remarked, that resulted in negotiations on particular issues exploding into a whole range of existential struggles, making compromise extremely difficult to achieve.[42] For the solid waste sector as a whole, the practical consequences of this immobilizing political dynamic have been disastrous.

Hence, it is clear from the above analysis of the parameters of Leba-non's environmental policy domain, and of the "sub-domain" in solid waste management, that those interested in fostering the emergence of an institutionalized and ruled-based sector in postwar Lebanon had to con-tend with the contrary interests of, and factionalized competition between, the country's postwar economic and political elite classes. Historically rooted in the very structures of the state and reinforced by the political dynamics of the war and postwar settlement, the power of these elite classes would be wielded—both at the level of the state and within civil society itself—to ensure that the emerging environmental policy domain would be uninstitutionalized, widely dispersed, and politically penetrated. In short, rather than using their political power to promote serious policies of environmental protection, these political elites would use environmentalism—with all of the human, associational, and financial resources that came with it—to reconsolidate and grow their own factional bases of political power.

Yet opportunities for environmental activists to promote a serious environmental agenda using forms of "intelligent agency" still existed. As was the case in the realm of women's politics, the informal, fragmented, and competitive nature of elite networks leave associational actors with a variety of strategic opportunities. Crucial to capitalizing on them, however, was the ability of environmental associations to carve out autonomous space in Lebanon's political economy within which environmental deliberations, projects, and campaigns could be carried out. This was attempted in two principal ways—through the creation by environmental activists and scientists of vibrant associations, backed up by links with environmental actors within global civil society; and through the establishment of institutional platforms from which to launch environmental campaigns—be they formal coalitions of environmental associations or informal policy networks that brought the former into alliance with members of Lebanon's elite political classes. What follows is an examination of the initial success of these efforts. This is followed by a more sobering analysis of the subsequent challenges that Lebanon's associational actors in the field of the environment have had in institutionalizing these successes within the constantly shifting but historically entrenched structural context that surrounds them.

## Probing Postwar Opportunities for "Green Politics": The Rise of Environmental Advocacy Networks

Lebanon's dynamic postwar environmental sector owes its origins to the initiative and courage of a number of independent and isolated activists during the war and early postwar period; these were the pioneers of the country's *ecologisme de base*, which, Karam has argued laid the basis for the "invention" of the environmental field in the country. A variety of individuals, in particular, stand out for their personal contributions. These included the tireless efforts of botanist Ricardo Haber, who, in the midst of the civil war, succeeded in laying the foundations for the subsequent and dramatic growth of the country's postwar conservation movement.[43] They also include the courageous advocacy efforts of Hafez Jreih and the Committee for the Protection of Enfeh, coercively intimidated by developers and their political backers wanting to build a port on the location of the town's declared national archeological site. Jreih not only succeeded in protecting the site; in alliance with an emerging informal national network of NGOs, he also managed to link the case of Enfeh to the broader and successful campaign against the privatization of the country's coastal area. Stressing the critical importance of the seemingly isolated Enfeh experience, Karam described it as acting like "*une ecole pour les ecologistes.*"[44] Similarly important learning experiences were gained by the advocacy work of the Matn-based Lebanese Committee for Environment and Development—efforts whose roots went back to the early 1980s in the midst of the civil war—against quarrying and the powerful and politically backed commercial interests that were associated with it. With the demand for building materials skyrocketing in the early postwar period, quarrying quickly emerged as Lebanon's postwar Eldorado, one in which both the Syrians and leading members of Lebanon's political elite, such as the interior minister for much of the 1990s (and the Matn-based member of parliament), Michel Murr, were highly implicated. Using an innovative mix of repertoires that revolved around networking with locally affected communities, civil society activists, the media, and leading local oppositional politicians, the persistence of the Matn-based group contributed to the emergence of quarrying as one of the country's serious environmental issues. Moreover, while the destruction wrought by the quarrying industry continued unabated at the national level—leading Zakhia to describe it as literally "eating up" the Lebanese mountains—quarrying in the Matn did subside considerably and was actually stopped for a time in the late 1990s.[45]

*The Emergence of Environmental Associations in Postwar Lebanon: The Case of Green Line*

To better understand the nature of the opportunities that emerged for environmental activists in the immediate postwar era in Lebanon, I conducted a series of interviews with the founding members of the country's premier postwar environmental NGO in the 1990s, Green Line, imaginatively named after the wartime demarcation line between East and West Beirut, which, due to the dangers and, hence, lack of crossing between the two zones, became one of the city's only "green spaces." Green Line was formed within the Faculty of Agricultural Sciences on the campus

of the American University of Beirut (AUB)—the coming together of
two groups: a small but young and well-educated echelon of foreign-
trained academics and scientists, who had grown up in Lebanon in the
1960s and 1970s; and a younger group of alumni who had stayed in the
country during the war and had been involved with civil relief and resistance campaigns. Many also had connections with global environmental
associations, especially Greenpeace, synergetic linkages that Green Line
strategically used in the 1990s to provide its campaigns with a transnational dimension. While this core group initially coalesced around Shadi
Hamadeh, a foreign-trained and politically connected agronomist who
had been a self-described "independent leftist anarchist" during his days
as a student at AUB in the 1970s, Green Line was more a collective than
a one-man show. "It was a great group," remembered another of Green
Line's founding members, Hala Ashur. "We spent a lot of hours shouting,
debating, taking stands . . . it was a very fruitful diversity."[46]

Critical to their decision to form Green Line was the desire for
the return of peace and stability to the country and the recreation of a
national public sphere, previously segregated into wartime cantons; "the
government was coming back," commented Hamadeh, the association's
first president. Equally crucial was the desire to shape the nature of the
country's emerging public sphere—to be a "prime mover" in the postwar political field, especially given the intensifying discussions around
the postwar reconstruction program. Hamadeh, for example, recollected
that "yes, this was the thing that gave civil society members a sense of
opportunity . . . it was these debates" with another of Green Line's leading activists, Mirvat Abu Khalil, remarking that there was "a breath of
fresh air" after the war and a sense that this was "our turn."[47] Adding
politicized energy to this hope were deep concerns that opportunities
to openly debate the country's reconstruction agenda would be lost in
the excitement emerging around the political figure of Rafiq Hariri, that
"guru of investment [and] money," as Ashur described him, who threatened to dominate the reconstruction agenda with his non-statist agenda
of markets and privatization. "We should be within a group to say "no"
to that . . . [in order to] preserve what is remaining after the war."[48] In
short, Green Line had very politicized beginnings, and many of its core
founders, already trained in the agricultural sciences, gravitated toward
the larger field of the environment because it seemed to offer them a
unique channel through which to participate in these larger reconstruction debates.

Several factors contributed to the association's unique positioning in
postwar Lebanon. First, Green Line's founding group were all convinced
of the futility of doing politics "as usual." At the end of the war, remarked

Abu Khalil, not only was the country "totally divided by sectarianism," but "political discourse had lost its content. . . . It didn't have any real political agenda—neither the right nor the left—because they were all identifying themselves with sectarian groups." As a result, she added, "there was a real need to start something new," and the environment, it was hoped, could be that new cause. For starters, it had the potential to act as "a unifying platform" around which people could revive their political interests and challenge the political elites of the country without having an explicit political affiliation, especially given the abuse to which the country's environment had been subjected to "by the warlords."[49] Given its potentially more defined and issue-oriented focus, it also was an issue that might allow activists to target—and at the same time be shielded by—the policy-making process rather than become involved in the political process as a whole. Further enhancing the perceived depoliticizing qualities of environmentalism was its relationship with science, something that seemed to give it that extra "epistemic edge" that many hoped would translate into "leverage with the political class" and that could act, as Karam has insightfully suggested, as both a tool for collaboration with, and opposition to, public authorities.[50] Hence, Lebanon's emerging coterie of postwar environmental activists harbored a sense of cautious optimism, excited by the opportunities that a focus on environmentalism offered yet deeply wary of the political dangers. As Hamadeh remarked, "in Lebanon, you have to be very careful. . . . Anything could be assimilated by political parties. As they say in Arabic, you have to walk between the rain drops!"[51]

All of Green Line's founding members look upon the 1990s as a "golden age" for the association and the environmental advocacy sector as a whole. Green Line became a hub in Ras Beirut for volunteerism, mobilizing more than 200 volunteers at its peak without devising recruitment strategies. Noted Hamadeh, "it simply grew by itself." Contributing to this quick growth was the sense that environmental associations were at the top of the emerging postwar advocacy sector—they were new; the issues affected all regardless of sectarian affiliation; and, as a result, the movement was able to draw on a wide variety of new recruits—those active in NGO networks, those returning to Lebanon in the postwar world, and those in academia. Green Line's volunteer membership also was distinguished by its gender balance—with more than 50 percent being women, not only within the various project committees but also within the Executive Council.[52] All of this contributed to what Ashur described as a "beneficial diversity" within the association.[53] Further facilitating the emergence of its volunteer base was Green Line's internal governance style. While, on the surface, its formal procedures and institutions resembled those of other NGOs, it actually operated in a more informal, inclusive, and transparent manner, promoting forms of governance described as being "horizontal" rather than "vertical."[54] This resulted in a remarkable degree of fluidity and freedom within Green Line in the 1990s that led several founding members to speak of a unique "democratic spirit" and "common sense." As another member of the core group, Salmon Abbas, remarked with respect to the sense of integrity within Green Line in the 1990s, "[we were all] fighting for what we believed was right."[55] Finally, backing up these internal strengths were Green Line's partnerships with a small but loyal coterie of foreign donors.[56]

One of the underlying criteria for activities undertaken by Green Line volunteers was that they promote some kind of advocacy—avoiding both pure scientific research and/or pure service provision, each of which could divert and swallow the association's advocacy voice. While there remained a wide space between these two poles that led to intense debates within Green Line's publicly open Tuesday Executive Committee meetings, the ensuing tension resulted in an interesting mix of projects and campaigns.[57] Veering toward the "service provision" side of the ledger was Green Line's successful "School Garden Project," one that attracted the association's largest base of volunteers. The project's immediate activities consisted of an annual training program to assist in the establishment of plant nurseries, composting programs, as well as vegetable, fruit tree, and livestock cultivation within selected private and public schools. The project also had a number of broader goals. The first was to raise public awareness of green spaces and agriculture, both severely neglected within the Lebanese public sphere as a whole; noted Adnan Melki, the chair of the committee within Green Line, "we wanted educated people to be farmers." The project's second goal was to promote its sustainability by encouraging the participation of all relevant stakeholders in the project's decision-making processes—whether or not they were members of Green Line. This included teachers, school administrators, parents, environmental NGOs, municipalities, as well as the relevant ministries of the state (Agriculture, Environment, and Education). This flowed into the third project goal, which was to create "a successful model" that could be incorporated into a regular state program—one partially fulfilled when the Ministry of Education, a participant in the School Garden project, agreed to mandate the establishment of environmental clubs in all public schools. In short, the School Garden project reveals some of the underlying principles that guided Green Line's activities—ones that revolved around its determination to encourage and assist the state in assuming its national public responsibilities while avoiding the long-standing temptation within the NGO world to replace, and hence weaken, the state.[58]

It was Green Line's politicized and well-publicized advocacy activities in the 1990s, however, that put the NGO on the national map. This began with Green Line's groundbreaking campaign in 1991 against the extraction of sands from the beaches in Tyre.[59] However, Green Line's most challenging and sustained postwar advocacy campaign revolved around the unresolved case of wartime toxic waste dumping. Toxic wastes had originally been imported into Lebanon in 1987, with thousands of barrels clandestinely being dumped along the shore or within the mountains.[60] Inadequately dealt with at the time—Makdisi describing the issue as being surrounded by "a web of official deceit"[61]—the file was reopened in the early 1990s after barrels of toxic waste, which local villagers described as "containers of fear,"[62] were rediscovered. Scientists involved in the previous investigations and Green Line jumped into the fray. Supported by a broader network of civil society associations that had formed an "emergency committee" on the toxic waste issue in 1994, they played an important role as advocate and intermediary—supporting scientific studies on the chemical makeup of the toxic waste, "cajoling" Greenpeace to become involved in the issue, which led to them establishing an office in Beirut to coordinate their campaign n 1994 (later turned into a permanent office in 1996),[63] acting as a liaison with the Lebanese Army that had, for its own public relations and political reasons, become interested in the issue itself, and eventually establishing fragile lines of communication and cooperation between Greenpeace and the Hariri government—the prime minister having visited the Rainbow Warrior when it first arrived off the Beirut coast in the hope, argued the Greenpeace representative in Lebanon, Fuad Hamdan, that "they could contain us."[64] At one point, the Lebanese government tried once again to brush the issue under the carpet, denying that Lebanon was still harboring toxic waste from the 1980s, declaring the toxic waste file closed despite efforts to clandestinely get rid of the waste, and even going so far as to indict Fuad Hamdan and Pierre Malychef, the investigating scientist. It was only the continued lobbying of Green Line, the "aggressiveness, volume, and sheer persistence" of Greenpeace's advocacy work, and "the promising evolution of the Basel Convention" in the 1990s[65] that laid the groundwork for a constructive approach later taken by the new MOE, Akram Chehayeb, after his appointment in late 1996.[66] Hence, Green Line's facilitating and persistent advocacy efforts proved to be remarkably successful in pressuring the country's reticent political leaders to address the issue of toxic waste, especially given the degree to which former militia leaders and high-ranking politicians were implicated in the scandal. More than any other, it was this campaign that consolidated Green Line's reputation as one of the country's leading postwar civil society associations. When asked retrospectively about Green Line's campaign, Hamadeh answered that the key to success was the vigilant defense of its autonomy. Indeed, throughout the 1990s, Hamadeh remarked that "we were extremely fierce about our political independence," and it was this that allowed it to balance its role as an activist environmental association with the practical need to get work done and keep the channels of communication between competing parties open. With respect to the high-stakes toxic waste file, in particular, Hamadeh added that it was this balancing act that allowed Green Line both "to survive" and to come out with its independence intact.[67]

Hence, the associational rise of Green Line in the 1990s was the product of intelligent agency able to take advantage of contingent internal and external opportunities. Organizationally, for example, Green Line's leadership under the stewardship of Hamadeh was able to marshal the various human, financial, and network resources available locally and internationally to knit together a vibrant, scientifically credible, and globally networked environmental advocacy association from scratch. This leadership proved particularly crucial in mediating between the various personal, professional, and political tendencies within the association, translating these incipient tensions into "positive" and "synergetic" associational integrity and independence.[68] Equally important, however, was the political context within which Hamadeh and Green Line were working in the 1990s, dominated as it was by the national reconstruction agenda of the Hariri government and widespread and cross-communal elite participation in it. While this did nothing to reduce the large and politically enforced power asymmetries between "political" and "civil society" that advocacy associations had to contend with, it did provide environmental associations like Green Line with a focused target for its advocacy efforts—"the Hariri system," as one Green Line activist labeled it. As Lebanon entered the twenty-first century, however, and the country's reconstruction agenda—with the focused opportunities for advocacy that it provided—began to seriously wane, one began to see this common ground whittle away. Not only did this lead to the decline of both Hariri the politician and, with it, Hariri the discursive target for environmentalists, it also brought back to the surface and intensified the deep and fragmenting internal divisions in the country. As we shall see, these divisions began to penetrate more intensely the realms of civil society, adversely affecting not only the dynamics of advocacy politics in general but also the internal politics within NGOs—such as Green Line—themselves. Before examining these subsequent transformations, however, we turn first to an analysis of the broader environmental NGO sector in early postwar Lebanon and its efforts to build more collective advocacy networks.

*The Emergence of Environmental NGO Networks in Postwar Lebanon*

As is clear from the profile of Green Line above, advocacy associations are only as effective and influential as the networks of which they are a part. In its initial campaign against sand extraction in Tyre, for example, Green Line's collaboration with a local NGO, the media, as well as with scientists from the National Scientific Research Council (NSCR) was crucial in generating the kind of impact that the event produced. Similarly with the prolonged campaign over the dumping of toxic waste in the country, Green Line not only relied on its transnational connections with Greenpeace; it also garnered the support of selective officials within the Lebanese state, local scientists, as well as a substantive gathering of civil society associations. In short, effective advocacy depends on effective networking.

In recognition of this fact, a small, pioneering group of Lebanon's emerging community of environmental NGOs in the early postwar years decided to establish a national committee of environmental NGOs to be called the Lebanese Environmental Forum (LEF).[69] On the surface, the meeting proved successful—an agreement to create the LEF was reached; it was subsequently recognized by the Ministry of the Interior and designated as the official national forum for environmental associations in the country; and its membership grew constantly, reaching more than 50 by the end of the 1990s and more than 150 by the mid-2000s. However, even at its initial meeting in Tripoli in 1993, divisions quickly emerged. On the surface, those differences seemed to emanate from the endemic "identity" problems within the environmental field as a whole—it lacking a "well-defined center" that makes the formulation of a clear and effective discourse, vision, and "strategic posture" more complicated.[70] In Lebanon (as elsewhere), this has translated into differences in orientation and discourse between conservation-oriented "greens" and more sustainable development-oriented "browns"—representatives of the latter at one point describing the conservation agenda as "an old way of thinking." These agendas were not necessarily contradictory, nor were they, in theory, far apart. Many of Green Line's projects, such as the grass-roots reforestation network, were in part conservation oriented. Similarly, there were many conservationists in Lebanon critical of the one-sided reconstruction emphasis on growth. Nevertheless, the symbiosis between the two tendencies within environmentalism in Lebanon—vital if one hoped to cultivate a more powerful environmental movement in the country—was never strong enough, a weakness that must be understood within "the hostile context of power" in which Lebanon's non-state environmental actors were operating.[71]

Many of the original members of the conservation-oriented LEF, for example, were of an older generation—steeped in a conservative, confessional mind-set; "it is like an archive!" commented one of LEF's original foreign backers.[72] Wary of taking politicized stances, they preferred to cooperate with rather than agitate against the reemerging state. As one of Green Line's leaders recognized, "it was a critical time . . . the civil war ha[d] ended . . . and they were trying to calculate their priorities."[73] When a Green Line representative suggested at LEF's first organizational meeting that they, as a group, make a statement against the extraction of sands from the beaches in Tyre, an enterprise that would have brought them into confrontation with Berri's political network, the majority of the representatives vetoed the suggestion and turned their attention to the "more pressing" proposal of sponsoring a series of environmental stamps.[74] This trend endured within the LEF—avoiding advocacy when it came to some of the difficult issues related to such issues as quarrying, industrial pollution, waste management, and toxic waste, preferring to focus instead on issues relating to tree planting, conservation, ecotourism, and occasionally hunting.[75]

Of deeper concern was the way in which sectarian criteria seemed to seep into the workings of the LEF. Assad Serhal, the first president of the LEF, admitted the prevalence of this dynamic but justified it on several counts. Suspicions were running high in the early postwar period, and it was "enough" to simply get these groups to sit around the same table with each other—"we had to start somewhere," he added. Moreover, most NGOs in the LEF were local ones, often emanating from areas controlled by powerful politicians and former militia leaders. Hence, while some tried to hide this fact, Serhal openly recognized that most NGOs in the LEF were "in some kind of relation" with these local powers. Finally, Serhal stressed that the sectarian dynamics within the LEF were not necessarily a problem, suggesting that their resulting representativeness "gives us a strength" when approaching the political class, much as Ghassan Sayegh argued with respect to the NGO Forum. "This is something I really stress," remarked Serhal., "it is not Assad Serhal as a Shi'a going to talk to Nabih Berri as a Shi'ite leader the way we do it in Lebanon. Now, it is this Shi'a and Maronite and Druze and Sunni, we all go . . . as an environmental group." If it results in "all of these influential people [getting] interested in the environment," he added, "why not?"[76]

Of greatest concern from the perspective of LEF's critics, however, were signs that, rather than being a platform for civil society advocacy, the LEF was being transformed into a platform through which broader political interests could monitor and penetrate the activities of Lebanese civil society. In short, there were well-grounded fears that the LEF was being absorbed into the hegemonic dynamics of Lebanon's reconsolidating postwar patron–client networks. During the first elections for the LEF's executive committee, for example, it was clear that political factions were working to guarantee their electoral success through the creation and/or recruitment of a number of compliant associations—sometimes referred to as "mushroom NGOs."[77] The presence of these nonenvironmental economic and political interests at the heart of the LEF suggested that the forum's muted and compliant environmental advocacy was not a strategic decision on the part of the membership—as Serhal had implied—but the result of an imposed and clientelized political logic—one that Zakhia described as le compromis tabouli.[78] Given its monopolization of the center of Lebanon's environmental civil society, the ineffectual LEF weakened advocacy efforts of less compliant environmental associations and networks, confusing their campaigns and discursive messages and putting off many potential volunteers. Symbolic of this disaffection was the withdrawal of Lebanon's most serious environmental activists from membership in the LEF—including the immediate departure of Zakhia after the initial series of meetings in 1993 who saw the writing on the wall.

Yet from the dormant ashes of the LEF emerged a promising, if more informal, environmental advocacy network—al-multaqa' al-bi'a, also known as Green Forum after the NGO that sparked its creation. Green Forum—the NGO—emerged out of the amalgamation of the Matn-based Committee for the Environment and Development and a small coterie of scientists and students based at the Lebanese American University (LAU). Given its national orientation and its links to academia, Green Forum was a Green Line–type NGO that was self-classified as being "militant" in approach—rejecting all connections with sectarian leaders, refusing donor finance that could compromise its independence, and working for the common good.[79] Unlike Green Line, it had roots in a local community (the Matn), and it was exclusively focused on advocacy (rather than combining this with a project-based approach). One of Green Forum's main goals was to create a national dialogue and framework for the discussion of environmental problems—sponsoring seminars, workshops, and publications (such as the monthly environmental magazine al-minbar al-akhdar) on a range of issues from quarrying, to solid waste management and recycling, to the destruction of the country's coastal area, to the raising of environmental awareness across the country. Having initially tried but failed to join the LEF (indeed, excluded by the LEF itself), Green Forum quickly became the focal point for an alternative, informal, and unofficial network of environmental associations—grouping within it some of the country's most dedicated "greens."[80]

Yet committing oneself to advocacy politics is one thing; knowing how to do this effectively within the postwar Lebanese context is another. Interviews with those involved with Green Forum, for example, revealed a quiet sense of frustration with its approach—"timid," remarked one; "primarily reactive," suggested another; "scared shitless," suggested a third.[81] Part of the problem emanated from the lack of collective leadership—decisions about participation in activist campaigns being made on an association-by-association basis.[82] There also was the emerging problem relating to the increasing diversion of many environmental associations into project, as opposed to advocacy, work at the national level; "lots of NGOs fall into this trap," commented Green Forum's Hani Abu Fadil, if only because they needed the money to survive. The members of Green Forum also had difficulty formulating a longer-term national vision or action plan. However, the most serious dilemma for activists within Green Forum was the manner in which they were constrained—though not co-opted, as in the case with the LEF—by the Lebanese context. On the one hand, it was clearly difficult to rely on enduring alliances with the political class for support, even strategically targeted and sympathetic members, given the constantly shifting political dynamics in the country. As Abu Fadil explained, "here in Lebanon, it's very difficult. You never know . . . what's the main power. Sometimes it is . . . religious, sometimes it is economic, sometimes it comes as an outside power. . . .Yani [I mean] . . . These politicians, they are ready to change their position very, very, easily and this will make it much more difficult for us to work." On the other hand, it also was dangerous to try to mobilize, let alone sustain social protests on the environment given the power of the elite class to undercut grassroots support. Things can change "very fast," noted Abu Fadil, and can evolve into situations whereby those mobilized around one issue "[become] divided into political groups which have nothing to do with the issue you [were initially] concerned with." Unable to trust the system or to strongly challenge it from below, therefore, Green Forum members seemed to have little option but to apply subtle forms of pressure from within its own parameters. In comparing Green Forum's more "diplomatic" approach to the more aggressive one of Greenpeace, for example, Abu Fadil stressed that "we will not isolate any politicians . . . neither will we go with [one] group against another." Instead, he explained, "we will try and reach politicians through their people," in effect, working to "stretch" without succumbing to the logic of patron-clientelism. While this could, and sometimes did, lead to success on an individual-case basis, Abu Fadil realized that it did not translate into a strong environmental movement. As he concluded pessimistically, "environmentalism is not yet a force in Lebanon that is going to change anything. It is very, very weak."[83]

Hence, political elites in symbiotic relationship with certain associational actors within the emerging postwar environmental sector proved to be effective "prime movers," helping to both establish and gain control over the official civil society institution representing environmental associations at the national level—the LEF. This blocked any potential that the LEF held as a platform for national environmental advocacy. At the same time, however, a group of more autonomous environmental associations, most of which were active at the local level, began to converge into an informal network spearheaded by autonomous associations such as Green Forum and Green Line, providing this group with a potential alternative platform on which to promote its national causes. However, while the LEF had its own clear access to the political class via traditional clientelist networks, the question remained as to how the network around Green Forum would be able to carve out its own avenues of access to political society and the state—especially in light of its opposition to the political class as a whole. It is to an analysis of the sudden emergence of the MOE as the agent providing political access that we now turn, precipitated by the appointment of Chehayeb, a Druze politician with interests in the environment, as its minister.

*Consolidating Environmental Networks in Postwar Lebanon: Chehayeb and the NGO-ization of the MOE*

The most interesting aspect of the environmental activism of the Chehayeb ministry in the late 1990s was that, fundamentally, its motivations did not emanate from civil society but from a rival, disadvantaged Druze political network under the leadership of Walid Jumblat. While solidly in control of the Shouf region, the position of the Druze within Lebanon's confessional system of power as a whole declined considerably from its heady prewar days in the 1960s and 1970s under the leadership of his father, Kamal Jumblat. Prior to the war, the Druze community had compensated for its small size by adopting a progressive political agenda that served to nibble away at the client base of rival networks. With the demise of the political left in postwar Lebanon, however, Walid Jumblat, eager to consolidate a national base of power, began to consider environmentalism as a new political resource. With the appointment of a PSP partisan, Chehayeb, to the newly created (though weak) MOE in 1996, Jumblat, already felt to have a personal interest in environmental questions, found himself with a chance to test the environmental waters in Lebanon and, if found suitable, to prepare *un terrain politique*.[84]

Chehayeb himself was no stranger to the environmental NGO community. A high school science teacher and a parliamentary deputy by profession, he also had been involved in a variety of environmental activities in the early postwar period, participating in the "emergency committee" on the toxic waste issue and supporting the various campaign efforts against quarrying; indeed, one activist described him as "a militant against quarries."[85] In 1995, he also was appointed president of a new Shouf-based environmental NGO—the Association for Forestry, Development, and Conservation (AFDC). In short, as Abu Fadil remarked with respect to his appointment as minister of the environment, "the connection was there before he came to the Ministry."[86] Indeed, Zakhia, who subsequently worked closely as a legal advisor with Chehayeb throughout the latter's stint as minister, described him as someone in whom he had great confidence, adding that, given his Druze heritage, with its instinctive attachment to the land, "he was not like the people that come from the cities who are predators."[87]

The MOE that Chehayeb had inherited, however, was in shambles. Elevated from the status of a Ministry of State for the Environment in 1993, little was accomplished in its first three years as a full-fledged ministry despite the provision of external assistance by the United Nations Development Programme (UNDP) in the form of experts from the Rio-mandated Capacity 21 (C21) Program. In fact, for the first year of its existence, the MOE was actually located in the minister's house. Moreover, when the project manager for the C21 program arrived one year later, the MOE had only thirteen employees, most of whom were administrative rather than technical staff, and even had trouble providing stationary and a computer. Tasked with the responsibility of establishing a variety of theoretical and legal frameworks—such as the MOE's organizational structure, guidelines for the undertaking of environmental impact assessments, and the overarching code of environment—the C21 advisor remarked that "of the two years I spent on the project, I can say that we've done . . . little."[88] Part of this problem stemmed from the unstable succession of ministers to the portfolio—one of whom died (Joseph Moghaizel), none of whom had expertise in the environment, and some of whom were even suspected of being implicated in the activities against which environmentalists were campaigning. Part of the problem also stemmed from the preoccupation of the MOE with overwhelming and politically sensitive environmental problems in the mid-1990s concerning toxic waste, incineration, and solid waste management. A more underlying explanation for the incapacity of the fledgling MOE, however, was its lack of political support. The C21 advisor, for example, described it as never being granted a clear mandate by the country's political class despite progress in negotiations at the bureaucratic level, a refusal symbolized by the unwillingness of the Council of Ministers to pass the newly formulated Code of the Environment.[89] All of this pointed to a determination on the part of the country's political class not to allow concerns about environment protection—especially in the form of power to conduct environmental impact assessments—to impinge on the crucially important task of promoting postwar economic growth, let alone complicate the already difficult equation around dividing up the reconstruction spoils. It also pointed, commented the C21 advisor, to a refusal—and perhaps inability—on the part of that same political class to think about the environment "in a holistic way," relegating it instead to matters of pollution, with some concession to the idea of protecting nature.[90]

Hence, the appointment of the NGO-friendly Chehayeb to the MOE in late 1996 was greeted with enthusiasm by the environmental NGO community as a whole, enthusiasm that grew further as a result of Chehayeb's clear intent to transform the MOE into a node for environmental advocacy at the national level. One of his immediate promises, for example, was to clean up the toxic waste scandal that had reemerged again in 1996, a promise that was subsequently fulfilled when the waste was successfully repatriated.[91] Further bolstering Chehayeb's credibility was Jumblat's decision to close his quarries and his subsequent vocal assistance in pushing for the closure of others. As Zakhia remarked when commenting on Jumblat's action, he was the only politician demanding that "more" be done for the environment.[92] Chehayeb also was supported by an increased budget from the UNDP's C21 Program, which was deliberately enhanced to assist this more promising minister.[93] With this assistance in place, Chehayeb quickly set about increasing the administrative capacity of the MOE. This entailed bringing in more qualified staff, most of whom (though belonging to the Druze confession) had preexisting associational and environmental credentials;[94] developing and improving some of the legal instruments for environmental protection in the country (for which consultants such as Zakhia were hired);[95] and building more institutionalized mechanisms for outreach to the various stakeholder communities in the country—notably the private sector, municipal governments, and (most importantly for our purposes) NGOs. It was this latter series of initiatives that revealed one of Chehayeb's main goals during his tenure as minister—to promote a broader and more inclusive national dialogue on environmental issues, much along the lines advocated by Green Forum and the coterie of NGOs around it. Ideally, argued his public awareness advisor, Chehayeb's goal was to broaden the meaning of the environment and move these discussions out of the "salons" and into the "heart of each household" in the country.[96]

The most distinctive feature of the MOE under Chehayeb, however, was its propensity to act more like an advocacy NGO than a government institution. The MOE, for example, quickly became a meeting place for environmental NGOs—in stark contrast to its first few years—with some of Lebanon's most progressive environmentalists, particularly those associated with Green Forum, being in and out of the ministry on a daily basis. Chehayeb was described as becoming "the chapeau" or central networking node for all NGOs—"there were no groups . . . outside," commented Abu Fadil, even those from the LEF.[97] To assist in the MOE's attempt to rein in and regulate the quarrying industry, for example, Chehayeb welcomed the active collaboration of Green Forum members in the formulation of the Master Plan for Quarrying, in campaigning for the closure of illegal quarries, and even in helping to carry out a series of de facto inspections of a large number of operating quarries (450 of 750).[98] Similar synergies emerged between Green Line and the Chehayeb ministry, especially with respect to the creation within the MOE of an "Ozone Office" as a first step in Lebanon's compliance with the Montreal Protocol and the Vienna Convention.[99] Perhaps the highest-profile case of Chehayeb's environmental advocacy activities, however, was his collaboration with the NGO campaign to protect the coastal area. Born out of courageous local initiatives such as that of Hafez Jreih in Enfeh, a network of NGOs spearheaded by Green Line began to organize a series of public awareness-raising events about the illegality of wartime commercial developments on the coastal area.[100] It was out of these events that a national campaign to save the coastal area emerged, one that targeted impending discussions within the Lebanese parliament on a proposal to grant fifty-year leases that would have, in effect, privatized areas of the Lebanese coast that were by law supposed to be accessible to the public. When the proposal came up for discussion in the parliament in 1998, embedded in the budget bill for that year, Chehayeb not only helped these NGOs organize demonstrations against it, but he also left his chair as a government minister in the midst of the deliberations and joined the NGOs in their protests.[101] Hence, where the National Council for Lebanese Women (NCLW)—examined earlier—failed in its opportunity to act as an advocacy platform for NGOs, Akram Chehayeb and the newly created MOE succeeded.

Of further potential significance with respect to Chehayeb were his consistent efforts to consolidate and institutionalize these alliances between environmental advocacy networks within civil society and the ministry. He was reputed to have repeated often to his NGO colleagues: "I will not stay forever here. You are the ones who will take the work afterwards."[102] To strengthen some of the organizational and legal parameters for the MOE, for example, Chehayeb sought to grant NGOs the right to have access to the decision-making table of the proposed Higher

Council for the Environment—a proposal that was subsequently vetoed by the interior minister, Michel Murr.[103] However, it was his efforts aimed at strengthening the capacity of environmental associations and networks themselves on which Chehayeb wagered a good deal of his political capital. These included plans to establish a jointly administered NGO-ministry fund designed to distribute capital to promising NGO projects and initiatives—a reinvigorated and systematic version of the existing system whereby funds were doled out on an ad hoc and often politicized basis by the minister himself. His most ambitious initiative was the attempt to unify and, hence, institutionalize a coordination mechanism between the two principal environmental NGO networks—Green Forum and the LEF. Efforts had been made by others—notably foreign donors—to bring the two networks together with little success, mainly because all were designed to subvert the LEF itself, efforts that the LEF resisted. Chehayeb hoped to do better, given his favorable relations with the LEF, and organized a national congress of ecological associations in July 1998. This attempt also failed, however, blocked by the mutually reinforcing alliance between members of the LEF and the MOI under Murr—the former wanting to maintain control over the official national environmental NGO forum, the latter seeking both to maintain his control over Lebanon's NGO sector as well as contain the efforts of Chehayeb to expand the power of both his ministry and his political network.[104] These failures left the Chehayeb team disappointed and their initiative to strengthen relations between Lebanon's environmental NGO sector and the ministry in tatters, especially given the impending change in government that spelled the end to Chehayeb's tenure as minister. Interviewed less than one year after the debacle, Chehayeb's C21 adviser, Mounir Abu Ghanem, remarked that "I am still confused. . . . I don't know what to do," adding more pessimistically with respect to the resultant return to more informal NGO advocacy work that "where this tendency would lead, I don't know but I cannot see a future [for it]."[105]

Chehayeb's efforts as minister of the environment, nonetheless, remain significant. Clearly, the structural parameters surrounding his tenure within the MOE remained unchanged. While some piecemeal successes were achieved with respect to the closure of some quarries, for example, the larger business of quarrying, within which the political class and its Syrian "protectors" were heavily implicated, carried on with impunity. As Abu Fadil remarked in recognition of the limits to the underlying political—rather than associational—sources of power behind the Chehayeb ministry and the networks that he tried to empower, "the ones who have quarries are much stronger than Jumblat."[106] In fact, with the one exception of its success with respect to preventing the formal privatization of the coastal area, Chehayeb's ministry accomplished very little in terms of results on the ground and never had any of its draft legislation passed into law by the parliament. Chehayeb was further constrained by the contradictions of his political relationship with Jumblat, who, though genuinely interested in the protection of the environment, was first and foremost a political leader of a minority confession fighting for its share of the country's resources. The result, as Zakhia recognized, was that while Chehayeb was given the political space to raise important but contentious environmental issues and discourses, his strategic positioning placed him in an ambiguous, Janus-faced position, on the one hand promoting more holistic and rule-based approaches to the environment while on the other hand continuing to play and be rooted in a more factional political game. As Zakhia concluded, *"la limite de Chehayeb, c'est la politique,"* or, as Abu Khalil of Green Line put it, "he couldn't go to the end."[107]

Despite the absence of concrete results, however, the Chehayeb period continues to represent for environmentalists in Lebanon the pinnacle of their "golden age." Karam described the Chehayeb experiment as having contributed to the "partial institutionalization" of the norms and rules that challenged the free-flowing and unruly nature of Lebanon's postwar clientelist dynamics.[108] In this sense, while it may not have had much bargaining success, it did have success at the deliberative and cognitive levels. In his empirically rich and cogent analysis, Karam gives several reasons for his optimistic conclusions. First, environmental activists succeeded in placing their issues on the national public agenda—in short, they "de-localized" many environmental issues and, in doing so, "enlarged the public sphere."[109] They accomplished this in part through the strategic and legitimizing use of legal and scientific expertise, one that Karam argues established their "right" to participate in policy debates.[110] This also was accomplished through the construction of a "causal story" that linked the country's burgeoning environmental problems to a broader critique of the narrowly based and elite-enriching reconstruction process. Finally, symbolized by the ability of the MOE to stave off attempts by the MOI to absorb its functions, the new environmental field in Lebanon, despite the recognized fluidness of alliances and personal and political interests from which it was constituted, had nonetheless achieved "an institutional stability" and "a certain continuity"—much as Karam has argued for the broader civil associational sector as a whole. [111] In short, rather than succumbing to the asymmetrical power relations within the emerging environmental policy domain, environmental advocacy associations succeeded in "stretching" their clientelist dynamics, opening up greater public space within which independent and nonaffiliated environmental policy advocacy can expand.

### The Instrumentalization and Fragmentation of Environmental Advocacy in Postwar Lebanon

From its "golden age" in the 1990s, Lebanon's environmental policy domain and the processes of institutionalization that were under way regressed substantially in the 2000s, suggesting that the opportunities for unified associational activism in the 1990s were at best contingent and fleeting in nature. There are three factors that help to explain these reversals. First, the various platforms on which environmental advocacy depended in the 1990s were significantly weakened, or disappeared altogether, in the course of the following decade. This was symbolized by the withdrawal of nodal environmental networks and associations representing more independent voices of accountability within the field of policy advocacy. This made it difficult to sustain advocacy campaigns, let alone project their influence into the realms of political society. The second factor narrowing the political opportunities for NGO environmental advocacy was the consolidation, after his departure from the MOE, of a more factional-oriented environmental network around Chehayeb. In effect, this "Chehayeb network" positioned itself as a gatekeeper into political society for environmental activists—establishing clear network hierarchies in the realm of environmentalism within Lebanese civil society. Finally, the attempt by environmental activists to promote a wider and more holistic understanding of the environment—prevalent in their campaigns against the unsustainable growth-oriented reconstruction agenda in the 1990s—has increasingly taken a back seat to a more narrowly based "green" environmentalism that focuses on conservation and eco-tourism. In addition to those NGOs already focusing on conservation issues—many of which have been compliantly associated with the LEF—an important driver of this process has been the country's political elite, who have shown a growing interest in the potential benefits that conservation can bring to their wider political fortunes—it being "a layer," as one member of a prominent landed family remarked, within a wider political arsenal.[112] Particularly interesting is the emergence of a coinciding of interests between the country's landed elites and foreign donors, the former having the influence and power—particularly over local populations—to effectively deliver programs offered by the latter. The result has been a "greening" of several elite-based political networks, providing them with resources to consolidate control over their "own" territories and spheres of influence while, at the same time, establishing "buffer zones" between them and their rival political networks. Hence, it is in the conservation field of Lebanon, bound up as it is with these larger political questions of territoriality and power, that one sees the clearest examples of the penetration of elite hegemonic power into the very heart of the Lebanon's environmental advocacy field.

*The Weakening of Nodal Environmental Advocacy Actors and Networks*

After a promising decade of campaigning and institutional growth in the 1990s, the environmental advocacy sector witnessed a dramatic weakening of its voice—symbolized by the virtual disappearance of the two most prominent civil society associational advocacy platforms in the country, Green Forum and Green Line. Green Forum (the NGO), for example, imploded in the wake of a series of personal, electoral, and strategic conflicts in the early 2000s, and, as discussed below, so did the associational network along with it. Green Line's decline has been gradual but discontinuous, symbolized by its increasing internal difficulties in attracting volunteers, let alone candidates to run in its internal elections. These internal challenges were fed by the increasing polarization of politics within the country as a whole—a process that became more pronounced with the election of Lahoud to the presidency in 1998 and intensified dramatically with the assassination of Rafiq Hariri in 2005 and the Israeli war against Lebanon and Hezbollah in 2006. As processes of political polarization intensified at the national level, opportunities for environmental advocacy shrank accordingly, intensifying and politicizing debates within (and between) associations about what the best strategic options were for continued advocacy work.

Interestingly, when members of Green Line were asked about its decline, most pointed to the emergence of problems *within* the association. These internal problems revolved around the growing dominance of some of the initial founding core group within the Executive Council, one activist remarking that they had become like an overprotective "family," making it difficult for new voices in the association to be heard.[113] Paralleling this collective version of the "founder's syndrome"—so often seen in the world of NGO governance—was the gradual erosion of Green Line's informal, open, and deliberative internal governance processes. There had always been discussions with Green Line as to whether it should formalize its governance system. These had become more intense as the success of the association grew, symbolized by the increased inflow of volunteers and donor finance. Indeed, in his last year as president, Hamadeh recommended that Green Line develop a two-tiered structure by adding a more professionalized management structure to its volunteer base—a proposal rejected by the Executive Council as a whole for fear that it would weaken Green Line's volunteering principles, move the association too far away from its advocacy roots, and transform the association into "a company."[114]

As if to contain these voices and protect the Green Line tradition, how-ever, a gradual and subtle process emerged, with the executive increasingly exerting its formal authority by vetoing project initiatives emanating from the committees if they strayed too far away from the association's tradition of advocacy. While one of Green Line's former presidents justified these developments on the grounds that the association could not maintain its "disorderly" form of governance over a sustained period of time, it also was clear that this exertion of executive authority gradually led to an "escalation of tension" within.[115]

However, while these internal struggles were ostensibly over ques-tions of internal governance, they also represented more underlying splits between the advocacy-oriented executive and the young volunteer base, which, as political tensions in the country began to heat up and economic opportunities diminished, became more and more wary of involvement in politicized advocacy activities. Former Green Line executive members, for example, complained of facing increasing difficulties in attracting vol-unteers to demonstrations.[116] Further exacerbating these tensions was the increasing propensity of the executive to encourage the association to move in the opposite direction, justified on the grounds that Green Line's "independence" did not have to translate into a stance of "neutrality."[117] As one member of Green Line's founding group remarked, the dilemma facing Green Line had not been one of "whether" to enter the political fray but of "how deep" to go.[118] In the early years, for example, conten-tious political questions over such issues as whether to attend conferences in which Israel was represented or whether to work with donors and/or private sector actors with problematic human rights and/or environ-mental records were decided on a case-by-case basis. In the following decade, however, the approach shifted toward making more definitive statements and policies on these matters, the cumulative effect of which was to increase the level of internal contestation within the association. As one of Green Line's founders retrospectively admitted, the effect of moving in this direction was to effect a "split" in the association, after which "politics came in."[119]

These fragmenting effects were not immediate but gradual and cumulative—precipitated by a constant flow of politically polarizing events from the U.S. invasion of Iraq in 2003, to the assassination of Hariri in 2005, to the Israeli war against Hezbollah in the summer of 2006, to the outbreak of civil conflict in May, 2008, most of which, while outside the immediate mandate of environmentalism, generated strong, conflicting demands within Green Line's membership. Hariri's assassina-tion, for example, opened up critical debates within the association as to whether it should officially attend the funeral. On the one hand, Green

Line had always made a point in its campaigns of targeting environmental abuses rather than politicians. As one of the founding members emphasized while spearheading the vigorous campaigns to protect the public beach at Ramlet al-Baida in Beirut, most of which had been sold to private interests linked to Hariri, "we are not hostile to this project in particular but to all projects that close public access to the beach. Beirut must not become the only Mediterranean city without a public beach."[120] On the other hand, Hariri had clearly been at the antagonistic center of many advocacy campaigns—from those against the privatization of the coastal area, to those demanding the creation of green spaces in Beirut (targeting the Hippodrome and the Hariri-dominated Beirut municipality that opposed its campaign),[121] to those aimed at protecting the country's public beaches. Noted a former president of Green Line, "we never liked the Hariri system," with the huge legacy of debt that it has left for the average Lebanese to pay back, adding further that it was really "the Syrians and the Saudis that brought him here." Hence, the debates about whether to attend Hariri's funeral were intense and went long into the night, eventually resulting in the decision to boycott the event officially. Indicative of the degree of political discord within the association over this matter, however, the executive took six months before issuing a press release.[122]

What were, until 2006, manageable tensions within Green Line transformed into destructive ones with the Israeli war against Lebanon and Hezbollah in the summer of 2006. Initially, the July War rejuvenated Green Line after several years in which its volunteer base had begun to whittle away—symbolized by the return of the association's media prominence and role as a central node for volunteering, NGO networking, and "civil resistance" in the country;[123] it was "a golden opportunity" to rebuild the association, remarked one of its founding members.[124] However, as Candice Raymond has remarked with respect to the informal coalition of civil society associations that met regularly at Zico House during the war (where Green Line also was housed), this wartime-motivated mobilization, while revealing an underlying vitality to Lebanon's "associative tissue," also uncovered "an extreme diversity in the perception of the conflict, of its causes and of its implications in terms civil society action." This diversity intensified as the war dragged on and led to the emergence of radical fault lines—both between and within associations.[125] Two wartime civil society working coalitions within which Green Line took a leading role—the Coalition of Civil Organizations for Life (CSO Life) and the Oil Spill Working Group, which was a response to the destruction of the coastal oil storage facilities by Israeli jets—became unhinged as a result of internal political disputes. Green Line, along with seventeen other associations, for example, split from the former coalition in pursuit of their desire to critique U.S. support for Israel's war, symbolized by their public refusal to accept assistance from the U.S. Agency for International Development (USAID).[126] This was paralleled by a similar process of fragmentation within the Oil Spill Working Group, precipitated by Green Line's strong public critique of the participation of the politically affiliated *Bahr Lubnan*—an NGO formally linked to Rafiq Hariri's family—in the actual oil spill cleanup operations, which, it argued, should be the responsibility of the state. These public critiques not only disrupted the viability of the respective NGO coalitions, but they also had "a major effect" inside Green Line, symbolized by a dramatic increase in political and sectarian tension between the association's Christian, Sunni Muslim, and Shi'a Muslim members; "it was a mess," noted one of Green Line's executive members.[127] Indeed, in the wake of the July 2006 war, Green Line found itself being increasingly labeled as a Shi'a association and charged with being affiliated with the March 8 political faction, accusations that contributed to a dramatic decline in its already weakened volunteer base.[128]

Paralleling the weakening of Green Line has been the shrinking of environmental advocacy networks outside the confines of the LEF. Though active into the 2000s, for example, the informal network of advocacy associations around Green Forum eventually petered out as Green Forum itself collapsed amid a range of personal and strategic disputes. As the network around Green Forum gradually dissolved, a new network cautiously began to take form.[129] Indeed, the group was described as having "really good synergy," having among its members an array of impressive activists on social and environmental issues, most of whom focused their energies on particular regions and localities. They met once a month and held the occasional workshop on such issues as capacity building and donor relations. They also were involved in limited policy advocacy—especially with regard to an ultimately ineffectual National Solid Waste Campaign launched in 2003. Yet, by and large, they acted cautiously and were wary of becoming too formalized and vocal lest they be "eaten by a big NGO."[130]

In the course of the tumultuous year that was 2005, however, a wider array of environmental activists, including those within this informal gathering, began to perceive the emergence of an opportunity to do more. The departure of the Syrians, for example, inspired some cautious hope that the political arena could open up in the country; "there's a new wind in the country," remarked one environmental activist.[131] Eager to position themselves within the newly emerging political arena, thoughts of "reintegrating" the LEF began to circulate within the environmental community—precipitated by the impending elections for its executive committee. It is here that the more destructive politicking began—exacerbated by the developing tensions in the broader political arena between the March 8 and March 14 camps. Initially, a series of negotiations between the old guard of the LEF and its challengers—most of whom were members of this successor to Green Forum—was held to try and create a shared list of candidates, negotiations that the "old guard" of the LEF rejected. This left little option but an electoral showdown between the two competing factions—a competition that quickly opened the door to an intense and politicized process that resulted in the reconsolidation of the old guard's power. There were a variety of dynamics that acted as institutional "feed-back mechanisms": the penetration of wider political struggles into the politics of the LEF, the mobilization of support around these nonenvi-ronmental political poles, and the neutralization and/or co-optation of more neutral NGOs in the electoral process as a whole. Indeed, an NGO representative active in the process pointed to clear cases of "manipula-tion on the inside of the LEF." Of the participants interviewed about the electoral process, all spoke of the elections as being dominated by com-petition between groupings of environmental associations affiliated with different national political figures—(Randa) "Berri's NGOs" versus "Bahia Hariri's NGOs," with "Jumblat's NGOs" acting as a kind of mediating force. While it is highly doubtful that the elections within the LEF actively interested these politicians directly—one activist remarking in response to my query in this regard, "Do you think they really care?"—what is nonetheless interesting about this LEF electoral process is the degree to which NGOs organized and spoke about the electoral competition in these terms. Indeed, by all accounts, the electoral competition was quite vicious—with LEF membership lists being increased at the last minute by the addition of "fictive" associations; with accusations of duplicitous politicking, particularly on the part of "Jumblat's representative," AFDC; and with the free flowing of vitriolic and politicized campaign rhetoric, particular among the various NGOs working in the Shi'a regions of the South.[132] Further paralleling the dynamics of elections within the Lebanese Women's Council, one of the younger NGO representatives also spoke of the existence of a generational dynamic, the old guard not wanting to give up their "posts and power" to a younger generation of environmental activists.[133] With the subsequent reelection of most of the old guard to the executive council—who promptly reelected the same president and secre-tary general who had held their posts since the mid-1990s—the attempt to take over and revive the LEF as an institutionalized platform from which to publicly promote environmental advocacy causes was lost. This engendered a significant degree of disillusionment and cynicism among the country's larger environmental NGO community, one describing the LEF as "a hopeless cause," with others deciding to withdraw from active national advocacy work altogether.[134]

Further debilitating the work of environmental activists was the withdrawal of the MOE as an active agent of advocacy within the Lebanese public sphere. Indeed, after its period of intense NGO-like collaboration with environmental associations during the period of the Chehayeb ministry, the MOE has become increasingly closed to the environmental NGO community itself, removing a crucial political intermediary in its attempts to access the state. Because it is a weak "second-tier" ministry—it having few services to deliver and few benefits to offer during elections—the ministry has usually been relegated to an opposition politician from one of the smaller confessions. Chehayeb was no exception to this rule—except that he rode on the coattails of his communal leader Jumblat's attempts to regain a seat at the center of political power in the country. As a result, both before and after Chehayeb, there has been a parade of lesser ministers of the environment, none of whom has stayed for long and few of whom have had any experience in environmental matters. Hence, with the brief exception of the Chehayeb period, the MOE has not had any significant energy or political weight behind it. This resulted in what one UNDP official described as "the non-lobbying power of the Ministry of the Environment" and eventually led the UNDP, once the main donor partner of the ministry, to move away from it as its main environmental focal point.[135]

Its more restricted approach to environmental associations, however, stemmed from bureaucratic developments within the ministry itself—namely the appointment by the Hoss government of a new director general (DG) in 1998. A young and talented professional with scientific expertise in the field, the new DG assumed his post determined to transform the MOE into a professional and "system-based" one, thereby increasing its influence beyond its weak position within the state.[136] When he first joined the MOE in 1998, for example, he described it as "a wreck."[137] There were only thirty-one employees (up from the thirteen that Chehayeb had inherited), with only one designated position for an environmental scientist. By 2003, there were fifty-two employees, and these were joined by an additional fifty temporary project staff and/or consultants who were externally funded by the World Bank, the UNDP (Capacity 21), and the European Union (Management Support Consultant Program [MSC]) and many of whom came with strong scientific training in such fields as hydro-geology, toxicology, and environmental engineering. This set the stage for "a very intensive time within the ministry" that consisted of formulating draft laws and draft implementation decrees on such matters as environmental impact assessments (EIAs), sectoral environmental assessments (SEAs), draft laws for such sectors as quarries and solid waste management, establishing the legislative requirements for compliance with international environmental conventions, as well as further reformulating a broader and overarching Code of the Environmental (444), all of which, if accepted by the Lebanese state, would have transferred significant authority to the ministry.[138] By 2003, the MOE also was moved from its original and slightly marginal location in Antelias in East Beirut to the Beirut downtown central district, making it in theory much more accessible to central decision makers and the general public.

Most relevant for the relationship between the MOE and environmental associations, however, were the efforts of the DG to root out corrupt practices from within the ministry—a campaign whose origins paralleled the "anticorruption" campaign of the Hoss government. He noted, for example, that "a good 50 percent of what I do is fight corruption."[139] He correctly surmised, for example, that most NGOs had connections to the ministry in the past via "patron–clientelist ties"—many of which were cultivated through a small grants program that had been run out of the small ministry budget and distributed on the discretion of the minister himself. As a result, the grants program was promptly canceled, leading to a dramatic drop-off in the ministry's ties with the NGO community. Indeed, one environmental activist described the ministry as being regrettably "absent" from the activist work of NGOs in the environmental field and, at times, hostile to it.[140] This anticorruption vigilance also led the MOE to become increasingly closed and bogged down in administrative and procedural delays; "it's a bottleneck," I heard over and over again with respect to dealings of both NGOs and foreign donor agencies with the MOE, with one commentator going so far as to remark that it has become like "a prison, *haram*. It's becoming a Syrian regime!"[141] All of this has created a dynamic whereby an increasing number of NGOs and foreign donors have avoided working with the MOE altogether, encouraging an already strong tendency in the foreign donor community to distribute development finance in the (often patrimonial) manner that they see fit. In short, efforts to systematize the operations of the MOE and, in effect, shield it as much as possible from the damaging effects of the penetration of political interests into its affairs have had a paradoxical effect on its position within the environmental policy domain. On the one hand, the MOE has successfully begun a process of professionalizing its work; on the other hand, the approach has seen the withdrawal of the MOE as a central, public, and political actor in environmental policy advocacy. For advocacy NGOs, this has resulted in the removal of a crucial node in the environmental policy network, one that helped both to unify the environmental advocacy field and to provide it with channels of access to the state in the "golden age" of the 1990s.

Hence, environmental activists have seen the gradual weakening of the various platforms for environmental advocacy that had emerged in the 1990s. Once-prominent advocacy NGOs have struggled to survive in the face of debilitating political divisions in the country. Promising advocacy networks and coalitions also have shrunk in size and ambition, contained by networks of clientelized environmental associations that have penetrated the advocacy field and, through the LEF, monopolized its institutional center. Finally, the MOE, having briefly emerged as a unifying force for environmental advocacy in the 1990s, has withdrawn from politicized advocacy work. All of these developments have resulted in the considerable shrinking and scattering of opportunities for environmental advocacy in the post-Chehayeb era. Rather than representing the death of environmentalism in the county, however, Lebanon has seen the rise of more hybrid forms of environmental advocacy, ones that, although promoting environmental sustainability, do so from within the prevailing clientelist political order of the country and in ways that strengthen—rather than stretch—its logic. It is to the emergence of those instrumentalizing environmental networks in Lebanon that we turn our attention now, first examining the consolidation of a factional network around Chehayeb before analyzing the broader use of environmentalism in the field of conservation as a mechanism for consolidating control over both land and politicized territory.

*Consolidating the "Chehayeb Network": From AFDC to the*
*Creation of the Lebanese Green Party*

Most of the NGOs and civil associations in postwar Lebanon have been the product of the political and social structures that surround them— whether created by or affiliated with structures relating to class, community, or clan. These have been joined by a small minority of associations that have tried to free themselves from these structural surroundings and work to promote social and political transformation. In the environment, this group was represented by NGOs such as Green Line, many of whose membership looked on environmentalism as offering a new way of doing politics and, potentially, of reviving the left. In the middle of these polar types of associations exist a third—NGOs with a foot in both camps, being both professionalized service delivery and policy advocacy associations with significant degrees of technical expertise while also maintaining strong links to powerful elements within the country's political society.

In the environmental sector, the Association for Forests, Development, and Conservation (AFDC) clearly represents an example of this

hybrid, Janus-faced NGO. From its humble origins in the town of Ramliyya in the Chouf region in 1994, AFDC has grown to become a dominant NGO player within the forestry and conservation sectors as well as
within NGO networking more generally. In 2008, it was able to support
a professional staff of more than twenty employees, including a full-time
fundraiser, most of whom were based in its headquarters in downtown
Beirut. It also supported four regional centers in the Shouf, Jbeil, Akkar
in the North, and Hasbiyya in the South, all of which sustained a volunteer base of about 300 individuals. Facilitating AFDC's growth has been
its ability to attract foreign donor funds—particular after the war in the
summer of 2006, when the size of its budget increased considerably from
U.S.$500,000 to U.S.$2 million. It has partnerships with a diversified number of large donors—from the EU-Life Program, to USAID, to Coopera-
zione Italiana, to the World Bank, to its traditional donors such as the
World Wildlife Fund, and it has gained a reputation for its ability to win
contracts in a competitive bidding process. The core of its work has been
in local reforestation,[142] and its greatest policy-level success has come in
the area of forest fire prevention. This was precipitated by a serious outbreak of forest fires in the country in the summer of 2007, ones that led
to the MOE hiring AFDC as the coordinator of the National Campaign
on Forest Fire Prevention. AFDC also acquired—indeed, was the only
NGO to do so—a seat on the Inter-Ministerial Committee on Forest Fire
Management. Moreover, even after the formal dissolution of that committee in 2008, AFDC staff continued to play a lead role, establishing and
helping to equip an "operations room" designed to coordinate forest fire
emergency responses. Remarked AFDC's executive director in 2008, "we
are coordinating all of the efforts."[143]

This was unprecedented access to a state decision-making process
for an NGO—parallel to that granted to Arc en Ciel in the field of disability examined below. How did AFDC manage to get its foot inside the
policy-making and implementation door? A series of interrelated factors
were at work here. First, AFDC's case was strengthened by the experience
it had gained over a number of years in the area of forest fire prevention.
In addition to its work on the ground, which included the training of
volunteer firefighting units, AFDC also had produced a "fire risk" map in
2004—in collaboration with Green Line—that turned out to be remarkably accurate during the forest fire crisis of 2007. This had impressed
Prime Minister Fuad Siniora and helped to open the door to collaboration with AFDC. Indeed, it also was the view of officials within the MOE
that AFDC had built up a significant degree of expertise on the issues of
forest fires in the country—especially in relation to the appalling lack of
knowledge of responsible Lebanese officials. As the DG of the ministry

commented with respect to AFDC's success, "it is not all about advocacy and activism. You have to supplement it with sound scientific judgment, research, you name it."[144]

However, AFDC also had clearly reached this stage because of its links with Chehayeb and his broader Druze political networks—though it also has spent much energy trying to dispel the notion. "AFDC is not Druze, AFDC is not PSP, AFDC is not Akram Chehayeb," stressed its former and long-standing executive director—adding that transcending AFDC's confessional origins had always been "a strategic imperative" if it wanted to grow, work in all of the regions, and have "added value" at the national level.[145] Nonetheless, the existence of some kind of relationship to these networks has always been apparent. While dispelling its confessional origins, for example, it was clear that Jumblat was supportive of AFDC "from the beginning." Indeed, Chehayeb was appointed AFDC's first president as a way to "protect the association from Jumblat and his people," implying that a more independent association would have had a difficult time surviving in the Aley/Shouf region.[146] The relatively monolithic influence that the Jumblat network held over the Shouf region also provided AFDC with a secure institutional base, something that contrasted with other regions, especially in the South of the country, where intense political competition between political factions often squeezed NGOs out.[147]

However, AFDC's embeddedness within the broader political networks of the Shouf region not only provided the association with a stable base of protection, but they also facilitated its work in the environment as a whole. While AFDC has never received any direct assistance from the Lebanese state for its regional centers, for example, it has received assistance in kind in the form of the provision of electricity, water, and roads to its centers—classic forms of political patronage in Lebanon. Moreover, it also is clear that its ambiguous arm's-length relationship to Jumblat's political network did not hurt the ability of AFDC to attract external assistance—particularly from more politicized external donors such as USAID, which, in the wake of the July 2007 war, was eager to support the March 14 faction, of which Jumblat was a leading member at the time. Most importantly, however, AFDC has been able to capitalize on political connections wielded by Chehayeb and Jumblat to gain access to those with decision-making power in the regions where they have wanted to work as well as with the central state itself. Indeed, the former executive director of AFDC spoke of having "over-exploited Akram's connections." His successor was even clearer about the benefits of using these political connections: "Why not use politicians to do your agenda? Why not? The main objective is conservation," adding that "you have to take them as major partners. . . . Anywhere you go, you can't do anything without

the permission of this political guy. So, either we sit and don't work or
we build alliances with them in partnership. . . . Of course, it's not the
perfect situation but at least it makes you move and makes you work."[148]

Are there limits to the extent to which Chehayeb's network will go to
promote environmental causes? Are they constrained from going "to the
end," as Abu Khalil remarked with respect to the Chehayeb ministry itself?
On the one hand, the network has used its prominence to play a significant role in campaigning on several environmental issues, especially with
respect to quarrying and solid waste management where AFDC acted as
the co-chair of the national NGO campaign, and hunting where it spearheaded the passage of a new—though unenforced—hunting law. AFDC
itself adopted the role of mediator within broader environmental NGO
networks—playing an important if not more ambiguous and opaque role
with respect to the failed attempts to revitalize the LEF. Finally, members
of the executive of AFDC also featured prominently in the 2008 revamped
executive of the Lebanese Green Party, initially dormant after its creation
in 2002. In short, it is clear that the network of environmentalists around
Chehayeb have positioned themselves to play a central and nodal role in
the country's environmental policy domain.

On the other hand, there also are signs that "the Chehayeb network"
was not as inclusive a network structure as it had appeared. Having once
collaborated together on a significant EU-Life project, for example, relations between AFDC and Green Line considerably soured, a deterioration
that coincided with the ascension of Jumblat into the ranks of the governing March 14 coalition after 2005 against which Green Line was seen as
politically hostile.[149] Neither has the opaque politicking of AFDC during
the LEF elections endeared it and the broader "the Chehayeb network"
in the minds of independent, nonaffiliated environmental associations.
Perhaps muddying the waters the most, however, was the strategic decision to create "its own" Green Party. Musings about creating a Lebanese
Green Party had circulated in a variety of associational and political
circles in the postwar period. Principle among its civil society advocates
had been Habib Maalouf, one of the founders of the Matn-based Committee for Environment and Development, a critically minded journalist
on environmental matters for as-Safir newspaper, a driving force behind
Green Forum, and a self-proclaimed leader of "the environmental left" in
Lebanon. Never convinced of the long-term efficacy of Green Forum and
of NGO advocacy more generally, Maalouf had always set his sights on
the creation of a Lebanese Green Party. Complicating that goal, however,
had been the preemptive decision by Chehayeb to form his own, and
Lebanon's first, Green Party. To Maalouf and others within the environmental sector, the decision was a clear attempt at both capitalizing and

keeping close tabs on the environmental movement as a whole—pushing the "troublemakers" such as Maalouf to the sidelines.[150] While efforts were made to bring Maalouf and other active environmentalists back into the party, they were rejected in light of the party's dubious origins and unclear political relationships. It was impossible for environmentalists to imagine, for example, that the party could be independent of Jumblat[151]—a conclusion that a visiting delegation of the German Green Party also was said to have reached.[152] Moreover, as Maalouf remarked in highlighting its ambiguous status as "a party within a party," there was the further question of its relationship to the PSP.[153] Further muddying the waters was the party's relationship to the March 14 movement. The final nail in the coffin for Maalouf, however, was the party's opaque links to the interests of "capital" and, in particular, to Sukleen—symbolized by the appointment of Phillip Skaff, the president of an advertising company responsible for promoting Sukleen's public relations campaign, as the Green Party's president in 2008.[154] This also was questioned by an executive member of the Green Party itself, who expressed concern that Skaff's appointment had come about as a result of a series of mutually beneficial yet hidden exchanges, especially for Sukleen, which had been eager to sanitize its problematic image.[155] Concluded the executive member, "it's business," adding that "nothing is transparent, nothing is clear, nothing is proper . . . it's unfortunate. There are people who simply want money. There are people who work for another goal. . . . [But], there are few people who work for the environment."[156]

Hence, there has been a gradual but significant realignment of environmental advocacy in postwar Lebanon. Environmental platforms emanating from politically unaffiliated sources have dramatically weakened, replaced by the emergence of platforms embedded within the political structures of the country. While they have garnered the cooperation and collaboration of NGOs within the field, they also have constrained them, seen most clearly in the influence that "the Chehayeb network" has established within broader advocacy circles. However, what is perhaps most interesting about the emergence of the Green Party is the degree to which it has garnered the participation not only of those associations directly affiliated with Chehayeb, such as AFDC, but also of a wider array of associations and actors within Lebanese civil society as a whole. As such, "the Chehayeb network," given its capacity to bridge divides between civil and political society, has emerged as a subtle but effective instrument of political hegemony in the country—on the one hand, promoting environmental causes in alliance with a variety of civil society actors yet, on the other, clearly doing so within a broader confessional political framework. As such, it must be understood more as a mechanism to modernize and

strengthen the existing political structures in the country rather than one
that could challenge them politically.

*Land, Territorial Control, and the Politics of Conservation in*
*Postwar Lebanon*

Encroachments by elements within Lebanese political society into the
country's environmental policy domain have been particularly evident in
the sub-environmental field of conservation. Initially, the emergence of
a conservation movement in Lebanon, though rooted in activities that
predate the postwar period,[157] owed its origins in the postwar period to
the work of a few dedicated individuals and NGOs. We have already
mentioned the pioneering work of Ricardo Haber, whose activism led to
the creation of the first of many protected areas in the country. This was
joined by the networking abilities of Assad Serhal, long-standing director of the Society for the Protection of Nature in Lebanon (SPNL) and
first president of the conservation-oriented LEF, who orchestrated the
arrival of a Global Environmental Facility (GEF) project, administered by
the IUCN and the UNDP, designed to promote the creation of a more
sustainable and institutionalized system of grassroots conservation in the
country.[158] From these early days of the postwar period, conservation-
oriented associations and initiatives have subsequently flourished, ranging
from the protection of the beautiful Matn-based Jabal Mousa by a wealthy
industrialist,[159] to the regeneration of the 'Ammiq wetlands in the Western
Beqa by the Skaff family in cooperation with an international Christian
conservation NGO,[160] to the resurrection of the traditional *Hima'* system
of regulating land use by the SPNL,[161] to the promotion of sustainable
local development in the remote, tribal areas of the Jourd in the north-
eastern region of the Beqa by a Beirut-based NGO called Mada (examined
below). Facilitating these initiatives has been donor financial and technical
assistance, all of which has led to the proliferation of conservation projects
and various kinds of natural reserves throughout the country.

However, before making pronouncements about the apparent success of advocacy efforts in the field of conservation, it is essential that
the analysis be placed in the broader political context of one simple question—why have elements within Lebanon's elite political classes become
interested not only in supporting the work of conservation associations
but also in actively participating in conservation initiatives themselves? I
propose three ways of answering this question, each of which points to
the instrumentalization of conservation for broader political goals. First,
conservation-oriented environmental advocacy does little to constrain
general processes of economic accumulation by the country's postwar

economic elite; at best, it promotes the creation of "islands" of conservation in the larger sea of "generalized constructability."[162] This limited reach
of conservation activities is accentuated by the fact that much of the land
designated as protected has been public land anyway, land that is limited
in quantity and that entrepreneurs have no legal right to develop. Second, conservation has proven to be a useful way for powerful politicians
and landowners to reconsolidate "sovereignty" over local territory—while
attracting the financial support of foreign donors in the process. Previous analysis of the GEF-funded protected area project in the 1990s, for
example, reached the conclusion that rather than promoting "grassroots
in situ biodiversity conservation," the project facilitated the emergence
of "environmental monopolies," especially in the Barouk reserve in the
Shouf region, which, though public land, also lies within the political
realm of the Druze leader Walid Jumblat.[163] Conservation also has proven
useful for landowning families interested in reestablishing control over
their estates and the villages that surround them. In that sense, conservation must be seen as part of broader efforts to consolidate the territorial power bases of certain "family systems" in the country.[164] Finally, the
politics of conservation in postwar Lebanon also must been seen as part
of a wider sectarian competition for land, one commentator referring
to the "systematic buying of land" by a variety of communal parties.[165]
This communal dimension to the land question has deep roots in the
country, linked both to the high inelasticity for land in the first place
as well as to the long-standing fear of the political implications of land
purchases by foreigners—from fear about land purchases by Palestinians
in the prewar period that led to the adoption of a complete ban on land
sales to foreigners in 1969, to fear of intensified foreign land speculation,
especially from the Gulf region after the Hariri government reversed the
ban in 2000, to concerns about the purchase of land by Hezbollah.[166] In
response to these emerging fears, "conservation alliances" have begun to
emerge in the postwar period, designed to create territorial buffer zones
between the encroaching communities.

A case in point is the emerging conservation regime around the
'Ammiq wetland in the West Beqa. Traditionally, the land in the vicinity
of the 'Ammiq wetland had been cultivated by tenant farmers and/or used
for grazing goatherds. During the war, cultivators and herders progressively began to encroach on the land closer to the wetland itself, in effect
"nibbling" away at its viability and destroying its natural role as a water-
accumulating "sponge" for the land around it.[167] Concern about these
developments were first raised in the mid- to late 1990s by an expatriate
British high school science teacher in Zahle who had been using the wetland as a field site for his students and who, with eventual support from

an international Christian conservation NGO called A Rocha, embarked upon efforts to convince the local community to save it. These efforts soon encountered serious political resistance. First, while the wetland was predominantly the property of the Skaff family, long the leading family in the West Beqa region, there were fifty-four other smaller landowners with a stake in its future, something that complicated negotiations over the establishment of a conservation regime immensely; indeed, the A Rocha representative described these negotiations as being, at times, "almost impossible." Even more challenging was the existence of a "Mafia-like" corruption ring in the estates around 'Ammiq that had emerged during the war and that involved collusion between stewards, tenant farmers, and goat grazers aimed at squeezing more production out of the land beyond the terms of the existing contracts with the landowners. It was the resultant expansion of cultivation and grazing that contributed to the destruction of the 'Ammiq wetland. Michel Skaff, the Skaff family member most concerned with the affairs of 'Ammiq, spoke of there being 10,000 heads of sheep and goats on land with a capacity for 3,000 during the war.[168] The most serious obstacles blocking the establishment of a conservation regime around the wetland, however, were the links between the "Mafia-like" corruption ring and broader political networks associated with both the Syrian Social Nationalist Party (SSNP) and its Syrian protectors. Indeed, when the A Rocha representative and the Skaff family began to talk about promoting conservation around the 'Ammiq wetland, opposition quickly emerged from within these rival networks. Efforts were made, for example, to belittle and mock the conservation initiative in the eyes of the local communities—it being described as "a typical feudal initiative" aimed at taking land away from farmers and giving it "to birds," and there were further efforts to link the water-saving purposes behind the initiative to efforts to enhance the flow of water to Israel, the mention of which, noted Michel Skaff, was "an open license to kill."[169] Indeed, there were attempts on the lives of both Michel Skaff as well as the A Rocha expatriate representative himself. Through connections with the SSNP, there also were efforts to bring the Syrians, whose relationship with the Skaff family had been tenuous at best throughout the war and postwar period, into the fray.[170] By 2000, however, after three years of tense maneuvering, Skaff "cut the head" off the corruption ring. With its members reputedly fleeing to Syria, an opportunity for the launching of a broader set of conservation initiatives was now open.

One of the most interesting aspects of these subsequent conservation initiatives was the way in which they revolved around broader goals of strengthening "the family system" of governance within the West Beqa region. Citing the apparent success of American strategies in the Sunni tribal regions of western Iraq after "the surge" in 2006, for example, Skaff stressed the importance of working with existing local authority structures such as the family as a way of stabilizing and improving local governance systems. In the context of West Beqa, he believed conservation-related initiatives could promote this agenda in three distinct dimensions. Of crucial importance was the way in which conservation-related ideas provided a justification for the "disciplining" of relations with those who worked on their estates, ejecting grazers and tenant farmers who were not from the area and/or not supportive politically and putting in place measures to improve the cultivation regime for those who remained.[171] This allowed the family to regain "the upper hand" on their estates—not by "crushing" the users of the land, noted Skaff, but by showing them a bit of generosity, an approach that placed them "100 percent under your control at the end of the day."[172]

Second, environmentalism and conservation also could be useful in extending the regional influence of the family. For example, Skaff spoke of establishing programs of environmental governance in the wider set of villages beyond their estates—including anything from the establishment of regional grazing corridors, to the promotion of eco-tourism, to the improvement in solid waste management facilities. As a way of facilitating these visions, Skaff entered into informal negotiations with a variety of foreign donors such as the World Bank to find financing—all of which was designed to strengthen a locally generated and family-centered model of governance. "In the absence of policy [and] in the wider absence of government," noted Skaff, "you are inclined to go along with these lines, generating your own ways of governing your region." For Skaff, crucial to this vision was the promotion of "sustainable development." "It's not just about buying land," remarked Skaff. "I tell the children—buying land you've got the deeds, legal things. This gives you 50 percent of the ownership. The full ownership is when you exercise authority on the land, what you call sovereignty . . . even if the land is not yours." Added Skaff, "the secret of success is not to get greedy. In the family system, everybody needs to eat."[173]

Finally, Skaff spoke of strengthening the family system in the area through the establishment of conservation alliances. The core alliance was between West Beqa and the Shouf—between the Skaff and the Jumblat clans—that Skaff remarked resembled the "small Lebanon" prior to the 1920s, with attempts at forming a parallel alliance with the Franjieh clan in the Zghorta region, where the protected area of Horsh Eddin is located. Symbolic of the interconnectedness of these alliances was the appointment of Skaff to the boards of a variety of environmental associations affiliated with Jumblat and the Shouf, such as the Arz as-Shouf Society of Jumblat, which managed the Barouk Protected Area; the Lebanon Mountain Trail Association (LMT); and the Green Party itself. Helping to further seal these emerging alliances has been donor support, the most significant being a project to develop networks of technical cooperation between nature reserves in the country, supported by a 1.4 million Euro, three-year grant from the Agence Francaise de Developpement in 2008. On the one hand, these alliances are aimed at improving technical environmental cooperation across related eco-zones within the Mount Lebanon region. On the other hand, however, they harbor a deeper sectarian logic, Skaff speaking of conservation as a way of giving one "presence" in an area in ways that can fill in "the gaps" between rival political factions, especially in the region of Jezzine on the southern edge of the Shouf, described as "very politicized" in terms of the competition for land between four major communities.[174] While the politicized purposes of these alliances were articulated with great caution,[175] it was nonetheless clear that conservation has emerged as an interesting layer in the broader sectarian political game, providing the Skaff family and its allies with a publicly oriented discourse through which to promote their factional goals; as Skaff remarked himself, it provided "a soft way" to their achievement.[176] Herein lies an excellent example of the ways in which environmental discourses, resources, and actors have been absorbed by those representing existing political structures in the country and used to rejuvenate and reinforce their positions of dominance, all the while promoting compliant forms of conservation. In effect, it is a case of patrons using—and promoting—environmentalism to strengthen both their relationship with their clients and as well as their broader territorial "sovereignty."

Whether clients—or the NGOs that represent them—can use environmentalism to strengthen their bargaining position with patrons, however, remains a more difficult proposition in postwar Lebanon. One final case study in the conservation field—which concerns an association called Mada—is particularly revealing of these dilemmas facing NGOs interested in promoting socioeconomic and political change. Mada described itself as a nonaffiliated environmental organization committed to promoting sustainable economic relationships between local communities and their environment. It also has been committed to long-term partnerships at the local level and is guided by principles of openness and dialogue, transparency, an acceptance of diversity, nonsectarianism, and the promotion of a culture of human rights. As a result, Mada has targeted some of the most isolated and vulnerable communities in the country—first, the al-Jourd region of northern Hermel, and, subsequently, the more isolated areas of Akkar, which is the poorest region in Lebanon. Finally, Mada has been committed to being a creative, learning, and democratic association.

Its first members were described as being "highly motivated volunteers coming from all over Lebanon and sharing the idea that Mada should not be an NGO like the others and should keep experimenting [with] new ideas and practices." In one of its self-assessments, it also described itself as creating "a space for constant learning [and] reflection." Hence, as one former board member remarked, there was something "unique" and "unbelievably interesting" about its approach to the environment and its understanding of ecology, adding that "no one on the board [really thought] in terms of classic development thinking." [177]

Mada was born out of a yearlong camping expedition in the al-Jourd region of Hermel in the late 1990s by its two founders, during which excellent contacts were established with the local population—a complex mix of internally competing Shi'a tribal groups and smaller Sunni families. Upon returning to Beirut, they were determined to support the local development and environmental protection of the area and decided to launch an innovative project—creating both an NGO (Mada) and a private local company (al-Jord) that would collaboratively launch and manage a series of development and eco-tourism projects. The purpose of the initiative was to improve the local livelihoods of people in the area while at the same time preserving its "exceptional environment." They wrote of trying to exploit its "natural, historical, cultural and aesthetic resources . . . in a non-aggressive, eco-touristy way allowing for projects that are both income generating and sustainable." While recognizing that the project would result in the integration of the region into "a wider global economic system," Mada nonetheless remained committed to the creation of "an independent local economic system capable of sustaining and managing its own development." In keeping with the principles of local development and ecological sustainability, Mada would be a share-holder in al-Jord, thereby ensuring influence and accountability over the latter's policies as well as access to its profits—profits that would then be reinvested to promote local sustainable development and human capac-ity. It was hoped, hence, that while the two entities would have different "missions," they would share the same overall "vision."[178]

In the early stages of the initiative, Mada implemented a number of projects, many of which were designed to enhance the profile and repu-tation of the company al-Jord itself—establishing, among other things, a small chicken farm, a pilot project in organic farming, the promotion of honey production, the opening of several wells, and the renovation of a small, local café. In its report on its experience in al-Jourd, Mada remarked that, initially, it felt it had been successful in introducing into the community "a sense of the importance of their environment as a capital asset in the future development of the area." Moreover, with respect to the company al-Jord, in the early years of the project, investors were lining up to offer their support. However, the project quickly unraveled, and for interesting reasons that cut to the heart of the difficulties of promoting local development in areas where the state's presence is weak, if nonexistent. According to Mada's analysis, for example, it became clear that its partner, majority owner of the al-Jord company, did not share the same values of local development or the same respect for legal agreements. Instead, he operated according to a "tribal" logic—using both the company and Mada's presence in the area to aggrandize his own power and that of his clan within the broader but weakening tribal system, whose unifying structure had begun to disintegrate in the wake of the dislocating effects of the civil war. The result was clashes on numerous issues between Mada and its local partner in al-Jord—the latter using the company to expand the clan's private land ownership, open up a sand quarry that Mada described as "an environmental crime," ignore an agreed-on transfer of land to Mada needed for a development project, and, most disconcertedly for Mada, manipulate the distributional benefits of some of the development projects (such as fruit tree planting and road building) for the purposes of demonstrating and exerting clan power, something that Mada argued revealed "the realities of a vulnerable population oppressed and unable to fight for its rights." Representatives from Mada also referred to the emergence of a fundamental conflict between "modern institutional management based . . . on specific ethical principles and a tribal culture of power and violence." Unable to find a successful mediated solution, Mada eventually pulled out of the project and filed a lawsuit against the company, the purpose of which was "to set a precedent" in the area and make "a clear statement" to the community that development in the area can only proceed if the rule of law—rather than that of clan and tribal power—is applied.[179]

What the "rule of law" would actually mean in the context of Lebanon's weak state and strong sectarian system, however, was not entirely clear—something that was to become increasingly apparent to Mada as it pursued its second major environmental initiative—the creation of a national park in the northern Lebanese region of Akkar. Like in al-Jourd, Mada's staff worked patiently and assiduously in the area over a number of years, conducting studies on such things as the region's biodiversity and socioeconomic status and cultivating dialogue with the various local stakeholders on key issues related to the establishment of a national park. This time, they targeted the fourteen municipalities in the designated area of the projected national park, some of which they had already made contact with as a result of their previous initiative in al-Jourd. As one of Mada's founders remarked, this was a refreshing change from past experience, giving them "legally recognized legal partners" with which to work as opposed to the "tribes and gangs" of the al-Jourd region.[180] Moreover, capitalizing on their extensive knowledge of the area, Mada began to act as a "clearinghouse" to which interested donors could turn for information and advice in finding appropriate local recipients and projects for its funds. Mada also set itself up as a kind of "platform" on which local fledgling associations could lean for support. The result has been the proliferation of a series of socioeconomic activities and projects in the area since Mada's arrival—based on "the participatory approach." In short, Mada began to emerge as a vital "development node" in the area. Remarked one of Mada's staff, "we're present, we're there, and we're not related to project cycles."[181] This, in turn, contributed to the cultivation of strong, trust-filled, and increasingly institutionalized relationships between Mada and a number of key municipalities in the area—evidenced by the signing of agreements of protocol with four of the municipalities, the creation of a technical committee on which sat all of the mayors, and the establishment of a "charter" in which the overall goals associated with the establishment of a national park are articulated. Finally, Mada also has begun to act as a mediator between the local municipalities and the state—establishing contact with and lobbying the CDR, the MOE, and other authorities with partial and overlapping jurisdiction over the area. Of key concern were the questions of land use, land tenure, and their relation to both the timing and content of a "national park" designation. The CDR has been a particularly crucial "network" link for MADA in this regard, helping it to promote its national park idea with both donors and the state and acting as a conduit through which Mada also can make contact with and lobby "the political class."[182] Interesting, Mada staff also argued that this explicit relationship with CDR has bolstered the credibility of its own association and of its project of creating a national park within the local communities and municipalities.[183]

However, Mada's project for a national park in the north eventually stalled—facing two principle dilemmas that symbolize the challenge of doing development and advocacy work in Lebanon. These challenges relate to the fragmentation of both society and the state and the resultant prevalence and power of informal political dynamics. These first arose with respect to the long-standing disputes between the two main communities in the area over land ownership in what is supposed to be the "core" area of the national park—disputes caused by the confused state of the region's land registration records for both public and private land. One Mada staff member described there being a "long trail" of documents—many of them false—and unresolved court cases, a situation that has been complicated by the unilateral occupation and cultivation of land

by groups allied to Syrians during the civil war.[184] Mada tried to act as a
mediator between these competing local groups—paralleling their unsuccessful experience in al-Jourd—but, given the periodic outbreak of violent
hostilities, the challenge of promoting social dialogue and peace has been
clearly beyond that which a single NGO can solve.[185] It needed the intervention of a powerful external actor like the state that could introduce
institutionalized and unified frameworks through which local disputes
could be mediated, if not resolved. In short, Mada needed the Lebanese
state to act as a "third-party enforcer." The problem for Mada, however,
was that it was not clear which portion of the state to "bring in." Ideally,
Mada wanted to empower the relevant and formal public authorities such
as the CDR and the MOE—having them agree on a formal designation
for the national park that would facilitate the resolution of land disputes
in the area, if only by declaring much of the land public. Yet the process
of involvement, particularly of the MOE, has been tentative, reluctant, and
contradictory—one Mada staff member going so far as to describe these
more formal bureaucratic arms of the state as being "scared" to get more
fully involved in the area.[186]

The real problem, however, was that the formal bureaucratic apparatus was not where the real power within the Lebanese state lay. Rather,
for Mada to have power, it needed to hook up with the myriad informal shadow networks associated with class, community, and clan, which
meant that "bringing the state back in" required Mada's engagement with
these more powerful, informal, and ultimately less accountable political
forces. Eager to promote genuine grassroots ownership of local environmental initiatives, jealously protective of its associational autonomy, yet
cognizant of the fact that its initiative to create a national park in the
Akkar region needed political support and protection, Mada, in dialogue
with the local municipalities in the area, entered into the process of deciding how it would "go political," or, in other words, which political leader
and network in Lebanon it should approach for support and/or protection. What emerged as the most realistic, but also problematic, option
was to approach the Sunni-oriented Future Movement of Sa'ad Hariri.
Mada staff, for example, believed that there were a number of factors that
could make this an interesting proposition for Hariri's Future Movement:
it could provide some political benefits, given their interest in consolidating stronger clientelist ties with Sunni population of the area, something
that the municipal leaders in the area of the national park all recognized;
most importantly, however, allocating a "reserve" to Hariri would fit into
the sectarian logic of postwar Lebanese politics—providing Hariri with
his own environmental "piece of the patronage pie." As one of Mada's
staff members remarked, if Hariri adopted the Akkar national park as

his own, "then everyone could have a park in Lebanon. Jumblat has his, Nabih Berri has his. OK, let Hariri have his. Just take it. Why don't you have a park for the Sunni people? . . . He's the only political leader that doesn't have a protected area."[187]

Here is the dilemma for nonaffiliated advocacy associations in Lebanon in a nutshell: Lebanon clearly offers space for individuals and associations to formulate and promote progressive, equity-oriented discourses and projects. In the fields of conservation and the environment, Mada represented one of the best, with its emphasis on promoting locally owned processes of sustainable development in the context of its overall critique of classic development thinking and practice. Yet Mada's experience also taught them some important cautionary lessons. The first related to the danger of reifying "the local," where even the most remote local actors and arenas are implicated in—if not instrumentalized by—the broader and fragmenting political dynamics in the country. The second concerned the need for a broader overall framework for grassroots environmental work than an NGO could provide. This, however, often required establishing a relationship with political forces that worked in a hierarchical and subordinating fashion, one at loggerheads with Mada's own principles and goals. While Mada did claim to have worked "with big NGOs with sectarian/political goals . . . whilst trying to protect [itself] from their policies,"[188] how such a relationship could be negotiated and sustained in practice and over the long term to the benefit of the local population and the environment in the Akkar and without strengthening the kind of hegemonic political dynamics that are antithetical to these goals remained to be seen.

## Conclusions

Once a stunningly beautiful country, Lebanon has witnessed a dramatic deterioration of its environmental heritage and resources over the last few decades. Its mountains are being slowly eaten away by the persistent proliferation of unregulated quarrying; its fresh water resources and coastline are being constantly threatened by the inability of the state and industry to adequately regulate the discharge of hazardous waste materials, most of which flow untreated into the Mediterranean Sea; and, outside Beirut, the country is awash with unregulated solid waste dumps, the most notorious being the mountain of waste that continues to blot the coastline of the city of Saida. Adding to this mix of environmental degradation is the reduction in Lebanon's forest cover, which has been exacerbated by the prevalence of forest fires in the hot summer months; the unrelenting and unplanned construction of buildings throughout the country, especially damaging along the Mediterranean coastline; and the unchecked increase in levels of air pollution caused by effluences from industry and the disproportionately high and increasing number of automobiles in the country. For a small country with densely populated urban areas, this level of environmental degradation is unsustainable.

On the surface, the Lebanese state has not completely ignored the issue of environmental degradation in the post–civil war era. A MOE was created early in the postwar period, various environmental conventions have been signed, and the state has entered into many co-financing arrangements with foreign donors on development projects with an environmental focus. Yet what has not emerged within postwar Lebanon is a defined and institutionalized environmental policy domain within which a clear set of rules has been agreed upon that can structure policy deliberations and guide policy implementation. Rather, the policy-making process within the field of the environment remains fragmented and deeply penetrated by informal networks of power linked to community, clan, and class. The result has been the almost complete immobilization of the Lebanese state when it has come to regulating and, by implication, constraining the accumulative unruly clientelistic practices of the country's elite networks of privilege.

In the postwar period, an impressive array of environmental associations have tried to rectify this situation by sparking advocacy and public action campaigns on a variety of local and, in some cases, national environmental issues. These associations also began to coalesce into a number of associational networks, each competing to influence the emerging environmental policy-making apparatus of the postwar Lebanese state. Further aided by well-placed colleagues within the Lebanese media and universities, the burst of activism by the MOE in the late 1990s, and the support of environmental advocacy networks at the global level, Lebanon's coterie of environmental activists succeeded in catapulting environmental issues, discourses, and norms into the mainstream of Lebanon's postwar public sphere. Indeed, given the ability of many of these environmental associations and networks to sustain these activities in the face of the challenges and political upheavals of the post-2000 era, it can be argued that they have contributed to the partial institutionalization of the country's emerging environmental policy domain—one in which the unruly clientelist practices of Lebanon's postwar elites had to contend with at least normative challenges at a discursive and deliberative level emanating from components of the country's civil society.

Yet efforts to further the process of consolidating and institutionalizing Lebanon's emerging environmental policy domain have been stymied by the "veto" power of the country's political elites, who, in the name of preserving factional rights, have used their asymmetrical power to out-network environmentalists and block their efforts to constrain their own accumulative practices. At the policy level, for example, political elites have effectively mobilized their intra-elite networks and alliances—often extending transnationally from Damascus to beyond—to block efforts to establish more stringent environmental rules. This is symbolized most profoundly by the difficulty in promulgating an overarching Code of the Environment, let alone establishing clear rules with respect to such activities as Environmental Impact Assessments and quarrying. Political elites also have systematically subverted and/or exploited the inflow of external donor assistance in the field of the environment to strengthen their own factional political power. The misuse of donor finance was seen most clearly in the solid waste sector; its instrumentalization most clear in the emerging geopolitics of conservation, linked as it was to the consolidation of political control over territory. Finally, and of greatest relevance for the arguments of this book, political elites have penetrated deep into the life of civil society, using their asymmetrical power to plant their own associational representatives, build their own networks of politically compliant environmental associations and political parties, and divide and weaken the advocacy efforts of their rights-based associational rivals. While, on the one hand, this has resulted in the partial "greening" of elite clientelist networks, on the other hand, it has resulted in the transformation of many environmental components of civil society into mechanisms for the reproduction of communal, clientelist, and class power. Hence, while environmental advocacy associations have been pushing for a unified and rules-based environmental policy domain, the dominant thrust of civil society in the environmental field has facilitated the efforts of the country's elite political class to capitalize on the advantages of environmentalism to strengthen their own factionalized bases of power while keeping its rule-bound imperatives at bay.

# 6

# Chehabism from Below?

## *Disability Advocacy and the Challenge of Sustaining Policy Reform*

"Why should the handicapped always have to beg? Why shouldn't it become a right?"[1]

Lebanon has become the home to one of the most vibrant disability sectors in the Middle East. Paradoxically, it was a sector that only began to develop more fully out of the ravages and disabling effects of civil war. Supported by the rise of a global disability movement that was itself spearheaded by the rising consciousness of people with disabilities themselves, several disability advocacy networks emerged within wartime and postwar Lebanon, all seeking to build an institutionalized national policy domain within which a rights-based disability policy framework could be promoted. As with activists within the women's and environmental fields, all looked to the Lebanese state as the locus of their reform efforts—hoping that the postwar period would provide opportunities to reform state institutions and, in particular, social policies as they pertained to people with disabilities. Indeed, with the creation of a policy deliberation council on which people with disabilities were represented, the implementation of a service delivery program designed to provide technical aids on the basis of "rights" rather than "belonging," and the passage of a comprehensive law on disabilities whose norms mirrored those within relevant international conventions, it appeared that associational activists within the disability field had succeeded where other associational advocacy movements had failed—in effect, creating a policy framework for a rights-based disability policy domain from scratch.

Sustaining these reforms, let alone expanding on their success, however, has proved to be an exercise in frustration. Material resources have been scarce in the public realm, limiting the capacity of the state to follow through on its commitments to the delivery of such basic life-giving needs as technical aids to people with disabilities; and state capacity has been limited, especially with respect to its ability to mainstream new disability policies across its various ministries. The most formidable obstacles, however, have been political. On the one hand are Lebanon's political class, who, for the most part, remain uninterested in the task of formulating national social policies in such areas as disability, preferring instead to instrumentalize distributions in the social field for their own particularist political advantage. On the other hand lie many of the large social welfare and disability institutions, variably linked to the main confessions or political parties of the country, that have been able to instrumentalize the sectarian dynamics that underlie the preexisting social policy framework of the state in ways that allow them to carve out a claim to a portion of state resources and fend off challenges to their autonomy from competitors and reformers. In short, this case study of disability politics provides paradigmatic examples of two central arguments of this book. First, it clearly reveals the existence of asymmetrical power relations within Lebanese civil society, symbolized here by the power disparities between disability advocacy networks and confessionally linked disability institutions. Second, it reveals the degree to which the sectarian political framework in Lebanon is instrumentalized as much by elements of civil society as by elements within political society, thereby contributing to the reproduction of a weak and fragmented disability policy arena.

The chapter is divided into three sections. The first examines the historical roots of Lebanon's disability policy domain as it entered the postwar period—roots that have long generated powerful dynamics leading to the exclusion and marginalization of people with disabilities in the country. The second section analyzes the rise of disability advocacy networks, ones that revolved around two, sometimes competing, subnetworks, both of which sought to take advantage of the perceived opportunities of the emerging postwar period to advance policy reform and reshape the Lebanese state in the social welfare field. It was as a result of these efforts that the more formal institutional parameters of Lebanon's disability policy domain were created. The third section documents the resilient, hegemonic power of informal sectarian dynamics, instrumentalized and reproduced as they were by the powerful elements within Lebanese civil and political society. The chapter concludes by arguing that while significant successes have been achieved at the levels of both policy discourse and social awareness, particularly among people with disabilities themselves, rights-based institutional reform at the national level remains at best piecemeal and precarious, subject to constant contestation from the resilient hidden networks that surround them.

## The Historical Roots of Lebanon's Disability Policy Domain

Increasingly large proportions of peoples with disabilities are living in the developing world. It is further estimated that people with disabilities are among the poorest and most marginalized of its population groups.[2] In her study as part of the Disability Knowledge and Research (KaR) Programme in the United Kingdom, Rebecca Yoe argues that people with disabilities are "overrepresented among the poorest of the poor," and estimates further that more than 10,000 die every day of extreme poverty, a situation which she argues is "the inevitable and logical result of existing global relations."[3] A recent report by the World Bank on disability within the Middle East and North Africa (MENA) region offers a similar portrait of people with disabilities as being poorer as a group than the general population, more likely to have income levels below the poverty line, and less likely to have savings and other assets. It further describes people with disabilities in the MENA region as having higher illiteracy rates, poorer nutritional status, and higher rates of unemployment and underemployment, and stresses that the situation is particularly bad for women with disabilities. Finally, it argues that individuals living in poverty are more at risk for becoming disabled than the non-poor. In short, the World Bank report concludes that people with disabilities in the MENA region are often trapped in a "life-long cycle of poverty."[4]

Why are so many people with disabilities among the poorest of the poor? One the one hand, KaR argues that it is difficult to establish exactly what the linkages are between disability and poverty, writing of them as being "deceptively complicated."[5] Part of the complication emanates from the challenges of defining terms such as disability and poverty, both of which are highly contested. Moreover, the linkages between disability and poverty can be particularly difficult to pinpoint given the manner in which disabilities cut across all societies.[6] Not only can the costs of having a disability vary depending on such factors as class, age, ethnic status, and especially gender, but they also can vary from disability to disability. Seddon and Lang, for example, refer to the existence of "a social hierarchy of impairment" in which those who are physically impaired (and male) often dominate the access points to the market, state, and international development apparatuses—a reality symbolized by the omnipresent use of the wheelchair as the symbol of the disability movement.[7] In recognition of the "misleading and monolithic" nature of the term "the disabled," which implies that disabled persons are all "the same," Oxfam has recommended that the category of "the disabled" be disaggregated.[8]

Yet, despite these complex challenges of analysis, the KaR Programme nonetheless writes of there being "ample evidence of the interconnected and multilayered symbiotic relationship between poverty, impairment, and disability."[9] This section examines three interconnected frameworks for understanding the persistent marginalization of peoples with disabilities. These revolve around the questions of social attitudes, capitalism, and the state—especially with respect to the latter's ability to promote a transition from "charitable" to "rights-based" systems of social welfare. People with disabilities, for example, have faced long-standing discriminatory social attitudes, ones often reinforced by traditional religious and familial social institutions. Research on the treatment of people with severe intellectual disabilities in the premodern Middle East, for example, reveals horrendous cases of inhumane practices by religious authorities.[10] While such official practices have long disappeared, the religious realm continues to treat people with disabilities in a discriminatory and paternalistic manner. During an early postwar symposium on "Disability and Religion" hosted by a disability nongovernmental organization (NGO) in Beirut, for example, that was attended by clerics of the main religious communities in Lebanon, Nawaf Kabbara, a physically disabled activist about whom we shall hear much more, argued that the continued inaccessibility of the vast majority of churches and mosques was proof that Lebanon's main religious leaders were not yet open to accepting the disabled in their midst "as human beings." Further troubled by the notions of "charity" and "care" that permeated religious discourse, Kabbara challenged religious leaders and institutions by asking them whether they were capable of adopting "the speech of rights and push[ing] it further all over society to raise the cause of disability from the level of care and shelter to that of integration and participation."[11] Also coloring attitudes toward people with disabilities have been systems of family honor. One scholar of disability in the developing world and the Middle East writes of "Arab culture" treating disability as "shameful, an ordeal to be endured by the family," something that often resulted in Arab families "fail[ing] to admit that they include a disabled person for fear that this would be considered a disgrace and lower the family's standing."[12] Girls and women have been particularly affected by these discriminatory family attitudes.[13]

Powerful though these attitudes have been and still are, however, it would be misleading to label them as "traditional." For example, the same cultural and religious traditions that have given rise to these attitudes may also carry within them discursive resources that can be used to challenge negative attitudes toward people with disabilities.[14] Moreover, research on the preindustrial world has described people with disabilities as often being "embedded" in their societies and, hence, able to participate "to varying degrees" in a wide variety of economic activities, especially with respect to rural production, which was described as allowing disabled people "to make a genuine contribution to daily economic life."[15] Finally, marginalizing attitudes toward those with disabilities also have been embedded within modern, medical approaches toward questions of rehabilitation. By defining disability as being the result of a physical impairment alone rather than as something caused by the sociopolitical context, for example, "the medical model" has served to reaffirm attitudes that look upon people with disabilities as being "broken," "victims" of tragic circumstances and "objects of pity."[16] Indeed, given the pervasive power of the medical model within the disability field, these attitudes have not only contributed to the paternalistic structuring of rehabilitation services in ways that "exact control over the lives of disabled people,"[17] but they also have had a hegemonic influence on the consciousnesses of people with disabilities themselves, leading to situations in which they have participated in their own "internalized oppression."[18] Hence, while the application of the medical model has certainly "made important contributions to the care, training, and opening up of new opportunities for people with disabilities in the developing world," it also has been done in ways that have kept them separate, excluded, and marginalized from society.[19] In short, despite improvements in the medical treatment of impairments, "modern" disability policy domains continue to be penetrated and underpinned by powerful and long-standing attitudinal forces that reinforce processes of marginalization.

A second school of thought within the field of disability studies links the persistent socioeconomic marginalization of people with disabilities to the worldwide growth and penetration of capitalist markets. It has been modern capitalism, argue Marta Russell and Ravi Malhotra, especially its emphasis on the commodification of labor with its parallel demands for such physical qualities as speed, strength, and dexterity, that has led to the systematic socioeconomic marginalization of disabled people, forging "a break with the slower, more self-determined and flexible work pattern into which many disabled people had been [previously] integrated." This, they argue, has made disabled people "less fit" to do the industrial tasks at hand and relegated them "to the bottom of the market."[20] Hence, "just as capitalism forces workers into a wage relationship, it equally forcefully coerces disabled workers out of it."[21]

Many disability scholars do not accept this direct relationship between capitalism and the poverty and marginalization of the disabled.[22]

Nonetheless, that people with disabilities are by and large excluded from labor markets in developing countries remains an irrefutable reality and something that the KaR Programme concludes was one of the principle reasons for their marginalization.[23] In Lebanon, for example, statistics compiled for the Population and Housing Survey in 1996 reveal a horrendous picture of exclusion. Almost 42 percent of people with disabilities were unemployed, more than seven times the rate of unemployment in the general population, and even these statistics were regarded as understated, given the high rate of "discouraged workers" (defined as those who have stopped looking for work altogether) who were "overwhelmed by the obstacles they face in getting a job."[24] Moreover, women with disabilities were described as facing "double discrimination" given their already low rates of participation in the labor force, and in a further discouraging finding, it appears that younger disabled people have had a more difficult time finding employment than their older counterparts.[25] Of those select few who do have stable jobs, a significant number are self-employed, a situation that, it was argued, also points to "the inaccessibility of the disabled to the mainstream labour market."[26] Further indicative of the "precarious nature" of economic opportunities for people with disabilities in Lebanon is the fact that very few of those employed seemed to have access to or can earn enough to pay into the National Social Security Fund (NSSF or *daman*), one of the only (and increasingly inadequate) sources of social protection in the country, accessible only to those working in the formal sector.[27] This has had particularly serious implications for poorer families having to make "catastrophic health payments" as a result of the emergence of family members with disabilities, contributing to a broader dynamic in Lebanon of "health-induced poverty."[28] Finally, and consistent with the more general trend in other developing countries toward the "informalization of labor," it is clear that most employed people with disabilities in Lebanon have been forced to find their niche in the informal sector, which offers very low pay and low security. One Lebanese study revealed, for example, that more than 60 percent of disabled income earners it surveyed were being paid less than the (already low) minimum wage, a situation that worsened with the dramatic slowdown in economic growth in the late 1990s.[29] In short, the nature of the labor market in Lebanon, embedded as it is within the country's laissez-faire economic system, generates powerful mechanisms of exclusion for disabled people. With growing pressure from the global arena to preserve and deepen Lebanon's laissez-faire economic system, symbolized by myriad project and trade agreements signed by Lebanon in the postwar era with Western bilateral and multilateral organizations such as the European Union, the World Bank, and the World Trade Organization, disabled groups are concerned that such potentially disabling dynamics emanating from the external push to open up Lebanese markets further are only likely to become stronger.

With the marketplace proving to be a fundamental barrier to the socioeconomic inclusion of people with disabilities, what has been the role of the state? Has it been able to become the lead actor in constructing a more rights-focused policy domain for people with disabilities? In the West, for example, it is clear that the basic livelihood of people with disabilities has improved dramatically with the emergence of autonomous welfare states. Not only have they formulated more progressive laws and policies, integrating peoples with disabilities into modern rights-based systems of welfare provision, but they also have worked to find a balance between institution- and community-based approaches to rehabilitation. In short, modern welfare states in the West have been "third-party supporters" for emerging disability activists, acting at times as an ally in their struggles to secure their full rights as citizens.[30] In much of the developing world, however, disability policy domains are underpinned by weak states (and politically penetrated markets) that remain embedded within resilient social structures linked to class, kinship, and community, a condition described by social policy experts as "negative permeability."[31] In his work on the challenges of constructing rights-oriented welfare state regimes, for example, Geof Wood argues that states in much of the developing world are not "impartial," cannot act as third-party enforcers, and are often instruments of "dominant classes and segments . . . [that] see state control as a crucial means of their own accumulation and reproduction." In these situations, argues Wood, it is unlikely that the state will create "corrective" social policy mechanisms that can compensate for its own failings, let alone those of the market, a reality that explains why debates between those determined to construct a more rights-based social policy regime quickly move to discussions about the role that civil society actors can play in compensating "for the inequities of the state."[32] Consistent with the arguments in this book, however, Wood further argues that, to varying degrees, civil society turns out to be equally embedded within these same penetrating structures of class, kinship, and community—a parallel form of "negative permeability" that complicates visions of a progressive civil society compensating for the inadequacies of the market and the state.[33] Hence, rather than seeing the emergence of "welfare state regimes" prevalent in developed countries, many developing countries witness the emergence of "informal security/insecurity regimes" in which social welfare provision is fulfilled by a diverse set of actors and institutions often operating on the basis of a informal clientelist logic that tends to be highly personalized, segmented, preferential, discretionary, subordinating, and sometimes predatory.[34]

Although these informal security/insecurity regimes are able to provide some welfare protection, they have several drawbacks. First, the acceptance of welfare security from these channels by the poor comes at the cost of their "adverse incorporation" into webs of clientelist relations, creating forms of "dependent security" that are "mediated through relationships of power and inequality" and that "foreclose future options for autonomous security by reproducing limited room for maneuver and limited choice."[35] It is what Wood calls the "Faustian bargain" that provides the poor with contingent security while generating longer-lasting sociopolitical dependence.[36] Second, because they are grounded in asymmetrical power relations, these patterns of social provisioning are characterized as much by exclusion and marginalization as they are by contingent inclusion, generating insecurity as much as security.[37] Finally, because they are "shaped" by and "intimately linked" to specific historical processes that often find their origins in colonial patterns of governance, these particularist and inequitable patterns of social provisioning have become institutionally "sticky" and resistant to change and reform, reproduced by socioeconomic and political elites determined to preserve the clientelist status quo in the social policy domain and prevent the state from formulating and enforcing new viable alternatives.[38] In short, efforts to construct more disciplined, rights-based social policy domains within many developing countries (under which disability policy usually falls) have to deal with the reality of numerous preexisting and historically entrenched clientelist networks that subordinate their welfare clients and "negatively" permeate the state in order to diffuse attempts to construct more centralized and coherent social policy fields.

The Lebanese system of welfare provision—to which people with disabilities are subject and on which they depend—falls squarely into this model of an "informal security/insecurity regime." First, the limited role of the Lebanese state in the social policy domain has its roots in the late Ottoman and French mandate period. The Ottomans, for example, had traditionally limited their social expenditures, with the social welfare field being mostly urban based and carried out by local charities, religious foundations, and foreign missionaries.[39] This began to change during the mandate period. First, the size of social provisioning by the state increased dramatically, "if still insufficiently," channeled into the increased subsidization of schools, hospitals, public health facilities, and campaigns targeted at such things as the regulation of food vendors and public baths.[40] Indeed, pushed by exponential increases in public demand for social welfare goods—the mandate state being described as "a magnet" for a multitude of republican-based social demands—Lebanon witnessed in the period between the two World Wars the emergence of a distinctly "colonial" welfare state.[41] This meant, however, that the provision of increased social welfare was not based on a rights-based social contract "binding state and society" together in a mutual commitment to higher taxes, but on a more fleeting arrangement funded by the influx of "stopgap" revenue from the metropole aimed at forestalling demands for independence. Second, instead of placing the state at the center of this emerging system of welfare provision, the French approach essentially subsidized the myriad and increasing number of private social welfare institutions embedded within networks linked to clan and community—in effect, consolidating a distinct system of welfare pluralism that bore close resemblance to models discussed above of "informal security/insecurity regimes." Indeed, fueled by an asymmetrically structured process of "triangular bargaining" between French officials, clientelist elites, and subaltern movements, this emerging "paternalist" system of welfare pluralism during the mandate period—complete with its subordinating consequences for a variety of subaltern social groups, including the disabled—was described as becoming increasingly "cast in stone."[42]

It was not that efforts to build up a more viable state-centered system of social welfare provisioning in the country were absent. During the Chehabist era in the 1960s, as we have seen above, a host of social institutions were created that revolved around the Office of Social Development, complete with a system of regionally based Social Development Centers (SDCs), the National Social Security Fund, in addition to national hospitals and the Lebanese University. This was accompanied by a significant increase in state expenditure in the broader area of socioeconomic development as a whole that added up to close to a third of the country's national revenue in these sectors—a percentage equivalent to that being spent in neighboring Syria at the time.[43] In the post–civil war era, the creation of a separate Ministry of Social Affairs (MSA) in 1993, along with the emergence of some institutionally separate foreign-funded social welfare programs, have added to this mix. These were to be backed up by the creation of an overarching Economic and Social Council within which would be represented substantive participation from civil society.

Yet, these initiatives and institutional developments have not altered the prevailing pattern of social welfare provisioning established during the mandate years. First, the role of the Lebanese state within the social welfare field remains limited and constrained. For example, there has been no concerted effort to formulate a viable social policy for the country in the post–civil war period, Myriam Catusse calling it *une question residuelle* for the most of the major political parties and political elites.[44] Symbolic of this has been the proliferation of numerous studies on the social sector, carried out by a confusing array of different institutions and financed, for the most part, by foreign donors—none of which has been able to offer "a global perspective" on the country's social problems.[45] Neither has the newly created MSA—described as a "middle level ministry" with a relatively limited budget[46]—been able to take a lead role in the social policy field. An overwhelming proportion of its budget, for example, has been historically predetermined, locked in by a series of contracts with the large social welfare institutions that are continually renewed and never put out to tender or subjected to monitoring exercises.[47] Indeed, a report for the European Union's Economic and Social Fund for Development (ESFD)—administered within the CDR and not the MSA—estimated that more than 50 percent of state expenditure on social welfare was channeled through private sector institutions, an amount that was, it argued, in comparative terms "extremely high."[48] Hence, the role of the MSA in the social welfare field has been extremely limited and constrained, confined for the most part to the more traditional task of subsidizing the work of private institutions while offering at best only limited, piecemeal, and short-term needs-based assistance to "the collateral victims of development," such as orphans, delinquent children, women, and the disabled through its various regionally based Social Development Centers (SDCs).[49]

The dominant actors within the social welfare sector remain the intermediary social welfare institutions, the vast majority of which are linked to clan and community. Indeed, as we have discussed above, the war and postwar periods have seen a relative explosion of the number of these institutions that has overwhelmed the nascent influences of the previous Chehabist reforms. Because the vast majority of these institutions are financially independent and, hence, autonomous from the state, it has been virtually impossible to devise mechanisms to coordinate and regulate their activities. Western donors, as a result, have been highly critical of the fragmented nature of the country's social welfare regime, one characterized by a lack of legal and administrative clarity and coordination between the myriad of institutions that make up the sector.[50] Indeed, as Rana Jawad concludes in her study of "welfare particularism" in postwar Lebanon, "everyone does their own social policy"—a reality that results in each institution deciding where to locate its social welfare institutions and to whom to deliver its social welfare benefits.[51] It has been the social welfare institutions rather than the MSA, for example, that determine which patients have access to its institutions, and it is the social welfare institutions rather than the MSA that determine their own criteria for care, despite musings by the MSA about devising universal standards.[52] As a result of this highly fragmented social welfare policy domain, the quality of social welfare services has been highly variable and their distribution throughout the country highly uneven, concentrated for the most part in the Beirut and Mount Lebanon regions of the country and severely lacking in areas such as the Beqa and Akkar, a pattern that has been particularly pronounced with respect to institutionalized service provision for the disabled.[53]

However, perhaps the greatest consequence for equitable social welfare delivery in the country has been the effective "veto power" that the powerful networks of familial and communal social welfare institutions have had over efforts to reform the system. When he was the United Nations (UN) Development Programme/World Bank adviser on poverty to the MSA, for example, Adib Nemeh experienced this veto power firsthand in reaction to proposals being formulated after 2000 to redirect MSA's funding away from institutionalized care for children and toward increased MSA subsidization of family-based care—something that had been called for by the UN Convention on the Rights of the Child, which the Lebanese government had ratified. Despite efforts to preempt potential opposition through a process of prior consultation, however, these proposals elicited a vigorous and comprehensive countercampaign on the part of the large, sectarian-based institutions that included their collective institutional lobbying at the highest levels of the state. Delegations were sent to meet with and lobby Hariri, Berri, and much of the religious leadership of the country, and press statements were released accusing the World Bank of forcing sectarian-based institutions to throw poor children out of their institutions and onto the street. Not surprisingly, the combined effect of this campaign was to force the minister to put a "freeze" on the entire reform-oriented planning process.[54] "It is a very, very fragile equilibrium," notes Nemeh, in recognizing the extreme sensitivity of the various sectarian social service networks to challenges to their autonomy, adding that it was this fragmented structural reality within the country's social welfare sector that made it very difficult to "change anything."[55] An EU report on Lebanon's social welfare regime concludes much the same, arguing that the resistance of "entrenched institutional political-sectarian influences" will make "even minor reforms concerning one or the other of the many different institutions dealing with social affairs very difficult to get adopted and implemented."[56] Hence, disability activists working to create a community-oriented and rights-based disability policy domain in postwar Lebanon face a formidable array of normative and institutional obstacles. Similar to the dynamics within other policy domains, such as that relating to women and the environment, a crucial aspect of these obstacles is represented by the long-standing recursive dynamics between certain components of political and civil society—in this case, between the Lebanese state, the MSA, and the numerous social welfare institutions with close ties to the various confessional communities and political parties. Protected by their implicit "veto power," these dynamics have served to preserve the autonomy of the latter and reinforce the fragmentation of the broader social welfare policy domain.

However, as argued all along, these dynamics are not all encompassing and provide spaces for "restricted forms of agency." What follows is an examination of how they emerged within wartime and postwar Lebanon within the field of disability and the effect these agents had on the construction of a more defined and rights-oriented policy domain. There were several factors that helped to forge political opportunities for disability activists. The first was the rise of the global disability movement, initiated by people with disabilities themselves. It not only led the way in promoting new norms within the disability field grounded in a rights-based framework, norms symbolized by the 2006 ratification of the UN Convention on People with Disabilities, but it also offered support—both material and moral—to emerging associational actors within Lebanon. This assistance would prove crucial in helping postwar disability advocacy networks take advantage of the social and political space that was an inherent feature of the country's fragmented social and political environment. Spearheaded by the rise of associations run by people with disabilities, several disability advocacy networks—all sustained by partnerships and networks at the global level—emerged within postwar Lebanon working to promote normative, institutional, and legal change on which a new rights-based disability policy domain could be established. It is these networks, through the forging of strategic linkages with actors within Lebanese political society, that successfully pushed for the reform of state institutions within the disability field that the former hoped would transform the state into a "third-party enforcer" of the rights of disabled people in the country.

## The Rise of Disability Advocacy Networks and the Promotion of Rights-Based Institutional Reform in Postwar Lebanon

Political opportunities for advocacy can emerge in the unlikeliest of situations. This was certainly the case for those concerned about the plight of Lebanon's people with disabilities during its long civil war period. On the one hand, the civil war witnessed the virtual collapse of the Lebanese state, the immobilization of the Office of Social Development, and the destruction of the few rehabilitation institutions for people with disabilities that existed[57]—all this in addition to the disabling human effects of war itself. On the other hand, the war also had a paradoxical effect on the country's fledgling disability sector—one that led to the rise of disability advocacy movement in the country. After providing a brief snapshot of the disability sector on the eve of the postwar period, the section dives into an analysis of the efforts of these emerging disability advocacy networks. We first examine the emergence of a pioneering network of disability associations established during the civil war period and run by people with disabilities. Supported by the prior rise of a disability movement at the global level, these associations, through their participation in various antiwar campaigns, succeeded in giving peoples with disabilities a voice at the postwar disability policy-making table. This is followed by an analysis of the efforts of a second associational advocacy network made up of a small group of disability service providers who were eager to back up the call for disability rights with progressive, state-led programs of disability service delivery on the ground. Taking advantage of favorable political conjunctures in the early postwar period, this latter disability network was successful in carving out autonomous policy space inside the state within which to pursue its reformist agenda. Finally, this section analyzes the advocacy campaigns that led to the passage of a comprehensive law on disabilities in 2000 (Law 220)—a law that established the formal legal parameters of a new disability policy domain for the country.

*Out of the Disabling Environment of Civil War:*
*The Rise of Associations Run by People with Disabilities*

At the onset of the civil war, Lebanon's disability sector was rudimentary at best. At the core of the sector were a few large rehabilitation institutions embedded within the main sectarian communities of the country. These were joined by some long-standing disability institutions whose origins go back to Western missionary initiatives. Of more recent creation were a number of specialized, service-oriented institutions that began to emerge after the Second World War, ones that catered to each of the four main disability groups in the country (the deaf, the blind, the mentally challenged, and the physically impaired). It was these institutions, whose emergence by and large paralleled the Chehabist era in the country, that began to make more serious and professionalized inroads into the enormous challenges facing people with disabilities in the country. The civil war generated a new burst of disability institution building of all kinds. Some of these were linked to the various militia structures in the country—a prime example being the creation of the Lebanese Welfare Association for the Handicapped (LWAH) in 1985, which had direct ties to the AMAL Movement and would go on to play a decisive role in the early postwar politics of disability.[58] There also were a myriad of politically unaffiliated institutional initiatives motivated by humanitarian and professional concerns, such as Sesobel (1975) and Zawraq (1985), both established to cater to the needs of children with intellectual disabilities.[59] Finally, the war witnessed the remarkable emergence of new kinds of advocacy associations, run by and for peoples with disabilities, examined in more depth below.

Yet, despite this increasing institutionalization of disability services, the disability sector as a whole has by and large been characterized by the socioeconomic exclusion of people with disabilities in the country. First, entire regions of the country—particularly the North, the South, and the Beqa Valley—remained completely unserviced and, in effect, abandoned by the country's disability institutions. An employee with the World Rehabilitation Fund (WRF) in Lebanon, for example, remarks that the WRF was always finding new cases, "especially in remote areas."[60] The situation was particularly dire for Lebanon's Palestinian community, which was excluded from the services offered by both the OSD and the myriad of private social welfare institutions. Even in areas where one found a concentration of disability institutions, namely Beirut and Mount Lebanon, there was little to no outreach to families with disabled members in the communities within which they operated. The professionalization of the sector also was extremely limited, there being virtually no specialists in physiotherapy and/or occupational therapy in Lebanon at the start of the civil war.[61] Exacerbating these marginalizing dynamics within Lebanon's disability sector was the absence of any national policy, let alone national standards, for the provision of disability services, a reality that has left the institutions within the disability sector accountable to no one. Indeed, as funding for disability did begin to increase as a result of the civil war, accusations began to emerge that the recipients of this funding—most of which were the larger rehabilitation institutions linked to the sectarian communities—were treating disability as if it were "a lucrative business."[62] According to Lina Abou-Habib, Oxfam-UK's wartime representative in Lebanon, who had been active in promoting associations run by people with disabilities, the absence of mechanisms of accountability, let alone "clear human development goals," within the country's disability sector effectively left the disabled "at the mercy of the rehabilitation industry."[63]

A report written for the Middle East Council of Churches in 1983 on the services available to people with intellectual disabilities is extremely revealing of the dire situation that existed in Lebanon during its civil war years. At this time, there were an estimated twenty mental health institutions in the country—some with religious affiliation, others being founded on a more secular and volunteer basis, and none of which was regulated by the state. Indeed, Ali Dehbozorgi, the report's author, described the Office of Social Development (OSD) as having "no choice other than to accept just about anyone who intend[ed] to open an institution for the mentally handicapped."[64] This had a number of dire consequences. Diagnoses, for example, were done in an unscientific and "haphazard manner,"[65] and, consistent with the conclusions of Abou-Habib, he also pointed to evidence of increasing numbers of people, unchecked by adequate diagnostic procedures, being placed within disability institutions where they were subject to systems of "forced labour and virtual exploitation."[66]

The testimonies of people with disabilities in Lebanon attest to their frustrations with the exclusionary and exploitative environment that surrounded them. Sylvana Lakkis, for example, who was disabled by polio in her youth and who would go on to become the longtime postwar president of the Lebanese Sitting Handicapped Union (LSHU), expressed her frustration with the endemic levels of discrimination in Lebanese society—epitomized by her segregated education away from home and her inability to find employment despite advanced overseas university training in translation. "Every step of my life," argued Lakkis, "was a battle . . . to be able to live like other people. Nothing was easy. I was disabled and Lebanon was not prepared for people like me."[67] Further depicting Lebanese society as treating the disabled as if they were "a bag of potatoes," Lakkis would go on to dedicate her life to working in the public domain on behalf of people with disabilities.[68] Amer Makarem, who was blind since birth and went on to establish the pioneering Youth Association for the Blind (YAB) in 1988, expressed similar frustrations with his exile within specialized schools for the blind, ones that "cut [him] off from any meaningful contact with the world beyond the confines of the institution."[69] Pointing to this tendency toward separating people with disabilities from society as "the root cause of the problem," Makarem would dedicate his life and the work of YAB to promoting the "integration" and, as we shall see, subsequently the "inclusion" of the blind in Lebanon into the regular educational system.

In the West, things began to change in positive directions for people with disabilities in the 1960s and 1970s, changes that would later reverberate throughout much of the developing world. Leading the way were parents of the disabled and, most importantly, a self-help movement of people with disabilities themselves, who began to challenge the power structures that surrounded them and lobby to promote new norms around which questions of disability should be framed. For the disabled, for example, it was clear that "the medical model" had taken power out of their hands and put it into those of both the rehabilitation centers where many of them lived as well as the disability associations that were created, in theory, to represent them. As a result, in the 1960s and 1970s, people with disabilities began to act, challenging the hegemonic voice of medical professionals within the existing disability institutions and associations and forming their own "self-help" associations from which to lobby for recognition of their right to a voice. By the early 1980s, these tensions reached a boiling point, symbolized by a split within Rehabilitation International (RI), the most significant international disability association at that time, which led to the creation of Disabled Peoples International (DPI), an international advocacy association exclusively run by and for people with disabilities. Among the founding principles of DPI were that persons with disabilities had the right to influence all measures taken on their behalf, that all forms of segregation be ended, and that the system of isolating disabled people within institutions be rejected.[70] Diane Dreidger, DPI's historian of its formative years, described its emergence as being the result of the determination of the world's disabled to throw off "the yoke of paternalism and 'charity'" that surrounded them and "to wrestle power from those with money and technical resources who would not grant them control."[71]

The creation of DPI, along with the other uni-disability coalitions such as the World Blind Union, the World Federation for the Deaf, and Inclusion International, had a catalytic effect on movements of people with disabilities worldwide, providing encouragement for those interested in establishing both associations and multi-disability advocacy coalitions run by people with disabilities.[72] This facilitated a revolution in international funding for self-help initiatives that placed disability closer to the mainstream in international development policy circles. These developments were further buoyed by the UN decision to declare 1981 as the International Year of Disability, followed soon after by the designation of the decade that followed as the International Decade for Disability. Finally, it led to stronger representation of people with disabilities within international policy forums, especially within the UN. This gave disability activists the opportunity to lobby for a global redefinition of the meaning of disability away from its medical foundations toward one grounded in the reality of the disabling environments created by the sociopolitical context within which people with disabilities found themselves.[73] It was from these achievements that two further crucial developments flowed: the establishment of the World Program of Action (WPA), which Driedger described as "a declaration of emancipation for disabled peoples around the world";

and the formulation of the Standard Rules for Equalization of Opportunities for Peoples with Disabilities, which was ultimately adopted by the UN General Assembly in 1993—though only after some aggressive lobbying tactics on the part of disabled activists that included the storming of the UN General Assembly in 1987.[74]

As was the case with respect to both environmental and women's activism in postwar Lebanon, the timing of these developments at the global level opened up significant opportunities for disability activists within Lebanon who were facing a deteriorating situation as a result of the civil war—a beneficial conjuncture symbolized by the support of the emerging international disability advocacy movement for a peace march organized by people with disabilities against the Lebanese civil war in 1987. One of the organizers of the 1987 peace march was Nawaf Kabbara, a young academic from a prominent family in Tripoli who had been disabled in a car accident in 1980. Having returned from doctoral studies in the United Kingdom in 1984, Kabbara, appalled by the unending nature of the civil war, saw an opportunity for disabled people in the country to raise their own profile by contributing to, if not leading the way, in a broader civil society antiwar movement. Their first action consisted of a hunger strike at Green Line in Beirut in 1985—one that almost cost them their lives. Their second attempt, in October 1987—the organization of the four-day, three-hundred-kilometer antiwar march through all of the various militia checkpoints from the north to the south of the country (marching through the cities and traveling between them by car)—turned out to be wildly successful, especially given the dangerous context within which it was carried out. Having started with one hundred marchers (fifty of whom were disabled), they ended up with thousands cheering them on in the streets and hundreds of thousands more following their progress as a result of the significant media coverage, both nationally and internationally. Campaigning for the rights of all Lebanese citizens and not just those with disabilities, Kabbara described the march as "a turning point in the history of disability in Lebanon. At a stroke, we moved from being a marginalized group that has to be "looked after" to a political force to be reckoned with."[75] Though the effect of the march on the peace movement itself was fleeting, its effect on Lebanon's fledgling disability movement was long lasting. Not only did it succeed in putting "the disability issue firmly on the map in Lebanon,"[76] but it also helped to raise awareness among the country's disabled community itself. The story of Nabil Abed, for example, who went on to become a leading disability activist in the north of the country in the postwar period, is not an uncommon one. He described his participation in the 1987 peace march as changing his life, transforming him from a "nonchalant participant" in disability advocacy to a committed one, willing to dedicate himself "to living the problems of the handicapped."[77]

The peace march, in fact, turned out to be the tip of the iceberg, giving greater exposure to numerous grassroots initiatives and movements concerning people with disabilities in the country. Some of these initiatives emanated from the select groups of parents of children with disabilities who were angered by the institutionalized isolation and social marginalization of their disabled daughters and sons—especially with respect to their exclusion from the regular school system or their institutionalization in special schools away from home. In the midst of the civil war, some began to self-organize in pursuit of more humane solutions that could keep their families together. Mousa Charafeddine, for example, who became a leading activist on behalf of the disabled in the postwar period, described many parents of intellectually disabled children (of whom he was one) coming together at the grassroots level in order to establish day care centers.[78] While these were necessarily limited initiatives, constrained by the exigencies of war and having little finance, rudimentary facilities, and no accreditation, let alone assistance from the state, many have grown into significant and successful institutions. Charafeddine, for example, has transformed his fledgling Friends of the Disabled Association (FDA), established in 1978 in conjunction with a group of concerned parents, into a significant player in the postwar period, symbolized by the establishment of its center in the Chouf mountains (Mechref) in 1999.[79] In short, as was the experience within the West, select parents of disabled children began to emerge as pioneering agents of change during the challenging circumstances of the civil war in Lebanon, promoting the development of more accountable, humane, rights-based, and community-oriented services for people with disabilities in the country.

The most significant agents of change in wartime Lebanon, however, were disabled activists themselves. The war had resulted in an enormous increase in the number of disabled people in the country, many of whom ended up staying within one of the country's rehabilitation centers.[80] It was there that they, along with their civilian disabled sisters and brothers, experienced both the restrictions of institutionalized life and the hardships of life once discharged—the latter exacerbated by the absence of rehabilitation services that "went beyond the medical."[81] It was these frustrations, for example, that motivated the founders of the LSHU—the first association administered by and for people with physical disabilities in Lebanon, established in 1981. A volunteer, nonsectarian-based association with local branches in Beirut, Sidon, the South, and the Beqa, the LSHU has placed special emphasis on enabling "people with disabilities to speak on their own behalf to government and the public about their human

rights."[82] Its activities revolved around providing community-based rehabilitation (CBR) services by way of home visits, raising awareness among
the families of the disabled, and trying within the limited means at its
disposal to confront barriers to the participation of the people with disabilities within their local communities—efforts that included the development of sporting leagues for the disabled, including the first basketball
team for women with disabilities in the Middle East.[83]

Other successful associational initiatives followed. The Philanthropic
Association for the Disabled (PADC), now a thriving politically unaffiliated CBR center in Nabatiyya, was established in the late 1980s by four
individuals with disabilities who started with little more than their determination, a room donated by the International Red Cross, and "a Peugot
504." Armed with its own informal mapping surveys of the spread and
extent of disability in this much neglected southern area and supported
by a few strategic donors, it proceeded to establish a system of outreach,
bringing much-needed services such as physiotherapy to the doorsteps of
the disabled. Describing the demand unleashed by their initiative as intensive—necessitating their need to cooperate and refer cases to the larger
disability institutions in Tyre, Sidon, and later Sarafand, those involved
with the PADC initiative, with the crucial support of strategic donors,
were able to sustain their momentum and institutionalize their successes.[84]

Similar success stories also emerged in the underserviced northern
regions of the country. It was in Tripoli, for example, that Nawaf Kabarra
set up a branch of the Friends of the Handicapped (FOH) to promote
CBR, awareness raising, and lobbying through volunteer action. It was in
the latter that FOH excelled—the most successful campaign being that to
target the only rehabilitation institution in the North, run by the Social
Services Association. By all accounts, the conditions in its Abu Samra
Center in Tripoli in the late 1980s were horrendous—there being no heat-
ing, no hot water, little privacy in the vast dormitories, and little freedom
for what were termed "the inmates." Through a sustained and at times
confrontational campaign of advocacy—including the mobilization of disabled activists within the center, networking with civil associations within
the Tripoli area, and coordination with the local media, all of which was
said to have created a "furor" in a city already embroiled in civil conflict—the FOH effected significant improvements in both the governance
of the center and the conditions within which people with disabilities
within lived. These included the firing of its president and board chair-
man, the breaking up of dormitories to allow for more individual privacy,
improvements in the quality of food, the greater professionalization of its
services, and greater provisions for CBR. Indeed, in the postwar world,
the Social Service Association in Tripoli has been transformed into a

respected rehabilitation institution in the North, recognized by the MSA as a regional center for disability service provision and one with which FOH has now established cooperative relationships.[85]

Hence, Lebanon's wartime disability activists laid important building blocks for the emergence of a vibrant postwar disability movement. Through the establishment of numerous associations run by people with disabilities and through innovative and often courageous social action, they brought the issue of disability into the national spotlight, where it never had been before. Especially important in this regard was the opening up of possibilities and of hope within the consciousness of many people with disabilities and their families that they had an equal right to the benefits of Lebanese citizenship, challenging marginalizing attitudes long entrenched within Lebanese society. With the strategic assistance of wartime donors and supported by the rise of new movements of people with disabilities in the global arena, Lebanese disability activists also began to introduce alternative ways of delivering essential and basic services, based on models of CBR. Although the fledgling disability associations were only able to deliver these services in a piecemeal and localized fashion given the meager resources at their disposal and limitations imposed by the civil war, their increasing use and promotion of the discourse of CBR set the scene for the emergence of more energized debates over disability policy in the postwar period—ones that would pose serious challenges to the hegemony of institutionalized care provided by the large sectarian-affiliated rehabilitation centers that had long been supported in an unquestioned manner by the Lebanese state. As Kabbara remarked in explaining the sense of opportunity that resonated within disability advocacy circles on the eve of the postwar period, "there was now a disability movement to respond to."[86] It was in response to all of these accomplishments that Coleridge, in his comparative study of disability movements in the Middle East region and beyond, concluded that Lebanon's wartime disability activists had succeeded in constructing "one of the most vigorous and progressive disability movements in the region."[87]

The challenge, however, was to translate this grassroots and discursive success into influence and policy reforms at the national level in the postwar period. Indeed, with the creation of a separate Ministry of Social Affairs (MSA) responsible for disability policy in 1993, the establishment soon thereafter of a National Council for Disabled People (NCDP) on which associations run by people with disabilities were represented, the creation of a new program of service delivery to the disabled called the Rights and Access (RA) Program, and the subsequent passage by the parliament of a comprehensive law (Law 220) on disabilities in 2000, it appeared that disability activists not only managed to establish their own foothold within the administrative apparatus of the Lebanese state; they also were able to effect significant changes in the norms and policies that governed policy in the disability sector as a whole. What we turn to now is an examination of the complex and hidden dynamics that both enabled and constrained these policy initiatives in the early postwar period. This entails an examination of the emergence and struggles between competing policy networks within the disability sector and of the crucial role played by political actors in mediating between them.

*The Hidden World of Disability Governance: Competing Disability Policy Networks and the State in Postwar Lebanon*

There were a variety of competing disability policy networks in early postwar Lebanon, each with different structures, densities, and access to the political center. Two were "associative" networks—one being the cross-sectarian network of awareness-raising and advocacy associations run by people with disabilities discussed above, the other being a small, tight, like-minded network of disability associations, emanating from within the Christian communities of the country, whose emphasis was on establishing a better administrative framework through which CBR services could be offered. It was the latter that would turn out to be the driving force behind the formulation and implementation of the Rights and Access program. However, while both policy networks seemed to share similar values, they remained distinct in terms of their makeups, the resources at their disposal, and their ease of access to elements within Lebanese political society, all of which generated significant suspicion and tension between the two. Standing in the way of both policy networks was a third—one that bore a strong resemblance to the small, closed "policy communities" in the broader literature on policy networks as a whole—that consisted of the larger rehabilitation institutions determined to maintain the status quo that guaranteed them both preferential access to, albeit limited amounts of, state financing as well as autonomy from state regulation. Consistent with the findings of the literature on "policy communities," it was the institutions that made up this latter network—through their powerful alliances with actors within the Lebanese political arena—that would act as a major source of policy inertia.[88]

What brought these networks together into a more defined policy arena was the decision by the Hariri government in July of 1993 to create a separate Ministry of Social Affairs (MSA)—with designated responsibility for disability. This was followed by the decision of the newly appointed MSA minister, the former Lebanese Forces commander and instigator of the Sabra and Shatila massacres in 1982, Elie Hobeika, to create a twelve-member National Council for Disabled Peoples (NCDP).[89] What was novel about the NCDP was its inclusion of associations run by people with disabilities—the official makeup of the council being four representatives from the MSA, four from the rehabilitation institutions, and four from associations run by disabled people. The network of disabled activists looked on the creation of the NCDP—especially their own representation—as a huge success story, one for which they had long lobbied.[90] While they had initially been skeptical of trapping disability affairs within one ministry—wondering whether the establishment of a higher interministerial committee on disability would have given them more national exposure—they were nonetheless encouraged by the speed with which the initiative had been taken and by the surprising degree of interest and determination shown by their new "minister of handicapped affairs" in listening to the concerns of the various actors within the sector.[91] "[Hobeika] gave us a space," noted one disability advocate, who described the first few years of the NCDP as being "very exciting."[92] While having only advisory power, the NCDP—meeting twice a month for the first year of its existence—agreed to an ambitious reform agenda that included the initiation of a reformist project called the Rights and Access Program (RA) and the formulation of a comprehensive law on disabilities. Given the diversity of interests, the level of mistrust, and the power asymmetries sitting at the same NCDP table, these were significant accomplishments.

The first of these reform initiatives, the RA program, was envisaged as a comprehensive package designed, in the words of its creators, to build a disability sector based on "rights rather than belonging." One of the principle building blocks of the RA program was the disability card to be distributed to all people with disabilities in the country. Its purpose was multiple—designed both to facilitate the community-based delivery of disability services as well as to provide a means to build up a national base of statistics on disability. A second building block of the RA program was the development of administrative capacity within the MSA-NCDP. Using the statistical base provided by the information from the disability cards, for example, the RA program envisaged the development of a more accurate system of disability classification—one based not on medical criteria alone but one that also took into consideration the social and political context within which the Lebanese disabled lived. As one official in the MSA-NCDP remarked, what may be a slight impairment in a country like Canada may be a more serious disability in Lebanon. Indeed, the RA Committee within the NCDP at one point in its work had already identified more than 155 types of impairments—35 more than in the classification system of the World Health Organization.[93] A third building block of the RA program was the development of a system of standards—with respect to both technical aids for people with disabilities as well as the quality of rehabilitation services provided by the various disability centers in the country. One of the first initiatives in this regard was the publication of the *Dalil al-Khadimat* (Guide to Services) in 1998, a first step in providing Lebanon's disabled with the opportunity to make autonomous choices free from clientelist influences as to where they can find the best care. The final building block of the RA program was the decentralization of service delivery to the various regions of the country, thereby beginning the process of supporting CBR. In an interesting twist to the decentralization approach, the local MSA-NCDP centers were to be housed and run out of local disability NGOs rather than the local SDCs of the MSA itself.

The RA program, with its underlying philosophy of promoting CBR, represented, in theory, a significant challenge to the position of the large, communally affiliated rehabilitation institutions. The question is, how did it ever see the light of day, especially in the tense early postwar environment when sectarian suspicions were at their height? While the wartime network of disability advocacy associations run by people with disabilities did succeed in challenging the normative hegemony of the "institutionalized" and "medically oriented" system of rehabilitation in the country, it would be difficult to attribute the introduction of this program, except in the most indirect of ways, to their influence. Indeed, in the early postwar period, there were a number of factors that significantly weakened their network. The first were financial—exemplified by reductions in donor assistance, on which these associations largely depended. This financial situation was exacerbated by the difficulty faced by these associations in accessing finance through the MSA, let alone from Lebanese society.[94] Further compounding these challenges was the commitment of these associations to a comprehensive program of providing both advocacy and CBR services. Unable to support both, donors presented disability advocacy associations with some difficult choices: find ways to compensate for falling aid budgets through income-generating activities, implement strategic restructuring away from service provision toward advocacy, and/or establish mechanisms of coordination and cooperation among the members of the network as a way of both rationalizing service-provision activities and/or establishing a stronger collective advocacy voice. In response to these pressures, for example, FOH, after having failed in its efforts to implement several innovative income-generating schemes—such as the establishment of a telephone-request "White Taxi" service in Tripoli—was forced to dramatically reduce its activities in the early postwar period, resulting in a dramatic reduction in the number of paid employees in

1990, most of whom were disabled.[95] Finally, further limiting the impact of this network was the divisiveness and competition within it. Donors tried to reverse these fractious dynamics by triggering the creation of formal cooperation and coordination mechanisms. The World Rehabilitation Fund (WRF), Oxfam, and DPI were most active in this regard, funding workshops and conferences within and across the various disabilities as a way of rationalizing activity in the field and promoting professionalism and transparency—both of which donors viewed as being sorely lacking.[96] Yet these efforts ultimately proved unsuccessful. In fact, the once-unified wartime network has effectively split into two distinct subnetworks. One revolved around Nawaf Kabbara (FOH and the National Association for the Rights of the Disabled [NARD]), who took the lead in establishing the Lebanese Council for Disabled Peoples (LCDP)—a network of about thirteen disability NGOs officially affiliated with DPI; the other revolved around the figures of Sylvana Lakkis (LSHU) and Amer Makarem (YAB), who went on to establish the "Inclusion Network," which would win a significant World Bank grant in 2005.

Disability advocacy associations, therefore, sat down at the new NCDP table in a weakened position, especially vis à vis the network of large rehabilitation institutions whose dominant position within the disability field they were challenging. While continuing their bold critiques into the postwar period, disability activists were under no illusions as to their own influence, one describing the large rehabilitation institutions as being "very, very, very strong. They have money, they have traditions, [and] they have ignorance that support them—they have everything."[97] Indeed, in light of the political and religious support that they could call on, one UN adviser to the MSA in the 1990s described the network of rehabilitation institutions as being "more powerful than the minister."[98] Among the largest and most influential of the institutions was the Lebanese Welfare Association for the Handicapped (LWAH), which was directly affiliated with the AMAL Movement and run by "the Queen of the disabled," Randa Berri. Facilitated by its political connections at the highest levels that gave the LWAH political cover and often resulted in the MSA ministerial portfolio being given to AMAL-affiliated politicians, LWAH quickly became one of the largest disability institutions in postwar Lebanon, symbolized by the construction of its large rehabilitation center in 1996 on formerly public land at Sarafand in South Lebanon—one that disability activists sarcastically called "the city of the handicapped." An equally powerful disability player was Dar al-Aytam, one of the oldest and largest orphanages and disability institutions in the country that was run by Mohammad Barakat as part of the Social Welfare Institute. Barakat was a staunch defender of the need for institutionalized care for people with disabilities in Lebanon and often fought back at attacks by disability advocacy associations, arguing that they were all talk and no action—especially when it came to meeting the tremendous demand for rehabilitation services; "if you want to talk, go to Lakkis, Kabbara, Makarem, and Charafeddine. I have no time . . . as an institution to use our time and our system to go with them."[99] Not wanting to change the rules of the game and facing their own daunting postwar costs of reconstruction and renewal, disability institutions were angered by the attempt by the reformist disability NGOs "to steal their bread"[100]—one disability activist remarking in response to this antagonism in the early post–civil war years that, if funds from crucial foreign donors continued to fall, they would be left "shivering in the dark in front of tycoons like Berri and Barakat."[101] Hence, while continuing to be aggressive in their lobbying and advocacy campaigns, the network of advocacy associations run by people with disabilities recognized that it had little immediate political leverage. As Kabbara himself recognized, "we are weak. We cannot stop MSA from giving money to Nabih Berri's organization . . . nor," he added in reference to the significant petty corruption within the system, "to the hundreds of NGOs that do not exist."[102]

Instead, the push for reforms to the disability sector came from a second associational network—one that revolved around a small group of service-oriented disability associations within the Christian communities—that both conceived and maneuvered to have the RA program accepted within the MSA. The network was deliberately kept narrowly based due to fears of politicization, and it was founded on the belief that reforms needed to be pushed not by vocal advocacy but by quiet and professionalized diplomacy.[103] At the center of the network was Pierre Issa, one of the founders of a small wartime disability NGO called Arc en Ciel that played the lead role within the RA program and that would go on to become one of the most important service providers and disability advocacy associations in the postwar period, with ten centers scattered throughout the country.[104] A man of deep Christian faith—the result of a conversion experience in the midst of the civil war period—Issa also had significant expertise in management and information technology and, crucially, had strong connections within elite Christian political circles. In meetings between the small network of disability activists within the Christian community at the end of the civil war in which the framework for the RA was first agreed on, for example, it was Issa who was targeted by the network as the one "with the possibility" in terms of his connections at the political level.[105] While Issa has always denied being part by a larger "superstructure,"[106] it was clear that Arc en Ciel, under the leadership of Issa, was able to play the confessional card to its advantage within the MSA. Indeed, one activist described these internal dynamics as being determined by a three-way confessional power-sharing agreement between institutional representatives of the Sunni, Shi'a, and Christian communities, with the MSA acting as mediator—a system of "three-part-heit," as it was sarcastically called.[107] As one of Issa's network colleagues stressed, "he had to bargain, he had to bargain, he can't do it any other way."[108] As a result of these hidden negotiations, Arc en Ciel acquired authority over and protection from within the MSA that allowed it to promote the RA reforms.[109] This protection was facilitated and enforced by the long-standing director general of the MSA throughout the war, Naamat Kanaan, who was described as having a knack, despite the over-arching political constraints that surrounded her, of carving out small, autonomous spaces within which to carry out more effective social work and who, as a result of growing up with a disabled brother, was particularly interested in the cause of the disabled.[110] Indeed, according to one UN consultant with the MSA, the RA program was one of its most protected social programs.[111] Offering further proof of the emergence of a special relationship between Arc en Ciel and the MSA was the location of the main offices of the RA program in the Beirut premises of Arc en Ciel. In short, in what in effect was a fascinating experiment in NGO-led reformism using the strategy of institutional layering—"Chehabism from below," so to speak—the network of disability associations around Arc en Ciel, assisted by the decisive political mediation of Hobeika and Kanaan, was able to carve out for itself a significant degree of autonomous space within the MSA to pursue its reformist-oriented agenda.

The question that remained, however, was how far these reforms could go. Kabbara, for example, described the "bargain" as being limited in scope and not extending into the area of disability financing; nor would it have the scope to threaten the autonomy of the larger rehabilitation institutions through the establishment of a tighter regulatory framework.[112] Issa's strategic vision, on the other hand, was expansive. At its heart was a functionalist model of change—one grounded in the belief that the gradual introduction of modernizing technological influences would be the key to unlocking the door to reform. These would unleash the real mechanism for change, people with disabilities themselves, who, through access to more information about the types and standards of service being offered and the improved nature of the services themselves, would emerge as a powerful social force challenging the defenders of the institutionalized status quo. In short, Issa's strategy was to win the hearts and minds of people with disabilities—the users and target groups, as Issa described them in his more private sector–oriented, technocratic language. As he subsequently argued, "they are our only force. Hence, we must help them; we must pay attention to our clients." In the meantime, however, Issa stressed the need to work quietly, "bringing reforms in through the back door." In a clear critique of the disability advocacy associations with which Arc en Ciel would end up clashing on numerous occasions, he argued that "if you work in broad daylight, you are going to get hit," adding that "I cannot insult the Minister of the Interior and, at the same time, ask him for a permit to bring medicine into prisons."[113]

A decade after the establishment of the NCDP and the launching of the Rights and Access Program, those responsible for it were convinced of its effectiveness. "The system works," stressed Issa in an interview in the fall of 2001, arguing that he had seen incremental yet tangible proof that the large rehabilitation institutions—particularly those servicing the physically disabled—were beginning to change their ways.[114] In part, this was the result of the ability of the RA program within the NCDP to recruit a few well-qualified and committed staff, giving the disabled, for the first time, an important "bureaucratic ally."[115] There also were attempts to begin a process of random field visits, phone calls, and evaluations of institutions, efforts that had uncovered some abuses in the system.[116] The NCDP even threatened to deny accreditation to one of the larger institutions for the disabled, and it was only after the provision of technical advice from the RA program that accreditation was subsequently given.[117] The RA program also has had some success in stopping the distribution of substandard technical aids such as hearing aids, glasses and wheelchairs, improvement that also is the result of a more demanding and more aware disabled community.[118] However, for Issa, the most important indication of progress in the implementation of the RA program concerned the movement of users away from institutionalized care toward more CBR that integrated the families back into the system. While he could not provide statistical proof of this trend at the national level, Issa stressed that his own experience with Arc en Ciel—which has managed a dramatic increase in demand for technical aids such as wheelchairs and prosthetics since the launching of the RA program—did suggest that something significant was afoot.[119]

Hence, what developed within the MSA in the initial postwar period was a two-track disability policy. On the periphery existed a small and marginally funded enclave of professionalism and transparency within the RA program. Within the core, however, lay the more dominant and entrenched system that distributed the majority of public income earmarked for the disability sector on the basis of the more opaque political and confessional logic. How far the former was able to transform the latter was at the heart of reformist debates within the disability sector in Lebanon in the 1990s. Those within the RA program, committed to their largely functionalist model, were optimistic about the degree to which the introduction of professionalism could begin to positively infect the larger system. "We know that it's not an easy thing," remarked Issa, "but it is not impossible."[120] On the other hand, those with a more political orientation looked on this optimism as naïve. "Where is their political understanding of disability?" asked Kabbara, who instead stressed the need for broader-based political action as the only way of injecting accountability into the system.[121]

*Creating a More Formalized Disability Policy Domain:*
*The Campaign for Law 220*

If the politics around the RA program represented the rising influence of the network of associations around Arc en Ciel, the politics around the disability law represented the return to form of the network of disability advocacy associations run by people with disabilities. Initially, they had been extremely discouraged by developments within the NCDP, where the project of law was being formulated, especially after the resignation of Hobeika in 1994, which had led to a dramatic reduction in its activities. Of even greater concern to disability activists, however, was the emergence of resistance on the part of political elites to the proposed disability law (Law 220) itself—designed to establish a comprehensive set of rights for people with disabilities in the country. This was symbolized by the decision of the Hariri government to send the draft law proposal back to the MSA and the NCDP for further development, President Elias Hrawi arguing that it was too advanced, "fit for Sweden, not Lebanon."[122]

Initially, the advocacy NGOs reacted to this discouraging turn of events by continuing to target the large disability institutions and their embedded relations with officials within the MSA. It was the institutions, for example, whom they argued had captured the ear of Hariri's cabinet and discouraged it from passing the law; it also was the institutions that they argued were preventing the MSA from opening up funding opportunities to a broader array of disability NGOs. In response to these concerns, they created their own "shadow committee" of the NCDP, published the results of a study of budget allocations within the MSA in the press, and demanded publicly that the existing members of the NCDP resign.[123] Not only did this evoke the ire of and sour relations with those in the MSA, but it also resulted, according to Lakkis, in mild threats from various arms of the security services that paralleled the broader crackdown on civil society activism.[124] By the late 1990s, however, strategic recalculations on the part of the disability activists resulted in their campaigns being increasingly targeted outside the narrow confines of the MSA and the

NCDP. At the root of this recalculation was their realization that they would not be able to compete with the larger rehabilitation institutions in terms of service provision, especially given the absence of a viable state backing them up. While accepting that "we had to pass through that experience,"[125] therefore, the LSHU, along with the other disability advocacy associations, began the process of returning to their roots. This entailed a two-pronged strategy of continuing their awareness-raising and advocacy campaigns, on the one hand, while seeking ways to "mainstream" disability through the establishment of better linkages within broader civil and political circles outside the narrow confines of the disability field, on the other.

Already active throughout the early postwar period with respect to campaigning for greater accessibility within the country,[126] for example, the LSHU, concerned about the languishing enthusiasm for the proposed disability law, launched a series of campaigns promoting disability rights and the new project of law. These included the hosting of events in celebration of the International Day for the Disabled (December 3), lobbying local municipal councils throughout the country, and the organization of numerous conferences on disability rights, particular in more outlying areas such as the South and the Beqa Valley. Lakkis of the LSHU was also active in making the links between gender rights and those of women with disabilities, using the occasion of International Women's Day to speak about problems of double discrimination faced by women with disabilities.[127] In 1998, they also launched a ten-day "Disability Rights" campaign—that included "parties" as opposed to "demonstrations"—on the Corniche in West Beirut and in Nabatiyya as a way of circumventing the government ban on the latter, and a competition within selected Lebanese schools for the student who could write the best story concerning the need to promote the rights of people with disabilities.[128] It was in 1999, however, that the LSHU got down to its most serious lobbing and networking activities on behalf of the new project of law—organizing a series of round tables and workshops with all of the leading and relevant civil society actors and hosting an international symposium on disability, which they convinced President Emile Lahoud to sponsor, that culminated in a sit-in of more than 600 people in front of the National Museum.[129]

Those associated with the MSA and the RA program were deeply concerned about the public exposure LSHU was giving to the proposed project of law—exposure that they argued might jeopardize its chances of being passed by sparking objections to its highly ambitious provisions. Indeed, Lakkis at one point described officials within the MSA-NDCP as acting as if "we [were] making a big crime."[130] The disability advocacy associations were not unaware of the importance of quiet, behind-the-scenes lobbying at the elite level. Kabbara had always gravitated easily to this level of activity, and the LSHU, traditionally more focused on the grassroots, had begun to use its networking with civil society associations such as the Lebanese Association for Democratic Elections to establish more useful connections with Lebanese parliamentarians.[131] Particularly fortuitous in this regard was the emergence of the Salim al-Hoss government in 1998 that followed in the wake of the resignation of the Hariri government, the former having much closer relations with civic activists than the latter. Indeed, Lakkis described Hoss's interest as being crucial in having the disability law finally passed. At the same time, however, she argued that "in the end, we also had to lobby. It was not enough just to make the usual contacts and meetings because we had too many issues and, of course, we were not always the priority. . . . In the end, we had to demonstrate."[132] Kabbara, who also had been active in campaigning for the passage of the disability law using both NARD and the newly created NGO network LCDP, perhaps summed up the strategic commitment of the disability advocacy associations to politicized and public advocacy the best. In describing to the author his "theory of the mosquito," for example, Kabbara noted that "first, [mosquitos] won't let you sleep and, second, they sometimes bite you, true? The mosquito is very small but very effective. We are very small and very weak but could be effective in not letting the political society sleep."[133]

The comprehensive law on disabilities was finally passed by the Lebanese parliament in June 2000, made possible by the receptiveness of Prime Minister al-Hoss to the demands of Lebanon's emerging disability movement. For those who labored for years within the disability advocacy movement, its passage was a major success. Kabarra, for example, described the final product as "a marvel . . . it covers almost everything,"[134] and, as Lakkis proudly exclaimed, "now, we have rights!"[135] There was an equal sense of euphoria among those associated with the RA program, they now having a sustainable legal platform on which to pursue their reformist agenda. In short, rising out of the ashes of civil war, Lebanon's various postwar disability associative networks had helped to carve out from scratch a defined disability policy domain, one grounded on principles of universal rights of the disabled. Not only did their efforts contribute to the expansion of the Lebanese postwar public sphere, but they also contributed, in a modest way, to the postwar reconstruction of the Lebanese state. At the same time, however, it remained a policy domain that was characterized by large power asymmetries between the various competing policy networks, network asymmetries across which state actors sometimes tried to mediate—note the success of Hobeika—

but that they were unable to overcome or challenge. Indeed, as we shall see, more often than not, those network actors resistant to reform were able to use the political and financial resources provided by the state to reinforce their asymmetrical veto power within the system. Hence, in the face of the "stickiness" of the hidden dynamics within the state (and the MSA), Lebanon's dynamic community of disability activists and associations, having spent the 1990s trying to institutionalize reforms in the public disability sector, were forced to retreat from their efforts to reform the state in the 2000s and rechannel their energies to improve the conditions for people with disabilities in the country in other directions. While the results on an associational level have been impressive—ranging from rising levels of awareness among people with disabilities, to the increasing prevalence of rights-based CBR discourse in the country, to the greater if still piecemeal access of the disabled to community-based services, the sector as a whole remains atomized and its benefits unevenly spread, held back by a political system whose dynamics reinforce rather than challenge the prevailing fragmented status quo.

## "We Cannot Wait for the State": The Disabling of Reforms in Lebanon's Postwar Disability Sector

The fragility of institutional reform, especially in polities characterized by deep, polarizing, and institutionalized political divides, became readily apparent in the politically tumultuous period of time in Lebanon after 2000. Disability activists had hoped to use this time to follow up on their initial gains of the 1990s by promoting the implementation of their various reformist initiatives and, hence, transforming the role of the state into a supporter, if not enforcer, of rights-based disability reform. However, this cautious enthusiasm quickly dissipated. On the surface, it would be easy to blame the subsequent "disabling" of institutional reform in the fledgling disability sector on the vagaries of national, regional, and global politics that came to dominate Lebanon in the wake of September 11, 2001. Yet such a focus on contingent political developments serves to mask the underlying and deeply entrenched political dynamics that structure relations within Lebanon's social policy domain and militate against reformist initiatives, regardless of the prevailing political climate. In short, the gains made by disability activists in the post–civil war period remained bounded and highly constrained by three features of the prevailing institutional order: the extremely limited interest of Lebanon's political class in rights-based as opposed to clientelist-based service delivery reforms, the limited autonomy of the country's bureaucratic class as enforcers of new bureaucratic norms, and the hidden but formidable veto power of sectarian-affiliated disability institutions that has allowed them to both preserve and reproduce the particularist dynamics within the disability sector as a whole.

### The Languishing of Law 220: Financial Austerity or the Lack of Political Will?

Law 220 created a comprehensive set of normative obligations on the part of the Lebanese state to promote the rights of the disabled and their integration as equal citizens into Lebanese society. For these norms to be translated into actual policies and programs, however, they needed to be joined by a series of decisions and implementing decrees that would oblige the bureaucratic arms of the Lebanese state to pursue their implementation. On the surface, some of this policy infrastructure *was* immediately created—epitomized by the creation of joint committees in the areas of education, health, and employment between the MSA and the respective ministries. Yet, in similar fashion to the gender focal points distributed throughout the Lebanese state, the work of these interdepartmental disability committees has languished, and they have failed to emerge as drivers in the promotion of more comprehensive reform of state policies, caught between competing bureaucratic interests and a lack of commitment to implementation on the part of the country's political class. This has resulted in what critiques of the development industry have called a process of "policy evaporation," one characterized by its inability to "mainstream" disability into its broader policy-making apparatus.[136]

The limited implementation of Law 220 with respect to the promotion of employment opportunities for people with disabilities is a case in point. Law 220, for example, enshrines the right of the people with disabilities to work. In order to fulfill this right, the law stipulates that the public sector must reserve 3 percent of its jobs for people with disabilities, the same stipulation being applied to private sector companies with employees in excess of sixty. Firms not complying with these obligations are supposed to be subject to fines, with the money being transferred into a social fund to support those people with disabilities unable to find work. Law 220 further obliges the state to ensure that people with disabilities have suitable training and job placement services—actions that were to be overseen by the National Office of Employment, within which was to be created a joint MSA–Ministry of Labour (MOL) Committee on Employment. The initial actions within the MOL were encouraging. The joint committee was immediately created, and the MOL publicly announced that it would punish those private sector firms that did not comply with the new 3 percent employment quota system. There also were modest attempts to promote vocational training for people with disabilities. Yet, announcements did not add up to effective new public policies. First, the private sector took little interest in complying with the new 3 percent quota—its participation on the joint committee being extremely limited. Contributing to this lack of interest was the refusal of the Ministry of Finance to create the necessary financial infrastructure to implement the system of penalties and fines—a refusal that effectively prevented the MOL from enforcing this part of the law. As one observer remarked, it was clear that "the private sector's priorities [were] far more important than those of the disabled."[137] Disability activists also were appalled by the lack of awareness on the part of officials within the MOL associated with the joint committee on employment—one of them having suggested at one point that the MOL should allow companies to employ people with disabilities at half the cost as a way of making them comply with the 3 percent quota. "It's incredible," remarked one activist, who went on to sarcastically ask, "Who's paying you? Are [they] working with the government or with the . . . companies?"[138] Indeed, the activist further lamented the inability of the state to enforce the penalty system against private corporations—arguing that "you know, in eight years, if all the companies paid at least [the fines] that they had to pay for not employing 3 percent of disabled people, they would have had . . . millions of dollars. They could do plenty of work. They would have been able to finance many projects to be able to employ the people who are disabled."[139] Instead, little systematic progress has been made on the employment file for people with disabilities in the wake of the passage of Law 220, effectively maintaining the status quo of state discrimination.[140] As another disability activist concluded, the net result of the state's efforts with respect to the inclusion of people with disabilities in both labor market and unemployment insurance schemes was "zero."[141]

A watchdog report on the status of Law 220 issued in 2005, five years after the passage of the law, by the Lebanese Council of Disabled Peoples (LCDP)—the advocacy coalition initiated by Nawaf Kabbara in the late 1990s—provided a full rundown of the areas where the Lebanese state has been neglecting its legal obligations to people with disabilities. With respect to health, for example, the right to free hospitalization and outpatient medical services was unfulfilled, held back by the inability and/ or unwillingness of the state to cover the expenses and, as a result, by the refusal of most hospitals to acknowledge the dispensations associated with the disability card. Similar problems were being experienced with respect to transportation, with new tenders for public buses failing to include

any orders for accessible ones despite stipulations in the law that 15 percent of all public transportation be accessible to people with disabilities.
Customs exemptions for imported cars for people with disabilities also
were being distributed on a highly restrictive basis—effectively depriving
many of a crucial element in their efforts at social integration. Neither
were there any efforts to train the police and civil servants with respect
to the enforcement of special parking privileges for people with disabilities; as Kabbara later remarked ten years after the passage of Law 220,
"[P]eople need to know that there will be big penalties if they park their
car in front of a [wheelchair] ramp."[142] With more than 50 percent of all
people with disabilities in the country remaining uneducated, the LCDP
report also lamented the fact that the vast majority of people with disabilities continued to be excluded from regular schools due to their physical
inaccessibility as well as to the continued resistance of parents, school
administrators, and educational bureaucrats. Many special-needs schools,
such as those for the deaf, for example, complained that they continued to
have to seek special dispensation for their students to take regular school
exams.[143] Indeed, while reporting on a few improvements in services for
people with disabilities in the country in the wake of Law 220,[144] the
overall conclusion was that "none of the main articles enabling a person
with a disability to be independent and integrate has been applied." The
result was that people with disabilities in Lebanon remain "victims of
peace just as they were victims of war."[145]

The response of Lebanon's advocacy networks of associations run
by people with disabilities was to redouble their efforts at lobbying the
state. Despite their previously antagonistic relations, for example, the two
subnetworks of disability associations increasingly began to coordinate
their campaigns, at one point participating in a joint sit-in in front of the
parliament in the fall of 2004. This was followed by a flurry of mutually
supported advocacy initiatives—designed to take advantage of the political opening in the wake of the departure of the Syrians after the Independence Intifada in the spring of 2005. The LCDP, for example, launched a
nationwide campaign and petition calling on the government to declare
2005 to 2015 as the Lebanese Decade for Disabled Peoples, within which
a systematic schedule would be established for implementing Law 220.
Supported by EU assistance, LCDP delegates traveled throughout the
country seeking the support of all of the major religious and political
leaders, a process that culminated in the spring of 2005 in the presentation of the petition to the new Prime Minister Fuad Siniora. While the
response of religious leaders was described as "a disappointment," the
response of several political leaders was initially more encouraging—the
major political parties being described as "competing with each other to

sign the petition."[146] Indeed, one year later, Siniora hosted a conference with disability activists in which he agreed to pursue issues relating to the implementation of Law 220, a response that Kabbara remarked hopefully was "just one small drop, but still, it comes as a refreshing shower at a time the parched soil of the cause seems to get dryer."[147]

In addition to the petition, the LCDP also tried to raise awareness about disability rights by nominating its own members to run as candidates in the elections in 2005—one for a Maronite, Sunni, and Shi'a seat, respectively. Kabbara, who was the only one of the candidates to actually make it onto an electoral list and run and who, in the end, garnered an impressive 64,000 votes in his eventual loss, argued that because the various political parties in the country failed to include disability issues as part of their electoral platforms, "we have decided to take the initiative on our own."[148] Paralleling and complementing these efforts of the LCDP during the 2005 elections was the "My Rights" campaign of the LSHU and the YAB aimed at countering the numerous and formidable challenges faced by disabled voters during elections. The vast majority of polling stations in the country, for example, were inaccessible,[149] a problem compounded by the fact that the staff at the polling stations were "minimally aware" of the voting rights of people with disabilities.[150] More fundamental, however, was the low level of awareness shown by most politicians with regard to disability issues. When disability activists met and lobbied with the various political parties asking them to include disability issues in their campaigns, the response and level of interest were limited. Indeed, politicians were described as continuing to act in clientelist ways by offering potential disabled voters services in exchange for political support.[151] Hence, despite extensive media and billboard campaigns in both the 2005 and the subsequent parliamentary elections in 2009, the continual targeted lobbying of political actors, and the provision of individualized support for disabled voters, the various campaigns of disabled activists have had only a limited impact at the political level.[152] Perhaps nothing symbolized this marginalization of disability issues from the political arena more than the persistence of problems associated with the inaccessibility of polling stations—a study by the LSHU revealing that fewer than one-half of 1 percent of the 1,741 polling stations in the 2009 elections were fully accessible.[153]

Hence, the mere existence of Law 220 has failed to transform the Lebanese state into a prime mover in the disability sector. Part of the problem is financial. Implementing Law 220 is an expensive proposition, especially given the severe economic constraints on state finances in the postwar period and the refusal of the country's political elite, supported by its various foreign benefactors associated with the various Paris donor conferences, to deviate from its laissez-faire economic system—though, as disability activists have repeatedly argued, these projected costs have been exaggerated and neglect the longer-term financial benefits of moving toward a more rights-based and community-oriented approach.[154] There also remains the problem of low social and political awareness, despite the numerous public advocacy campaigns launched by disability activists; "they really don't understand," noted Amer Makarem with respect to the attitudes of Lebanon's political and administrative classes toward Law 220.[155] Even if more finance and greater political awareness existed, however, implementing and enforcing the law would still be difficult in the face of the informal political dynamics that underlie the Lebanese state. In his explanation for why the implementation of Law 220 has been so limited, for example, Makarem argued that "the law is not really part of the culture of decision-makers. [It] is not obligatory, they can avoid it, they can neglect it."[156] Kabbara's explanation went even closer to the mark, stressing that "the Lebanese political system is only sensitive to issues related to the traditional power base in the country," adding that the various civic components of Lebanon's civil society remained "weak in terms of affecting the power game in the country."[157]

*Sectarian Dynamics and the Political Immobilization of the NCDP*

The implementation of Law 220 was clearly hampered by the weakness of the Lebanese state and the absence of political awareness, let alone a political champion, on the part of the country's political and administrative elite. Yet what about the bureaucratic arm of the state responsible for disability—the MSA and the NCDP? The literature on policy advocacy, for example, stresses that bureaucratic platforms within the state can act as "critical points of leverage" for policy advocacy movements. As we have already examined, while the NCLW failed to play that role with respect to postwar women's advocacy, the MOE initially had greater success, symbolized by its cooperation with postwar environmental advocacy movements in the late 1990s. Endowed with primary responsibility for issues of disability within the state, the MSA and the NCDP were, in theory, positioned to play that same role of bureaucratic champion—acting as advocates for the disabled within the state. Indeed, the staff of the MSA has been looked on as "positive and outgoing in its support of disability rights."[158] The NCDP, however, as the advisory policy-making body for disability in the country, has not been able to support those few dedicated officials and the pockets of bureaucratic capacity with collective resolve or vision, an inability that can be attributed to its own immobilizing factionalism caused by the penetration of broader political conflicts into the heart of its proceedings. It is to an analysis of the intertwining of policy debates with political and sectarian dynamics within the NCDP, particularly acute in the years after the assassination of Hariri, that we turn now.

There existed multiple layers of potential factionalism within the NCDP. Some actors within the network of disability activists, for example, continued to harbor suspicions about the enduring cozy, politicized relationships between the MSA and the large, politically connected rehabilitation institutions. These concerns manifested themselves in the stipulations within Law 220 for restructuring the NCDP, one that some disability activists argued would weaken their voice on the council. The number of seats, for example, was increased from twelve to eighteen members, six of whom were appointed by the MSA, thereby giving the MSA effective control of more than one-third of the representation. Of further—if paradoxical—concern was the inclusion of four additional seats for people with disabilities, delegates for which would be elected by people with disabilities themselves. While on the surface this seemed to be an inclusive provision, several disability activists questioned whether the electoral process would actually work to their benefit, especially given that the largest concentration of disabled voters remained dependent on the services and, hence, subject to the influence of the larger rehabilitation institutions. In short, by creating a framework within which clientelist elections could flourish, disability activists looked on the proposals to "democratically" restructure the NCDP as potentially leading to the fragmentation and co-optation of the disability movement itself. Noted Lakkis, in drawing parallels with the manipulation by political elites of the labor union movement in the country in the mid-1990s, these proposals will "keep us divided."[159] As a result, several key disability activists initially decided to remain outside the NCDP, refusing to get "wrapped up" in its increasingly politicized dynamics.[160]

Subsequent interviews with several members of the NCDP confirmed the infusion of confessional and political dynamics into its proceedings. Although representation on the NCDP was based on functional categories and, with the exception of the MSA delegates who were appointed, determined through an electoral process, there nonetheless emerged an unwritten consensus within the council that representation also should be confessionally balanced. This led to the emergence of some interesting representational anomalies. Because the National Rehabilitation and Development Center was the only Druze rehabilitation institution in Lebanon, for example, it became permanently represented on the council. On the other hand, because there were numerous rehabilitation institutions within the Shi'a communities, they were forced to share representation among themselves or bargain their way into the position of becoming one of the appointments of the minister.[161] Given the desire of most to be on the council, if only to see what the other players in the field were up to,[162] the result was a significant degree of intrasectarian politicking over questions of representation. Indeed, one disability activist described religious and political affiliation as "invading" the distribution of posts, with representation emerging through processes of political bargaining and compromise. The result, he added, was a disability council that was "inclusive but dysfunctional."[163]

Further complicating the deliberations of the NCDP was the penetration of questions relating to political affiliation, ones which escalated in importance after the assassination of Hariri and the emerging antagonism between the March 8 and March 14 coalitions. The situation became particularly acute in 2005 with the awarding of the MSA ministerial portfolio to a March 14 politician, Nayla Mouawad, for whom political affiliation in the post–February 14, 2005, era in Lebanon was described as "everything."[164] This not only disrupted previous patterns of negotiations and relations within the MSA-NCDP, traditionally presided over by ministers affiliated with the AMAL movement, but it also set the scene for further politicization given that many of the associations on the council at this time were more or less affiliated with March 8—including the Lebanese Welfare Association for the Disabled run by Randa Berri and linked to the AMAL Movement and the al-Jarha Association directly affiliated with Hezbollah. NCDP representatives said that Mouawad rarely called meetings and that, when she did, they were held on the partisan turf of her own home; they also spoke of the partisan distribution of contracts as well as foreign aid for disability—an influx of the latter having come into the MSA in the wake of the Israeli–Hezbollah struggles in the summer of 2006; and further concern was expressed over her decision to rescind the appointment of a Lebanese delegate to the negotiations surrounding the new UN Convention on the Rights of People with Disabilities—ostensibly for partisan reasons.[165] In short, the various associational representatives on the NCDP, in addition to the minister, acted as channels through which broader political struggles penetrated into the heart of its proceedings, effectively immobilizing it as a deliberative and advisory body.

*"Islands of Rights": The Limited Scope of the Rights and Access Program*

While the failure of the MSA and NCDP to promote the implementation of Law 220 was certainly a disappointment, there was more guarded optimism with respect to the RA program. We have already examined its early success—improvements in the delivery of life-giving technical aids to people with disabilities and the development of technical expertise within the MSA with respect to the disability sector as a whole, something that it was hoped would increase the levels of accountability and transparency in the system. Indeed, a glance at some of the annual reports of the RA program suggests that its levels of activity, knowledge, and capacity did increase. In 2004, for example, the RA program was able to continue its steady if unspectacular increase in the distribution of disability cards, registering more than 5,000 new people with disabilities. It also succeeded in processing more than 8,000 requests for various tax and custom duty exemptions and in distributing more than 4,500 technical aids. Indeed, since the beginning of the RA program in 1997, the total services rendered to people with disabilities in the country were estimated to be about 2.5 million.[166] Moreover, in terms of the delivery of technical aids in 2004, it was of further interest that while the largest number continued to be distributed in the Mount Lebanon region (35 percent), there also were signs that the previously marginalized areas of the country—the Bekaa (16 percent), the South (17 percent), Nabatieh (9 percent), and the North (17 percent)—were beginning to be better serviced.[167] Hence, when disability activists were asked whether the program had improved the distribution and quality of technical aids in the country, most responded that things were better than before.[168]

It also was clear, however, that the RA program, initially designed to be the driver of more far-reaching reforms to the state's role in the disability sector, has been unable to escape its enclave status within the MSA, remaining a rational-legal link within a broader clientelist-sectarian chain. These limitations are the result of several factors—some material, others political. Financial austerity, for example, placed severe limits on the extent to which the program can deliver its promised goods. In 2001, for example, Pierre Issa estimated that the state had been able to cover at most 30 percent of the costs of technical aids distributed, leaving the rest to be paid for by local disability institutions and foreign donors.[169] By 2004, the Annual Report of the RA program reported that the program was only able to finance the delivery of technical aids for a few days each month—leading to the effective closure of the program for the remainder.[170] This was lamented by one senior disability official, who argued that this placed the program in a difficult situation that forced it to choose which technical aids were worthy of financing and which ones were not—something that constituted a grave violation of the principle that all disabled people, of whatever socioeconomic background, have equal rights.[171] Indeed, Adib Nemeh, a UN consultant within the MSA who had closely followed developments within the disability sector, admitted that the sustained financial austerity had created opportunities for petty corruption—giving those bureaucrats and/or NGO personnel administering the program discretion as to who would be given distributional priority.[172] Moreover, because the demand for technical aids remains extremely high and unmet by the state or the small sector of foreign-funded disability NGOs, people with disabilities have been forced to approach potentially more politicized, subordinating, and less professionally exacting sources of support—what Wood described more generically as their "Faustian bargain."[173] An official from a prominent foreign donor in the disability sector in Lebanon, for example, described her office as being constantly contacted by ministers of parliament requesting technical aids such as wheelchairs and water mattresses for their political clients and constituents. Indeed, in perhaps the starkest indication of the persistence of the prevailing clientelist logic within the disability sector despite the achievements of the RA program, this same donor official recalled facing demands for the particularistic distribution of technical aids from Social Affairs ministers themselves.[174]

However, not only did the situation of sustained financial austerity limit the functioning of the RA program itself, but it also hampered its ability to gradually redirect the broader funding patterns of the MSA away from institutionalized care and toward CBR. First, while Issa had envisioned the MSA-RA program being able to play an increasingly regulatory role within the disability field as a whole, in reality, both the RA program and the MSA remained understaffed and, at one point in the post–Law 220 days, was forced to reduce its staff complement, sparking threats of strike action on the part of some of its officials.[175] Hence, when asked about the regulatory capacity of the MSA, the responses were not surprising. The executive director of one major rehabilitation institution, for example, remarked that they rarely received staff visits from the MSA, while another described many of their staff as being underqualified to investigate what they actually paid for. Hence, while arguing that "we should know who's working and who's not, who's professional and who's not," in reality, it was concluded that "there's no system of control."[176]

However, perhaps the most significant factor limiting financial flexibility in the already underfunded disability sector was the long-standing MSA system of per diem financing that consumed most of its revenue. As many disability activists recognized, the continued dominance of the per diem system—one that funded overnight stays within institutions—posed serious obstacles to reform in the disability sector, preventing newer organizations in the disability field from being able to finance CBR strategies. As one disability activist admitted, "the system is pushing us towards institutionalization."[177] A 2005 report by the LCDP, for example, estimated that only 6 percent of MSA funding in the disability field went toward the provision of technical aids that might have facilitated the ability of disabled people to better integrate into the community, while more than

90 percent was scattered over contracts with sixty-six different disability institutions, many of which continued to promote institutionalized care.[178] As a result, the MSA, described as being "overwhelmed" by requests for both greater amounts of and increases in per diem financing, had little revenue to fund alternative activities, let alone act as a leader by keeping up with the latest rights-based developments in the field.[179] Ultimately constraining the policy flexibility of the MSA, however, was the entrenched position of the larger rehabilitation institutions, which insisted on maintaining the system of per diem payouts, especially advantageous within the field of disability where these payments were higher—"bigger money," as one observer called them.[180] Indeed, despite anecdotal murmurings of ongoing petty corruption within the system—the result, in part, of the MSA's tendency to accept the lists of patients forwarded to it by the various rehabilitation institutions without medical reverification[181]—little effort has been made by actors within the disability field as a whole to challenge publicly the prevailing system. "What's the point," argued a representative from one of the large social welfare institutions in the country that also caters to people with disabilities, "it only gets one into political problems."[182] Similar views were expressed by the representative of another disability institution that had been actively involved in the small reformist disability network associated with the formulation of the RA program. After responding to questions about its initial desire to dismantle the per diem system with "oh . . . this was the dream!," he went on to explain that subsequent efforts to critique the system openly were simply too politically difficult. "If you accuse," he argued, "then they say you are against the Shi'a because the Ministry of Social Affairs is mostly [linked] to the Shi'a. So, nobody dare says anything. This is the problem with our ministries today. It's . . . confessional."[183] In short, the large and powerful institutionalized players within the disability sector take advantage of—indeed instrumentalize—the prevailing sectarian climate within the country to carve out and/or maintain their access to MSA funding and preempt attempts by reformists to challenge their hegemonic access. The result is an entrenched disability policy domain within postwar Lebanon—strengthened and reproduced by the instrumentalized sectarian framework that surrounds it—that remains resistant to the kind of functionalist transformation envisioned by those who initially crafted the RA program. Rather than spread its dynamics throughout the disability sector of the state, the RA program has remained a constrained rational-legal island amid a larger politicized and clientelized sea. As Kabarra starkly but clearly remarked with respect to the political economy of funding within the MSA: "We are in Lebanon. The big bosses, the big sharks, use the Ministry of Social Affairs to finance their activities. These activities

are directly linked to political favors . . . They take money because they
have political support. . . . That's it. Full stop!"[184]

## Conclusion: Disability Advocacy in the Absence of the State

In the face of the fragmentation and political penetration of Lebanon's
social policy domain—qualities that have blocked the emergence of a
more robust state role in the disability sector—disability activists interested in advocating for CBR policies have refocused their energies away
from the collective endeavor of reforming state institutions and policies at
the national level toward a more incremental strategy of promoting CBR
initiatives at the project level—consolidating and expanding the various
"islands" of progressive disability service provision and rights promotion
in the country. Crucial in facilitating these efforts has been the support of
disability networks at the regional and global levels—networks on which
disability institutions and associations within Lebanon have always and
historically depended. Before outlining my concluding analysis of disability politics in postwar Lebanon, I briefly examine the impacts of some of
these transnational advocacy efforts.

The most important contribution of external networks to advocacy
within Lebanon's disability sector has been financial. Most associations
and institutions within the field, for example, have a difficult time keeping
up with running costs, let alone investing in professional training, new
technologies, and/or the building of new facilities—contributions that,
as we have seen, are beyond the capacity of the MSA. As a result, the
implementation of initiatives and projects in the field of CBR has usually depended on resources from outside the country. Frustrated with
the ineffectiveness of the interministerial committee of employment and
disability, for example, Roland Tamrouz, the executive director of Zawraq, an institution concerned with people with intellectual disabilities,
ultimately ended up pursuing his own "supported employment" initiative
after receiving support from a civil society promotion program (AFKAR)
funded by the European Union.[185] The pilot project—which he argued was
the first of its kind in the Middle East—turned out to be an encouraging
success, resulting in the employment of more than twenty individuals
with intellectual disabilities in such economic enterprises as textile fac-
tories, supermarkets companies, as well as placements within fast-food
franchises such as Burger King and Pizza Hut.[186] With the help of long-
standing foreign donors, the LSHU also has implemented a successful
pilot project, setting up the first job placement center in Lebanon for
people with disabilities in the Beqa. Within one year of its establish-

ment, the center had begun the process of creating a network of support among employers and local municipalities and had succeeded in finding employment for ten individuals.[187] Perhaps the most significant donor contribution to the strengthening of advocacy networks within post-2000 Lebanon, however, came with the decision of the World Bank to award its Community Development Project loan earmarked for the disability sector to the "Inclusion Network"—a consortium of small disability advocacy associations that included the LSHU, the YAB, and the Lebanese Down Syndrome Association, whose goal was to promote "inclusion" rather than merely "integration" of the disabled into both the workforce and the educational system.[188] This decision was significant for a number of reasons. First, the Inclusion Network was chosen over two other consortiums, both of which were made up of a number of the influential players in the field—one consisting of seven of the large disability rehabilitation centers and headed by the AMAL-backed Lebanese Welfare Association for the Handicapped (LWAH), the other by the increasingly influential and expanding Arc en Ciel, backed up by the Rene Mouawad Foundation. Given the long history of acrimony and power asymmetries between these three rival disability networks, it was not surprising to hear Lakkis of the LSHU describe the awarding of the loan as "a great victory for us."[189] Apart from advancing the Inclusion Network's agenda of educational and employment inclusion,[190] however, the project was described as having significantly improved its previously limited access to the state itself. Amer Makarem, the project's managing director, who was particularly concerned with the inclusion of blind students into the regular school system, noted that after the awarding of the loan, the door of Ministry of Education "started opening for him," giving the Inclusion Network "a certain power with the ministers."[191] Whether policy "inclusion" would add up to policy "change" at the level of the state, however, was open to question, even from within the National Inclusion Network itself. In its final report to the World Bank, for example, it emphasized that despite the initial success of the initiative, it was not sufficient to merely "convince[e] officials in the ministries of the importance of inclusion. . . . It rather requires a change in the ministries' policies, rules, personnel, and budget. Since that requires a long time to happen, associations and civic society institutions will remain the main players."[192]

A parallel development has been the increasing participation and integration of associational leaders of Lebanon's disability sector into regional and global advocacy networks. The examples are numerous. It was Nawaf Kabbara, for example, who played a catalytic role in establishing the Arab Organization for Disabled People (AODP); Pierre Issa of Arc en Ciel has been active in franchising the "Rights and Access" model within neighboring Arab states; and numerous other activists have taken leading roles on the boards of several international disability associations—from Rehabilitation International to Inclusion International to the World Blind Union. Paralleling these efforts has been the active participation of Lebanese delegates in the formulation and promotion of the UN Convention of the Rights of People with Disabilities passed by the UN General Assembly in 2006, helping to push the issue of disability into the mainstream of the global human rights movement.[193] While, on the one hand, these efforts represent the deflection of advocacy energy away from the Lebanese political arena, on the other hand, there is evidence that they also have contributed to an advocacy "boomerang" effect within the Lebanese disability arena itself.[194] This is symbolized by the increasing use of "CBR-oriented" language revolving around concepts such as integration and inclusion by the large disability institutions themselves—even if the actual meanings attached to these terms differ substantially.[195] As one long-standing donor representative in Lebanon remarked, "nobody talked before about inclusion and now inclusion is becoming important. Nobody talked about integration and . . . [now] everybody's talking about all kinds of integration: economic integration, social integration, etc. All these issues were not there when we started." Added another local activist, "you hear less and less religious ideology, you hear more and more human rights ideology."[196] Interestingly, this convergence on a discursive level also seems to have impacted relationships within the disability field as a whole—helping to generate a mildly cooperative détente between rights-based and institutional-based disability networks. Both the "Inclusion Network" and the LCDP—disability networks whose core purpose is to advocate for the rights of people with disabilities—now include some of the large disability institutions as their members. This has been supplemented in small ways by the implementation of several joint inclusion-oriented pilot projects.[197] Disability activists attribute these changes in discourse and, to a much more limited extent, practice to the normative power of their global alliances. They can "feel it," argued one disability activist, adding that the initial feeling of insecurity that many of the small advocacy associations run by people with disabilities felt vis à vis the large disability institutions has now diminished. "I don't feel that they are stronger, even if they have lots of money and huge institutions. . . . When we talk about "inclusion," we are stronger than them and they can't stand against us. . . . Now, they cannot say what they used to say before."[198]

The most important potential source of advocacy power, however, will remain Lebanon's people with disabilities themselves. In the wake of more than two decades of globally supported advocacy activities, there are certainly signs that the overall situation of people with disabilities in the country has improved. Indeed, many of those I interviewed in the disability sector spoke of there being "an awakening" among Lebanon's people with disabilities. There are more people with disabilities out on the streets and participating in the country's public sphere—though still only a small percentage. There is greater access to basic life-giving services—though still highly inadequate; and there are signs that people with disabilities, always having been acutely aware of their own needs, are beginning to articulate their concerns in terms of "rights"—though this has not coalesced into the emergence of a strong grassroots disability social movement. The nature of progress was summed up well by one disabled activist, who remarked that, "before 1990, disabled people had no dreams. There are now dreams with ambitions—to study, to have a specialization, to work, to marry . . . the mentality has changed."[199]

One should not get carried away by this sense of optimism. It certainly remains the case that this chance to cultivate dreams continues to elude a large proportion of the country's people with disabilities—especially those who are poor, those who are women, those with multiple disabilities, those who live in remote regions, and those who are Palestinian and live within refugee camps in Lebanon—who have weak access to the "islands" of improved and rights-based disability service provision that has arisen in the post–civil war period. It also is clear that, even for those who can begin to cultivate more ambitious "life dreams," the collective fulfillment of those dreams continues to be blocked by the resilient resistance of the political system to creating the institutional conditions needed to make the aspirations of the country's people with disabilities a genuine and more universalized possibility. In short, most of the country's people with disabilities continue to find themselves in positions of vulnerability to the disabling socioeconomic and political environment that surrounds them.

What is changing, however, in large part due to the networking and lobbying of a relatively small number of associational activists for disabled rights, is that the building blocks for significant reform in the disability sector are beginning to be put in place. Where, once, disability issues were discursively framed in terms of charity, if not dishonor, now they are beginning to be referred to in terms of rights. Where, once, disability service provision was monopolized by large disability institutions often linked to powerful sectarian political networks, now this monopoly on service provision for the disabled is being challenged by the numerous disability associations, including those run by people with disabilities, that have proliferated in the country since the 1960s, especially during the war and post–civil war period, and that have been trying to promote community-based as opposed to institution-based rehabilitation services.

And where, once, disability institutions remained completely autonomous and unaccountable, now the building blocks of a more formal policy domain have been put in place, creating institutionalized opportunities for accountability-generating deliberation over disability norms and practices. In short, advocates for the disabled have made enormous strides over the last two decades, taking advantage of the limited and shifting opportunities provided by the complex Lebanese social and political systems. That they have not been able to "bring the state in" as an ally and third-party enforcer of new rights-based disability norms and practices—these remaining relegated to the normative periphery and bureaucratic trenches of its activities—attests not only to the relative weakness of their own advocacy networks but also to the limited autonomy of the Lebanese state itself in relation to powerful communal and clientelist networks—including their associational components—that colonize and use the state to reproduce their own factional autonomy and power.

# Conclusion

Lebanon's current political system has deep historical roots, dating back to developments in Mount Lebanon in the mid-nineteenth century. As a result of the contingent interaction between structural transformations in the region and the political machinations of European powers, Ottoman officials, and various local factions, a hybrid mix of republican and communal power-sharing institutions were established to govern the area. These, in turn, precipitated a series of reactions from elite political actors—"feedback" dynamics, in the terminology of historical institutionalism—that had the effect of privileging informal and factionalized political dynamics relating to communalism and clientelism at the expense of democratic ones that required the strengthening of centralized, formal institutions. With the imposition of the French mandate state in Lebanon in 1920, these asymmetrical effects were further reinforced and have become "sticky" over time, leading to a situation whereby the Lebanese polity has become increasingly resistant to institutional change or, in other words, "path dependent." Even with the destabilizing effects of its long civil war, which could have opened up opportunities for significant change in its regime structure, Lebanon's confessional democracy was in the end resuscitated, its reestablishment underpinned by a series of "reversals" in state formation that had the effect of entrenching these political legacies more deeply.

As this study has shown, however, Lebanese politics is not all about sectarianism—hegemonic though its dynamics can be. Rather, the Lebanese political field remains vibrant, full of a diverse set of political orientations and movements. This should not be surprising for a number of reasons. First, as Pierson reminded us at the beginning of this study, there is nothing within the analysis of "path dependence" that implies that a particular political trajectory is "locked in." Rather, there always exists some room for "restricted" and "intelligent" forms of agency able to take advantage of cracks that exist within any system of political domination. The 2011 popular mobilizations in the Arab world have reaffirmed this important truth. Second, our analysis of the Lebanese case reveals these cracks to be seemingly quite large. Its political system, for example, is a paradigmatic case of "dispersed domination"—on the one hand, characterized by a powerful, factionalized, and entrenched regime structure, while, on the other hand, featuring a weak state incapable of penetrating and extending a unified and institutionalized set of political rules deep into Lebanese society. It is precisely this absence of "unified domination" by the Lebanese state—let alone by any one of the various communal and clientelist factional networks in the country—that has given numerous if shifting opportunities for "restricted agency" to a wide array of actors within civil and political society. In the pre–civil war period, these included the increasingly militant mobilizations of labor unions and students, the efforts by new associational elements to address problems of unequal socioeconomic development, the drive to reform state institutions by President Chehab and his networks of technocrats and security officials, as well as the more radical efforts to mobilize powerful countermovements by Kamal Jumblat and the Lebanese left. Even given the reversals in socioeconomic development and state formation brought about by the civil war, one nonetheless saw the rise of a similar, if self-limiting, vibrancy in the post–civil war period, symbolized by the numerous civil reform movements that include the rights-oriented advocacy networks examined in this book.

In analyzing forms of "restricted agency" within Lebanon, this study has directed its particular focus on the role of civil society actors, narrowing in on the activities of associative networks that emerged in the post–civil war period advocating for rights-oriented policy reform within the areas of gender relations, the environment, and disability. Despite the vibrancy, creativity, and determination of those who were a part of these associational networks, however, it is important to remember that their efforts started from a position of double disadvantage. Not only were they calling for reform to policies and institutions in a polity that exhibited strong "path-dependent" qualities, but they also were operating within a broader civil society whose structural underpinnings generated and privileged associational forms that were linked to the prevailing sociopolitical order. Just as the market and the state in contemporary Lebanon have been composed of a fractious array of forces linked to communities, clans, and classes, so too has its civil society, producing an environment whereby associations representing new social and political forces have been forced to contend with an array of associational elements that not only represent more entrenched forms of structural power but also reproduce them.

Nonetheless, reformist associational networks within all three policy domains had important achievements despite the discouraging context.

First, they have been notably successful in institutionalizing their presence within Lebanon's postwar civil society, contributing to broader processes of political reconstruction. In large part, this success has been the result of the normative commitment, determination, and strategic calculations of associational actors themselves—finding ways to take advantage of the constricted political opportunities available to them, transcending the unfavorable structural context that surrounded them, and constructing associational platforms and networks capable of sustaining their presence in the Lebanese public sphere over the longer term. Particularly crucial to this success has been the support of advocacy and development networks in the global arena, providing select, if fluctuating, financial support and opportunities for their local initiatives just at the time when the civil war was coming to an end. As was more generally argued by Keck and Sikkink, the influence of these global advocacy networks "boomeranged" back into the Lebanese political arena, helping local associational actors to sustain their presence, if not increase the resonance of their voices, in the post–civil war period.

These associational networks have used their institutionalized presence in Lebanon's postwar civil society to achieve important, albeit limited, policy successes. First, associational advocacy networks in all three fields have contributed to an ongoing, if highly contested, process of rights-based discursive change. All of the major actors within the disability field, for example, now speak of their work in terms of integration rather than charity—even if the meaning, let alone practice, of this terminology is subject to varying interpretations—and this rights discourse is now backed up by law. This is a notable achievement. Environmental discourses linked to such notions as "sustainable development" and "community-based conservation" also have flooded into the Lebanese public sphere in the post–civil war period, and their meaning has been sharpened by the courageous advocacy campaigns of Lebanon's small coterie of environmental activists, even if these same discourses have also been instrumentalized by factional political forces for their particularistic and often contradictory benefit. However, while discourses relating to gender equality also have become prominent within Lebanon's postwar public sphere, their collective impact has been limited, challenged by the historically entrenched discourses associated with neo-patriarchy as well as the emerging ones revolving around norms of gender complimentarity rather than equality that are prominent within the country's Islamist movements. In short, the advocacy movements examined above have had "cognitive" successes, though the more their discourses have directly challenged historically entrenched institutional power (as has been the case with respect to norms of gender equality), the less impact they have had.

The second series of policy successes—ones that vary widely from one advocacy field to the next—revolves around the injection of energy and some limited forms of accountability into processes of policy dialogue. Again, this has gone furthest within the field of disability, symbolized by the creation of the National Council for Disabled Peoples (NCDP), on which the representation of disabled people was secured, and which proved to be particularly effective in laying out some initial parameters for a reformed disability policy domain in the first years of its existence. While the NCDP subsequently became highly factionalized and, as a result, immobilized as an effective forum of policy dialogue, the resilience of disability advocacy networks combined with their willingness to engage with their policy network rivals has ensured that forms of policy dialogue have continued to take place, albeit in informal and fragmented ways. After the period of intense consultation and cooperation in the mid- to late 1990s between the Ministry of the Environment and environmental associations, institutionalized processes of policy dialogue in this sector also became much harder—confined for the most part to crisis-driven and fleeting moments within particular environmental subsectors such as forest fire prevention. For women's associations trying to promote norms of gender equality, however, significant high-level policy dialogue has been virtually nonexistent, this despite the pioneering creation of the National Commission for Lebanese Women—the country's first "machinery" for women in the postwar period. While part of the explanation for this failure revolves around the ways in which policy demands for gender equality directly challenge powerful institutional legacies, those associations advocating for gender equality have been unable to circumvent these obstacles by forging effective policy—as opposed to personal—linkages with influential political actors at the highest level of the state. While this has been a challenge for all associative networks, especially with respect to sustaining high-level nodal linkages over time, women's associative networks also have had a particularly difficult time in creating them.

The most understated successes of Lebanon's coterie of postwar associative networks, however, have been their ability to forge working relations with bureaucratic enclaves within the Lebanese state—an achievement that could be described as representing a form of "institutional layering" at the level of the state's "trenches." Again, the clearest and most institutionalized example of this is found in the disability sector with the creation and ongoing development of the Rights and Access Program. While not examined in this book, environmental associations, particularly within the solid waste recycling field, also struck up similar forms of cooperative relations with various municipal governments in the country. However, perhaps the most encouraging development in this respect has been the ability of women's advocacy associations—especially those working on the issue of violence against women—to establish working relations with the various Social Development Centers affiliated with the Ministry of Social Affairs, linkages that facilitated their access to some of the poorer women of the country living in remote areas. While these initiatives remain small islands of progressive bureaucratic rationality, they nonetheless represent successful, if piecemeal, experiments that have been able to instrumentalize parts of the state as a "third-party" facilitator—though not a "third-party" enforcer—of rights-oriented social development work.

However, the further one goes up the policy ladder—from changes in policy discourse to improvements in policy deliberation to actual changes in policies and programs themselves—the less associational networks have achieved. Indeed, with respect to the formulation and implementation of broad-based policy change, their achievements have been virtually nonexistent. The ultimate question is, why? What are the main factors that have so constrained agents of reform throughout Lebanon's modern history—including those agents emanating from civil society? As we have argued throughout this book, the answer—a highly discouraging one—is found in the historical processes that have contributed to the deep entrenchment and reproduction of sectarian political life in the country. These dynamics—the cumulative product of various forms of elite networking that have been able to instrumentalize in a factionalized manner the central institutions and commanding heights of the Lebanese state—have continued to privilege informal sectarian political processes over those linked to the country's parallel tradition found within its democratic rules and institutions. While the most powerful forms of networking have been at the national, regional, and global levels, forms of networking within civil society also have been crucial to sustaining the hegemony of informal, factionalized power, facilitating its penetration deep into the social fabric of the country.

The examples in this study are numerous. In the field of gender relations, not only do the majority of associations within the Lebanese Women's Council (LWC) have deep ties to their respective confessional communities and leadership, but many of them also have instrumentalized these ties in order to sustain their associational privileges, thus helping to "reproduce" the pillars of the sectarian political order within the women's sector as a whole. In the environment sector, there has been a parallel proliferation of "mushroom" associations, created and/or co-opted by factional economic and political elites, that have worked either to fend off challenges to their predatory economic practices or, in the field of conservation, to act as mechanisms for asserting factional "sovereignty" over valuable strategic territory. The sustained neutralization of the Lebanese Environmental Forum (LEF) as a unified mechanism for effective environmental lobbying within the postwar public sphere has been a powerful testament to the effectiveness of these practices. Finally, in the field of disability, there has been a long tradition emanating from French statecraft during the mandate period of the large social welfare institutions instrumentalizing their political connections and confessional identities to preserve their autonomy and immobilize efforts to create a unified and rule-based social policy domain. In short, numerous and powerful components of Lebanon's civil society have been active participants in reproducing the country's sectarian political order. It is this dynamic—one that has deep historical roots within modern Lebanese political practice—that has made the social and democratic aspirations of Lebanon's determined community of rights-oriented associational activists particularly difficult to fulfill.

# Notes

## Chapter 1

1. For a discussion of the theory and the historical evolution and practices associated with sectarian democracy in the Lebanese context, see Chapter 2.

2. One of the few English language studies that, in part, examines questions of associational life in Lebanon is Samir Khalaf, *Lebanon's Predicament*, New York: Columbia University Press, 1987. The most significant study of civil society politics in Lebanon is a recent one in French by the Lebanese scholar Karam Karam, *Le Mouvement Civil au Liban: revendications, protestations et mobilizations associatives dans l'apres guerre*, Paris: KARTHALA Editions, 2006. See also Karam Karam, *Revendiquer, Mobiliser, Participer: Les associations civils dans l'apres guerre*, These, Docteur de L'Universite Paul Cezanne–Aix Marseille en Science Politique, October 30, 2004.

3. See (ed.) Richard Augustus Norton, *Civil Society in the Middle East*, Volumes I and II, Leiden; Konynklijke Brill NV, 1994 and 1996. A recent exception is Anne Marie Beylouny, *Privatizing Welfare in the Middle East: Kin Mutual Aid Associations in Jordan and Lebanon*, Bloomington: Indiana University Press, 2010.

4. For an excellent analysis of civil society in post–civil war contexts more generally, see Roberto Belloni, "Civil Society in War-To-Democracy Transitions" in (eds.) Anna Jarstad and Timothy Sisk, *From War to Democracy: Dilemmas of Peacebuilding*, Cambridge: Cambridge University Press, 2008, pp. 182–210.

5. See Robert Bates, Avner Greif, Margaret Levi, Jean-Laurent Rosenthal, and Barry Weingast, *Analytical Narratives*, Princeton: Princeton University Press, 1998, p. 10.

6. Alexander George and Andrew Bennett define process tracing as "attempts to trace the links between possible causes and observed outcomes," describing it as a particularly useful methodology when analyzing the complexity of "sequential processes within a particular historical case." They further identify several facets of process tracing—one of which is guided by "hypotheses and generalizations," which fits with my own historical institutionalist-guided approach.

See Alexander George and Andrew Bennett, *Case Studies and Theory Development in the Social Sciences*, Cambridge: MIT Press, 2005, p. 6, p. 13, and p. 211.

7. Bates et al; op. cit., 1998, p. 12.

8. George and Bennett, op. cit., 1998, p. 216.

9. Paul Pierson, *Politics in Time: History, Institutions, and Social Analysis*, Princeton: Princeton University Press, 2004, p. 21.

10. James Mohoney and Kathleen Thelen, "A Theory of Gradual Institutional Change" in (eds.) James Mahoney and Kathleen Thelen, *Explaining Institutional Change: Ambiguity, Agency, and Power*, Cambridge: Cambridge University Press, 2010, p. 7. See also Giovanni Capoccia and R. Daniel Kelemen, "The Study of Critical Junctures: Theory, Narrative, and Counterfactuals in Historical Institutionalism" in *World Politics*, 59, April 2007, pp. 341–369.

11. Atul Kohli, *State-Directed Development: Political Power and Industrialization in the Global Periphery*, New York: Cambridge University Press, 2004, p. 409.

12. Ruth Berins Collier and David Collier, *Shaping the Political Arena: Critical Junctures, the Labor Movement, and Regime Dynamics in Latin America*, Princeton: Princeton University Press, 1991, p. 29.

13. Pearson, op. cit., 2004, p. 53.

14. Jack Knight, *Institutions and Social Conflict*, New York: Cambridge University Press, 1992, pp. 172–173, p. 188. See also Gretchen Helmke and Steven Levitsky, "Informal Institutions and Comparative Politics: A Research Agenda" in *Perspectives on Politics*, 2, 4, December 2004, pp. 725–740.

15. Knight, op. cit., 1992, p. 188.

16. Ibid., p. 126.

17. Ibid., pp. 192–193.

18. Ibid., p. 150.

19. Kohli, op. cit. 2004, p. 409.

20. Katznelson, op. cit, 2003, p. 297.

21. Pierson, op. cit, 2004, p. 52.

22. Knight, op. cit., 1992, p. 174.

23. James Mahoney, *Legacies of Liberalism: Path Dependence and Political Regimes in Central America*, Baltimore: Johns Hopkins Press, 2001, p. 11.

24. Pierson, op. cit., 2004, p. 73.

25. Katznelson, op. cit., 2003, p. 282.

26. Adam Seligman, *The Idea of Civil Society*, New York: The Free Press, 2002, p. 14.

27. Michael Foley and Bob Edwards, "The Paradox of Civil Society" in *Journal of Democracy*, 7, 3, July 1996, p. 38.

28. John Ehrenburg, *Civil Society: The Critical History of an Idea*, New York: New York University Press, 1999, p. 223.

29. Jenny Pearce, "Civil Society, the Market, and Democracy" in (eds.) Peter Burnell and Peter Calvert, *Civil Society and Democratization*, London: Frank Cass, 2004, p. 96.

30. Edwards and Foley, op. cit, 1996, p. 39.

31. Ehrenburg, op. cit., 1999, pp. 241–244.

32. Geoffrey Hawthorn, "The Promise of 'Civil Society' in the South" in (eds.) Sudipta Kaviraj and Sunil Khilnani, *Civil Society: History and Possibilities*, Cambridge: Cambridge University Press, 2001, p. 286.

33. Joel Migdal, "The State in Society: An Approach to Struggles for Domination" in (eds.) Joel Migdal, Atul Kohli, and Vivien Shue, *State Power and Social Forces: Domination and Transformation in the Third World*, 1994, p. 28.

34. Ibid. p. 20.

35. Sunil Khilnani, "The Development of Civil Society" in (eds.) Sudipta Kaviraj and Sunil Khilnani, *Civil Society: History and Possibilities*, Cambridge: Cambridge University Press, 2001, p. 24.

36. Omar Encarnacion, "Civil Society Reconsidered" in *Comparative Politics*, April, 2006, p. 373. See also Omar Encarnacion, *The Myth of Civil Society: Social Capital and Democratic Consolidation in Spain and Brazil*, New York: Palgrave, 2003.

37. Ehrenburg, op. cit., 1999, p. 235.

38. See Hawthorne, op. cit., 2001, p. 285. See also Laurence Whitehead, "Bowling in the Bronx: The Uncivil Interstices between Civil and Political Society" in (eds.) Peter Burnell and Peter Calvert, *Civil Society and Democratization*, London: Frank Cass, 2004, p. 29.

39. Dietrich Rueschemeyer, Evelyne Huber Stephens, and John D. Stephens, *Capitalist Development and Democracy*, Chicago: University of Chicago Press, 1992, p. 51.

40. Ibid. p. 5

41. Ibid. p. 8

42. Ibid. p. 274.

43. Whitehead, op. cit., 2004, p. 12.

44. Ibid., p. 14.

45. Reuschmeyer, Stephens, and Stephens, op. cit., 1992, p. 54.

46. Ibid., p. 269.

47. Ibid., p. 272,

48. Ibid., p. 271.

49. Ibid., p. 274.

50. See Gordon White, "Civil Society, Democratization, and Development: Clearing the Analytical Ground" in (eds.) Peter Burnell and Peter Calvert, *Civil Society and Democratization*, London: Frank Cass, 2004, p. 12.

51. Diane Singerman, "Civil Society in the Shadow of the Egyptian State: The Role of Informal Networks in the Construction of Public Life" in (ed.) Jim Gelvin, *The Civil Society Debate in Middle East Studies*, Los Angeles: UCLA Near East Center Colloquium Series, 1996, p. 92.

52. See Whitehead, op. cit., 2004, p. 24.

53. See Keith David Watenpaugh, *Being Modern in the Middle East: Revolution, Nationalism, Colonialism, and the Arab Middle Class*, Princeton: Princeton University Press, 2006.

54. Hawthorne, op. cit., 2001, p. 285.

55. Whitehead, op. cit., 2004, p. 39.

56. Peter Evans, "Development Strategies Across the Public-Private Divide" in *World Development*, 24, 6, 1996, p. 1034.

57. Jack Knight and Henry Farrell, "Trust, Institutions, and Institutional Change: Industrial Districts and the Social Capital Hypothesis" in *Politics and Society*, 31, 4, December 2003, p. 560.

58. Knight, op. cit., 1992, p. 126.

59. Migdal, *State in Society: Studying How States and Societies Transform and Constitute One Another*, Cambridge: Cambridge University Press, 2001, p. 59.

60. Migdal, op. cit., 1994, p. 18.

61. Migdal, op. cit., 2001, p. 22.

62. Ibid., p. 19.

63. See Jonathan Fox, "The Difficult Transition from Clientelism to Citizenship: Lesson from Mexico" in *World Politics*, 46, 2, 1994.

64. Douglas Chalmers, "Civil Society Links to Politics: The Importance of Second Level Institutions," unpublished paper, March 2000, p. 11.

65. Elizabeth Friedman and Kathryn Hochstetler, "Assessing the 'Third Transition' in Latin American Democratization: Civil Society in Brazil and Argentina" in *Comparative Politics*, 35, 1, 2002, p. 23.

66. Ibid., p. 25.

67. White, op. cit., 2004, p. 13.

68. This phrase is an adaptation from that used by David Levy and Peter Newell in "Business Strategy and International Environmental Governance: Towards a Neo-Gramscian Synthesis" in *Global Environmental Politics*, 2, 4, November 2002, pp. 84–101.

69. Fox, op. cit., 1994, p. 153.

70. Chalmers, op. cit., 2000, p. 15.

71. Joseph Wong, *Healthy Democracies: Welfare Politics in Taiwan and South Korea*, Ithaca: Cornell University Press, 2004, p. 27.

72. Heydemann, op. cit., 2004, p. 23.

73. Margaret Keck and Kathryn Sikkink, *Activists Beyond Borders: Advocacy Politics in International Politics*, Ithaca: Cornell University Press, 1998, pp. 8–9.

74. Roger Gould, "Uses of Network Tools in Comparative Historical Research" in (eds.) James Mahoney and Dietrich Rueschemeyer, *Comparative Historical Analysis in the Social Sciences*, Cambridge: Cambridge University Press, 2003, p. 242.

75. David Knoke, *Political Networks: A Structural Perspective*, Cambridge: Cambridge University Press, 1990, p. 3. David Knoke defines policy domains as "meso-structural aspects of power built by the participants' social relationships." He goes on to argue that they usually consist of actors having "a common interest in certain types of public policies (but not identical preferences) who must take one another into account in their efforts to influence those policy decisions. Every domain encompasses a diversity of controversial policy matters and numerous

claimant groups and public authorities, each seeking in varying degrees to influence the ultimate decisions about matters of importance to them and to their constituents" (p. 9).

76. Ibid., p. 3.

77. Ibid., p. 9.

78. Heydemann, op. cit., 2004, p. 26.

79. Migdal, op. cit, 2001, p. 108.

80. R. Rhodes and D. Marsh, *Policy Networks in British Government,* Oxford: Oxford University Press, 1992, p. 259.

81. Ibid., p. 260.

82. Ibid. See also Douglas Chalmers, "Associative Networks: New Structures of Representation for the Popular Sectors?" in (eds.) Douglas A. Chalmers, Carlos M. Vilas, Katherine Hite, Scott B. Martin, Kerianne Piester, and Monique Segarra, *The New Politics of Inequality in Latin America: Rethinking Participation and Representation,* Oxford: Oxford University Press, 1997, p. 555.

83. Rhodes and Marsh, op. cit, 1992, p. 14.

84. Hydemann, op. cit., 2004, p. 13.

85. Chalmers, op. cit., 1997, p. 546.

86. Rhodes and March, op. cit., 1992, p. 14.

87. Ibid., p. 250.

88. Keck and Sikkink, op. cit, 1998, p. 207.

89. Ibid., p. 29 and p. 204.

90. Chalmers, op. cit, 1997, p. 575.

91. Ibid.

92. Writes Chalmers, "If (and, of course, it is a big 'if'), popular sectors in associative networks are able to develop cognitive skills, and if elites can develop the capacity to hear what they are saying, such networks represent arenas in which outcomes will not be determined uniquely by the fundamental political resources with class, property, social status, or access to the means of coercion." Ibid., p. 576.

93. Keck and Sikkink, op. cit., 1998, p. 27.

94. Ibid., p. 25.

95. Keck and Sikkink, op. cit., 1998, p. 201.

96. Ibid., p. 27. Keck and Sikkink give, as an example, the decision of transnational women's groups to focus on the issue of violence against women as a way of attacking patriarchy in an indirect manner, a lesson that, as we shall see, was only partially and belatedly learned by activists on behalf of women within the postwar Lebanese context.

# Chapter 2

1. See Max Weiss, *In the Shadow of Sectarianism: Law, Shiism, and the Making of Modern Lebanon,* Cambridge: Harvard University Press, 2010, p. 6.

See also Max Weiss, "The Historiography of Sectarianism in Lebanon" in *History Compass*, 7, 1, 2009.

2. See Julie Peteet, "Imagining the 'New Middle East'" in *International Journal of Middle East Studies*, 40, 4, 2008, p. 551.

3. See Fanar Haddad, *Sectarianism in Iraq: Antagonistic Visions of Unity*, London: Hurst and Company, 2011, p. 2. See also Paul Kingston, "Sectarianism, Paternalism, and Patriarchy: Reflections on Culture and Politics in Lebanon," Review Article in *MIT E-Journal of Middle East Studies*, http://web.mit.edu/cis/www/mitejmes, October 2002.

4. Ussama Makdisi, "Moving Beyond Orientalist Fantasy, Sectarian Polemic, and Nationalist Denial" in *International Journal of Middle East Studies*, 40, 4, 2008, p. 559.

5. See Eric Davis, "A Sectarian Middle East?" in *International Journal of Middle East Studies*, 40, 4, 2008, p. 555.

6. Weiss, op. cit., 2010, p. 235.

7. See Ussama Makdisi, *The Culture of Sectarianism: Community, History, and Violence in Nineteenth-Century Ottoman Lebanon*, Los Angeles: University of California Press, 2000, p. 17.

8. See Arend Lijphart, "Consociational Democracy" in *World Politics*, 21 January 1969; and *Democracy in Plural Societies: A Comparative Exploration*, New Haven: Yale University Press, 1977.

9. Weiss, op. cit., 2010, p. 11

10. Ibid.

11. This "low culture" focus is the approach of Fanar Haddad's recent study of sectarianism in contemporary Iraq. See Haddad, op. cit., 2011.

12. Makdisi, op. cit., 2000, p. 137. This is evident in the mistakes that intervening foreign powers have made in both Lebanon and, more recently, Iraq, where their isolation of "sect" as a driving political variable has led to a self-fulfilling prophecy of "sectarianization." Fanar argued, for example, that in both of these cases—Lebanon in the mid-nineteenth century and Iraq after 2003—foreign actors "reduced society to a simple confessional division and proceeded to formulate policy from that sociological standpoint inevitably lending sectarian identity added political relevance." Fanar, op. cit., 2011, p. 12.

13. See John McGarry and Brendan O'Leary, "Iraq's Constitution of 2005: Liberal Consociation as Political Prescription" in *I*CON*, 5, 4, 2007, pp. 670–698.

14. See Peteet, op. cit., 2008, p. 550.

15. See Sami Farsoun, "E Pluribus Plura or E Pluribus Unum? Cultural Pluralism and Social Class in Lebanon" in (ed.) Halim Barakat, *Toward a Viable Lebanon*, Washington, DC: Center for Contemporary Arab Studies, Georgetown University, 1988; and Donald Horowitz, *Ethnic Groups in Conflict*, Berkeley: University of California Press, 1985, pp. 41–54.

16. Sami Zubaida, *Islam, the People, and the State*, London: Routledge, 1989, p. 146.

17. Albert Hourani, "Lebanon: The Development of a Political Society" in *The Emergence of the Modern Middle East*, London: Macmillan Press Ltd./St. Antony's College, 1981, p. 127.

18. At the height of the autonomous principality, its territorial reach extended to the coastal cities of Tyre, Sidon, Beirut, and Tripoli before being reduced to Mount Lebanon by the Ottomans in 1841, territorial borders that remained in place until the French created the modern state of Lebanon based on the Greater Lebanon model in 1920.

19. Georges Corm, *Le Liban Contemporaire: Histoire and Societe*, Paris, France: Editions La Decouverte, 2003, p. 78. Corm writes of the ease of passing back and forth from one community to the other, especially but not exclusively at the level of elites, and argues that this symbiosis would prove crucial in laying some of the foundations for the emergence and persistence of the Lebanese entity.

20. In the mid-nineteenth century, Traboulsi writes of peasants in Mount Lebanon demanding "full equality and complete freedom" for commoners vis à vis their feudal lords, something that he refers to as a "peasant democratic component." Fawwaz Traboulsi, *A History of Modern Lebanon*, London: Pluto Press, 2007, p. 31.

21. Jens Hanssen writes, for example, of striking Beirut port workers adopting "the very language of universal principles enshrined in the Ottoman constitution." Jens Hanssen, *Fin de siècle Beirut: The Making of an Ottoman Provincial Capital*, Oxford: Oxford University Press, 2005, p. 109.

22. Traboulsi, op. cit., 2007, p. 77. See also Karam, op. cit., 2006, p. 49. Akarli similarly argues that the influence of the ideals of the French Revolution on the representatives of the reinstated administrative council was "unmistakable." Akarli, op. cit., 1993, p. 178.

23. Akarli, op. cit., 1993, p. 190. In the context of municipal politics in late-Ottoman Beirut, Jens Hanssen has similarly argued that its "participatory institutions brought along important modifications of existing patterns in the politics of notables, in terms of power-sharing, compromise, and cooperative decision-making for the sake of public welfare." See Hanssen, op. cit., 2005, p. 161.

24. Makdisi, op. cit., 2000, p. 16.

25. Sami Farsoun defines "sect classes" as representing a fusion of the socio-economic and the communal in such a way that it generates a "differentiated, unevenly stratified, polarized, and antagonistic" set of social relations between the communities. See Farsoun, op. cit., 1988, p. 100. See also Claude Dubar and Salim Nasr, *Les Classes sociales au Liban*, Paris: Presses de la Fondation Nationale des Sciences Politiques, 1976; Roger Owen, "The Economic History of Lebanon, 1943–1974: Its Salient Features" in (ed.) Halim Barakat, *Towards a Viable Lebanon*, Washington, DC: Center for Contemporary Arab Studies, Georgetown University, 1988, p. 28; and Roger Owen, "The Political Economy of Grand Liban, 1920–1970" in (ed.) Roger Owen, *Essays on the Crisis in Lebanon*, London: Ithaca Press, 1976.

26. See Corm, op. cit., 2001, p. 76.

27. This dynamic was especially pronounced during the era of the *mutasari-fiyya* as the area's old feudal elites, desperate to maintain their social and political prestige in the newly emerging political order, competed intensely for administrative offices, thereby transforming "public service into a highly politicized pursuit." Akarli adds that it was the ability of these factional elite actors to take advantage of the *mutasarifiyya's* confessional framework that helps to explains why the system of confessional quotas under the *mutasarifiyya* became so rigid "for virtually all positions within its administrative apparatus" by the end of the period. See Akarli, op. cit., 1993, p. 157. See also Nizar Hamzeh, "Clientelism, Lebanon: Roots and Trends" in *Middle East Studies*, 37, 2001, pp. 167–178.

28. Samir Khalaf argues that while these peasant revolts "evinced attributes of collective solidarity and class consciousness rare among movements in small and highly factionalized sociocultural settings . . . [they] rarely remained in pure form . . . [and] either merged with intercommunal tensions, rampant at the time, or were deflected into confessional hostility." See Samir Khalaf, "Peasants, Commoners, and Clerics: Resistance and Rebellion, 1820–1860" in *Civil and Uncivil Violence in Lebanon: A History of the Internationalization of Communal Conflict*, New York: Columbia University Press, 2002, p. 63. See also Samir Khalaf, *Lebanon's Predicament*, New York: Columbia University Press, 1987.

29. Traboulsi, op. cit., 2007, p. 26.

30. Akarli, op. cit., 1993, p. 149.

31. The right of women to vote was achieved in Lebanon in 1953. Initially, elections were designed as a two-stage process, with the actual parliamentary deputies being elected by an electoral college in the second stage. This was replaced by direct universal (male) suffrage in 1934.

32. See Thompson, *Colonial Citizens: Republican Rights, Paternal Privilege, and Gender in French Syria and Lebanon*, New York: Columbia University Press, 2000, p. 114. See also Meir Zamir, *Lebanon's Quest: The Road to Statehood, 1926–1939*, London: I.B. Taurus, 1997, p. 30.

33. See Theodor Hanf, *Co-Existence in Wartime Lebanon: Decline of a State, Rise of a Nation*, Oxford: Center for Lebanese Studies, 1993, p. 68; see also Corm, op. cit., 2003, pp. 90–92.

34. Ibid. Zamir described the attitude of the French High commissioners to the Syrian-Lebanese mandate as being that "as long as Lebanese politicians did not interfere with French interests in the mandated territories, it was preferable to leave them to their own devices." See Zamir, op. cit., 1997, p. 44.

35. Kais Firro, "Ethnicizing the Shi'is in Mandatory Lebanon" in *Middle Eastern Studies*, 42, 5, 2006. See also Kais Firro, *Inventing Lebanon: Nation and State Under the Mandate*, London: I.B. Taurus, 2003, p. 106.

36. Max Weiss further argues that the establishment of the Jafari court system (with branches in Beirut, Sidon, Nabatiyya, Marja'yun, Ba'lbak, and Hirmil) had a number of important effects, including the bureaucratization of Shi'i law, aggrandizing the authority of Shi'a judges, the reorientation of Shi'a society toward

Beirut, and the restructuring of relationships between the Shi'a and other Lebanese sectarian communities. See Max Weiss, "Institutionalizing Sectarianism: The Lebanese Jafari Court and Shi'a Society under the French Mandate" in *Islamic Law and Society*, 15, 2008, pp. 371–407. See also Firro, op. cit., 2003, pp. 158–172.

37. One of many telling examples of the forced communal institution-building process is provided by the Protestant community within Lebanon. The Protestant community had a deep and active history in Lebanon, having received millet status under the Ottomans in 1854—indeed, it was the "last millet" recognized by the Ottoman state. Yet it was not until 1936, sparked by the reaffirmation by the mandate state of the responsibility of the various religious communities to regulate their own personal status issues as well as by its first divorce case, that the community was forced to unify and institutionalize itself. It responded by writing up its own laws of personal status, establishing a court system, and uniting the community under the umbrella of the Supreme Council for the Evangelical Community, all of which were officially registered and sanctioned by the Lebanese state one year later. By the 1970s, the Protestant community had further developed its legal institutions with the establishment of four permanent courts in Beirut, Zahle, Tripoli, and Sidon. Interview with Dr. Habib Badr, Near East School of Theology, Beirut, 31 March 2004.

38. Thompson, op. cit., 2000, pp. 168–169.

39. See Meir Zamir, op. cit., 1997, p. 28.

40. Figures in Kais Firro's book, for example, suggest that 171 members of landowning families or merchants owned 50 percent of all cultivable land in Lebanon in the Mandatory period (though no exact year was specified, and this percentage would have varied significantly from region to region of the country). See Firro, op. cit., 2003, p. 87.

41. Elizabeth Picard, *Lebanon—A Shattered Country: Myths and Realities of Wars in Lebanon*, Teaneck, New Jersey: Holmes and Meier, 1996, p. 48.

42. This included major upgrades to the port of Beirut, the building of a new commercial center for the city, the construction of more than 1,500 miles of roads, the development of communication facilities, and the improvement of infrastructure related to sanitation and health. See Zamir, op. cit., 1997, p. 40.

43. Picard notes, for example, that it was only after 1939 that the parliamentary representation of the commercial and financial bourgeoisie increased to an average of 25 percent. Picard, op. cit., 1996, p. 48. For discussion of France's infrastructural policies, see Marwan Buheiry, "Beirut's Role in the Political Economy of the French Mandate, 1919–1939" in (ed.) Lawrence Conrad, *The Formation and Perception of the Modern Arab World*, Princeton: Darwin Press, 1989; and Carolyn Gates, *The Merchant Republic of Lebanon: The Rise of an Open Economy*, London: The Center for Lebanese Studies and I.B. Taurus, 1998.

44. See Caroline Gates, *The Historic Role of Political Economy in the Development of Modern Lebanon*, Oxford: Center for Lebanese Studies, 10, September 1989, p. 14.

45. Firro, op. cit., 2003, p. 91.

46. See Picard, op. cit., 1996, pp. 52–53.

47. A *zaim* is defined as "the recognized leader of a community who has the power to speak for his clients as a group or as individuals." See Arnold Hottinger, "*Zuama* in Historical Perspective" in (ed.) Leonard Binder, *Politics in Lebanon*, New York: Wiley, 1965.

48. Zamir, op. cit., 1997, p. 33.

49. Firro, op. cit., 2003, p. 151.

50. Firro in fact argued that communalism was "the only true basis of legitimacy" for Lebanon's factional elites. Ibid., p. 115.

51. Ibid., p. 125.

52. Maronite negotiators, for example, pushed strongly for guarantees of communal protection from France and increasingly demanded that the office of president, hitherto open to any community, be restricted to a Maronite Christian. On the other hand, the political discourse of Sunni political elites increasingly began to coalesce around demands for communal equality—ones that included appeals for more seats within the parliament, a greater hold over the Office of the Prime Minister, and more jobs within the burgeoning administration, which had reached almost 5,000 employees by the late 1930s. While Shi'a political elites had long been demanding their share of state resources for their marginalized communities in the Bekaa and the South—demands that usually took the form of requests for more roads, more schools, and less taxation—their elites, too, intensified the process of communal demand making in the wake of the 1936 treaty, hoping to avoid being crowded out in the wake of intensifying Sunni demands. See Corm, op. cit., 2003, p. 92 and p. 120; and Firro, op. cit., 2006, p. 755.

53. Firro, op. cit., 2003, p. 152.

54. See Weiss, op. cit., 2010, p. 18. See also Farid el-Khazen, *The Communal Pact of National Identity: The Making and Politics of the 1943 National Pact*, Oxford: Center for Lebanese Studies, 1991, p. 5. Albert Hourani reached the same conclusion, describing the National Pact not as symbolizing a "deeper or wider agreement about the nature of Lebanon or the purposes to which its political system should be used," but rather as being the product of "a temporary change of mood" among factionalized Lebanese elites. Hourani, op. cit., 1981, p. 140 and p. 172.

55. See David Hirst, *Beware of Small States: Lebanon, Battleground of the Middle East*, New York: Nation Books, 2010, pp. 22–44.

56. Zamir, for example, describes the uproar that surrounded a decision by the Maronite Prime Minister Emile Edde to "rationalize" government expenditures in 1929, one that was projected to result in the closure of one hundred public schools, most of which were attended by Muslim students. Not only did this decision precipitate an outcry within Lebanon's Muslim communities, but it also sparked "well-orchestrated" press campaigns and public demonstrations in neighboring Arab countries. Zamir, op. cit., 1997, p. 78.

57. Hanna Ziadeh, in fact, argues that the role of the British has been "systematically underplayed" in national accounts of the National Pact. See Hanna

Ziadeh, *Sectarianism and Intercommunal Nation-Building in Lebanon*, London: Hurst and Company, 2006, p. 113; and Firro, op. cit., 2003, p. 209.

58. While the Ottomans had registered only thirty-one associations (in part the result of their Law of Associations only having been formulated and passed in 1909), the mandate period witnessed the official registration of "a dizzying array" of associations that, by the end of 1942, numbered more than 400 in Beirut alone, with another 338 in the rest of the country. Thompson, op. cit., 2000, p. 91.

59. Zamir, op. cit., 1997, p. 31. Among the most dynamic were movements of workers, women, and the educated middle classes, spawning a diverse array of organizations from employee-only unions and labor federations with a strong antisectarian ethos, to the country's first women's organizations that were described as having carved out a significant presence within the civic order, to several nonsectarian political forums, movements, and parties. These included the Syrian Nationalist Socialist Party (SNSP) of Antun Saadeh; the Lebanon People's Party that eventually transformed into the Lebanese Communist Party (LCP); as well as a multisectarian "gathering" called the National Democratic Congress that emerged in the late 1930s and whose platform called for popular suffrage, the direct election of the president, and progressive direct income taxation to replace the existing, regressive system of indirect taxation. Firro argues that these initiatives emerged, by and large, from elements "outside the strata of Lebanon's existing political elites" and were designed to lay the socioeconomic and political foundations for the development of a more integrated political arena. See Thompson, op. cit., 2000 for an excellent study of the associational activism of women and workers during the mandate period. See also Firro, op. cit., 2003, p. 130; and Traboulsi, op. cit., 2007, pp. 103–104.

60. See, for example, Samir Khalaf, "Family Associations" in *Lebanon's Predicament*, New York: Columbia University Press, 1987, p. 161.

61. See Karam, op. cit., 2004, p. 51; and Thompson, op. cit., 2000, p. 96; Bernard Hillenkamp, "From the Margins to the Centre? Kurds and Shi'a in a Changing Zokak el-Blat in West Beirut" in Orient-Institute, *History, Space and Social Conflict in Beirut: The Quarter of Zokak el-Blat*, Beirut: Orient Institute, 2005, pp. 213–246; and LCPS, op. cit., undated.

62. See Traboulsi, op. cit., 2007, pp. 102–103.

63. Firro, op. cit., 2003, p. 115; and Traboulsi, op. cit., 2007, p. 102. The mobilizational capacity of *al-Kataib*, for example, was estimated to have reached 8,000 within its first year and almost 30,000 by the end of the mandate period. Thompson, op. cit., 2000, p. 193. See also Wade Goria, *Sovereignty and Leadership in Lebanon, 1943–1976*, London: Ithaca, 1985, p. 47.

64. Zamir, op. cit., 1997, p. 233.

65. Ibid., p. 208.

66. The proposals were aimed at reestablishing the role of the state and civil law in matters relating to personal status—imposing stricter requirements on the registration of religious marriages with the state, giving civil law jurisdiction over matters where religious law was either vague or silent, and, most significantly,

giving citizens the right to disavow their religious affiliation altogether—all of which would have created segments of the Lebanese population that lay completely outside the authority of Lebanon's religious communities, in effect creating a "nineteenth civil confession" in the country. Thompson, op. cit., 2000, p. 152.

67. The French eventually withdrew their proposal, concluding in its wake that the country's personal status law system was "locked in an iron cage" as a result of alliances between religious clerics, nationalist politicians, and their subaltern followers. Ibid., p. 154.

68. Picard, op. cit., 1996, p. 71.

69. Pierson, op. cit., 2004, p. 52. See also Mahoney and Thelen, op. cit., 2010, pp. 1–37.

70. These gradual processes of institutional change become important when they reach a "collective threshold," which Pearson defines as a "big effect" that can lead to nonlinear institutional change, away from a particular critical juncture. Pearson adds that while one needs to guard against painting "an overly deterministic picture of social processes" delinked from the "causal chain" of factors that actually trigger collective action, these sources of institutional change can nonetheless be quite promising because of their potential to challenge asymmetrical power relations that underpin processes of institutional reinforcement. Pierson, op. cit., 2004, pp. 83–86 and p. 102.

71. Ibid., p. 137. See also Thelen, op. cit., 2003, p. 225.

72. Thelen cautions us about the potential of this roundabout strategy of institutional reform, arguing that it needs to be placed in the overall context of the "self-reinforcing" rather than "corrective" nature of institutional change in the political realm, adding further that it is really "changes in power relations that hold the key to creating openings." Thelen, op. cit., 2003, p. 125 and p. 217.

73. See Thelen, op. cit., 1991, p. 9; and Thelen, op. cit., 2004, p. 216.

74. Thelen, op. cit., 1991, p. 7.

75. Owen writes of the explosion of industrial production at this time, contributing close to 25 percent of gross domestic product and emanating from more than 300 large plants. With increasing percentages of this production being exported to the Arab world and, in particular, to the oil-rich states of the Gulf region, Owen concluded that "certainly, the way was open for the country to become a major Middle Eastern industrial—as well as financial—power." Owen, op. cit., 1985, p. 37.

76. Some estimates suggest that annual growth rates were as high as 7 percent per year between 1950 and 1974. Ibid., p. 33.

77. Salim Nasr, "The Crisis of Lebanese Capitalism: Backdrop to Civil War" in *MERIP*, 73, 1978, p. 3.

78. Ibid., p. 4.

79. Ibid., pp. 5–6.

80. Gates, op. cit., 1989, p. 37. Michael Johnson has similarly argued that the interests of local industrial capital in Lebanon's pre–civil war period were subordinated to the interests of international and local financial capital. See Michael

Johnson, *Class and Client in Beirut: The Sunni Muslim Community and the Lebanese State, 1840–1985*, London: Ithaca Press, p. 35.

81. Nasr, op. cit., 1978, p. 8.

82. Khalaf, op. cit., 2002, p. 170. See also Tawfiq Gaspard, *A Political Economy of Lebanon, 1948–2002: The Limits of Laissez-faire*, Leiden and Boston: Brill, 2004, p. 93; and Nasr, op. cit., pp. 8–10.

83. Petran, op. cit., 1987, p. 75; Traboulsi, op. cit., 2007, p. 157; and Gaspard, op. cit., 2004, p. 166.

84. See Traboulsi, op. cit., 2007, pp. 145–146.

85. See Hudson, op. cit., 1968, p. 178; and Hanf, op. cit., 1993, p. 176.

86. See Collier and Collier, op. cit., 1991.

87. In the late 1950s, for example, it was estimated that more than 97 percent of all enterprises in the service sector and 98 percent of all enterprises in the industrial sector were family proprietorships or partnerships. See Yusif Sayigh, *Entrepreneurs of Lebanon: The Role of the Business Leader in a Developing Economy*, Cambridge: Harvard University Press, 1962, pp. 52–54. See also Arthur Mills, *Private Enterprise in Lebanon*, Beirut: American University of Beirut/Center for Public Sector Projects and Studies, 1959. More recently, Franck Debie et al. suggest three political reasons why the family firm has been able to persist, relating to its ability to capture various kinds of "rent" linked to protection, its cartelization of the import business, and its access to diaspora capital. See Franck Debie, Danuta Pieter, avec la collaboration d'Eric Verdeil, *Le paix et la crise: le Liban reconstruit?*, Paris: Presses Universitaires de France, 2003, p. 37.

88. Gaspard, op. cit.; 2004, p. 65. Hanf reported that by 1980, there were 165 separate trade unions in addition to 18 trade union federations. Theodor Hanf, "Homo Oeconomicus-Homo Communitaris: Crosscutting Loyalties in a Deeply Divided Society: The Case of the Trade Unions of Lebanon" in (eds.) Milton Esman and Itamar Rabinovich, *Ethnicity, Pluralism, and the State in the Middle East*, Ithaca: Cornell University Press, 1988, p. 175.

89. Khalaf emphasizes in his pre–civil war research on Lebanon's fragmented labor movement that workers' loyalties were directed more "towards the workplace and the employers rather than to some general industry-wide or occupational form of association," an orientation that constituted a "serious drain on workers' commitment to the labor movement." Khalaf, op. cit., 1987, pp. 43–44.

90. With respect to processes of labor co-optation at the Regie des Tabacs, see Malik Abisaab, *Militant Women in a Fragile Nation*, New York: Syracuse University Press, 2010, p. 150. See also Tabitha Patran, *The Struggle Over Lebanon*, New York: Monthly Review Press, 1987; and Traboulsi, op. cit., 2007, p. 168.

91. With respect to the use of the Lebanese Army to disrupt 1,965 worker disruptions at the Hadath plant of the Regie des Tobacs, see Abisaab, op. cit., 2010, pp. 169–170.

92. Gaspard, op. cit., 2004, p. 65; and Baroudi, op. cit., 1998, p. 533. These figures seem to be disputed. Hanf, for example, estimates that membership in the

trade union movement had reached 24 percent of the total labor force by 1980, a figure that Hanf argued "compared to the level of organization in the United States of America or Mexico." Hanf, op. cit., 1988, p. 175.

93. In his study of pre–civil war urban Druze migrants, for example, Nazih Richani described them as "individualistic, competing with one another for work, customers, and patrons." In his class analysis of prewar Lebanese politics, Johnson described the menu people as a whole as a "desperate" social force, "lacking in any clear direction." See Nazi Richani, "Class Formation in a Civil War: The Druze of Mount Lebanon" in *MERIP*, January–February, 1990, pp. 27–28; and Johnson, op. cit., 1985, p. 38.

94. Farid el-Khazen, *The Breakdown of the Lebanese State in Lebanon, 1967–1976*, London: I.B. Taurus, 2000, p. 177.

95. See Hudson, op. cit., 1968, p. 302.

96. See Traboulsi, op. cit., 2007, p. 155.

97. With respect to President Chamoun's more confrontation approach to reforming the Lebanese political system that ultimately resulted in a "revolt of the pashas." See Johnson, op. cit., 1985, p. 156. See also Caroline Attie, *Struggle in the Levant: Lebanon in the 1950s*, London: I.B. Taurus, 2004.

98. These included the power to make decrees, the power to veto legislation, the power to appoint the prime minister and the cabinet, as well as the power to dissolve the parliament.

99. See Hudson, op. cit., 1968, pp. 309–312. See also Oren Barak, *The Lebanese Army: A National Institution in a Divided Society*, New York: SUNY Press, 2009.

100. Ibid., p. 303.

101. Institut International de Recherche et du Formation en vue de Developpement Integral et Harmonize.

102. These ranged from the Central Bank, to National Litani Authority, to the Office of Social Development (OSD) with its plans for a series of Social Development Centers spread throughout the country.

103. See Goria, op. cit., 1985, p. 72; and Rex Brynen, *Sanctuary and Survival: The PLO in Lebanon*, Boulder: Westview Press/Pinter Publishers, 1990.

104. See Adel Beshara, *Lebanon: The Politics of Frustration—The Failed Coup of 1961*, London: Routledge/Curzon, 2005, p. 144.

105. Hudson, op. cit., 1968, p. 135.

106. Johnson, op. cit., 1985, p. 141; and Traboulsi, op. cit., 2007, p. 143.

107. Traboulsi, op. cit., 2007, p. 138.

108. El-Khazen, op. cit., 2000, p. 181.

109. Johnson, op. cit., 1985, p. 149.

110. See Kamal Salibi, "Lebanon Under Fuad Chahab, 1958–1964" in *Middle East Studies*, 1966, p. 213.

111. Picard, op. cit., 1996, p. 76.

112. Petran, op. cit., 1987, p. 87. See also Trabousli, op. cit., 2007, p. 143; and Hudson, op. cit., 1968, p. 319.

113. Beshara, op. cit., 2005, p. 59.

114. Michael Young has articulated this dimension of Lebanese society in a similar manner, describing Lebanon somewhat optimistically as "a country of liberal spaces." See Michael Young, *The Ghosts of Martyrs Square: An Eyewitness Account of Lebanon's Life Struggle*, New York: Simon and Schuster, 2010, p. 120. See also Ahmad Beydoun, "Confessionalism: Outline of an Announced Accord" in (ed) N. Salam, *Options for Lebanon*, London: I.B. Taurus, 2004, in which he similarly argues that it is the "endemic disunity" of the Lebanese system that allows for the possibility of public space.

115. Hudson, op. cit., 1968, p. 148.

116. Ibid., p. 211.

117. Ibid., p. 225.

118. Ibid., p. 248.

119. Ibid., p. 225.

120. Ibid., p. 169.

121. Ibid., p. 330. El-Khazen reaches similar conclusions about the pre–civil war Lebanese political system becoming "more democratic" and "more open." El-Khazen, op. cit., 1991, p. 24.

122. Nazih Richani, *Dilemmas of Democracy and Political Parties in Sectarian Societies: The Case of the Progressive Socialist Party of Lebanon 1949–1996*, New York: St. Martin's Press, 1998, p. 51.

123. See Farid el-Khazen, "Lebanon's Communal Elite-Mass Politics: The Institutionalization of Disintegration" in *The Beirut Review*, 3, Spring 1992.

124. Richani, op. cit., 1998, pp. 57–59. See also Goria, op. cit., 1985, p. 31 in which Jumblat is quoted as keeping open the possibility of using violence to back up his socialist ideas despite his sympathy for Gandhi.

125. Picard writes, for example, of the growth of a Palestinian associational infrastructure—epitomized by the emergence of hospitals, social welfare institutions, research centers, press centers, and information agencies; she also writes of the growth of Palestinian economic infrastructure—complete with companies and banks; this was complemented by the growth of Palestinian political and military infrastructure, complete with the existence of several political factions and parties, all with their own militias. Picard, op. cit., 1996, p. 82.

126. Goria, op. cit., 1985, p. 93.

127. See Traboulsi, op. cit., 2007, p. 176.

128. Hudson, op. cit., 1968, p. 248.

129. Labib Zuwiyya Yamak, "Party Politics in the Lebanese Party System" in (ed.) Leonard Binder, *Politics in Lebanon*, New York: Wiley and Sons, Inc., 1968, p. 155.

130. Having started out with cross-sectarian representation in the 1950s, for example, "Jumblat's" PSP saw this dramatically reduced in the wake of the 1958 crisis with the withdrawal of many of its Maronite members. Indeed, with membership increasingly being made up of students, labor, and the "menu people," with the latter constituting the majority of the PSP by 1975, the PSP was pushed into becoming a clientelist mechanism for patronage delivery, Jumblat being

viewed by its rank and file as a "passport for jobs." Richani notes, for example, that "on Saturdays and Sundays, Jumblat received hundreds of people soliciting jobs, most of them from the menu strata. To them, he usually gave a card carrying a personal signature, to be given to the person in charge at the institution or bureaucracy where a job was available. In return for this favor, many job hunters became PSP members." Richani, op. cit., 1989, p. 52 and p. 82.

131. Ibid., p. 2.

132. Ibid., p. 52.

133. Petran, op. cit., 1987, p. 110.

134. See Sami Baroudi, "Economic Conflict in Postwar Lebanon: State-Labour Relations between 1992–1997" in *Middle East Journal*, 52, 4, Autumn 1998.

135. See Traboulsi, op. cit., 2007, p. 172.

136. See Petran, op. cit., 1987, p. 111.

137. Among the incidents of deadly violence perpetrated by the Lebanese state included two protesters killed while on strike at the Ghandour Chocolat and Biscuit Factory in November 1972, those killed while occupying the offices of the Regie des Tabac in Nabatiyya in January 1973, as well as the deaths of several more, including Marouf Saad, the Nasserist and deputy of modest social background, in the demonstrations of fishermen in Sidon in January 1975 protesting against the encroachment into local waters of the industrial fishing company Protein (of which the former president, Chamoun, was a major shareholder). Traboulsi, op. cit., 2007, p. 171.

138. Hanf argues that, for the most part, sectarian issues rarely seemed to come to the forefront in the day-to-day tussles of politics in post-independence Lebanon, with political elites, especially after the events of 1958, implicitly adopting an approach of "pragmatic accommodation." He further argues that this resulted in the constitutionally preeminent and Maronite-controlled office of president being transformed into "a de facto Maronite-Sunni duumvirate." See Hanf, op. cit., 1993, p. 91. See also Ziadeh, op. cit., 2006, p. 125.

139. In 1973, it was estimated that Christians controlled 67 percent of wealth in industry, 75 percent of wealth in commerce, and 71 percent of wealth in the banking sector, figures that had improved only moderately from the 1950s. See Traboulsi, op. cit., 2007, p. 162.

140. Having initially formed in opposition to Chehabist reforms, the *Hilf* became a more powerful political alliance after the 1967 war, reflected in its strong showing in the 1969 parliamentary elections. On the eve of the civil war, it would consolidate further with the formation of the Lebanese Front.

141. See Goria, op. cit., 1985, p. 127.

142. Helping to consolidate the pre–civil war power of the Kataib were the development of an extensive array of party offices throughout the country, the organization of summer camps to recruit Maronite youth, and its practice of the holding numerous rallies and military parades in the towns and villages of Mount Lebanon. See ibid., p. 66.

143. This power reached its symbolic apex with the *Kataib* rejection of proposals at the National Dialogue Committee in the fall of 1975 that was a crucial moment in the country's descent into civil war.

144. See Petran, op. cit., 1987, p. 154.

145. George Corm, "The War System: Militia Hegemony and Reestablishment of the State" in (ed.) Dierdre Collings, *Peace for Lebanon? From War to Reconstruction*, Boulder and London: Lynne Rienner Publishers, 1994, p. 219.

146. See Lewis Snider, "The Lebanese Forces: Their Origins and Role in Lebanese Politics" in *Middle East Journal*, 38, 1, 1984; and Marie Joelle Zahar, "Proteges, Clients, Canon Fodder: Civilians in the Calculus of Militias" in *International Peacekeeping*, 7, 4, Winter 2001.

147. See Richard Norton, *AMAL and the Shi'a: Struggle for the Soul of Lebanon*, Austin: University of Texas Press, 1987, pp. 90–91.

148. See Emmanuel Bonne, *Vie publique, patronage, et clientele: Rafic Hariri a Saida*, Universites d'Aix-Marseille: IRENAM and CERMOC, 1995; and Marwan Iskandar, *Rafiq Hariri and the Fate of Lebanon*, London: Saqi, 2006.

149. Some of the traditional zu'ama also developed their own militia structures. This included the Marada militia of the Franjieh clan, the Tigers of the Chamoun clan, and the PSP militia of the Jumblat clan, which was the most institutionalized of these more traditional entities, with Picard describing it as "an autonomous principality." See Elizabeth Picard, "The Political Economy of Civil War in Lebanon" in (ed.) Steven Hydeman, *War, Institutions, and Social Change in the Middle East*, Berkeley: University of California Press, 2000. See also Paul Kingston and Marie Joelle Zahar, "Rebuilding *A House of Many Mansions*: The Rise and Fall of Militia Cantons in Lebanon" in (eds.) Paul Kingston and Ian Spears, *States within States: Incipient Political Entities in the Post-Cold War Era*, New York: Palgrave MacMillan, 2004.

150. Elizabeth Picard, "Trafficking, Rents, and Diaspora in the Lebanese War" in Cynthia Arnson and I. William Zartman (eds.), *Rethinking the Economics of War: The Intersection of Need, Creed, and Greed*, Baltimore: Johns Hopkins University Press, 2005, p. 28.

151. Ibid., pp. 32–33. Picard added that, in certain cases, the militias even collectively negotiated with the enfeebled Lebanese state over the terms of dismantling the latter's own public import monopolies—such as crude oil and tobacco—and redistributed those rights to the various militia interests. The result was that, at the civil war's height, the "militia economies" roughly generated an annual income in the range of U.S.$900 million per year, a figure that William Harris breaks down as follows: drugs (U.S.$600 million), arms trafficking (U.S.$150 million), and protection money (U.S.$200 million). See William Harris, *Faces of Lebanon: Sects, Wars, and Global Extensions*, Princeton: Markus Weiner Publishers, 1997, p. 207.

152. Picard, op. cit., 2000, p. 298.

153. Ibid., p. 300.

154. With respect to the commercial motives behind militia military maneuvers, see Picard, op. cit., 2005, pp. 39–40.

155. S. Makdisi, op. cit., 2004, p. 74; and Picard, op. cit., 2005, pp. 49–50.

156. See Salim Nasr, "New Social Realities and Post-War Lebanon: Issues for Reconstruction" in (eds.) Philip S. Khoury and Samir Khalaf, *Recovering Beirut*, Leiden: Brill, 1993, p. 69; Salim Nasr, " 'The New Social Map.' " In *Lebanon in Limbo*, (eds.) T. Hanf and N. Salam. Baden-Baden: Nomos Verlagsgesellschaft, 2003, p. 143; and Traboulsi, op. cit., 2007, p. 239.

157. Nasr, op. cit., 2003, p. 152. See also Kamal Hamdan, "La Classe moyenne dans la guerre du Liban" in (ed.) Fadia Kiwan, *Le Liban aujourd'hiu*, Paris: CNRS Editions, 1994, pp. 193–203.

158. S. Makdisi, op. cit., 2004, p. 47.

159. Thierry Kochuyt, "La misere au Liban: une population appauvrie, peu d'Etat et plusiers solidarities souterraines" in *Revue Tiers Monde*, XLV, no. 179, Juillet–Sept., 2004, p. 518. See also Debie, op. cit., 2003, p. 150 and p. 167; and UNDP, "Towards a Regionally Balanced Development Program" in *Linking Economic Growth and Social Development in Lebanon*, Beirut: UNDP, 2000.

160. Samir Kassir chose to use "protectorate" instead of "occupation," arguing that the latter is "too simplistic a description of Syrian goals and practices in Lebanon." Samir Kassir, "A Polity in an Uncertain Regional Development." In *Lebanon in Limbo*, (eds.) T. Hanf and N. Salam. Baden-Baden: Nomos Verlagsgesellschaft, 2003, p. 100.

161. There were other positive stipulations in the Taif Accord that included the call for strengthening judicial independence, the creation of a national Social and Economic Committee, and the promotion of political decentralization.

162. The Taif Accord produced thirty-one amendments to the Lebanese constitution, the principal ones revolving around changes to the informal power-sharing formulas of the 1943 National Pact. Communal representation in the parliament was changed to a 5–5 ratio (Christian–Muslim), and the power of each of the three communally allotted executive offices of the state was divided on a more equal, if ambiguous, basis, thus eliminating the presidency as the unambiguously preeminent and "critical institution" within the Lebanese state. See Hudson, op. cit., 1968, p. 262. See also Sami Ofiesh, "Lebanon's Second Republic: Secular Talk, Sectarian Application" in *Arab Studies Quarterly*, Winter 1999; and Joseph Maila, "The Ta'if Accord: An Evaluation" in (ed.) Deirdre Collings, *Peace for Lebanon? From War to Reconstruction*, Boulder: Lynne Rienner Publishers, 1994, p. 38.

163. Nicholas Blandford, *Killing Mr. Lebanon: The Assassination of Rafik Hariri and its Impact on the Middle East*, London: I.B. Taurus, 2006, p. 51.

164. See Raymond Hinnebusch, "Pax Syriana? The Origins, Causes and Consequences of Syria's Role in Lebanon" in *Mediterranean Politics*, 3, 1, Summer 1998, p. 150.

165. For a rebuttal to those who argued that the Syrians agreed to a "trade-off"—accepting Lebanese autonomy in economic matters in exchange for political hegemony—see Reinoud Leenders, "Lebanon's Political Economy: After Syria, an

Economic Taif?" in *MIT-International Electronic Journal of Middle East Studies*, 2006, p. 42.

166. International Crisis Group, *Lebanon: Managing the Gathering Storm*, Middle East Report #48, December 2005, p. 8.

167. See Farid el-Khazen, "The Postwar Political Process: Authoritarianism by Diffusion" in (eds.) Theodor Hanf and Nawaf Salam, *Lebanon in Limbo: Postwar Society and State in an Uncertain Regional Environment*, Baden-Baden: Verlagsgesellschaft, 2003, p. 67.

168. The 1992 elections were based on twelve electoral districts, the 1996 elections were based on ten electoral districts, and the 2000 elections were based on fourteen electoral districts, as were the elections in 2005. See El-Khazen, op. cit., 2003, p. 64. See also Farid el Khazen, "Lebanon's First Postwar Parliamentary Election, 1992: An Imposed Choice" in *Prospects for Lebanon*, Oxford: Center for Lebanese Studies, 1998; Joseph Bahout, "Les Elites Parlementaires Libanaises De 1996" in (eds.) Joseph Bahout et Chawqi Douayhi, *La Vie Publique Au Liban: Expressions et Recompositions du Politique*, Beirut: CERMOC, 1997; and Thomas Scheffler, "Religious Communalism and Democratization: The Development of Electoral Law in Lebanon" in *Orient*, 44/2003, 1.

169. See Bassel Salloukh, "The Limits of Electoral Engineering in Divided Societies: Elections in Postwar Lebanon" in *Canadian Journal of Political Science*, 39, 3, September 2006.

170. El Khazen, op. cit., 1998, p. 69. See also Salloukh, op. cit., 2006.

171. El Khazen, op. cit., 1998, p. 70. For an alternative perspective on the vigor of the Lebanese parliament in the early postwar period, see Abdo Baaklini, Guillain Denoeux, and Robert Springborg, *Legislative Politics in the Arab World: The Resurgence of Democratic Institutions*, Boulder: Lynne Rienner Publishers, 1999, p. 101 and p. 109.

172. These included disputes over whether cabinet meetings should be held in the offices of the president or the prime minister, whether it was the prime minister or the Speaker of the Assembly who had the right to establish the agenda for debating and voting on legislation, and whether it was the president or the cabinet that held executive authority over the Lebanese Army.

173. Reinoud Leenders, "The Politics of Corruption in Postwar Lebanon," PhD diss., School of Oriental and African Studies, University of London, 2004, p. 187.

174. Reinoud Leenders, "Public Means to Private Ends: State Building and Power in Post-War Lebanon" in (ed.) Eberhard Kienle, *Politics from Above, Politics from Below: The Middle East in the Age of Economic Reform*, London: Saqi Books, 2003, p. 328. See also Reinoud Leenders, "Nobody Having Too Much to Answer For: Laissez-Faire, Networks, and Postwar Corruption in Lebanon" in (ed.) Steven Heydeman, *Networks of Privilege in the Middle East*, New York: Palgrave MacMillan, 2005.

175. Leenders, op. cit., 2004, pp. 140–141.

176. Kassir, op. cit., 2003, p. 101.

177. Ibid., p. 102.

178. See El Khazen, op. cit., 1998, p. 64; and El Khazen, op. cit., 2003, p. 102. Included within this group were a variety of political figures including Michel Murr, minister of the interior throughout much of the 1990s, who regularly interfered with the freedom of associational life, as well as dissident Maronite militia leaders such as Elie Hubayka, who would go on to play an interesting crucial role with respect to the rise of the disability sector in the postwar period.

179. El Khazen, op. cit., 2003, p. 102.

## Chapter 3

1. Karam, op. cit., 2004, p. 68; World Bank, *Lebanon Social Protection Note—Attachment II: Mapping and Review of Lebanese NGOs,* 21 October 2001 (written by Omar Trabousli with Bassam Ramadan and Shaha Riza).

2. World Bank, op. cit., 2001, p. 2; LCPS, op. cit., 1999, p. 25.

3. Ibid., p. 28.

4. Ibid., pp. 25–26.

5. Guillain Denoeux and Robert Springborg, "Hariri's Lebanon: Singapore of the Middle East or Sanaa of the Levant?" in *Middle East Policy,* VI, 2, October 1998, p. 160.

6. Ibid., p. 163. See also Tom Pierre Najem, *Lebanon's Renaissance: The Political Economy of Reconstruction,* Reading: Ithaca Press, 2000.

7. Debie, op. cit., 2003, p. 21.

8. Denoeux and Springborg, op. cit., 1998, p. 172.

9. Hudson, op. cit., 1968, p. 266.

10. Gaspard, op. cit., 2004, p. 220. See also Leenders, op. cit., 2004.

11. Interview with George Corm, Beirut, 14 December 2004.

12. Gaspard, op. cit., 2004, p. 219.

13. Ibid.

14. Leenders, op. cit., 2004, p. 190.

15. Leenders, op. cit., 2003, p. 329.

16. Efforts were made to reform and rationalize the Lebanese administration in the early postwar period, ones that revolved around the creation of the Ministry of State for Administrative Reform with its program for National Administration Rehabilitation. As Christophe Ingels argued, however, this program and ministry lacked domestic backers and was largely financed and supported by foreign donors. See Christophe Ingels, "L'administration Libanias au sortir du conflit civil," PhD diss., Political Science, L'universite Aix-Marseille III, 1998–1999, p. 189.

17. Ingels, op. cit., 1998, p. 146.

18. Ibid., pp. 281–282.

19. Ibid., p. 154. This contrasts somewhat with the argument by Denoeux and Springborg that Hariri sought to shield the "bureaucratic rationality" of the CDR from the neo-patrimonial dynamics of the Lebanese state. Given the levels of corruption associated with the CDR, however, it appears that the "two-headed state" that they talked about emerging in postwar Lebanon was really one state divided up into many neo-patrimonial pieces. See Denoeux and Springborg, op. cit., 1998, pp. 161–163.

20. See Laurie Brand, *Citizens Abroad: State and Emigration in the Middle East and North Africa*. Cambridge: Cambridge University Press, 2006, p. 163.

21. See Leenders, op. cit., 2004, p. 95, p. 158, and pp. 263–264.

22. Ibid., p. 189. One prominent Lebanese figure described the politics of distribution and corruption within the first postwar troika as such: "Hrawi is willing to sell all, Hariri is willing to buy all, and Berri is willing to take a commission on all!" Interview with Abdullah Ben Habib, Beirut, 9 December 2002.

23. One report estimated overall campaign costs in the 2000 election at more than U.S.$200 million, which was used "mainly to buy votes, entice voters to cast their ballots for certain candidates, or secure seats on winning lists." Salloukh, op. cit., 2006. These developments elicited several calls for electoral law reforms, especially concerning the establishment of limits on campaign expenditures. See Nawaf Salam, "Reforming the Electoral System: A Comparative Perspective" in (ed.) Salam, *Options for Lebanon*, London: I.B. Taurus, 2004, pp. 1–22.

24. Ghada Jabour, "Le prix des dons," MA Thesis, L'Ecole de Formation Sociale, University of St. Joseph, 2002, p. 86.

25. Ibid., p. 87.

26. See Elizabeth Picard, "La crise de institutions" in (eds.) Paul Balta and Georges Corm, *L'Avenir du Liban Dans le Context Regional et International*, Paris: Les Editions Ouvriers et Etudes et Documantation International, 1990.

27. See Lebanese Centre for Policy Studies, "Civil Society in Beirut," 1999. For a study of the wartime growth of militia-oriented social welfare institutions, see Judith Harik, *The Public and Social Services of the Lebanese Militias*, Papers on Lebanon, Centre for Lebanese Studies: Oxford, 1994.

28. Ibid., p. 20.

29. Hezbollah's institutions are not the only ones within these Shi'a Islamists circles. The late Shaikh Mohammad Fadlallah also spearheaded the creation of a significant social welfare infrastructure in both the dahiyeh and beyond that revolves around the widespread activities of al-Mabarrat Charitable Association. This is in addition to numerous other smaller, family-oriented associations and charitable groups that operate within the Shi'a community. See Deeb, op. cit., 2006, pp. 88–92.

30. Hezbollah's extensive social welfare infrastructure includes eight associations, the most important of which are the Islamic Charity Emdad Committee, the Martyrs' Association, and *Jihad al-Bina* Development Organization. The services that these associations have offered over the last twenty years include large-

scale health care delivery, the construction of major hospitals such as Al-Rasul al-Azam in the southern suburbs; the construction and running of a wide array of primary, secondary, and religious schools; the delivery of extensive programs of rural development; as well as a national micro-enterprise small loan program estimated at U.S.$4.5 million in 2001. See Judith Harik, *Hezbollah: The Changing Face of Terrorism*, London: I.B. Taurus, 2004, p. 92.

31. Catherine Le Thomas, "Formation et socialization: un projet de (contre)-societe" in (ed.) Sabrina Mervin, *Le Hezbollah: etat des lieux*, Arles, France: Actes Sud/Sinbad, 2008, p. 148.

32. Catherine Le Thomas, "Les scouts al-Mahdi: un 'generation resistante' " in (ed.) Sabrina Mervin, *Le Hezbollah: etat des lieux*, Arles, France: Actes Sud/Sinbad, 2008, p. 173.

33. LCPS, op. cit., 1999, p. 20.

34. Harik, op. cit., 2004, p. 92.

35. See Chapter 4 and Carol Dagher, *Break Down the Walls: Lebanon's Postwar Challenge*, New York: St. Martin's Press, 2000, p. 124.

36. Khalaf, op. cit., 2003, p. 132.

37. Deeb, op. cit., 2006, p. 170.

38. See Heiko Wimmen, "Rallying Around the Renegade" in *Middle East Report Online*, 27 August 2007, pp. 3–4.

39. Ahmad Beydoun, "A Note on Sectarianism" in (eds.) T. Hanf and N. Salam, *Lebanon in Limbo*, Baden-Baden: Nomos Verlagsgesellschaft, 2003, p. 87.

40. Interview with Fadi Abboud, president of the Lebanese Industrialist Association, Beirut, 13 December 2002. See also Debie, op. cit., 2003, pp. 140–141; and Hamdan, op. cit., 2004, p. 46.

41. Lebanon has been plagued by both skyrocketing levels of public debt in the postwar period and falling rates of growth that leveled off to 0 in 2000. By 2005, the size of the public debt reached the unprecedented level of 188 percent of gross domestic product at U.S.$41 billion in 2005. See ICG, op. cit., 2005.

42. Abdallah Dah, Ghassan Dibeh, and Wassim Shahin, *The Distributional Impact of Taxes in Lebanon: Analysis and Policy Implications*, Beirut: The Lebanese Center for Policy Studies, 6, 1999.

43. See MSA and UNDP, op. cit., 2000, p. 34. See also Ghallab, 2000.

44. Kochuyt, op. cit., 2004, p. 521. See also Kochuyt, op. cit., 2002, p. 34.

45. Karam, op. cit., 2004, p. 122.

46. Ibid., p. 89.

47. Baroudi, op. cit., 1998, p. 549.

48. Ibid., p. 533.

49. Ibid., p. 531.

50. Joseph Bahout, "A Division of Labor: The Amin-GCLW Saga Continues" in *Lebanon Report*, March 1994, p. 4.

51. See Karin Seyfert, unpublished PhD diss. on NGOs in postwar Lebanon, School of Oriental and African Studies, University of London, undated, p. 123.

52. Khalaf estimates that family associations alone made up close to 50 percent of all associations in the country in 1968 (477 of 1,094). See Khalaf, op. cit., 1987, p. 166.

53. See Gregoire Haddad, "Comprehensive Secularism: The Intellectual and Political Dimensions" in *Tayyar al-Mujtama'a al-Madani*, 6, April 1999, p. 1.

54. Karam, op. cit., 2004, p. 63. See Agnes Favier, "Logiques de l'engagement et modes de contestation au Liban: Genese et eclatement d'une generation de militants intellectuels," These Docteur, L'Universite Paul Cezanne–Aix Marseille III, 23 December 2004, p. 250.

55. See also "Report on Workshop on Information: Inter-NGO Forum on Lebanon," Cyprus, May 8–10, 1987. The participants included representatives from Amel, Solidarity and Development (SDPI), Secours Populaire Libanais, the Maarouf Saad Foundation, the Ghassan Khanafani Children's Foundation, Association Najdeh, the Mouvement Social Libanais, and the Middle East Council of Churches. International NGOs, such as Oxfam-UK, the Children's Fund (UK), NOVIB, the Mennonite Central Committee, and Christian Aid, also attended.

56. Ibid.

57. Ibid.

58. "General Report: Inter-NGO Meeting on Lebanon," Cyprus, 23–26 March 1988, p. 28.

59. Interview with Leila Zacharia, Association Najdeh, Beirut, 19 July 1995.

60. General Report, op. cit., March 1988.

61. "Meeting of the Coordinating Group, Inter-NGO Forum on Lebanon," 11 May 1987.

62. See "Meetings of the Steering Committee and the Information Group of the Lebanese National Forum for Social Development," British Refugee Council, London, 28 June 1988.

63. "Report of Meeting of National Forum for Social Development," 13 October 1988.

64. Oxfam memo, "ICVA in the Middle East," 6 March 1989.

65. Internal Oxfam correspondence, 27 February 1989.

66. Among the members of the LNF were the Higher Shi'a Council, the Maronite League, Dar el-Fatwa (Sunni community), the Druze Foundation for Social Protection, the Greek Orthodox and Greek Catholic Patriarcates, and the Lebanese Association for the Handicapped (linked to the AMAL Movement).

67. Ramzi Namaan, an active participant in wartime relief networks, described the LNF as a "clear representation of the regime" that played the game of relief and service delivery in war and postwar Lebanon in "the traditional way," in which "Christians have their own, Muslims have their own, and the Druze have their own. And guys, let's see how see can divide the cake." Namaan added that this resulted in the emergence of a "stratified hierarchy of power" under which emerged a whole generation of NGOs. Interview with Ramzi Namaan, 24 July 2008.

68. See Annual Report, YMCA Lebanon, 1993.

69. See Jon Bennett, "The Lebanese NGO Forum and the Reconstruction of Civil Society, 1989–1993" in (ed.) Jon Bennett, *Meeting Needs: NGO Coordination in Practice*, London: Earthscan Publications Ltd., 1995.

70. Interview with Ghassan Sayegh, Beirut, 7 August 1995.

71. Bennett, op. cit., 1993, p. 142.

72. See "Proceedings of the Conference on Social Development in Lebanon," Rene Maowad Foundation, Washington, DC, June 1995, in which both Sayagh and Moukheiber spoke.

73. See Paul Kingston, "Promoting Civil Society Advocacy in the Middle East at Home and Abroad: NGOs, CIDA, and the Middle East Working Group, 1991–2001" in (eds.) Paul Heinbecker and Bessma Momani, *Canada and the Middle East: In Theory and Practice*, Waterloo, Ontario: Wilfred Laurier Press, 2007, p. 128.

74. Interview with Ghassan Sayegh, 7 August 1995.

75. Interview with Ghassan Sayegh, 6 December 2001.

76. See Christine Crumrine, Power, Politics, and Prestige: The Business of INGO Development in Rural Areas of Lebanon," PhD diss., Center for Middle East and Islamic Studies, University of Durham, 2002, which provides a critical analysis of the YMCA's role as an implementing NGO for USAID's $60 million "Rural Community Development" program in Lebanon between 1997 and 2002.

77. Interview with Mohammad Barakat, 31 July 1995.

78. Interview with Gregoire Haddad, 25 July 1995.

79. Karam, op. cit., 2006, p. 67.

80. Interview with Joseph Farah, 2 June 1999. Farah added that "the LNF do not have a program together; the administration has a program." In that sense, he didn't really feel that the LNF was a truly collaborative institution in the way that le Collectif had tried to become.

81. Interview with Mayla Bakhash, 6 December 2001.

82. Ibid.

83. Interestingly, a study of the various associations within le Collectif revealed that more than 70 percent of its working revenue was raised internally, and, with certain associations, its use of local financial resources was as much as 93 percent. See Antoine Haddad, "Lebanese NGOs: Guidelines for a Common Strategy," Beirut: Middle East Council of Churches/Collectif des ONG au Liban, 1995.

84. Interview with Mayla Bakhash, 6 December 2001.

85. Karam, op. cit., 2006, p. 72.

86. Interview with Mayla Bakhash, 6 December 2001.

87. Ibid.

88. Interview with Joseph Farah, 2 June 1999.

89. Much of the material in this section is based on the excellent and extensive writing of the Lebanese political scientist Karam Karam, to whom I am greatly indebted. See especially Karam, op. cit., 2004; and Karam, op. cit., 2006.

90. Karam, op. cit., 2004, p. 73.

91. The oldest of the associations is the Lebanese Association for Human Rights (ALDHOM), established in the midst of the civil war in 1985 by Joseph Moghaizel in conjunction with his wife, Laure, and twelve other colleagues. Other critical associations within this core group were the Movement for Human Rights–Civil Rights (MDH), established in 1988 and which has been extensively involved in the field of human rights education; the Association for the Defense of Rights and Liberties (ADDL), established by a small group of lawyers and which has been at the forefront of legal battles defending the rights of associations; and the Lebanese Association for Democratic Elections (LADE), established in 1996 and which has been extensively involved in both democratic education and the monitoring of elections. See Karam, op. cit., 2006, pp. 99–111.

92. Karam, op. cit., 2004, p. 189.

93. Ibid., p. 89.

94. In 2000, for example, foreign sources of financial support made up 80 percent of the budget of ALDHOM, 70 percent of the budget of MDH, and 99 percent of the budget of LADE. Karam, op. cit., 2006, p. 150.

95. See Melhem Chaoul, "Demonstrations in Beirut" in (eds.) Barbara Drieskens, Frank Mermier, and Heiko Wimmen, *Cities of the South: Citizenship and Exclusion in the Twenty-First Century*, London: Saqi Books, 2007.

96. Karam, op. cit., 2004, p. 189.

97. Ibid., p. 167.

98. Ibid., p. 149.

99. Karam, op. cit., 2006, p. 217.

100. See Agnes Favier (ed.), *Municipalites et Pouvoirs Locaux au Liban*, Beirut: Centre d'etude et de recherché sur le Moyen-Orient comtemporain, 2001.

101. Karam, op. cit., 2004, p. 226.

102. These were Fadi Moughaizel of the Lebanese Associational for Human Rights (ALDHOM), who actually ran in the 1996 parliamentary elections for a seat in Beirut; Nawaf Kabbara, a disability activist and head of the Friends of the Handicapped, who ran for a seat in Tripoli; Paul Salem, founder and member of LADE and the Lebanese Center for Policy Studies (LCPS), who began a campaign for a seat in the Koura region before eventually dropping out; and Ghassan Moukheiber, founding member of ADDL, who ran for a seat in the Metn and, despite his small vote count, eventually won it after the other two candidates were disqualified.

103. Paul Salem, for example, argued that, in his case, he needed a minimum of U.S.$100,000 in order to run for parliamentary office in 2000, most of which was eaten up by the cost of being represented on one of the major electoral lists—a figure dwarfed by the more than U.S.$30 million that Hariri was estimated to have spent on his election in Beirut in that same year. See Karam, op. cit., 2006, pp. 273–274.

104. Ibid., p. 275.

105. Karam, op. cit., 2004, p. 462.

106. Ibid., p. 461.

107. In one interesting case, Nawaf Kabbara was accused of betraying his family's interests when he decided to run in Tripoli in competition with someone from his own family who was already a deputy—an experience that in his mind confirmed the existence of "a closed system of tribal and confessional . . . thinking [that] will not promote democratic values and practices." See AFKAR/OMSAR, *Les Organizations Non-Governmentales Au Liban: Realites et Perspectifs*, 2005/2006, p. 24.

108. See Young, op. cit., 2010, pp. 27–40. See also Rayan Majed, "L'engagement politique des etudiants dans l'intifada de l'independence: Etat d'ame ou formation d'un movement estudiantin autonome?," Memoire de Diplome d'Etudes Approfondies en Science Politique, Universite St. Joseph, October 2007, p. 31.

109. Quoted in Blanford, op. cit., 2006, p. 171.

110. See Oussama Safa, "Getting to Arab Democracy: Lebanon Springs Forward" in *Journal of Democracy*, 17, 1, January 2006, p. 30.

111. See Majed, op. cit., 2007, p. 45 and pp. 23–23.

112. See Chaoul, op. cit., 2007, pp. 159–160.

113. Majed, op. cit., 2007, pp. 14–15.

114. See Hirst, op. cit., 2010, p. 298.

115. Majed, op. cit., 2007, p. 20.

116. Young, op. cit., 2010, pp. 52–53.

117. See "Civil Society in Lebanon: Sensitive Political Issues Avoided—Interview with Omar Traboulsi," www.qantara.de/webcom/show_article.php/_c-593/_nr-8/i.html.

118. Majed, op. cit., 2007, p. 37.

119. Ibid., p. 51.

120. Blanford, op. cit., 2006, p. 167.

121. Majed, op. cit., 2007, p. 60. Majed attributed this to the communal legacies of the war and postwar period, whose influences had seeped into Lebanon's universities and "prevented the formation of autonomous, modern, rebellious, and independent individuals." Ibid., p. 64.

122. Hirst, op. cit., 2010, p. 312.

123. Blanford, op. cit., 2006, p. 211.

124. Hirst, op. cit., 2010, p. 312.

125. Halim Shebaya, "Intifada 2005: A Look Backwards and a Look Forwards" in (ed.) Youssef Choueiri, *Breaking the Cycle: Civil Wars in Lebanon*, London: Stacey International, 2007, p. 267.

126. See, for example, the following two articles on the rise of civic associational activism during Israel's "sixth war" on Lebanon in the summer of 2006. Candice Raymond, "Samidoun, trente-jours de mobilization civile a Beyroute," and Karam Karam, "Resistances civiles?" in (eds.) Frank Mermier and Elizabeth Picard, *Liban, une guerre de trente-trois jours*, Paris: La decouverte, 2007.

127. Indeed, Johnson describes Lebanon as having "a vibrant, multi-faceted, and often optimistic counter-cultural movement in [its] civil society. It informs

public discourse and even some aspects of public life. . . . [D]ifferent ideas are represented within it, but what is common is a belief in a united and secular country in which inclusive liberal nationalism can finally overcome those exclusive ethnicities, motivated by romantic ideologies of blood, honor, and vengeance." See Michael Johnson, "Managing Political Change in Lebanon: Challenges and Prospects" in Choueiri, op. cit., 2007, p. 139 and p. 164.

128. See Karam Karam, "An Analysis of Political Change in Lebanon in the Light of Recent Mobilization Cycles" in (eds.) Laure Guazzone and Danielle Pioppi, *The Arab State and Neo-Liberal Globalization: The Restructuring of State Power in the Middle East*, London: Ithaca, 2009.

# Chapter 4

1. Michelle Browers, *Democracy and Civil Society in Arab Political Thought: Transcultural Possibilities,* Syracuse: Syracuse University Press, 2006, p. 195.

2. CRTD-A, *Caught in Contradiction: A Profile of Gender Equality and Economy in Lebanon,* May 2006, p. 13.

3. Thompson, op. cit., 2000, pp. 97–100.

4. See Sonia Alvarez, "Latin American Feminisms 'Go Global': Trends of the 1990s and Challenges for the New Millennium" in (eds.) Sonia Alvarez, Evelina Dagnino, and Arturo Escobar, *Cultures of Politics/Politics of Cultures: Revisioning Latin American Social Movements,* Boulder: Westview Press, 1998, p. 297.

5. A charismatic feminist within the Progressive Socialist Party (PSP) named Janine Robeiz, for example, frustrated by the gender-limiting and ineffective structures of the party, used her close ties to Kamal Jumblat to successfully push for the creation of a women's department in 1974 and, only one year later, for a more autonomous women's organization—linked to but not run by the party—called L'union des femmes progressistes, a dynamic that was paralleled within other leftist parties such as Lebanese Communist Party (LCP), the Syrian Socialist Nationalist Party (SSNP), the Organization of Communist Action (OCA), and the Popular Nasserist Organization of Mustafa Saad. Interview with Selma Sfeir, 14 June 2008.

6. See Deeb, op. cit., 2006; Lara Deeb and Mona Harb, "Les autres pratiques de la Resistance: tourisme politique et loisirs pieux" in (ed.) Sabrina Mervin, *Hezbollah: etat des lieux,* Arles: Actes Sud/Sindbad, 2008; Mona Fawaz, "Action et ideologie dals les services ONG islamiques dans la banlieu sud de beyrouth" in (eds.) Sara Ben Nefissa, Nabil 'Abd al-Fattah, sari Hanafi, and Carlos Minani, *ONG et governance dans le monde arabe,* Paris: Karthala, 2004; and Anja Peleikis, *Lebanese in Motion: Gender and the Making of a Translocal Village,* London: Transaction Publishers, 2003.

7. Anne Marie Goetz, *The Politics of Integrating Gender to State Development Processes: Trends, Opportunities and Constraints in Bangladesh, Chile,*

*Jamaica, Mali, Morocco, and Uganda*, UNRISD, 1995, p. 39. See also Jeromy Shiffman, "Generating Political Priority for Maternal Mortality Reduction in 5 Developing Countries" in *American Journal of Public Health*, 97, 5, May 2007, p. 802.

8. Thompson, op. cit., 2000, p. 7.

9. Sofia Saadeh, *The Quest for Citizenship in Post Taef Lebanon*, Beirut: Sade Publishers, 2007, p. 56.

10. Suad Joseph, "Women Between Nation and State in Lebanon" in (eds.) Caren Kaplan, Norma Alarcon, and Minoo Moallem, *Between Women and Nation: Nationalism, Transnational Feminisms, and the State*, Durham: Duke University Press, 1999, p. 170.

11. See Laurie Brand, *Women, the State, and Political Liberalization: Middle East and North African Experiences*, New York: Columbia University Press, 1998, p. 3.

12. Farsoun, op. cit., 1988, p. 110.

13. Suad Joseph, "Elite Strategies for State-Building: Women, Family, Religion, and State in Iraq and Lebanon" in (ed.) Deniz Kandiyoti, *Women, Islam, and the State*, Philadelphia: Temple University Press, 1991, p. 191.

14. Suad Joseph, "Problematizing Gender and Relational Rights: Experiences from Lebanon" in *Social Politics*, Fall 1994, p. 282.

15. Suad Joseph, "Civic Myths, Citizenship, and Gender in Lebanon" in (ed.) Suad Joseph, *Gender and Citizenship in the Middle East*, New York: Syracuse University Press, 2000, p. 110.

16. Suad Joseph, "Women Between Nation and State in Lebanon" in (eds.) Caren Kaplan, Norma Alarcon, and Minoo Moallem, *Between Women and Nation: Nationalism, Transnational Feminisms, and the State*, Durham: Duke University Press, 1999, p. 175. As Joseph strongly asserted in another of her articles, "civil society cannot be theorized in a 'post-patriarchal' manner." See Suad Joseph, "Gendering Citizenship in the Middle East" in (ed.) Suad Joseph, *Gender and Citizenship in the Middle East,* New York: Syracuse University Press, 199?, p. 26.

17. As one social worker and women's activist noted, people are afraid of being excluded from community networks because "we cannot act without having a backup from someone. We don't have an identity if we are not integrated into a community. If we want to get married, if we want to have a child, get divorced, to register a child in school, we have to have a confession. . . . If we want to get access to things . . . , you have to have a confession." Interview with staff of Lebanese Council for Resistance to Violence Against Women, June 18, 2002.

18. See Denis Kandiyotti, "Bargaining with Patriarchy" in *Gender and Society*, Vol 2, 3, September 1988, pp. 274–290.

19. Interview with staff of Lebanese Council for Resistance to Violence Against Women, 18 June 2002.

20. See Tamar Kabakian-Khasholian, Afamia Kaddour, Jocelyn DeJong, Rawan Shahayoob, and Anwar Nassar, "The Policy Environment Encouraging C-section in Lebanon" in Health Policy and Planning, 83, 2007, p. 10. See also Rita Khayat and Oona Cambell, "Hospital Practices in Maternity Wards in Lebanon" in Health Policy and Planning, 15, 3, 2000, pp. 270–278.

21. It is estimated that there are 109,440 foreign workers in the country in 2005, most of whom are women and most of whom work in domestic service. See Lina Abou Habib, "The Use and Abuse of Female Domestic Workers in Lebanon" in *Gender and Development*, 6, 1, March 1998, pp. 55–56. See also Lebanese CEDAW Report, 2006. See also *Lebanon's Third Periodic Report—CEDAW*, 7 July 2006.

22. See Karam, op. cit., 2004.

23. Thompson, op. cit., 2000, p. 9.

24. Mounira Charrad, *States and Women's Rights: The Making of Postcolonial Tunisia, Algeria, and Morocco*, Berkeley: University of California Press, 2001, p. 9.

25. See Thompson, op. cit., 2000, p. 4 and p. 224.

26. Joseph, op. cit., 1994, pp. 280–281. Indeed, she argues that this process intensified in the post-civil war period, commenting that, after her field work in 1993, "I found that dealing with government agencies and officials necessitated, even more than before, that a person be embedded in and shielded by massive relational networks."

27. Ibid., p. 275.

28. Ibid., p. 272.

29. Joseph argues, for example, that "middle and upper-class women could and did maneuver with greater independence than did working class women [and] in some situations, Christian women had more spaces for movement than Muslim women." See Joseph, op. cit., 1999, p. 179.

30. Mounira Charrad also emphasizes the "structurally delimiting" nature of the sociopolitical environment within which women activists work and argues that, within this context, reforms would only occur "when they were in conformity with the interests of . . . political forces controlling the newly found state. They were rejected or avoided when they would have threatened alliances deemed critical to the existing political and social balance of power." See op. cit., 2001, p. 239.

31. Pierson, op. cit., 2004, p. 82.

32. CRTD-A, op. cit., 2006, p. 30.

33. Ibid., p. 25.

34. Samih Boustani and Nada Mufarrej, "Female Higher Education and Participation in the Labour Force in Lebanon" in (eds.) Nabil Khoury and Valentine Moghadam, *Gender and Development in the Arab World*, New York: Zed Books Ltd., 1995, p. 112. There has even been an increase in the number of women enrolled in vocational and educational programs, from 17.55 percent in 1982 to 34.2 percent in 1994. See CRTD-A, op. cit., 2006, p. 27.

35. See Anja Peleikis, *Lebanon in Motion: Gender and the Making of a Translocal Village*, London: Transaction Books, 2003, p. 153.

36. CRTD-A, op. cit., 2006, p. 21. See also Lamia Osseiran, "The Lebanese Council of Women: Mission and Expectations," Masters of Arts in International Affairs, Lebanese American University, June 2006, p. 31.

37. Ibid., p. 22.

38. Saadeh, op. cit., 2007, p. 76. She noted, for example, that while female teachers (45,000) outnumber male ones (13,000), there were only two female principals in primary and secondary schools.

39. Lamia Rustum Shehadeh, "Women in the Public Sphere" in (ed.) Lamia Shehadeh, *Women and War in Lebanon*, Gainesville: University of Florida Press, 1999, p. 59.

40. CRTD-A, op. cit., 2006, p. 2.

41. Ibid., p. 7.

42. Ibid., p. 24. Estimates of the number of households headed by women range from 6.6 percent to 14.2 percent. See *Lebanon's Third Periodic Report—CEDAW*, 7 July 2006, p. 20; and Ghena Ismail, "Women-Headed Households in Lebanon" in *al-Raida*, XIV, 76, Winter 1997, p. 21.

43. Shehadeh, op. cit., 1999, p. 68. Peleikis argues in a similar fashion that "the fact that more and more women in Lebanon are unmarried and engaged in wage labour combined with the fact that many of them remain unmarried throughout their lives, could lead to a major upheaval in the socially constructed image of women in Lebanese society—single women may in time become socially more acceptable. Gender relations hitherto taken for granted may be questioned and renegotiated from the vantage point of single women." See Peleikis, op. cit., 2003, p. 157ff.

44. Interview, 5 June 2008.

45. Yolla Polity Sharara, "Women and Politics in Lebanon" in *Khamsin: Journal of Revolutionary Socialists in the Middle East*, 6, 1978, pp. 6–15. In commenting on the fact that women's wartime party activities were, for the most part, limited to the provision of relief, Polity wrote that "everything was just as in the family. For women, the service jobs; for men, the noble jobs," and even if women did actually join the militias, she remarked that "their presence was considered to be neither natural nor obvious" (p. 14).

46. Interview, 11 April 2008.

47. Alvarez, op. cit., 1998, p. 308.

48. See Laure Moghaizel, "Les droits des femmes au Liban: Situation et perspectives dans le cadre de la construction nationale," Beyrouth: Commission nationale libanaise pour l'UNESCO, 29–31 March 1993, p. 27.

49. Osseiran, op. cit., 2006, p. 47.

50. Interview, 14 June 2008. In addition to the emergence of regional wartime coalitions of women's associations in both Sidon and Tripoli, Salma Sfeir, wartime head of the PSP-affiliated Union des Femmes Progressistes, further revealed that there had been an attempt to create a new national coalition of women's associations during the war, called the Alliance des Femmes Nationales Libanaises, that had been loosely affiliated with the LNM and, that at one point had grouped 24 members. Immobilized for much of the war and lacking in members from East Beirut, however, the membership decided to annul the coalition at the end of the war and to throw its institutional weight behind the rejuvenation of the LWC.

51. See Zeina Zaatari, "Women Activists of South Lebanon," PhD diss., University of California Davis, 2003; and Osseiran, op. cit., 2006.

52. Osseiran, op. cit., 2006, p. 50.

53. The following were the members of the original NGO Committee and, for the most part, represented the core of the postwar secular women's network: Dr. Aman Shaarani, Mrs. Nayla Mouawad, Ms. Habib Sadek, Mrs. Laure Moghaizel, Dr. Nour Selman, Mrs. Linda Matar, Mrs. Majida Kabbara, Mrs. Souad Salloum, Mrs. Mona Mourad, Mrs. Wadad Chakhtoura, Dr. Fadia Kiwan, Dr. Elham Kallab Bssat, Dr. Lamia Shehadeh, Mrs. Mona Khalaf, Dr. Fahmieh Sharafeddine, Mr. Walid Tibbi, Mrs. Nelly Helou, Mr. Nicolas Berbari, Mr. Moussa Maalouf, Mrs. Sonia Attiyeh, Mr. Samir Farah, and Mr. Youssef Gebai.

54. One member of the Beijing Group, Fadia Kiwan, for example, added that its lobbying of the state "came at a very good moment," as it coincided with the emergence of interest on the part of First Lady Mona Hrawi, whom Kiwan described as being "sensitized" to women's issues. Interview, 17 July 2008.

55. Osseiran, op. cit., 2006, p. 53.

56. Interview with Linda Matar, 11 April 2008.

57. Nelda LaTeef, *Women of Lebanon: Interviews with Champions for Peace*, London: McFarland and Company, 1997, p. 203.

58. This cautionary principle also was incorporated into Lebanon's third periodic report to the CEDAW in July 2006, which stated that "the attempt to place all legislation in one basket may hinder the possibility of amending any at all, considering that, based upon the experience of previous attempts, certain laws arouse latent sectarian sensitivities within the Lebanese context that cannot be ignored."

59. Iqbal Dughan, a lawyer and women's activist in the postwar period, similarly argued that some degree of social mobilization and support was important if legal campaigns were going to succeed. Noted Dughan, "we cannot use the court system without the people." Interview, 10 April 2008.

60. See Laure Moughaizel, op. cit., 1993, p. 21. For her own summary of her approach to legal activism, see pp. 17–18. Among the other legal changes effected by Moughaizel's campaigning and networking in the prewar period included gaining inheritance rights for non-Muslim women (1959), the right of women to choose their own citizenship (1965), and the recognition of independent travel rights for women (1974).

61. Interview, 3 July 2008.

62. Karam, op. cit., 2006, p. 101.

63. Sonia Ibrahim Attiya, for example, another pioneering lawyer in Lebanon and someone who also was part of the Beijing group, described herself as "belonging to no one." She has provided legal advice to many associations and organizations, among them being the NCLW, the LWC, the NGO Committee, the League of Women's Rights, and the Rassemblement National (*al-liqa' el-watani lil kada' ala jamii ashkal el tamyiz dod el mar'a*), with which she described herself as being at ideological loggerheads. Indeed, as a precondition for continuing her legal assistance to them, she has insisted that minutes be taken of their meetings, recording her disagreement with their more "political" approaches to women's legal advocacy work. Interview, 26 June 2008.

64. Dughan's association is called the League of Working Women in Lebanon. She also has been involved in efforts to raise awareness within the Order of Lawyers in Lebanon of women's issues. These efforts led, in 2005, to the establishment of an internal Commission for Women and, one year later, to the holding of a conference on CEDAW, though she admitted that it had been difficult to maintain interest, energy, and continuity in its work given the exigencies of a legal field and its practice of reelecting members on yearly basis. Interview with Iqbal Dughan, 21 July 2008.

65. Especially important was her husband, who was also a lawyer, a human rights activist, as well as a deputy in the first postwar parliament. For an account of what it was like to grow up with this husband-and-wife team of human rights activists, see Nada Moughaizel-Nasr, *Joseph et Laure*, Beirut: Editions Dar an-Nahar, 2008.

66. In its 2008 response to the third periodic report of the Lebanese government, for example, it described a variety of issues as being "insufficiently addressed" and, as a way of generating public pressure for improved compliance, encouraged the Lebanese government both to disseminate its critique in a widely publicized public forum and to sign the Optional Protocol that would provide nongovernmental parties with a more formal and direct voice in the CEDAW process. See CEDAW, "Concluding Observations of the Committee on the Elimination of Discrimination against Women: Lebanon," 1 February 2008, pp. 2–3.

67. Interview, 11 April 2008.

68. Interviews with Iqbal Dughan, 10 April 2008; and Lina Abou Habib, 18 July 2008.

69. See YWCA-Lebanon, *Gender Based Violence in Lebanon and the Middle East*, undated, p. 1.

70. See Keck and Sikkink, op. cit., 1998, who devote one of their case studies to the development of global networks concerned with the issue of violence against women.

71. Rouhana was not the first to attempt to establish an association dedicated to the issue of preventing violence against women. There had been an earlier attempt "by some elite women" in the early 1990s to establish a similar association, but it had been rejected, illegally, by the Ministry of the Interior. Indeed, the initial application of LCRVAW was also refused by the Ministry of the Interior, a refusal that was simply ignored by LCRVAW. Interview with Zoya Rouhana, 11 April 2008.

72. This has included an emergency helpline, the establishment of a Listening and Counseling Center (LCC), and the development of a network of social workers as well as of psychological, medical, and legal professionals to whom women victims could be referred.

73. Among the tactics commonly used by men against their wives and daughters that KAFA cited in one of its donor reports: isolation, downplaying and denying abuse, the use of force and threats, swearing, blaming the women for abuse, using children to make the mother feel guilty or afraid, hitting the

women on the head or stomach, throwing furniture, and taking advantage of the concept of the male "head of household." Among the destructive psychological consequences for women of this violence: feelings of entrapment, isolation, powerlessness, guilt, confusion with women having a difficult time separating their needs from those of others, chronic stress and anxiety, low self-esteem, self-rage, depression, and suicidal thoughts. Moreover, the report added that "the children who witness their mothers being abused also exhibit many of the same effects and they are at high risk of being abused by the batterer themselves." See KAFA, *Narrative Interim Report to Women's Empowerment Project: Kvinna Till Kvinna*, February–March 2006.

74. See Azza' Beydoun, *Crimes of Killing Women: In Front of the Lebanese Courts*, KAFA, 2008 (in Arabic).

75. Interview with Mona Khawli, 24 June 2008.

76. The February 2008 letter of CEDAW to the Lebanese government, for example, called on the state to enact "without delay" legislation on violence against women, including domestic violence, and requested that the state provide "detailed information in its next report on the laws and policies in place to deal with violence against women and the impact of such measures." See CEDAW, "Concluding Observations of the Committee on the Elimination of Discrimination against Women: Lebanon," January–February 2008, p. 5.

77. Among the donors listed are the Open Society Institute, which has provided "core" funding to KAFA; Save the Children–Sweden, the Global Fund for Women; Mama Cash, which provides small grants to new women's organizations; the EU's AFKAR program run out of OMSAR; Oxfam-Quebec; CIDA; the Canada Fund; the Australian Embassy; and ROSS, established by the Italians after the Israel-Hezbollah war of July 2006. Added Rouhana, "we are not [having] a lot of difficulty in finding funding." Interview, 11 April 2008.

78. Interviews with Laura Sfeir, 4 April 2008; and Zoya Rouhana, 11 April 2008.

79. The Tripoli office of LCRVAW has taken a more cautious approach to the issue than the office in Beirut. Indeed, Laura Sfeir stressed on several occasions how difficult the social and political environment has been in Tripoli with respect to work in the field of violence against women; "c'etait un peu difficile . . . beaucoup plus difficile qu'a Beirut. . . . surtout les premieres annees." She added that "a Beirut, les gens accuellent les nouvelles idees. Mais, ici a Tripoli, ils ont des ides un peu traditionalles. . . . Ils n'ont pas d'esprit ouvert." With regard to their work on issues of sexual violence and sexual abuse, for example, Sfeir remarked that "on en peut pas utiliser le meme mot a Tripoli" (one cannot use the same word in Tripoli). Indeed, one of the possible reasons for the split of LCRVAW into two associations in 2005 may well have been a dispute over whether one should adjust one's approach to cases of domestic violence against women depending on the social circumstances on the ground. Remarked Rouhana with respect to the Tripoli office of LCRVAW, "[T]heir approach is to try and reconcile the women and their husband. This is not our approach; our approach

is to name things by their name." Interviews with Laura Sfeir, 4 April 2008; and Zoya Rouhana, 11 April 2008.

80. Interview, 11 April 2008.

81. Interview, 18 July 2008; and CRTD-A, *Jinsiyati Campaign Newsletter*, Issues 1, 2, and 3, http://www.crtda.org.

82. Interview, CRTD-A, 18 July 2008.

83. Elinor Bray-Collins, "Muted Voices: Women's Rights in Postwar Lebanon," MA Thesis, Ontario Institute of Education, University of Toronto, 2003, p. 76.

84. Interview with Lina Abou Habib, 18 July 2008.

85. Interview, 18 July 2008. When CRTD-A initially established the network around the nationality issue, for example, it insisted on two founding principles— first, that it would accept nothing less than full equality, namely the right of women to grant citizenship and nationality to both their children and spouse; and, second, that its advocacy efforts would extend to all those living in Lebanon, including Palestinians.

86. Interview with Marie Dibs, 16 June 2008. With respect to membership in *al-Liqa*'s nationality campaign, for example, Dibs noted that it had attracted lots of interest from "veiled Sunni women from Tariq al-Jadid [a district in Beirut] and Tripoli" who were married to Syrians, Iraqis, and Palestinians. She also added that *al-Liqa* had asked the Hezbollah's Women's Association to join, which, "until now," they had not accepted.

87. Interview with Samir Diab, 24 June 2008.

88. One activist, for example, spoke about the emergence of some "weird, weird contradictions" with respect to deliberations over social security and labor law reforms, ones that concerned the question of whether one should lobby for social security benefits for women within polygamous households. While some answered "no," arguing that polygamy should be banned and that, therefore, one should not agree to work within that framework, those associated with *al-Liqa'a* argued that the focus should simply be on the labor law itself rather than on attacking the confessions. Interview, 18 July 2008.

89. A clear example of its more independent approach was its decision not to join the NDI-sponsored Lebanon Women's Network in 2002. In part, this was motivated by its unwillingness to accept American financial support; it also was predicated on its desire to work through a more grassroots-oriented network— such as its own—than that which the LWN seemed to be able to provide.

90. One of the more interesting NGO Committee projects, carried out with the support of AMIDEAST, was designed to promote both legal awareness and advocacy efforts at the regional level. Five regional teams of five women were created, each with the task of determining an area of legal discrimination on which it would like to focus before beginning the process of identifying and contacting key local politicians, religious officials, and family/clan leaders for the purposes of determining their level of awareness and, if possible, gaining their support for legal reform. The discriminatory laws chosen were as follows:

Beqa—honor crimes; the North and the South—questions of a woman's right to pass on her nationality; the Mountain—expanding the women's right of custody; and Beirut—women's divorce rights. The project manager, Abla Qadi, described it as "an extremely interesting exercise" and remarked that interest in the work throughout the various regions increased "like a snowball," providing women with a chance to "open up and feel that they were not alone." Interview with Abla Qadi, 19 June 2008.

91. See Islah Jad, "The NGOization of the Arab Women's Movement" in *al-Raida*, Volume XX, No. 100, Winter 2003, p. 44. See also Alvarez, op. cit., 1998, p. 26.

92. Interview, 24 June 2008.

93. See Browers, op. cit., 2006, p. 192.

94. Bernard Rougier, for example, argues that the Islamists wanted the election process for the Grand Mufti expanded to include all the "living forces" of the Sunni community—meaning all of the Islamic associations, mosques, and charitable foundations. See *Everyday Jihad: The Rise of Militant Islam among Palestinians in Lebanon*, Cambridge: Cambridge University Press, 2007, p. 129. See also J. Skovgaard-Petersen, "Religious Heads or Civil Servants? Druze and Sunni Religious Leadership in Post-War Lebanon" in *Mediterranean Politics*, 3, 1, Winter 1996; and "The Sunni Religious Scene in Beirut" in *Mediterranean Politics*, 1, 3, Summer 1998.

95. Interview with Mohammad Nuqayri, 13 April 2004.

96. Symbolic of Dar al-Fatwa's weakening postwar institutional capacity were various factors: the rise of numerous independent mosques, associations, and educational institutions—"anyone can build a mosque," noted Mohammad Sammack, Rafik Hariri's principal representative with Dar al-Fatwa; the lack of supervisory and sanctioning ability of Dar al-Fatwa with respect to preaching and educational instruction—in 2004, it had only three inspectors for the more than 500 mosques in the Beirut area; the difficulty of attracting orthodox-trained scholars to Dar al-Fatwa, with their scholarships to al-Ahzar in Cairo going unused; and the increased prevalence of corruption and bribery within the Sunni court system. Interviews with Mohammad Sammack, 30 March 2004; and Mohammad Nuqayri, 13 April 2004.

97. See Rougier, op. cit., 2007, p. 132.

98. See ibid., pp. 137–139.

99. Interview with Mohammad Nuqayri, 13 April 2004.

100. See Omayma Abdellatif and Marina Ottaway, "Women in Islamist Movements: Towards an Islamist Model of Women's Activism" in *Carnegie Papers*, 2 June 2008.

101. Mona Yakan to Paul Kingston, undated correspondence, 2008 (in Arabic).

102. Ibid.

103. Ibid.

104. Abdullatif and Ottaway, op. cit., 2008, p. 1.

105. Interview with Elias Khalife and Paul Rouhana, 8 April 2004.

106. Ibid.

107. Ibid. See also Dagher, op. cit., 2000.

108. Interview with Alexa Abi Habib, Middle East Council of Churches (MECC), 9 April 2004.

109. Dagher, op. cit., 2000, p. 195. Among the actions taken by the Vatican were the appointment of a powerful Papal Nuncio, Pablo Puente, who was described as "one of the sharpest diplomats Lebanon has known in recent years"; the taking of measures aimed at reigning in the more reactionary, right-wing elements of the church; the initiation of a seventy-two-part survey to all Maronite parishioners in 1993; the holding of a special Synod on Lebanon in Rome in 1995; the issuing of a post-Synod *Exhortation Apostolique* embedded within which were calls for greater social action by and within the church as well as calls for the creation of more opportunities for women's participation within the church; and, finally but not exhaustively, the (tremendously popular) visit of the Pope to Lebanon in 1997, during which he took a particularly strong interest in the lay and youth of the communities, over and above the objections of the Maronite bishops. Interview with Paul Rouhana, 25 April 2004. See also Dagher, op. cit., 2000; and Jean-Paul II aux Patriarches, aux Eveques, au Clerge, aux Religieux, aux Religieuses, et a Tous Les Fideles Du Liban, *Exhortation Apostolique Post-Synodale: Une Esperance Nouvelle Pour Le Liban*, 10 May 1997.

110. This renewal included the proliferation of outward symbols of belief such as bumper stickers, the incorporation of youth-oriented modern music into the liturgy, an increase in religious practices such as pilgrimages and church attendance, and an increase in the number of those entering religious vocations. Interview with Elias Khalife and Paul Rouhana, 8 April 2004.

111. Dagher, op. cit., 2000, p. 127. John Donahue, a longtime observer in Lebanon of Maronite politics, also remarked that progress in implementing the Synod's recommendations had been very slow, with the Association of Patriarchs and Catholic Bishops in the country having done "very little." Interview, 7 April 2004.

112. See "The Dynamics of the Lebanese Christians: From the Paradigm of the *'ammiyyat* to the Paradigm of Hwayyek" in (ed.) Andrea Pacini, *Christian Communities in the Arab Middle East: The Challenge of the Future*, Oxford: Oxford University Press, 1998, p. 221.

113. See H. E. Chahabi, *Distant Relations: Iran and Lebanon in the Last 500 Years*, London: Centre for Lebanese Studies and I.B. Tauris, 2006.

114. Roschanack Shaery-Eisenlohr, *Shi'ite Lebanon: Transnational Religion and the Making of National Identities*, New York: Columbia University Press, 2008, p. 33.

115. See Mallouk Berry, "Radical Transitions: Shifting Gender Discourses in Lebanese Muslim Shi'a Jurisprudence and Ideology, 1960–1979 and 1990–1999," PhD diss., Near Eastern Studies, University of Michigan, 2002, p. 21 for a list of the various institutions that emerged as a result of al-Sadr's activism, among them

being Bayt al-Fatat (a home for girls), Madrassat al-Tamrid (a nursing school), Madrassat al-Lughat (a language school), and the Zahra Cultural and Vocational Complex, which was later transformed into the Imam al-Sadr Foundation in 1984 after his disappearance, these being in addition to the numerous *husseiniyyats*.

116. See also Peleikis, op. cit., 2003, p. 137.

117. The appointment by the Iranian President Khatami of a woman judge, for example, was said to have sparked significant debates and reverberated strongly within the Shi'a communities of Lebanon. See Berry, op. cit., 2002, p. 156.

118. Berry, op. cit., 2002, p. 40.

119. Interview with Zoya Rouhana, 11 April 2008.

120. Berry, op. cit., 2002, p. 135.

121. Amin argued, instead, for the need to contextualize the Sharia, adding that it must "be woven into the fabric of reality . . . [and] become a humane project." See ibid., pp. 73–74.

122. It is interesting to note, for example, that Lara Deeb, in her field work on the Shi'a communities in the southern suburbs of Beirut, remarked that the status and image of Muslim women was one of the most consistently contentious issues that she encountered. See op. cit., 2006, p. 29.

123. Berry, op. cit., 2002, p. 82.

124. Deeb, op. cit., 2006. Mona Harb and Lara Deeb define the "Islamic sphere" as a decentered network of organizations aimed at the integration of everyday life into "the resistance society." See Mona Harb and Lara Deeb, "Les autres practiques de la Resistance: tourisme politique et loisirs pieux" in (ed.) Sabrina Mervin, *Le Hezbollah: etat des lieux*, Arles: Actes Sud/Sindbad, 2008, p. 226.

125. Zaatari, op. cit., 2003, p. 122.

126. See Mona Fawwaz, "Action et Ideologie dans les services" ONG islamiques dans la banlieu sud de beyrouth" in (eds.) Saran Ben Nefissa, Nabil 'Abd al-Fattah, Sari Hanafi, and Carlos Minani, *ONG et governance dans le monde arabe*, Paris: Karthala, 2004, pp. 341–367.

127. Peleikis, op. cit., 2003, p. 136.

128. See Zaatari, op. cit., 203, p. 114.

129. Amin has continued to uphold the man as head of the household, affirming his right to unilateral divorce and larger shares of inheritance, on the grounds that the family is not an institution that should change in tandem with social evolution; Fadlallah continued to avoid accepting the notion of gender equality as being unequivocally grounded in Islamic texts, something that Berry admitted would take "a very courageous theologian . . . under the current social and cultural norms of the Muslim community"; and Shams ad-Din, the most progressive Shi'a cleric, according to Berry, did not come close to providing an alternative "gender ideology." See Berry, op. cit., p. 65 and p. 137.

130. Shaery-Eisenlohr, op. cit., 2008, p. 40.

131. Peleikis, op. cit., 2003, p. 146. See also Deeb, op. cit., 2006; and Dalal el-Bizri, *L'Ombre et son double: femmes islamiques, libanaises et moderns*, Beirut: CERMOC, 1995.

132. This decision had been the product of a much longer lobbying effort by a network of human rights, political party, and women's activists in the early postwar period that had included Laure Moghaizel and Linda Matar. Salma Sfeir, president of the PSP's Union des femmes progressistes, which was involved in this campaign, for example, described the presence of "a significant lobbying effort" on the part of this network of activists that had culminated in the presentation of the draft law to President Hrawi at a large conference at the Carleton Hotel in early 1995. Interview, 14 June 2008.

133. See Nadia al-Cheikh, "The 1998 Proposed Civil Marriage Law in Lebanon: The Reaction of the Muslim Communities" in *al-Raida*, XVIII–XIX, Spring/Summer 2001, pp. 27–35.

134. See Saadeh, op. cit., 2007, p. 65.

135. Ibid., p. 70. I heard this view many times in my interviews with Christian clerics. It was argued, for example, that instituting an optional civil marriage code would, in essence, create a nineteenth sect in the country, most of whom would consist of Christians. "The nineteenth confession will paralyze the Christian community . . . and divide us in two," noted Elie Haddad, a Greek Catholic priest (and now bishop) with strong connections to LCRVAW. Concerned that this would "destroy the political balance" in the country and, hence, promote Muslim domination, Haddad emphasized that "it's a zero-sum game for Christians. . . . What was Hrawi thinking?" He concluded by saying that the only way that Christians would accept a civil marriage law would be if it were mandatory and applicable to all communities. Interview, 31 March 2004.

136. Interview with Hani Fahs, 12 April 2004.

137. Cheikh, op. cit., 2001, pp. 31–32.

138. Sherifa Zuhur, "Empowering Women or Dislodging Sectarianism? Civil Marriage in Lebanon" in *Yale Journal of Law and Feminism*, 14, 97, 2002, p. 185.

139. Nabih Berri, who had initially supported the draft legislation enthusiastically, also refused to subsequently receive the project in the assembly and later promised the religious authorities that he would not discuss any new project of law in the assembly touching on religious affairs without consulting them first—clear evidence of the hegemonic sway that religious authorities could exercise over their respective communal political representatives. See Karam, op. cit., 2006, p. 231.

140. Interviews with Alexa Abi Habib (MECC), 22 April, 2004; Hani Fahs, 12 April 2004; and Mohammad Sammack, 30 March 2004.

141. Interviews, 6 April 2004 and 11 April 2008. Laura Sfeir similarly spoke of cultivating close personal contacts with leading Sunni clerics in Tripoli, even suggesting that their reaction to the establishment of a LCRVAW office in the city was "less severe than that of others," with some clerics expressing interest in cooperating with LCRVAW's work. She also noted, however that, "at the same time that they say 'yes,' you are right," they also emphasized that "we can do nothing now." Interview with Laura Sfeir, 4 April 2008. Interestingly, as a way of nibbling away at the jurisdiction of the religious courts more indirectly, a small

group of judges, lawyers, and activists have embarked on an alternative strategic direction of taking advantage of the gaps and contradictions within the religious personal status codes to expand the jurisdiction of civil law. Interviews with Zoya Rouhana, 11 April 2008; and Nada Khalife, 30 June 2008.

142. See KAFA, *Guidelines for Women on Family Laws*, 2008; and interview with Zoya Rouhana, 11 April 2008.

143. Interview with Mona Khawli, 24 June 2008.

144. Ibid.

145. Karam, op. cit., 2006, p. 230.

146. See Cheikh, op. cit., 2001, p. 34. It was not until a month after the introduction of the draft bill, for example, that an associational network calling "the Gathering for an Optional Secular Personal Status Law" emerged, led by an association called the Movement for Human Rights, that brought together more than fifty NGOs, student associations, and political parties. In addition to periodic demonstrations, the network also managed to circulate a variety of petitions, both on university campuses with the help of numerous student associations, where more than 12,000 signatures were collected, as well as in the public at large, where more than 38,000 signatures were collected. While the network managed to stay together until 2002, eventually finding enough (ten) deputies willing to introduce a revised draft law into the parliament, it has since languished, as has the draft law itself. See Karam, op. cit., 2006, pp. 183–185 and pp. 229–231.

147. Interview with Aman Sharaani, 17 June 2008.

148. See Bray-Collins, op. cit., 2004.

149. Interview, 1 July 2008.

150. Interview with Zoya Rouhana, 6 April 2004.

151. Saadeh, op. cit., 2002, p. 454.

152. See Goetz, op. cit., 1995, p. 21.

153. Interview with Fadia Kiwan, 17 July 2008.

154. This remark was in response to the failure of an attempt to lobby for the creation of a Ministry for Women's Conditions in 1982, resulting instead in the creation of a low-level administrative body called "La Service de la femme et la famille." See Moghaizel, op. cit., 1993, p. 28.

155. Interview with NCLW member, 1 April 2008.

156. Interview with NCLW member, 9 April 2008.

157. An early evaluation of the NCLW, for example, argued that there was a need for a wider distribution of powers and responsibilities within its Executive Bureau because they were "too much centralized within specific individuals." See Omar Trabulsi, *National Commission for Women: Capacity Building and Action Plan Report*, UNIFEM, October 2001, p. 21. A similar criticism emerged from a second evaluation of the NCLW five years later, which argued that vague rules with respect to internal governance had facilitated the personalization of power within the Executive Bureau. See Fahima Sharaf el-Din, *Assessment of the National Women's Machinery in Lebanon*, EUROMED Role of Women in Economic Life Programme, October 2006, p. 16.

158. One of the initial internal fault lines within the decision-making process of the NCLW was that between its respective presidents (Mona Hrawi and
Madame Lahoud) and Randa Berri, the first and long-standing vice president of
the NCLW. Described as "a very bright woman, a brilliant woman" whose influence proved useful in some of the activities of the NCLW, particularly with respect
to the creation of ministry focal points, Berri also complicated the workings of the
NCLW with her maneuverings for symbolic and hegemonic influence—threatening (unsuccessfully) to block the first round of appointments to the NCLW in
exchange for her appointment as co-president rather than vice-president, and
blocking important meetings over the strategic direction of the NCLW because
they were going to be held in the offices of the First Lady rather than her own.
Indeed, given the fear that the NCLW could become a political fiefdom for Berri,
some female members of the parliament threatened in 1998 to lobby preemptively
against its very creation. Interviews with former members of the NCLW, 2008.

159. Interview, 17 July 2008.

160. See Omar Trabulsi, op. cit., 2001, p. 17.

161. Interview with NCLW member, 1 April 2008.

162. See Omar Trabulsi, op. cit., 2001; and Fahima Sharaf el-Din, op. cit.,
2006.

163. See Azza Beydoun, "Arguments Valid for Once Only" in al-Raida,
XXII, No. 111–112, Fall–Winter 2005–2006. The CEDAW Committee was particularly critical of the tendency of the NCLW and the Lebanese government to
site "cultural specificities" and "on-going development crises" as excuses for its
lack of progress in implementing the CEDAW Convention (p. 25). See also the
CEDAW letter to the Lebanese government (February 2008), in which it described
the NCLW as being "severely under-resourced and understaffed" and lacking
the authority to effectively promote the implementation of the Convention. It
also commented "with concern" on what it felt was "the lack of awareness in
the part of the State party about the importance of a strong and well-resourced
national machinery" and "the lack of political will to develop the necessary institutional capacity . . . in accordance with its obligations under the Convention."
See CEDAW, op. cit., 1 February 2008, p. 4.

164. Interview with NCLW member, 1 April 2008.

165. See Trabulsi, op. cit., 2001; and interview with a staff member of the
NCLW, 9 April 2008.

166. Interview with NCLW member, 1 April 2008.

167. Goetz, op. cit., 1995, p. 2.

168. Interviews with Azma Kurdahi, UNFPA-Lebanon, 2 June 2008; and
Mirna Sabbagh, UNDP-Lebanon, 17 June, 2008. One of the more interesting
NCLW projects, called WePass, was a women's empowerment program funded
by UNFPA (among other donors) aimed at raising awareness—particularly on
issues such as violence against women—among poorer women in ten outlying
villages in the South. The project tried to target villages left out of the bonanza
of aid that followed in the wake of the July 2006 war and that have both a

Social Development Center of the Ministry of Social Affairs and, ideally, some form of women's committee connected to a municipality. Although it had little to do with the policy work of the NCLW itself, the project was considered to have been a success, and there are now plans, first, to expand the project to an additional ten villages scattered throughout the country and, second, to integrate all twenty villages into the parallel project funded by UNFPA to reformulate the NCLW's national strategy. Interview with Zeina Mehzer, WePass Project Manager, 19 June 2008.

169. Interview with NCLW member, 1 April 2008.

170. These include Aman Shaarani, Linda Matar, and Iqbal Dughan—with Aman Shaarani being elected for a second term in 2008. Under Linda Matar's mandate, for example, there were two big conferences on the establishment of a system of quota for parliamentary elections. In 2010, this was eventually adopted within municipalities—though at a percentage of 20 percent rather than the 30 percent demanded by the LWC.

171. Interview, 11 April 2008.

172. Interview, 30 May 2008.

173. See Osseiran, op. cit., 2006, pp. 84–85. In a clear attempt to employ generational and familial hierarchies, for example, Osseiran recounted that when she was still musing about whether to run against Aman Shaarani, who had made it clear that she would only run for the LWC presidency "unopposed," several groups within the LWC pleaded with Osseiran not to be "rebellious," "impolite," and "disrespectful of the elderly" by staying in the race but to make sacrifices as if Aman Shaarani were her "mother." Interview, 6 June 2008.

174. Interview with Iqbal Dughan, 21 July 2008. It was her proposal that was vetoed by the Ministry of the Interior when she was the LWC president.

175. Sharara, op. cit., 1978, p. 6.

176. Interview, 24 April 2008.

177. Interview, 1 July 2008.

178. See Fadia Kiwan, *The Work of Women in Civil Associations*, Beirut: Friedrich Eberhardt Stiftung and the Lebanese Women's Council, 1994 (in Arabic).

179. Quoted in Osseiran, op. cit., 2006, p. 44.

180. Interviews with members of *al-Rabita*, 23 April, 24 April, and 4 June 2008. When speaking about the various topics of their lecture series, for example, they remarked that when it came to dealing with religious questions, their aim was to promote "the real religion," and they were especially insistent to emphasize the tolerant nature of Islam, especially as regards Judaism and Christianity. "We worship one God. . . . We are together, we are neighbors, we are together. . . . Fanaticism [on the other hand] is a divergence from Islam . . . [and] we have to be ready [to] fight this trend."

181. Interview, 24 April 2008.

182. Interview, 1 July 2008.

183. Interview, 21 July 2008.

184. Interview with Iqbal Dughan, 27 July 2008.

185. Interview, 1 July 2008.

186. Interview, 11 April 2008.

187. Interview, National Democratic Institute (NDI), Lebanon Office, 10 April 2008.

188. Aman Shaarani and Linda Matar, former presidents of the LWC, both unsuccessfully ran for a seat in the Lebanese parliament.

## Chapter 5

1. Interview with Abdullah Zakia, 23 May 1999.

2. See Raymond Bryant and Sinead Bailey, *Third World Political Ecology*, London: Routledge, 1997, p. 39.

3. Levy and Newell, op. cit., 2002, p. 85.

4. Ibid., p. 85.

5. Ibid., p. 94.

6. Ibid., p. 85.

7. Led by such associations as the World Wildlife Fund (created in 1961), Friends of the Earth International (created in 1971), and Greenpeace (created in 1972), the campaigning of these networks made several important achievements. These included the dissemination of a new ecological sensibility, the legitimization of a sense of global collective responsibility for the environment, and the facilitation of "the search for common ground" within the newly emerging global environmental policy domain. Keck and Sikkink, 1998, p. 132.

8. See Karim Makdisi, "Trapped Between Sovereignty and Globalization: Implementing International Environmental and Natural Resource Treaties in Developing Countries—The Case of Lebanon," PhD diss., Fletcher School of Law and Diplomacy, Tufts University, April 2001, p. 66.

9. Keck and Sikkink, op. cit., 1998, p. 126.

10. Douglas Torgeson, *The Promise of Green Politics*, Raleigh, NC: Duke University Press, 1999, p. 2.

11. Makdisi, op. cit., 2001, p. 57.

12. See World Bank, *The Cost of Environmental Degradation in Lebanon*, 2004. See http://siteresources.worldbank.org/INTMNAREGTOPENVIRON-MENT/Resources/Final_English_Lebanon.pdf.

13. Karam, op. cit., 2004, p. 343.

14. Ibid., p. 381.

15. Interview, 19 April 1999.

16. Makdisi, op. cit., 2001, p. 104.

17. Interview with Charbal Nahhas, 1 December 2008. See also "Au Liban, on peut construire n'importe ou et n'importe quoi," *Orient le Jour*, 11 March 2003.

18. See Picard, op. cit., 2005, pp. 39–40. See also Eric Verdeuil, op. cit., 2005, p. 39.

19. Makdisi, op. cit., 2001, p. 130.

20. Ibid., p. 4.

21. As one local environmental activist in the Zghorta area of the country commented with respect to the effects of the intense competition between the various political families in the area, "they know your weakness. They know everybody's weakness. They work on your weakness and they pull you back in. It's a prison, it's a jail system. . . . You try to get out and then they pull you back in. . . . It's frightening and you have no alternative. The government doesn't protect you." Interview, 27 October 2008.

22. Beydoun, op. cit., 2004, p. 87.

23. Interview with Nashat Mansour, 16 April 1999.

24. Levy and Newell, op. cit., 2002, p. 87.

25. Fuad Handan, "The Ecological Crisis in Lebanon" in (ed.) Kail Ellis, *Lebanon's Second Republic: Prospects for the Twenty-first Century*, Gainesville: University of Florida Press, 2002, p. 175.

26. Council for Reconstruction and Development (CDR), *National Physical Master Plan for the Lebanese Territory*, Final Report, December 2005.

27. Between 1992 and 1999, for example, the sector is estimated to have spent in excess of U.S.$3 billion, with annual expenditures estimated to be in the range of U.S.$200 million. See *Orient le Jour*, 27 August 2003.

28. Ibid.

29. This activist remarked that in 2008, Sukleen was charging more than U.S.$100 for each ton of waste—compared to U.S.$30 to $50 per ton in New York City and $20 per ton in Zahle—in addition to the 40 percent of the waste that they recycled and then sold for significant profit each year. Interview, 15 December 2008.

30. World Bank, *Implementation Completion Report on a Loan in the Amount of US$10.9 Million to the Lebanese Republic for a Solid Waste/Environmental Management Project*, 21 June 2004, p. 7.

31. Interview, 12 November 2008.

32. Ibid.

33. World Bank, op. cit., 2004, p. 11.

34. Ibid., p. 16.

35. Interview, 23 May 1999.

36. World Bank, 2004, op. cit., p. 16.

37. *The Daily Star*, 14 November 2003. Interestingly, in a later CDR report, it also called for both greater public consultation and public awareness raising with respect to waste management policy—especially on questions relating to the selection of sites—arguing that ignoring these local concerns could induce "trouble"—especially given its own estimate that the country would need on an annual basis an additional 40 hectares of land to satisfy its territorial need for landfill sites. CDR, op. cit., 2005, p. IV:8:3.

38. Interview, 12 November 2008.

39. Ibid., p. 6.

40. *The Daily Star*, 30 August 2003.

41. Ibid.

42. Interview, 12 November 2008.

43. In the late 1980s, Habre convinced Suleiman Franjieh Sr., head of one of the leading families within the Zghorta region of the country, to assist in the protection of Horsh Eddin—a mountainous forested area that he described as "a paradise" consisting of more than thirty-nine species of trees alone—and, by the 1990s, he also had cultivated interest among local groups in Tripoli for the protection of the Palm Islands. In 1992, Habre's efforts culminated in the formal establishment of Horsh Eddin and the Palm Island as protected areas by the Council of Ministers. See Kingston, op. cit., 2001, p. 64.

44. Karam, op. cit., 2004, p. 377.

45. Ibid., p. 370.

46. Interview, 24 November 2008.

47. Interview with Mirvat Abu Khalil, June 2008.

48. Interviews with Shadi Hamadeh, 29 March 1999 and 1 December 2008; and Hala Ashur, 24 November 2008.

49. Interview, 26 March 1999.

50. Karam, op. cit., 2004, p. 351.

51. Interview, 29 March 1999.

52. Interview with Adnan Melki, 25 November 2008.

53. Interview with Hala Ashur, 24 November 2008.

54. This "horizontal" form of governance was reflected in several commitments: (i) to remain as a volunteer-based rather than a "professionalized" association; (ii) to replace one-third of the Executive Council every three years; (iii) to keep Executive Council meetings open to everyone, even non-members; (iv) to give an enormous amount of autonomy to members to initiate projects without the immediate or prior need for approval by the Executive Council; and (v) to include the initiators of such projects as ex officio members on the Executive Council. Interview with Shadi Hamadeh, 29 March 1999; interview with Adnan Melki, 25 November 2008.

55. Interview, 2 December 2008.

56. In fact, Karam estimates that Green Line obtained 97 percent of its budget of U.S.$200,000 in 2000 from external sources. See Karam, 2006, p. 150.

57. Interview with Hala Ashur, 24 March 1999.

58. Interview, 25 November 2008.

59. This pioneering campaign struck at the heart of political power in the extremely sensitive early postwar years given the involvement of companies linked to the head of the AMAL militia, Nabih Berri. Described as "a scientific intervention" consisting of a Tyre-based symposium of coastal geologists and marine biologists hosted by a local NGO (*nadi al-tadamun*), the event proved both politically explosive—it being coercively disrupted by Berri's political thugs—and surprisingly successful in that not only was the sand extraction (temporarily) stopped but, with the help of the Lebanese media, the campaign catapulted an important environmental issue into the country's emerging postwar public sphere.

60. Karim Makdisi suggests that a large number of the barrels of this toxic waste were simply dumped into streams and/or the Mediterranean Sea. Others were sold for use as fertilizers, with the empty barrels sold and used for all sorts of public and private purposes such as storing rainwater. Argues Makdisi, it was mainly poor farmers who took advantage of these offers. See "Implementing Environmental Treaties in Developing Countries: Using Flows to Explain How Lebanon Dealt with Trade in Hazardous Waste," Paper Presented at the International Studies Association Annual Meeting 2006, San Diego, CA, 23 March 2006.

61. See Makdisi, op. cit., 2001, p. 308.

62. Makdisi, op. cit., 2006, p. 18.

63. Fuad Hamdan remarked that the decision to set up a more permanent office in Beirut was "a test to see if it was possible to work in the Arab world." He also remarked that "without Green Line, there would be no Greenpeace in Lebanon." Interview, 4 March 1999.

64. Ibid.

65. See Makdisi, 2001, op. cit., p. 308. With respect to compliance with international environmental conventions, for example, Makdisi's study further concluded that one of the most crucial factors was the formation of "informal transnational alliances" between non-state actors like Green Line and Greenpeace "that close the gap between the ideals of international law (as expressed in international treaties) and the realities on the ground (i.e., the uneven capacities and will of the relevant state players to comply with the treaties)." Ibid., p. 7.

66. This included the eventual decision by the Lebanese parliament to ratify all treaties (known as the Basel conventions) governing the transboundary movement of hazardous waste. See Makdisi, op. cit., 2006; and Green Line's Web site: www.greenline.org.lb.

67. Interview, 1 December 2008.

68. Adnan Melki, for example, praised Hamadeh for having effectively delegated responsibility and authority to a degree that was unusual in the associative world of Lebanon, adding that it was something that he seemed to do almost "without noticing." A further testament to Hamadeh's success in promoting a more collective approach to associative governance, noted Melki, was the fact that "many Lebanese who knew of Green Line [in the 1990s] never knew who its president was." Interview, 25 November 2008.

69. The three main sets of participants in this initial meeting were representatives from Green Line, Assad Serhal from the Society for the Protection of Nature–Lebanon (SPNL), and Abdullah Zakhia.

70. Torgeson, op. cit., 1999, p. 2.

71. Ibid., p. 20.

72. Interview, 13 April 1999.

73. Interviews, 2 April 1999 and 14 May 1999.

74. Interview, 23 May 1999.

75. One activist with direct experience with the LEF—having administered the UNDP-Life Program from its offices between 1995 and 1996—described its

rank and file as being far removed from the real environmental problems in the country, preferring instead to "put on their suits and ties, go and meet the minister and shake his hand, have free cocktails, and clap [in the hope that] they will send us to workshops in Brazil." In short, she argued, "they don't have a clue. They've never even been in the field or in a squatter settlement where sewers are running wild in the streets . . . they've never gotten themselves dirty." Interview, 19 April 1999. For a classic example of the promotional and uncritical environmental orientation of the LEF, see an article written by the LEF in the in-flight magazine of Middle East Airlines. "Think Green, Act Green: The Lebanese Environmental Forum" in *Cedar Wings*, 2001–2002.

76. Interview, 1 April 1999.

77. The most obvious example of this penetration is the presence of the NGO called *Amwaj al-Bi'a*, the environmental arm of Randa Berri's wider hegemonic involvement within the affairs of Lebanese civil society. Described by its first president as "an NGO without people," *Amwaj al-Bi'a* quickly established a dominant foothold within LEF and managed to jealously and continuously hold onto the position of secretary-general, in part through its influence over a number of LEF associational members from the South. It has not been alone, however, joined by a number of other NGOs—some linked to Jumblat, others linked to Murr, and still others linked to particular commercial and industrial interests such as the production of asbestos and cement and the importation of pesticides. The president of the LEF in 1999, Rifaat Saba, for example, was targeted by the Greenpeace representative in Lebanon, Ghassan Geara, for his links to asbestos industry in the country. See Hala Kilani, "Greenpeace lashes out at local activist" in *The Daily Star*, 15 April 1999, p. 3.

78. Interview, 23 May 1999.

79. Interview with Nashat Mansour, 16 April 1999.

80. These included those within Green Line (which remained a member of both groups in the 1990s), Paul Abi Rashid of Terre-Liban, Antoine Daher of the Committee for the Environmental Protection of Qobeiyat, Youssef Touk of the Committee for the Environmental Protection of Bcharre, and Habib Maalouf of Green Forum itself, who was also one of the country's leading environmental journalists, writing a weekly environmental column for *as-Safir* newspaper.

81. This last commentator made some interesting comments about the limited nature of environmental activism in Lebanon as a whole. Commenting on Green Forum's fear of mobilizing demonstrations, for example, she went on to argue that "in Lebanon, things are not going to go smoothly unless we show that we are strong and that we are not afraid. We've got to burn something, sometimes even if it pollutes. We've got to tie ourselves to trees, [we've got] to prevent trucks from getting to construction sites." Interview with Gaby Butros, SOS-Environment/AFSAD, 17 April 1999.

82. In the discussions about possible protests against industrial pollution within the Chekka region of the country, for example, associations proved reti-

cent to get involved given the proximity of powerful political figures (Franjieh in Zghorta and Karame in Tripoli). Interview, 26 March 1999.

83. Ibid.

84. Interviews with Abdullah Zakhia, 23 May 1999; and Hani Abu Fadil, 21 May 1999.

85. Interview, 19 April 1999.

86. Interview, 21 May 1999.

87. Interview, 23 May 1999.

88. Interview, 19 May 1999.

89. An EU report on the state of the environment in Lebanon noted that "the law establishing the MoE is ambiguous and fails to provide a clear basis upon which the MoE can develop its role in Lebanon or to interact and coordinate activities and responsibilities with other relevant organizations." While the law requires the MoE to "fight pollution from any sources," it failed to define violations or the principles for dealing with them." The report recommended the formulation of "an integrated environmental law." See METAP (Mediterranean Environmental Technical Assistance Program), *Lebanon: Assessment of the State of the Environment*, May 1995, p. 155 and p. 179.

90. Interview, 19 May 1999.

91. See Makdisi, 2006, op. cit.

92. Interview, 23 May 1999.

93. Interview with Lamia Mansour, UNDP, 25 May 1999.

94. One of Chehayeb's appointments was Nabil Abu Ghanem as his special advisor for environmental awareness. Like Chaheyeb, Abu Ghanem also had been a high school science teacher who had a long-standing interest in environmental issues. During the civil war, he had been in charge of a daily program for the Druze radio station *Sawt al-Jabal* called *Baladna Helu*. Another of Chehayeb's main appointments was Mounir Abu Ghanem as the project manager for C21. Abu Ghanem had been the founder of AFDC, to which Chehayeb had been appointed president, and, as we shall see, would go on to play a central role in the environmental field, building AFDC up into one of the major environmental NGOs in the country. Interview with Nabil Abu Ghanem, 21 May 1999; and interview with Mounir Abu Ghanem, 25 March 1999. For further comments on the merit-based nature of these appointments, see Karam, 2004, op. cit., p. 402.

95. These included a revamped Code of the Environment, a Strategy for the Environment, a Master Plan for Quarries, a Master Plan for Solid Waste Management, and the new C21 Strategy for Building the Ministry of the Environment. Zakhia described these efforts at improving the legal framework for environmental protection in the country as "un program serieux d'infrastucture." Interview, 23 May 1999.

96. Interview with Nabil Abu Ghanem, 21 May 1999.

97. Interview, 21 May 1999.

98. See Karam, 2004, op. cit., p. 405.

99. Ibid., p. 365. Karam argues that this initiative was crucial in helping to set the stage for the parliament's approval in 2001 and later in 2002 of a series of bills dealing with air pollution by, among other things, banning diesel taxis and mini-buses (p. 366).

100. It was estimated, for example, that more than 50 percent of the developed portions of the Lebanese coast were occupied by illegal constructions. See *Atlas du Liban: Territoires et Societe*, IFPO and CNRS, 2007, p. 107. It is interesting to note that, collectively, the LEF not only refused to attend the conference but, in addition, they lobbied for the conference not to take place and subsequently refused to sponsor the book when it was released. Interview with Abdullah Zakhia, 23 May 1999.

101. Interview with Mounir Abu Ghanem, 25 March 1999. See also Karam, 2004, op. cit., p. 403. Chehayeb later participated in a similar parliamentary sit-in that was demanding the closure of quarries in the (Murr-dominated) Metn region.

102. Interview with Mirvat Abu Khalil, 26 March 1999.

103. Interview with Abdullah Zakhia, 23 May 1999. Other key additions to the code were the commitment to creating "a green police"—likewise vetoed by Murr—and the stipulation that all major development projects be required to carry out a prior Environmental Impact Assessment (EIA), which, though included as part of the Environmental Code eventually passed in 2002, has not been activated by passage of the requisite implementation decrees.

104. The procedural stumbling block emerged over the issue of elections to an executive committee, after the two sides had agreed on a unified draft constitution. Chehayeb and Green Forum members hoped to reach a preelection agreement over a slate of candidates, avoiding the need for an actual election that would play to the advantage of the LEF given its larger associational numbers. In the end, however, the LEF insisted on having "democratic" elections that ultimately scuttled the entire deal. Interview with Mounir Abu Ghanem, 25 March 1999. See also Karam, 2004, op. cit., p. 404.

105. Interview, 25 March 1999.

106. Interview, 21 May 1999.

107. Interviews, 23 May 1999 and 26 March 1999.

108. Karam, 2004, op. cit., p. 437.

109. Ibid., p. 381.

110. Ibid., p. 388.

111. Ibid., p. 421.

112. Interview with Michel Skaff, 16 November 2008.

113. The most concerted attempt to break the hold of the founding core group on the executive came in 2004, when demands were successfully made for the holding of formal elections for the executive. The closeness of the election combined with constitutional provisions that in the case of a tie gives the seat to the longest-serving member worked to the advantage of the old executive and allowed them to maintain their control. Interview, 25 November 2008.

114. Interview, 2 December 2008.

115. Interview, 24 November 2008.

116. Interview, 10 December 2008.

117. Interview, 24 November 2008.

118. Ibid.

119. Ibid.

120. "Journee de solidarite pour le protection de la plage de Ramlet al-Baida," *Orient Le Jour*, 23 September 2003.

121. See Elizabeth Picard, "Beyrouth: la gestion nationale d'enjeux locauz" in (ed.) Agnes Favier, *Municipalites et Pouvoirs Locaux au Liban*, Beirut: CER-MOC, No. 24, 2001, pp. 295–318.

122. Interview, 10 December 2008.

123. See Candice Raymond, "Samidoun, trente-trois jours de mobilization civile a Beyrouth" in (eds.) Mermier and Picard, *Liban, une geurre de trente-trois jours*, Paris: La decouverte, 2007; see also Karam Karam, "Resistances civiles?" in Ibid., 2007.

124. Interview, 2 December 2008.

125. Raymond, 2007, op. cit., n.p.

126. One of the executive members of Green Line commented that this decision had created much tension and led to "hours of debate" within the association itself, adding that it was the kind of polarizing moment in the association and the country whereby "members [all] took positions." Interview with Hala Ashur,

127. Interview, 24 November 2008.

128. Particularly devastating was the decision of a large number of young wartime volunteers to leave Green Line and join a new association called Indy-Act. This was established by Wael Hmaidan, the former Greenpeace regional coordinator based in Lebanon, who, in conjunction with Green Line, had taken a lead role in the Oil Spill Working Group's advocacy campaign and has now turned his attention to Indy-Act and to campaigning on the issue of climate change.

129. In explaining its cautious beginnings, Youssef Touk, a long-standing environmental activist in the Bcharre region of Lebanon, remarked that "in the Middle East, we talk a lot but we do very little." With regard to Lebanon, he elaborated further, stating that "there is the LEF, there is this committee, there are hundreds of committees but nothing moves. Or, nothing moves in a positive sense. On the contrary, things are moving in a negative sense. As a result, we are frustrated and from time to time, this frustration leads us to meet again and to try and do something. But, we do not have lots of resources . . . [and] in Lebanon, the question of the environment is not . . . popular . . . and that is a double frustration." Moreover, adding with a further sense of exasperation, the situation in Lebanon is made worse by the fact that people in positions of political responsibility "do almost nothing." Hence, with respect to the new groupings of NGOs, Touk emphasized that "what was important was to work—to try to do something." Interview, 20 December 2008.

130. Interview, 15 December 2008.

131. Interview, 22 December 2008.

132. Interviews, 28 November 2008; 5 December 2008; 15 December 2008; 20 December 2008; 22 December 2008.

133. Interview, 15 December 2008.

134. Youssef Touk, for example, who was universally respected for his integrity as an environmentalist and whom some had hoped would be the president of the "new LEF," withdrew from environmental advocacy activities at the national level altogether after the LEF debacle, utterly disillusioned with the degree of political maneuvering and interference in the field; "I'm finished," he remarked in response to my question about his interest in the re-revival of discussions about reintegrating the LEF; "I no longer have confidence." Interview, 20 December 2008.

135. Interview, June 2008. See also Max Kasparek, "Lebanon: Evaluation of the Energy and Environment Programme—An Outcome Evaluation," Beirut: UNDP-Lebanon, December 2007.

136. Interview, 19 November 2008.

137. Interview, 29 November 2008.

138. Interview, 5 November 2008. See also Karim Makdisi, "NCSA Cross-Cutting Synthesis Report: Lebanon," Republic of Lebanon National Capacity Self-Assessment (NCSA), October 2007 for an evaluation (and critique) of the work of the ministry with respect to promoting compliance with respect to three international environmental conventions: UNCBD (Biodiversity), UNCFCCC (Climate Change), and the UNCCD (Desertification).

139. Interview, 29 November 2008.

140. Interview, 15 December 2008.

141. Interview, June 2008. Despite these difficulties, however, it also was clear that the cooperation of the Ministry of the Environment, especially for NGOs, was important if only because it could cause many problems in the implementation of projects. Commented the leader of one NGO in the conservation field, "you need the ministry, you need to be on good terms with the ministry, and sometimes you need permission of the ministry. . . . [Hence], keep them sweet but don't ever work with them. . . . That is basically how everyone tries to operate because they are just too difficult to work with. I know a number of NGOs that will never work with the ministry, never. They just try to avoid it completely." Interview, 28 October 2008.

142. AFDC, for example, was commissioned to write the country's first *State of Lebanon's Forests* report for the UNDP; it has held an annual reforestation campaign; it has been developing tree nurseries, especially at its center in Ramliyya; and it also has begun work on the cultivation and planting of what it calls "productive trees"—pine, olive, and carob trees. Through its regional centers, it also has programs promoting rural development through such initiatives as small income–generating and eco-tourism projects—all premised on the principle that conservation must go hand in hand with the promotion of development. Finally, its national office has been developing a number of programs in advocacy

and environmental education—most notably the USAID-funded program called *Hewarna*, aimed at promoting dialogue at an annual conference for Lebanese youth on matters relating to the environment.

143. Interview, 5 November 2008.

144. Interview, 7 December 2008.

145. Interview, 5 December 2008.

146. Ibid.

147. Ibid.

148. Interview, 5 November 2008. The former executive director contrasted AFDC's approach with that of Green Line, arguing that "Green Line never use these connections. . . . For them, advocacy is nagging, not engagement. [Our approach] is engagement. You are at the heart of the policy making process and you are trying to make trade-offs," adding that "where is this going to lead if you don't engage. . . . You can, OK, have your line of struggle for the environment but if you want to have achievable results, you have to use the system. You have to engage one way or the other." 5 December 2008.

149. Symbolic of this deterioration has been the launching of a legal case by Green Line and a group of environmental NGOs against the mayor of Beirut (within which Jumblat was named) for the latter's role in sanctioning the transfer of waste from the Normandy dump site in Beirut to a section of a quarry in Siblime owned by Jumblat, a transfer that the coalition of NGOs argued transpired in an untransparent manner without the proper environmental impact assessments being conducted. In response to this case, Jumblat's lawyer launched a countercase against Green Line within which it was accused of being one of those hundreds of illegitimate "mushroom" NGOs that have popped up throughout the country, statements that clearly have a political rather than a legal purpose behind them. Interviews with Green Line, 10 November 2008 and 10 December 2008.

150. Interviews, 2 June 2008 and 24 November 2008.

151. Interview 15 December 2008.

152. Interview, 2 June 2008.

153. In the meantime, Maalouf also had created his own Lebanese Environment Party, though his timing had been particularly unfortunate, established as it was in the month before Hariri's assassination in January 2005. Since that time, the party has been essentially moribund, to Maalouf's own admission, making no effort to attract more than its founding members and acting, at best, like a civil association through the implementation of a few environmental projects. Argued Maalouf, it was premature to try and create a real oppositional green party in the country; there was simply not enough public support. Interview with Habib Maalouf, 24 November 2008.

154. It also had been Phillip Skaff who had managed AFDC's National Forest Fire Campaign in 2007.

155. One leading environmentalist in the country, for example, actively involved in promoting "reducing, reusing, and recycling," was offered a U.S.$50,000 grant by Sukleen for his work—but on the condition that he appear on a Sukleen

advertisement to receive the check. This activist replied, in turn, that he would only agree to do this if Sukleen publicly supported the recycling campaign of his NGO—to which the company ultimately and revealingly refused. Interview, 15 December 2008.

156. Interview, 22 December 2008.

157. I was told by many conservation activists that the real founder of the conservation movement in modern Lebanon was George Tome, who, as a prewar employee with the National Center for Scientific Research (NCSR), conducted numerous pioneering scientific studies that laid the basis for much subsequent research in the postwar period.

158. See GEF/UNDP, *Strengthening of National Capacity and Grassroots In-Situ Conservation for Sustainable Biodiversity Protection*, Project Document, March 1997.

159. See http://www.jabalmoussa.org/.

160. See http://www.mectat.com.lb/Naturebook/nat7.htm.

161. See http://www.spnl.org/load.php?page=hima_leb&id=128&section=projects.

162. Interview with Charbal Nahhas, 1 December 2008.

163. See Kingston, op. cit., 2001, p. 64. See also "Donors, Patrons, and Civil Society: The Global-Local Dynamics of Environmental Politics in Postwar Lebanon" in (eds.) Jordi Diez and O. P. Dwivedi, *Global Environmental Challenges: Perspectives from the South*, Peterborough: Broadview Press, 2008.

164. It is interesting to note, for example, that contrary to the standard historical conclusions that land tenure systems in Lebanon are predominantly characterized by small-hold tenure, the country actually has one of the higher rates of land inequality in the world, a situation accentuated and consolidated during the "critical" period of the French mandate. See Michael Gilsenan, "A Modern Feudality? Land and Labour in North Lebanon, 1858–1950" in (ed.) Tarif Khalidi, *Land Tenure and Social Transformation in the Middle East*, Beirut: American University of Beirut Press, 1984, pp. 459–460; and Kais Firro, op. cit., 2003, p. 88. For statistics on Lebanon's Gini coefficient with respect to land inequality, see FAO's Statistical Yearbook, 2007–2008. Interview with Rami Zuraik, 20 November 2008.

165. Interview, 17 December 2008.

166. Ibid. See also Ana Maria Lucas, "Politics and Property" in *Now Lebanon*, 5 November 2010.

167. Interview with Chris Naylor, Director, A Rocha-Lebanon, 28 October 2008.

168. The scheme revolved around goat grazers and tenant farmers taking extra land around the wetland and then paying off the steward who worked for the landowner. Interview with Michel Skaff, 16 November 2008.

169. Ibid.

170. Ibid.

171. Michel Skaff spoke of reworking contracts for renting the land, refurbishing buildings, promoting soil conservation measures, increasing prices for tenant farmers, and changing crop rotations as examples of these measures. Ibid.

172. The economic benefits of these measures for the Skaff family seem to have been significant, Michel Skaff speaking of annual growth rates of 20 percent in the last decade that have resulted in the value of their assets tripling. He did add, however, that the family could have made tens of millions had it decided to simply extract top soil from the 'Ammiq wetland—"just like quarries." Ibid.

173. Interviews, 16 November 2008 and 14 December 2008.

174. Interview, 17 December 2008.

175. Skaff, for example, remarked that he was moving "slowly, slowly . . . because already, you feel that some people are getting nervous," adding that, as a result of the close proximity within which all live in the country, "any group that moves could be stepping on anybody's toes . . . and everyone is very jumpy. You need very, very, very clear demarcation lines, very fast, and you need to hold them and to be very serious." Interview, 16 November 2008.

176. Ibid.

177. See "Mada, Strategic Workshop, Batroun 28–28, 2007," www.mada.org. lb. Also see interview with Mona Fawaz, 3 November 2008.

178. Among the concrete goals of the project were to promote the development of small tourist enterprises, expand local employment opportunities, create a market for local produce, improve access to transportation facilities for the local population, better regulate the use of forest resources and goat grazing, and halt and find viable alternatives to two local sand quarrying enterprises. Integrally important to the success of all of these projects, however, was the promotion of greater social integration between the various competing families and tribal groups within the region itself. See Mada, *Support a Common Territorial Development Project in Upper Akkar*, November 2008.

179. Ibid.

180. Interview, 24 July 2008.

181. See National Park Steering Committee, "Support a Common Territorial Development Project in Upper Akkar," November 2008. Interview 24 July 2008.

182. The CDR, for example, included a designation for a national park in the North in its final report of the *National Physical Master Plan of the Lebanese Territory* (2005); it has lobbied the EU to include a budget line in its aid program for the creation of a national park in Akkar; and it has acted as a conduit for Mada to the recently created interministerial committee for matters relating to the development of both the North and Hermel-Balbak.

183. Interview, 12 December 2008.

184. Ibid.

185. Rami Zurayk and Mona Haidar, for example, similarly argued in the context of their evaluation of biodiversity reserve projects in Lebanon more generally that NGOs have usually found it difficult to adequately represent the

diverse and often conflictual array of interests that make up local communities, remarking that "local NGOs serve, at best, only as entry points and more than one entry point is needed in a complex society." They went on to argue that "in the absence of multiple entry points, projects quickly became hostage to the good will of one local group and reflect that group's priorities rather than the priorities of the whole community." See Rami Zurayk and Mona Haidar, "Biodiversity Conservation Priorities: Lebanon" in *Sharing Innovative Experiences: Examples of Successful Conservation and Sustainable Use of Dryland Biodiversity*, New York: UNDP, Volume 9, 2004, p. 16.

186. Mada's staff, for example, described the government as acting "weirdly" in response to outbreaks of violence between the two principal villages—Fnaideq and Akkar Atika—over the opening up of a road by one village in the central area of the proposed park in the summer of 2008, initially sending the Lebanese Army in to close it before subsequently reopening it on the orders of a local judge. "It's just not consistent," commented one of Mada's employees. "It just means that the government was subject to pressure and they couldn't handle it," adding that while the local judge was "nice but very weak," the state did not provide "space" for him to work. Interview, 12 December, 2008.

187. Ibid.

188. See "Self-Assessment Checklist," www.mada.org.lb.

## Chapter 6

1. Interview with Roland Tamruz, executive director of Zawraq, 2 June 1999.

2. Both the absolute numbers of people with disabilities and the proportion of them living in the developing world—where it is estimated that more than 80 percent of them live—have been on the rise since the 1970s.

3. Rebecca Yoe, "Disability, Poverty, and the New Development Agenda," KaR Programme, September 2005, p. 4.

4. World Bank, *A Note on Disability in the Middle East and North Africa*, 30 June 2005, p. 5. Adib Nemeh, a UN consultant with the Ministry of Social Affairs in postwar Lebanon, suggested that the disabled in postwar Lebanon were three times more likely to be subject to extreme poverty. Interview with Adib Nemeh, 27 October 2008.

5. Disability KaR, *Lessons from the Disability Knowledge and Research Programme*, www.disabilitykar.net, p. 9.

6. Barbara Harriss-White, "Disability" in *Encyclopedia of International Development*, London:
Routledge, 2005, p. 157.

7. David Seddon and Raymond Lang, "Mainstreaming Disability Issues into Development Studies—In Theory and Practice," Paper presented at the 14th annual meeting of the Disability Studies Association, Winnipeg, June 2001, p. 5.

8. See Lina Abou-Habib, *Gender and Disability: Women's Experiences in the Middle East*, Oxford: Oxfam, 1997, p. 14.

9. KaR, op. cit., p. 11.

10. A notable example was the description of practices at "the notorious convent" of Qazhiyya in Mount Lebanon, where monks were described as subjecting the intellectually disabled to internment in caves, confinement in chains, and torture revolving around the administration of such things as dousing with cold water, bleedings, and beatings—all justified as mechanisms to cast out demons. See Eugene Rogan, "Madness and Marginality: The Advent of the Psychiatric Asylum in Egypt and Lebanon" in (ed.) Eugene Rogan, *Outside In: On the Margins of the Modern Middle East*, London: I.B. Taurus, 2001, pp. 104–125.

11. NARD, WRF, and USAID, "A Symposium on Disability and Religion," 26 July 1995, p. 5.

12. Majid Turmusani, *Disabled People and Economic Needs in Developing Countries: The Political Perspective from Jordan*, Burlington, VT: Ashgate Publishing Company, 2003, p. 50.

13. Turmusani tells the story of a disabled woman in southern Lebanon who was left by her father to die in their half-destroyed house after an Israeli military offensive in 1978, reputedly because the cow was more useful to him than the girl. Ibid., p. 53. See also Lina Abou-Habib, op. cit., 1997; and Samantha Wehbi and Sylvana Lakkis, "Women with Disabilities in Lebanon: From Marginalization to Resistance" in *Affilia: Journal of Women and Social Work*, 25, 1, 2010, pp. 56–67.

14. Ibid., p. 58.

15. Marta Russell and Ravi Malhotra, "Capitalism and Disability" in *A World of Contradictions: Socialist Register,* 2002, p. 212.

16. See Janet Lord, "It Takes a Treaty: Elbowing into the Mainstream Human Rights Movement," paper delivered to the International Studies Association, Montreal, March 2004, p. 2.

17. Majid Turmusani, A. Vreede, and L. S. Wirz, "Some Ethical Issues in Community-Based Rehabilitation Initiatives in the Developing World" in *Disability and Rehabilitation*, 24, 10, 2002, p. 559.

18. Lord, op. cit., 2004, p. 5. See also Turmusani, op. cit., 2003, 107.

19. Turmusani, op. cit., 2003, p. 58.

20. Russell and Malhotra, op. cit., 2002, p. 212.

21. Ibid., 214.

22. See Joseph Melling and Bill Forsythe (eds.), *Insanity, Institutions, and Society, 1980–1914: A Social History of Madness in Comparative Perspective*, Studies in the Social History of Medicine, London and New York: Routledge, 1999; and Gerald Grab's review of the above book in *Medicine History*, 44, 3, July 2000, pp. 416–417, in which he praises the volume for eschewing "overarching generalizations" linking the oppression of people with intellectual disabilities with notions of "bourgeois productivity" (p. 416).

23. The KaR Programme concluded, for example, that people with disabilities found it difficult to find work in rural areas, to access vocational training

programs, and to access micro-credit schemes; and, as Barbara Harriss-White argues, the effects can be particularly devastating for poor families that experience impairment in midlife. For these families, argues Harriss-White, "impairment often comes as a shock . . . pitching them into debt and downward mobility through immediate loss of income, through the direct costs of care and the costs of future income forgone by those bearing the burden of care." See KaR, op. cit., p. 10. See also Harriss-White, op. cit., 2005, p. 157.

24. Sylvana Lakkis (LPHU) and Eddie Thomas (Oxfam-UK), "Disability and Livelihoods in Lebanon," paper presented to conference at the University of Manchester, UK, on "Staying Poor: Chronic Poverty and Development Policy," 9 April 2003, p. 5.

25. Ibid.

26. See National Inclusion Project, "Disability in Lebanon: A Statistical Report," Council for Development and Reconstruction and the World Bank—Community Development Project, 2007, p. 30. For more on the "inaccessibility of the labour market" in Lebanon and the role of family members in creating self-employment opportunities for people with disabilities, see also Samantha Wehbi and Y. El-Lahib, "The Employment Situation of People with Disabilities in Lebanon: Challenges and Opportunities" in Disability and Society, 22, 4, June 2007, pp. 371–382.

27. Ibid., p. 31. Lakkis and Thomas, for example, described Lebanon's employment insurance system as being "badly hit by the hyperinflation of the war years" and, given the resultant "extremely costly" nature of payments for both employers and employees, one that has encouraged employers to hire people informally as a way of avoiding the payment of high premiums. See Lakkis and Thomas, op. cit., 2003, p. 8.

28. See Nisreen Salti, Jad Chaaban, and Firas Raad, "Health Equity in Lebanon: A Microeconomic Analysis" in International Journal of Equity in Health, 9, 11, 2010.

29. The study concluded that most working-aged disabled people in Lebanon are "low-waged workers not covered by state retirement or health insurance." See Lakkis and Thomas, op. cit., 2003, p. 7.

30. Russell and Malhotra take a more skeptical view of the role of the state in the West, arguing that disability policy initiatives remain constrained by the commitment of political elites to the capitalist system. Indeed, they argue that the state has often imposed the harsh logic of the market on people with disabilities—promoting their segregation within newly created and "modern" institutions such as asylums, schools, and prisons; exploiting them as opportunities for profit making within the "rehabilitation industry"; and, at the most extreme, eliminating them altogether, whether through programs of forced sterilization, which were prevalent in the United States in the 1930s, or through their actual physical extermination, as was the case in Nazi Germany in the early 1940s. See Russell and Malhotra, op. cit., 2002, p. 215.

31. Geof Wood, "Informal Security Regimes: The Strength of Relationships" in (eds.) Ian Gough and Geof Wood, Insecurity and Welfare Regimes in

*Asia, Africa, and Latin America: Social Policy in Developing Countries*, Cambridge: Cambridge University Press, 2004, p. 49.

32. Wood, op. cit., 2004, p. 50.

33. Ibid.

34. Ian Gough and Geof Wood define the general notion of "welfare regimes" as "repeated systematic arrangements through which people seek livelihood security both of their own lives and for those of their children and descendants." They add that the use of the word "welfare," rather than denoting passive notions of charity, points to more active notions of the poor pursuing "their own sustainable survival and pursuit of well-being." See Ian Gough and Geof Wood, "Introduction" in Ian Gough and Geof Wood (eds.), *Insecurity and Welfare Regimes in Asia, Africa, and Latin America: Social Policy in Developing Countries*, Cambridge: Cambridge University Press, 2004, p. 7.

35. Wood, op. cit., 2004, p. 51.

36. Wood adds that "to be poor means, *inter alia*, to be unable to control future events because others have more control over them. This is why a sense of political economy is essential to understanding the constrained choices and options facing the poor. People are poor because of others." See Geof Wood, "Staying Secure, Staying Poor: The 'Faustian Bargain'" in *World Development*, 31, 3, March 2003, p. 456.

37. A perfect example of this is provided by Michael Gilsenan in his discussion of "the lords" in the context of late Ottoman and early-mandate Lebanon, who used their access to the state to restrict basic services to their local village and regional clients. These become "favors" that were "personally and arbitrarily awarded through the increasingly elaborate networks of patron-client relationships" and that worked to intensify and systematize power relations at the local level. Added Gilsenan, this contributed to what he called the "de-development" of life at local levels. Michael Gilsenan, "A Modern Feudality? Land and Labour in North Lebanon, 1858–1950" in (ed.) Tarif Khalidi, *Land Tenure and Social Transformation in the Middle East*, Beirut: American University of Beirut Press, 1984, p. 460.

38. See Naila Kabeer, "Re-Visioning the Social: Towards a Citizen-Centered Social Policy for Developing Countries" in *IDS Working Paper*, 191, January 2004, p. 36.

39. Thompson, op. cit., 2001, p. 74.

40. Thompson, op. cit., 2001, p. 155.

41. Ibid., p. 76 and p. 156.

42. Ibid., p. 79.

43. See Myriam Catusse, "Liban: la reforme sociale en panne?," unpublished seminar paper, CERMOC-Beirut, 29 February 2008, p. 16. See also A. Dagher, "L'etat et l'economie du Liban, action gouvernmentale et finances publiques de l'independence a 1975" in *Les Cahiers du CERMOC*, Beyrouth, No. 12, p. 21.

44. Ibid., p. 5.

45. Ibid., p. 11. See also Thierry Kochuyt, "La misere au Liban: une population appauvrie, peu d'Etat et plusiers solidarities souterraines" in *Revue Tiers Monde*, XLV, No. 179, Juillet–Sept., pp. 515–537.

46. Interview with Adib Nemeh, former UNDP adviser to the MSA, 25 October 2008.

47. CDR and ESFD, "Analysis of Institutional Set-Up and their Social Programs" in *Formulation of a Strategy for Social Development in Lebanon*, Volume I, December 2005.

48. Ibid.

49. Rana Jawad, "Religion and Social Welfare in the Lebanon: Treating the Causes or Symptoms of Poverty?" in *Journal of Social Policy*, 38, 1, pp. 141–156. Even the work of the MSA through its SDCs, however, is limited by the clientelist manner in which many have been created and operated. At the time of writing, there were eighty-six SDCs and fifty satellites in Lebanon, with plans to add another two hundred of the latter. In theory, both are designed to deliver services as well as facilitate development-type projects (training and/or income generating) with NGOs. Co-studies by the World Bank and the UNDP examining the distribution of SDCs in the country, however, reveal through a geographic information systems mapping project that many of the newly created SDCs were located "outside of the identified pockets of poverty" and concentrated disproportionately in the southern regions of the country, a distribution that has worked to the benefit of the AMAL Movement, which politically controlled the MSA for much of the post–civil war period. Indeed, Adib Nemeh, a UNDP/World Bank poverty advisor with the MSA, who during his assignment had lobbied hard to rein in the wasteful patronage dynamics associated with the creation of SDCs, spoke of the existence of concerted pressure being placed on the various ministers to create SDCs in the electoral districts of his party colleagues and allies, especially in the run-up to national elections. Interviews with Adib Nemeh, 25 October 2008; and Joumana Kalot, 28 October 2008. See also CDR and ESFD, op. cit., 2005, p. 129; and Ivo Gijsberts, "Inception Phase Mission: Social Sector Expert," ARLA Project, Office of the Minister of State for Administrative Reform (OMSAR), Lebanon, 19 March–7 April 2000.

50. CDR and ESFD, op. cit., 2005, p. 61.

51. Rana Jawad, "Human Ethics and Welfare Particularism: An Exploration of the Social Welfare Regime of Lebanon" in *Ethics and Social Welfare*, 1, 1, July 2007.

52. Interview with Joumana Kalot, op. cit., 2008.

53. Dr. Padmani Mendis, "Community-Based Rehabilitation Programme: Report of an Evaluation Mission 18th April to 2nd May, 1997," Arc En Ciel, Lebanon, p. 14.

54. Interview with Adib Nemeh, 25 October 2008.

55. Ibid.

56. CDR and ESFD, op. cit., 2005, p. 119. A postwar report on civil society in Lebanon by CIVICUS similarly concluded that "realistic pan-national policy formulation and consensus building was not possible under the present structure of civil society," adding that Lebanese civil society needed a "corrective movement." See Khaldoun Abou Assi, "An Assessment of Lebanese Civil Society," *CIVICUS Civil Society Index Report*, Beirut, 2006, p. 21. See also Ahmad Baalbaki and

Abdallah Muhieddine, *The Contribution of Non-Governmental Organizations in the Domain of Health, Education, and Social Welfare: A Study Through Reasoned Choice Sampling*, World Bank, June 1998.

57. Among the rehabilitation institutions affected were the Social Welfare Institute's facilities at Aramoun, destroyed during the Israeli invasion of Lebanon, and the Father Andeweg Institute for the Deaf, ransacked by the Syrians at the end of the civil war. Others, such as Jeanine Safa of the Institute de Reeducation Audio-Phonetique (IRAP), described how the local crises set off by the civil war forced their small school for the deaf to be transformed into a center for displaced people in its region. Lamented Safa, "la guerre a eclate IRAP." See Janet Duros McClearen, "Father A. J. Andeweg, Hussein M. Ismail, and the Development of Deaf Education in Lebanon," Master's thesis, University of Nebraska at Omaha, 2009, p. 61. Also see interview with Jeanine Safa, IRAP, 25 July 2008.

58. See www.lwah.org.lb. Other rehabilitation institutions created during the civil war and linked to one of the militias were the Mount Lebanon Rehabilitation Center (now the National Rehabilitation and Development Center) associated with the PSP of the Druze community and the Association al-Jarha of Hezbollah. See http://www.aljarha.net/english/index.php.

59. There is no Web site for al-Zawrak. For Sesobel, see http://www.sesobel. org/english/index.asp.

60. Interview, 24 July 1996.

61. Interview, Norwegian People's Aid—Lebanon, 4 November 2008.

62. Lina Abou-Habib, "Advocacy around Disability in the Midst of War: The Lebanon" in *Humanitarian Practice Network*, www.odihpn.org.asp?id=1068, 1998. See also Coleridge, op. cit., 1993.

63. Abou-Habib, op. cit., 1998. The financial incentives for crowding dormitories with disabled people was outlined by an administrator within the Mohammad Khalid Foundation, one of the large rehabilitation hospitals in the country, when he argued that "the more the number of beneficiaries they have, the more donations will come," adding that "the mentality . . . in the huge and large historical institutions is that the donor . . . should come and see hundreds of disabled, he should feel pity for them—'Oh my God, I have to help'—and he will give you money." Concluded this official, "[T]his is the barrier which stands [in the way of] the integration of the disabled." Interview, 9 March 1999.

64. See Ali M. Dehbozorgi, "The Mentally Handicapped in Lebanon: An Assessment and Appraisal of Services and Needs," MECC, August 1983, p. 22.

65. Dehbozorgi wrote, for example, that it was not uncommon for "an understimulated, poorly nourished, neglected child of a family with low socio-economic status who may have had, among other things, severe emotional and learning difficulties [to be] labeled as mentally handicapped"—a label that effectively denied that child the right to further growth and development as a result of "the constrictions imposed on him through institutionalization." Ibid., p. 23.

66. In one instance, he found mentally handicapped patients being kept on metal beds without mattresses; in another, he found patients being kept on beds that consisted of sponges soaked with urine and excreta. Another heart-wrenching

account of institutional neglect was his discovery of a person reduced to utter passivity as a result of having been kept in a bed for more than sixteen years, a case of horrendous inhumanity minimized only by the spirit of the person himself, whose "joyful face and shining eyes indicated that he was far from giving up hope." Ibid., pp. 38–41.

67. "Life Stories—Sylvana Lakkis: NGO Activist" in *al-Raida*, XVI, No. 8384, Fall/Winter 1998–1999, p. 70.

68. Ibid., p. 72.

69. Coleridge, op. cit., 1993, p. 198.

70. Diane Driedger, *The Last Civil Rights Movement: Disabled Peoples International*, London: Hurst and Company/St. Martin's Press, 1989, p. 54.

71. Ibid., p. 37.

72. By 1985, DPI already had a membership of more than 100 associations, up from forty at its founding meeting, with sixty-nine of them representing different countries. Driedger does add, however, that DPI's effect was weaker with respect to associations representing the deaf and the intellectually disabled as well as associations representing disabled women and the disabled poor. Ibid., p. 61.

73. Driedger added that the struggle over the definition of a disability was of crucial importance to DPI because "if you cannot define who you are on your own . . . , society will attempt to control you through its definition, in this case, the medical model." Ibid., p. 121.

74. Ibid., p. 97.

75. Nawaf Kabbara, "Daring for Peace" in *New Internationalist*, Issue 233, July 1992, www.newint.org/issue233/liberation.htm.

76. Coleridge, op. cit., 1993, p. 206.

77. Interview with Nabil Abed, 20 October 2008.

78. Interview, 3 February 1999.

79. See http://www.friendsfordisabled.org.lb/About%20FDA.html.

80. One survey by the MSA estimated that about 12 percent of disabilities in Lebanon can be attributed to war. See Marwan George Mansour, *Implications of International Policies on National Legislation: A Case Study of Law 220 for the Rights of the Disabled in Lebanon*, Master's thesis, American University of Beirut, 2001.

81. Coleridge, op. cit., 1993, p. 195.

82. "An Introduction to the Lebanese Sitting Handicapped Association and its Goals/Programmes/Achievements," undated document.

83. Ibid., p. 4.

84. Among the crucial early donors for PADC were the World Rehabilitation Foundation, Norwegians People's Aid, Middle East Council of Churches, Mennonite Central Committee, and Canada Fund. Interviews with Nada Ismail, executive director of PADC, 17 November 2008; and Ali Moushemish, 7 July 1996.

85. See http://www.ssatripoli.org/index.php. See also Coleridge, op. cit., 1993, p. 204.

86. Interview, 6 May 1999.

87. Coleridge, op. cit., 1993, p. 190.

88. See Rhodes and Marsh, op. cit., 1992, p. 259.

89. A National Council for the Welfare of Disabled Peoples had initially been created in 1973 within the then Ministry of Labour and Social Affairs, but, after rarely meeting between 1973 and 1975, it subsequently became dormant with the beginning of the civil war. See Nawaf Kabbara, "Lebanon" in (eds.) Jane Hodges-Aeberherd and Carl Roskin, *Affirmative Action in the Employment of Ethnic Minorities and Persons with Disabilities,* Geneva: ILO Office–ILO, 1997.

90. As far back as 1981, the LSHU had drafted proposals for a disability directorate and national disability assembly. By 1990, representatives from the Lebanese government were beginning to show interest in the idea and had entered into consultations with disability activists such as Nawaf Kabbara. Indeed, when the NCDP was created, one of its long-standing donor supporters described its lobbying as having been "instrumental" in getting it accepted. See Gordon Janzen, Mennonite Central Committee, Trip Report, 30 November–4 December 1992, Files of Oxfam-UK; and interview with Nawaf Kabbara, 6 May 1999.

91. Ibid.

92. Interview, Sesobel, 27 October 2008.

93. Interview with Hyam Fakhoury, NCDP-MSA, 15 March 1999.

94. Because they refused to have any sectarian affiliation during the war, a struggle that Mousa Charafeddine described as "our hardest and severest fight," most associations run by people with disabilities were effectively denied access to significant amounts of financing, even from within their own communities. As Amer Mukarem, the head of the Youth Association for the Blind, remarked, as a result of his refusal to affiliate YAB with his own Druze community, "we [found ourselves] out of the game." Interviews with Amer Makarem, 19 July 1996; and Musa Sharif ad-Din, 7 August 1996.

95. Interview with Nabil Abed, 20 October 2008. See also Coleridge, op. cit., 1993.

96. Interview, WRF, 6 August 1996.

97. Interview, 23 April 1999.

98. Interview with Adib Nehme, 25 October 2008.

99. Interview with Mohammad Barakat, 30 July 2008.

100. Interview, 3 February 1999.

101. Interview, 7 August 1996.

102. Interview, 2 December 2001.

103. Interview, 29 April 1999.

104. Arc en Ciel was created in the late 1970s by a group of disabled scouts from Beit Shabab, a rehabilitation institution that became closely associated with the Lebanese Forces. According to Joseph Salameh, a longtime volunteer with Arc en Ciel, the dream of its founders was to promote "independence and a well integrated society" for people with disabilities in the country. See Tony Long, "A Nation for Everyone" in *Now Lebanon,* 14 October 2009. See also http://www.arcenciel.org/fr/programmes/rehabilitation.htm.

105. Interview, 29 April 1999.

106. Interview, 29 November 2001.

107. Interview, 17 July 2008.

108. Interview, 29 April 1999. A representative of the Mohammad Khalid Foundation, one of the large rehabilitation institutions with direct ties with Dar al-Fatwa, described the "monopolistic relationship" that developed between the MSA and Arc en Ciel as not being "healthy." Nonetheless, he recognized that this was how decisions were taken within the MSA—the product of "secret alliances" in which "nobody knows who controls who." Interview, 9 March 1999.

109. It also was clear that Arc en Ciel benefited from its initiative. For example, the land that Arc en Ciel used to establish its main offices in Jisr al-Wati in Beirut, within which some of the main offices of the Rights and Access Program were based, was donated by the state, in much the same way that LWAD received its land to build its rehabilitation center in Sarafand. Interview, 2 June 1999.

110. Among the other initiatives and pet projects relatively free from political interference that Kaanan managed to carve out for the MSA in the postwar period—at least until her retirement in 2004—were the provision of special funding for select Social Development Centers and the work of the MSA in the area of the Rights of the Child. Interview with Adib Nemeh, 25 October, 2008.

111. Interview with Joumana Kalot, 28 October 2008.

112. Interview, 6 May 1999.

113. Interview, 29 November 2001.

114. Ibid.

115. Interview with Nabil Abed, 20 October 2008.

116. The most egregious examples were the filling of beds with able-bodied people in order to be able to claim greater amounts of MSA per diem subsidies— although the thousand cases or so that were discovered was felt to be surprisingly low. Interview, NCDP-MSA, 13 December 2001.

117. Ibid.

118. Interview, 30 June 2008.

119. Interview, 29 November 2001.

120. Ibid.

121. Interview, 2 December 2001.

122. See Zeina Osman, "Disabled Still Waiting for Law to be Passed to Improve Conditions" in *The Daily Star*, 6 February 1998.

123. Interviews, LSHU, 3 March and 12 March 1999. See also Ranwa Yehia, "Members of Association for Disabled Resign en Masse" in *The Daily Star*, 22 September 1998.

124. Interview with Sylvana Lakkis, 3 March 1999.

125. Ibid.

126. Taking advantage of the impending plans to rebuild the country's physical infrastructure, for example, disability activists—especially those concerned with questions of physical disabilities—had been quick off the mark in linking issues of accessibility to the broader agenda of reconstruction. Numerous demonstrations were held, often with the support of associations outside the

disability sector, within crowded areas of Lebanon's cities demanding wheelchair ramps and special parking spaces for peoples with disabilities—the very first of which was constructed as a result of their efforts in the Ain Mreisseh district of Beirut in 1991. Taking advantage of the popular resonance of sport in the country, the LSHU also held demonstrations highlighting the inaccessibility of the Beirut sports stadium, reconstructed by the Hariri government in time for the Pan-Arab Games in the summer of 1997. Perhaps the most effective networking and awareness-raising campaign focused on promoting accessibility in the downtown Beirut central district being reconstructed by Solidere, ones that, with the assistance of local and regional activists, resulted in the area being one of the most accessible in the country. See LSHU, "Annual Report," 1998. See also Riadh Tappuni, "Accessibility for the Disabled in the Beirut Central District," Report prepared for the Lebanese Company for the Development and Reconstruction of Beirut Central District (SOLIDERE) and the Economic and Social Commission for Western Asia (ESCWA), January 1994.

127. See "Statement by Sylvana Lakkis," Round Table on Women and Physical Disability—On the Occasion of International Women's Day, UN House-Beirut, 8 March 1999. See also Sylvana Lakkis, "Mobilizing Women with Physical Disabilities: The Lebanese Sitting Handicapped Association" in Lina Abou-Habib, *Gender and Disability: Women's Experiences in the Middle East*, Oxford: Oxfam, 1997, pp. 28–35; and Samantha Wehbi and Sylvana Lakkis, "Women with Disabilities in Lebanon: From Marginalization to Resistance" in *Affilia: Journal of Women and Social Work*, 25, 1, 2010, pp. 56–67.

128. See LSHU, "Annual Report," 1998. Interview with Sylvana Lakkis, 3 March 1999.

129. In her speech at the sit-in, Lakkis remarked that "our action in this sit-in is not to judge the past but to contest the present trend. We are warning of future tragedies. Why does Parliament not adopt the drafts of laws prepared by the National Committee for Disabled Affairs since 1996? Why are suggested legislations blocked by the government? What is the use of legislation without a budget to execute it? We ask for immediate action from Parliament and the Government. Our sit-in is the result of our social and life conditions and it is just the beginning." See Imad ed-Din Raef, "The Continuing Demands Campaign for the Disabled in Lebanon" in *Waw Magazine*, No. 14, 2007, pp. 18–23 for text of Lakkis's speech (in Arabic); and interview with Sylvana Lakkis, 11 December 2001.

130. Ibid.

131. Lakkis listed several deputies in the late 1990s who were among the allies of the LSHU: Butros Harb, Najah Wakim, Marwan Hamade, and Antoine Ghanem, who was reputed to be an ally of Elie Hobeika. One of the more crucial civil society allies for LSHU was Ghassan Moukheiber, who became its leading consultant on the issue of the disability law.

132. Interview with Sylvana Lakkis, 11 December 2001.

133. Interview with Nawaf Kabbara, 2 December 2001.

134. Interview, 2 December 2001.

135. Interview, 11 December 2001.

136. See Bill Albert, Andrew Dube, and Trine Riis-Hansen, "Has Disability Been Mainstreamed in Development Cooperation?" in Bill Albert (ed.), *In or Out of Mainstreaming? Lessons from Research on Disability and Development Cooperation*, Leeds: The Disability Press, 2006, p. 58.

137. Jessy Chahine, "4 Years On, Still No Law for Disabled Rights" in *The Daily Star*, 17 June 2004.

138. Interview, 25 July 2008.

139. Ibid.

140. To provide one of many examples, the press reported on the experience of one blind job seeker who, despite her excellent results on the civil service entrance exams, had her application referred to the MSA, where she was channeled toward sheltered and, hence, segregated workshop employment. See Maya Abou Nasr, "Jobs Harder to Find for Disabled" in *The Daily Star*, 5 August 2004.

141. Interview, 17 July 2008. Parallel research on the implementation of an employment quota system for people with disabilities in Jordan has shown its policies to have been similarly ineffective. Though Jordan's policy is less ambitious than that of Lebanon's—requiring that 2 percent of the workforce in firms with more than fifty workers be people with disabilities, Turmusani nonetheless argued that "little attempt has been made to implement and enforce policies addressing unequal opportunities in the workplace," adding that, as a result, the economic needs of disabled people in Jordan continue to be "almost totally unmet." See Turmusani, op. cit., 2003, p. 128.

142. See Taylor Long, "A Nation for Everyone" in *Now Lebanon*, 14 October 2009.

143. Interview, 25 July 2008.

144. Improvements included dispensations from paying municipal taxes, some exemptions from customs duties for communication and transportation devices, and partial improvements in the delivery of such technical aids as wheelchairs. Indeed, the LCDP report indicated that in 2004, the state provided 7,342 services for the disabled that included the provision of 707 moveable wheelchairs. It also approved 1,844 exemptions from customs for cars and 15,000 exemptions from municipal taxes. See Lebanese Council of Disabled People (LCDP), "Disability Report in Lebanon: Where Do We Stand Regarding the Application of Law 220/2000 and Admitting the Rights of the Disabled People in Lebanon?," *al-Raida*, XXII, No. 108, Winter 2005, p. 32.

145. Ibid., p. 34.

146. Ibrahim Abdullah, the president of the LCDP at the time and founder of the Lebanese Association for Blind University Students, highlighted Mohammad Raad of Hezbollah—who had been supportive of associational efforts to have Law 220 passed in the first place—and Michel Aoun of the Free Patriotic Movement—whose previous experience with disabled soldiers predisposed him toward supporting the petition and campaign—as being particularly sympathetic and aware of the issues. On the other hand, Abdullah criticized religious leaders

of not being engaged in the issues, of ignoring issues of accessibility to churches and mosques, and of "still look[ing] upon disability as charity work." Interview, 7 November 2008.

147. Nawaf Kabbara, "Abstract" in *Echoes of the Disabled*, pp. 54–55, p. 104.

148. Leila Hatoum, "Disabled Declare Their Candidacy for Elections: Seats in Parliament Are the Only Way to Secure Rights" in *Daily Star*, 15 May 2005.

149. Research by the National Association for the Rights of the Disabled (NARD) revealed in a survey of more than 600 public buildings, many of which were used as polling stations, that most were not accessible to disabled people, nor had the building regulations and codes been amended to comply with the stipulations of Law 220. See LCDP, op. cit., 2005, p. 33.

150. Samantha Wehbi, "Organizing for Voting Rights of People with Disabilities in Lebanon: Reflections for Activists" in *Equal Opportunities International*, 26, 5, 2007, p. 453. In a horrendous example of disregard for the needs of people with disabilities, Sylvana Lakkis recalled a story of one disabled voter who was carried to a fourth-floor polling station to vote and then left there. See Hayeon Lee, "With Dignity and Independence," *Now Lebanon*, 24 May 2009.

151. Participant observation research further revealed the existence of powerful political pressures on people with disabilities relating to clan solidarity, Samantha Wehbi observing that "because family members go to polling stations together, this pressure . . . continue[s] even when casting a ballot." See Wehbi, op. cit., 2007, p. 453.

152. This included the provision of transport to and from polling stations as well as a monitoring presence at polling stations that was designed to protect the right of the disabled to a politically free vote.

153. See Hayeon Lee, op. cit., 2009.

154. See Lebanese Physically Handicapped Union and the National Democratic Institute, *Lebanon Alternative Budget Project*, 2007, www.idasa.org.za/gbOutputFiles.asp?WriteContent=Y&RID=1857.

155. Interview with Amer Makarem, 29 July 2008.

156. Ibid.

157. Nawaf Kabbara, "Abstract" in *Echoes of the Disabled*, 47, December 2003, p. 57.

158. Ibid.

159. Interview, 12 March 1999.

160. Interview with Sylvana Lakkis, 22 July 2008. In his analysis of Law 220, Marwan Mansour reached similar conclusions about the impact of reforms to the structure of the NCDP, arguing that the changes left disabled peoples without "powerful representation." See Mansour, op. cit., 2001, p. 51.

161. Interview, 20 October 2008.

162. Interview, 21 June 2008.

163. Interview, 20 October 2008.

164. Interview, 30 June 2008.

165. Interviews, 30 June 2008; 17 July 2008; 7 November 2008.

166. See MSA, "The Achievements of the Program for Ensuring the Rights of the Disabled for 2004," Annual Report, Rights and Access Program (in Arabic), 2004, p. 3.

167. Ibid.

168. Interview, 20 October 2008.

169. Interview with Pierre Issa, 29 November 2001.

170. See "The Achievements of the Program for Ensuring the Rights of the Disabled for 2004," Annual Report, Rights and Access Program (in Arabic), MSA, 2004.

171. Interview with Hyam Fakhoury, 8 June 2008.

172. Interview with Adib Nemeh, 27 October 2008. Nemeh suggested that there may also have been abuse with respect to the distribution of the disability card itself, some non-disabled gaining access to it as a way of reaping some of its taxation and customs exemptions. When asked about the level of corruption, however, he remarked, "10 percent, 15 percent, 20 percent waste, we will never know."

173. See Woods, op. cit., 2003.

174. Commenting on a particular request from the minister of social affairs between 2005 and 2008, Nayla Mouawad, for artificial limbs, this aid official remarked, "If this is the minister, do you think that she has any substance, or she has any vision towards disabled people? She has her own calculations. She wants to help disabled people from her area so that they will elect her in the upcoming elections. This is how they think." Interview, 4 November 2008.

175. Interview, MSA, 13 December 2001.

176. See interviews, LWAH, 30 June 2008; and Dar al-Aytam, 30 July 2008.

177. Interviews, Zawraq, 2 June 1999; and al-Imdad, 21 June 2008.

178. LCDP, op. cit., 2005, p. 32. Interview, 21 June 2008.

179. Interview, Sesobel, 27 October 2008.

180. Interview with Adib Nemeh, 25 October 2008.

181. Ibid.

182. Interview, 21 June 2008.

183. Interview, 25 June 2008.

184. Interview, 2 December 2001.

185. See http://afkar.omsar.gov.lb/English/SITEUTILS/HOME/Pages/Home. aspx.

186. Interview with Roland Tamrouz, 25 June 2008.

187. See Claudia Cui, "Unlocking Job Opportunities for People with Disabilities," UNDP, 2005, www.undp.org.lb/unv/Claudia.cfm.

188. Inclusion is defined as "a process that culminates in the inclusion of a person in her or his natural environment according to her or his capacities and needs. In order for inclusion efforts to be successful, inclusion needs to take place at three basic levels: the family, the school, and society." See National Inclusion Project, *Disability and Inclusion in Lebanon: A Thematic Social Assessment of the Status of Inclusion in Society, Education, and Employment*, 2005, p. 7.

189. Interview with Sylvana Lakkis, 22 July 2008.

190. See "Final Report," National Inclusion Project, December 2007, www.yablb.org/downloadPdf.php?pdf=13.

191. Interview with Amer Makarem, 29 July 2008.

192. "Final Report," National Inclusion Project, December 2007, p. 11, www.yablb.org/downloadPdf.php?pdf=13. Interestingly, a related National Inclusion Programme has subsequently been adopted by the MSA in 2009 with funding from the Italian government, a development that affirms the catalytic role that well-placed donor assistance can make in promoting the voice and sustaining the influence of local advocacy networks. See http://www.nip-lebanon.com/inclusionpilotproject.asp.

193. See Janet Lord, "NGO Participation in Human Rights Law and Process: Latest Developments in the Effort to Develop an International Treaty on the Rights of People with Disabilities" in *Journal of International and Comparative Law*, Spring 2004; Lord, "Disability Rights and the Human Rights Mainstream: Reluctant Gate-Crashers?" in (ed.) Clifford Bob, *The International Struggle for New Human Rights*, Philadelphia: University of Pennsylvania Press, 2009, pp. 83–92; and Lord, op. cit., 2004.

194. For a discussion of the "boomerang effect," see Keck and Sikkink, op. cit., 1998, pp. 12–13.

195. When asked about the emerging unity of discourse, for example, one activist remarked that, in reality, "there is no unity of vocabulary in Lebanon. . . . Even integration issues are unclear. Everyone has his own version. So, how can you have common standards?" Interview, 2 June 1999.

196. Interview, 4 November 2008; interview, 29 April 1999. Mohammad Barakat, the representative of Dar al-Aytam, for example, also has initiated a program of "reverse integration" into his school for intellectually disabled children by incorporating intellectually abled children into the classroom. Interview, 30 July 2008.

197. A notable example is al-Mabarrat's pilot project, administered in cooperation with the Lebanese Down Syndrome Association, which is designed to promote the inclusion of mentally disabled children into the regular classrooms of its al-Kawthir School.

198. Interview with Amer Makaram, 29 July 2008.

199. Interview, 20 October 2008.

# Bibliography

## Selected Interviews

*General Postwar Associational Issues*: Albert Abi Azar, Paul Achcar, Fadi Abboud, Ziad Abdul Samad, Mayla Bahkash, Abdullah Ben Habib, Fatima Cheraffiddine, George Corm, Chris de Clerq, Joseph Farah, Samir Farah, Rima Habasch, Antoine Haddad, Gregoire Haddad, Salim al-Hoss, Golda Khoury, Kemal Mouhanna, Ghassan Moukheiber, Ramzi Naaman, Mona Saad, Paul Salem, Ghassan Sayegh, Omar Traboulsi, Layla Zacharia.

*Women's Issues*: Alexa Abi Habib, Lina Abou Habib, Sonia Ibrahim Attiya, Habib Badr, Azza Beydoun, Aman Shaarani, Wadad Chakhtoura, Fahmieh Charafeddine, Samir Diab, John Donohue, Iqbal Dughan, Elie Haddad, Abla Kadi, Mona Khalaf, Mona Khawli, Nada Khalifa, Fadia Kiwan, Asma Kurdaha, Roula Masri, Linda Matar, Zeyna Mehzer, Najwa al-Mousawi, Marie Nassif-Debs, Mohammad Nuqayri, Lamia Osseiran, Zoya Rouhana, Paul Rohanna, Mirna Sabbagh, Mohammad Sammak, Laura Sfeir, Salma Sfeir, Lamia Shehadeh, Nada Tabbara Soubra, Hind Soufi, Faeka Turkieh, Mona Yakan, Alia Berti Zein.

*Environmental Issues*: Salman Abbas, Paul Abi Rached, Hani Abu Fadel, Mounir Abu Ghanem, Nabil Abu Ghanem, Mirvat Abu Khalil, Hala Ashour, Sawsan Bou Fakhreddine, Gabi Butros, Edgar Chehab, Ali Darwish, Pierre Doumet, Moutasem el-Fadel, Mona Fawaz, Ricardo Haber, Amer Haddad, Shadi Hamadeh, Fuad Hamdan, Berj Hatjian, Wael Hmaidan, Faisal Izzeddine, Dalia al-Jawhary, Fifi Kallab, Ramez Kayal, Paul Khawaja, Mohammad Khawli, Habib Maalouf, Lamia Mansour, Nashat Mansour, Adnan Melki, Farouk Merhebi, Pierre Mouawad, Charbel Nahhas, Chris Naylor, Najib Saab, Rifaat Saba, Tony Saadeh, Oussama Safa, Ghada Sayagh, Assad Serhal, Michel Skaff, Salma Talhouk, Youssef Touk, Lina Yamout, Abdullah Zakia, Clement Zakia, Rami Zuraik.

*Disability Issues*: Nabil Abed, Ibrahim Abdullah, Jahda Abou Khalil, Lina Abou Habib, Mohammad Barakat, Randa Berri, Mousa Cheraffedine, Hyam Fakhoury,

Kamal Feghali, Mikhail Haddad, Reem Makki Haddara, Kamal Hamdan, Nada Ismail, Pierre Issa, Abdel Hafiz al-Ladiki, Nawaf Kabarra, Joumana Kalot, Nadim Karam, Yakoub Kassir, Dimitri Khodr, Sylvana Lakkis, Ali Moushamish, Khalid Mukhtar, Amer Mukarem, Adib Nemeh, Tawfiq Raskala, Farouk Rizk, Antoine Roumanos, Qasim Sabah, Fadia Safa, Jeanine Safa, Solange Sakr, Fadi Sayegh, Roland Tamroz, Omar Traboulsi, Samir Yaseer, Wafaa el-Yassir.


## Documents and Reports

AFKAR/OMSAR, Les Organizations Non-Governmentales Au Liban: Realites et Perspectifs, 2005/2006.

Al-Moubayad, Bissat L. "Role of NGOs and Civil Society: Case Studies from Lebanon." World Bank, Capacity Building Workshop, Beirut, 3–6 June 2002.

Assi, Khaldoun Abou. "An Assessment of Lebanese Civil Society," CIVICUS Civil Society Index Report, Beirut, 2006.

*Atlas du Liban: Territoires et Societe*, IFPO and CNRS, 2007.

Baalbaki, Ahmad, and Abdallah Muhieddine. *The Contribution of Non-Governmental Organizations in the Domains of Health, Education, and Social Welfare: A Study through Reasoned Choice Sampling*, World Bank, June 1998.

CEDAW, "Concluding Observations of the Committee on the Elimination of Discrimination against Women: Lebanon," 1 February 2008. http://www.bayefsky.com/pdf/lebanon_t4_cedaw_40_adv.pdf.

CEDAW, *Lebanon's Third Periodic Report*, 6 July 2006,

Council for Development and Reconstruction (CDR), *National Physical Master Plan of the Lebanese Territory* (2005). http://www.cdr.gov.lb/study/sdatl/English/NPMPLT.PDF.

Council for Reconstruction and Development (CDR), *National Physical Master Plan for the Lebanese Territory*, Final Report, December 2005. http://www.cdr.gov.lb/study/sdatl/English/NPMPLT.PDF.

Council for Reconstruction and Development (CDR) and the European Fund for Social Development (EFSD), "Analysis of Institutional Set-Up and their Social Programs." In *Formulation of a Strategy for Social Development in Lebanon*, Volume I, December 2005.

CRTD-A. *Caught in Contradiction: A Profile of Gender Equality and Economy in Lebanon*, Beirut: CRTD-A. May 2006.

CRTD-A. Jinsiyati Campaign Newsletter, Issues 1, 2, and 3, http://www.crtda.org.

Cui, Claudia. "Unlocking Job Opportunities for People with Disabilities," UNDP, 2005, http://www.undp.org.lb/unv/Claudia.cfm.

Dehbozorgi, Ali M. "The Mentally Handicapped in Lebanon: An Assessment and Appraisal of Services and Needs," MECC, August 1983.

GEF/UNDP. *Strengthening of National Capacity and Grassroots In-Situ Conservation for Sustainable Biodiversity Protection*, Project Document, March 1997.

Gijsberts, Ivo. "Inception Phase Mission: Social Sector Expert," ARLA Project, Office of the Minister of State for Administrative Reform (OMSAR), Lebanon, 19 March–7 April 2000.

Haddad, Antoine. "Lebanese NGOs: Guidelines for a Common Strategy," Beirut: Middle East Council of Churches/Collectif des ONG au Liban, 1995.

Jean-Paul II aux Patriarches, aux Eveques, au Clerge, aux Religieux, aux Religieuses, et a Tous Les Fideles Du Liban. *Exhortation Apostolique Post-Synodale: Une Esperance Nouvelle Pour Le Liban*, 10 Mai 1997.

KAFA; *Guidelines for Women on Family Laws*, 2008, http://www.kafa.org.lb/ StudiesPublicationPDF/PRpdf2.pdf.

———. *Narrative Interim Report to Women's Empowerment Project: Kvinna Till Kvinna*, February–March 2006.

Kasparek, Max. "Lebanon: Evaluation of the Energy and Environment Programme— An Outcome Evaluation," Beirut: UNDP-Lebanon, December 2007.

Kiwan, Fadia. *The Work of Women in Civil Associations*. Beirut: Friedrich Eberhardt Stiftung and the Lebanese Women's Council, 1994.

Lebanese Physically Handicapped Union (LPHU). "Statement by Sylvana Lakkis." Round Table on Women and Physical Disability—On the Occasion of International Women's Day, UN House–Beirut, 8 March 1999.

Lebanese Physically Handicapped Union and the National Democratic Institute. *Lebanon Alternative Budget Project*, 2007. www.idasa.org.za/gbOutputFiles. asp?WriteContent=Y&RID=1857.

Mada. "Mada, Strategic Workshop, Batroun 28–28, 2007." http://www.mada.org. lb/aboutus.php.

Mada. "Self-Assessment Checklist." http://www.mada.org.lb/aboutus.php.

Makdisi, Karim. "NCSA Cross-Cutting Synthesis Report: Lebanon," Republic of Lebanon National Capacity Self-Assessment (NCSA), October 2007

Mendis, Padmani. "Community-Based Rehabilitation Programme: Report of an Evaluation Mission 18th April to 2nd May, 1997," Arc En Ciel, Lebanon.

METAP (Mediterranean Environmental Technical Assistance Program), *Lebanon: Assessment of the State of the Environment*, May 1995.

Moghaizel, Laure. "Les droits des femmes au Liban: Situation et perspectives dans le cadre de la construction nationale." Beyrouth: Commission nationale libanaise pour UNESCO, 29–31 March 1993.

NARD, WRF, and USAID. "A Symposium on Disability and Religion," 26 July 1995.

National Council for Disabled Persons, Ministry of Social Affairs, Government of Lebanon. "The Achievements of the Program for Ensuring the Rights of the Disabled for 2004," Annual Report, Rights and Access Program (in Arabic), 2004.

National Inclusion Project. "Disability in Lebanon: A Statistical Report," Council for Development and Reconstruction and the World Bank—Community Development Project, 2007.

National Inclusion Project. *Disability and Inclusion in Lebanon: A Thematic Social Assessment of the Status of Inclusion in Society, Education, and Employment*, 2005.

National Inclusion Project. "Final Report," December 2007. http://www.yablb.org/downloadPdf.php?pdf=13.

National Park Steering Committee. "Support a Common Territorial Development Project in Upper Akkar." Mada Files, November 2008.

Naylor, Chris. "The Return of Ammiq Wetland." http://www.mectat.com.lb/Naturebook/nat7.htm.

Oxfam-UK Lebanon files, "Gorden Janzen, Mennonite Central Committee, Trip Report," 30 November–4 December. 1992.

Rene Maowad Foundation. "Proceedings of the Conference on Social Development in Lebanon," Washington, DC, June 1995.

Sharaf el-Din, Fahima. *Assessment of the National Women's Machinery in Lebanon*, EUROMED Role of Women in Economic Life Programme, October 2006. http://www.euromedgenderequality.org/image.php?id=110.

Tappuni, Riadh. "Accessibility for the Disabled in the Beirut Central District," Report prepared for the Lebanese Company for the Development and Reconstruction of Beirut Central District (SOLIDERE) and the Economic and Social Commission for Western Asia (ESCWA), January 1994.

Trabousli, Omar, with Bassam Ramadan and Shaha Riza. *Lebanon Social Protection Note—Attachment II: Mapping and Review of Lebanese NGOs.* World Bank, 21 October 2001.

Trabulsi, Omar. *National Commission for Women: Capacity Building and Action Plan Report*, UNIFEM, October 2001.

World Bank (Human Development Department, Middle East and North Africa Region). *A Note on Disability in the Middle East and North Africa,* 30 June 2005.

World Bank, *Implementation Completion Report on a Loan in the Amount of US$10.9 million to the Lebanese Republic for a Solid Waste/Environmental Management Project*, 21 June 2004.

World Bank. *The Cost of Environmental Degradation in Lebanon*, 2004. http://siteresources.worldbank.org/INTMNAREGTOPENVIRONMENT/Resources/Final_English_Lebanon.pdf.

YMCA-Lebanon, Annual Report, 1993.

YWCA-Lebanon. *Gender Based Violence in Lebanon and the Middle East*, undated.

## Articles and Books

"Civil Society in Lebanon: Sensitive Political Issues Avoided—Interview with Omar Traboulsi," http://en.qantara.de/Democracy-and-Civil-Society/684b233/index.html.

Abou-Habib, Lina. *Gender and Disability: Women's Experiences in the Middle East.* Oxfam: Oxford, 1997.

———. "Advocacy around Disability in the Midst of War: The Lebanon." In *Humanitarian Practice Network*, 1998. http://www.odihpn.org.asp?id=1068.

————. "The Use and Abuse of Female Domestic Workers in Lebanon." *Gender and Development* 6, no. 1 (March 1998): 52–56.

Albert, Bill, Andrew Dube, and Trine Riis-Hansen. "Has Disability Been Mainstreamed in Development Cooperation?" In *In or Out of Mainstreaming? Lessons from Research on Disability and Development Cooperation*, edited by Bill Albert, 57–73. Leeds: The Disability Press, 2006.

Al-Cheikh, Nadia. "The 1998 Proposed Civil Marriage Law in Lebanon: The Reaction of the Muslim Communities." *al-Raida* XVIII–XIX (Spring/Summer 2001): 27–35.

Alvarez, Sonia. "Latin American Feminisms 'Go Global': Trends of the 1990s and Challenges for the New Millennium." In *Cultures of Politics/Politics of Cultures: Re-visioning Latin American Social Movements*, edited by Sonia Alvarez, Evelina Dagnino, and Arturo Escobar, 293–324. Boulder: Westview Press, 1998.

Attie, Caroline. *Struggle in the Levant: Lebanon in the 1950s*. London: I.B. Taurus, 2004.

Baaklini, Abdo Guillain Denoeux, and Robert Springborg. *Legislative Politics in the Arab World: The Resurgence of Democratic Institutions*. Boulder: Lynne Rienner Publishers, 1999.

Bahout, Joseph. "A Division of Labor: The Amin-GCLW Saga Continues." *Lebanon Report*, March (1994): 4.

————. "Les Elites Parlementaires Libanaises De 1996." In *La Vie Publique Au Liban: Expressions et Recompositions du Politique*, edited by Joseph Bahout and Chawqi Douayhi, 17–89. Beirut: CERMOC, 1997.

Barak, Oren. *The Lebanese Army: A National Institution in a Divided Society*. New York: SUNY Press, 2009.

Baroudi, Sami. "Economic Conflict in Postwar Lebanon: State-Labour Relations between 1992–1997." *Middle East Journal* 52, no. 4 (Autumn 1998): 531–550.

Bates, Robert, Avner Greif, Margaret Levi, Jean-Laurent Rosenthal, and Barry Weingast. *Analytical Narratives*. Princeton: Princeton University Press, 1998.

Baylouny, Anne Marie. *Privatizing Welfare in the Middle East: Kin Mutual Aid Associations in Jordan and Lebanon*. Bloomington: Indiana University Press, 2010.

Belloni, Roberto. "Civil Society in War-To-Democracy Transitions." In *From War to Democracy: Dilemmas of Peacebuilding*, edited by Anna Jarstad and Timothy Sisk, 182–210. Cambridge: Cambridge University Press, 2008.

Bennett, Jon. "The Lebanese NGO Forum and the Reconstruction of Civil Society, 1989–1993." In *Meeting Needs: NGO Coordination in Practice*, edited by Jon Bennett, 118–144. London: Earthscan Publications Ltd., 1995.

Berins-Collier, Ruth, and David Collier. *Shaping the Political Arena: Critical Junctures, the Labor Movement, and Regime Dynamics in Latin America*. Princeton: Princeton University Press, 1991.

Berry, Mallouk. "Radical Transitions: Shifting Gender Discourses in Lebanese Muslim Shi'a Jurisprudence and Ideology, 1960–1979 and 1990–1999." PhD diss., Near Eastern Studies, University of Michigan, 2002.

Beshara, Adel. *Lebanon: The Politics of Frustration—The Failed Coup of 1961.* London: Routledge/Curzon, 2005.

Beydoun, Ahmad. "A Note on Sectarianism." In *Lebanon in Limbo*, edited by T. Hanf and N. Salam, 75–86. Baden-Baden: Nomos Verlagsgesellschaft, 2003.

———. "Confessionalism: Outline of an Announced Accord." In *Options for Lebanon*, edited by N. Salam, 75–96. London: I.B. Taurus, 2004.

Beydoun, Azza. "Arguments Valid for Once Only." *al-Raida* XXII, no. 111–112 (Fall–Winter 2005–2006): 22–26.

———. *Crimes of Killing Women: In Front of the Lebanese Courts*, KAFA, 2008 (in Arabic).

Blandford, Nicholas. *Killing Mr. Lebanon: The Assassination of Rafik Hariri and Its Impact on the Middle East.* London: I.B. Taurus, 2006.

Bonne, Emmanuel. *Vie publique, patronage, et clientele: Rafic Hariri a Saida.* Universites d'Aix-Marseille: IRENAM and CERMOC, 1995.

Boustani, Samih, and Nada Mufarrej. "Female Higher Education and Participation in the Labour Force in Lebanon." In *Gender and Development in the Arab World*, edited by Nabil Khoury and Valentine Moghadam, 97–124. New York: Zed Books Ltd., 1995.

Brand, Laurie. *Women, the State, and Political Liberalization: Middle East and North African Experiences.* New York: Columbia University Press, 1998.

———. *Citizens Abroad: State and Emigration in the Middle East and North Africa.* Cambridge: Cambridge University Press, 2006.

Bray-Collins, Elinor. "Muted Voices: Women's Rights in Postwar Lebanon." Master's thesis, Ontario Institute of Education, University of Toronto, 2003.

Browers, Michelle. *Democracy and Civil Society in Arab Political Thought: Transcultural Possibilities.* Syracuse: Syracuse University Press, 2006.

Bryant, Raymond, and Sinead Bailey. *Third World Political Ecology.* London: Routledge, 1997.

Brynen, Rex. *Sanctuary and Survival: The PLO in Lebanon.* Boulder: Westview Press/Pinter Publishers, 1990.

Buheiry, Marwan. "Beirut's Role in the Political Economy of the French Mandate, 1919–1939." In *The Formation and Perception of the Modern Arab World*, edited by Lawrence Conrad, 537–560. Princeton: Darwin Press, 1989.

Cammett, Melani, and Sukriti Issar. "Bricks and Mortar Clientelism: Sectarianism and the Logics of Welfare Allocation in Lebanon." *World Politics* 62, no. 3 (July 2010): 381–421.

Cammett, Melani Claire. "Partisan Activism and Access to Welfare in Lebanon." *Studies in Comparative International Development* 46 (2011): 70–97.

Capoccia, Giovanni, and R. Daniel Kelemen. "The Study of Critical Junctures: Theory, Narrative, and Counterfactuals in Historical Institutionalism." *World Politics* 59 (April 2007): 341–369.

Catusse, Myriam, and Alagha, Joseph. "Les service sociaux du Hezbollah: Efforts de guerre, *ethos* religieux et resources politiques." In *Le Hezbollah: etat des lieux*, edited by Sabrina Mervin, 113–140. Arles, France: Actes Sud/ Sinbad, 2008.

Catusse, Myriam. "Liban: la reforme sociale en panne?" Unpublished seminar paper, CERMOC-Beirut, 29 February 2008.

Chahabi, H. E. *Distant Relations: Iran and Lebanon in the Last 500 Years.* London: Centre for Lebanese Studies and I.B. Tauris, 2006.

Chahine, Jessy. "4 Years On, Still No Law for Disabled Rights." *The Daily Star*, 17 June 2004.

Chalmers, Douglas. "Associative Networks: New Structures of Representation for the Popular Sectors?" In *The New Politics of Inequality in Latin America: Rethinking Participation and Representation*, edited by Douglas A. Chalmers, Carlos M. Vilas, Katherine Hite, Scott B. Martin, Kerianne Piester, and Monique Segarra, 543–582. Oxford: Oxford University Press, 1997.

———. "Civil Society Links to Politics: The Importance of Second Level Institutions." Unpublished paper, March 2000.

Chaoul, Melhem. "Demonstrations in Beirut." In *Cities of the South: Citizenship and Exclusion in the Twenty-First Century*, edited by Barbara Drieskens, Frank Mermier, and Heiko Wimmen, 155–168. London: Saqi Books, 2007.

Corm, Georges. "The War System: Militia Hegemony and Reestablishment of the State." In *Peace for Lebanon? From War to Reconstruction*, edited by Dierdre Collings, 215–230. Boulder and London: Lynne Rienner Publishers, 1994.

———. *Le Liban Contemporaire: Histoire and Societe.* Paris, France: Editions La Decouverte, 2003.

Crumrine, Christine. "Power, Politics, and Prestige: The Business of INGO Development in Rural Areas of Lebanon." PhD diss., Center for Middle East and Islamic Studies, University of Durham, 2002.

Dagher, A. "L'etat et l'economie du Liban, action gouvernmentale et finances publiques de l'independence a 1975." *Les Cahiers du CERMOC*, Beyrouth, No. 12. 1995.

Dagher, Carole H. *Bring Down the Walls: Lebanon's Postwar Challenge.* New York: St. Martin's Press, 2000.

Dah, Abdallah, Ghassan Dibeh, and Wassim Shahin. *The Distributional Impact of Taxes in Lebanon: Analysis and Policy Implications.* Beirut: The Lebanese Center for Policy Studies 6, 1999.

Davis, Eric. "A Sectarian Middle East?" *International Journal of Middle East Studies* 40, no. 4 (2008): 555–558.

Debie, Franck, Danuta Pieter, avec la collaboration d'Eric Verdeil. *Le paix et la crise: le Liban reconstruit?* Paris: Presses Universitaires de France, 2003.

Deeb, Lara. *An Enchanted Modern: Gender and Public Piety in Shi'a Lebanon.* Princeton: Princeton University Press, 2006.

Denoeux, Guillain, and Robert Springborg. "Hariri's Lebanon: Singapore of the Middle East or Sanaa of the Levant?" *Middle East Policy* VI, no. 2 (October 1998): 158–173.

Disability KaR. *Lessons from the Disability Knowledge and Research Programme.* http://www.disabilitykar.net.

Driedger, Diane. *The Last Civil Rights Movement: Disabled Peoples International.* London: Hurst and Company/St. Martin's Press, 1989.

Dubar, Claude, and Salim Nasr. *Les Classes sociales au Liban.* Paris: Presses de la Fondation Nationale des Sciences Politiques, 1976.

Duros McClearen, Janet. "Father A. J. Andeweg, Hussein M. Ismail, and the Development of Deaf Education in Lebanon." Master's thesis, University of Nebraska at Omaha, 2009.

Ehrenburg, John. *Civil Society: The Critical History of an Idea.* New York: New York University Press, 1999.

El-Bizri, Dalal. *L'Ombre et son double: femmes islamiques, libanaises et moderns.* Beirut: CERMOC, 1995.

El-Khazen, Farid. *The Communal Pact of National Identity: The Making and Politics of the 1943 National Pact.* Oxford: Center for Lebanese Studies, 1991.

———. "Lebanon's Communal Elite-Mass Politics: The Institutionalization of Disintegration." *Beirut Review* 3 (Spring 1992): 53–81.

———. *Lebanon's First Postwar Parliamentary Election, 1992: An Imposed Choice—Prospects for Lebanon;* Oxford: Center for Lebanese Studies, 1998.

———. *The Breakdown of the Lebanese State in Lebanon, 1967–1976.* London: I.B. Taurus, 2000.

———. "The Postwar Political Process: Authoritarianism by Diffusion." In *Lebanon in Limbo: Postwar Society and State in an Uncertain Regional Environment,* edited by Theodor Hanf and Nawaf Salam, 53–76. Baden-Baden: Verlagsgesellschaft, 2003.

Encarnacion, Omar. *The Myth of Civil Society: Social Capital and Democratic Consolidation in Spain and Brazil.* New York: Palgrave, 2003.

———. "Civil Society Reconsidered." *Comparative Politics* 38, no. 3 (April 2006): 357–376.

Evans, Peter. "Introduction: Development Strategies Across the Public-Private Divide." *World Development* 24, no. 6 (1996): 1033–1037.

Farsoun, Sami. "E Pluribus Plura or E Pluribus Unum? Cultural Pluralism and Social Class in Lebanon." In *Toward a Viable Lebanon,* edited by Halim Barakat, 99–130. Washington, DC: Center for Contemporary Arab Studies, Georgetown University, 1988.

Favier, Agnes, ed. *Municipalites et Pouvoirs Locaux au Liban.* Beirut: Centre d'etude et de recherché sur le Moyen-Orient comtemporain, 2001.

———. "Logiques de l'engagement et modes de contestation au Liban: Genese et eclatement d'une generation de militants intellectuels." PhD diss., L'Universite Paul Cezanne—Aix Marseille III, 23 December 2004.

Fawaz, Mona. "Action et ideologie dals les services ONG islamiques dans la banlieu sud de beyrouth." In *ONG et governance dans le monde arabe*, edited by Sara Ben Nefissa, Nabil 'Abd al-Fattah, Sari Hanafi, and Carlos Minani, 341–368. Paris: Karthala, 2004.

———. "La reconstruction de Haret Hreik." In *Le Hezbollah: etat des lieux*, edited by Sabrina Mervin, 141–146. Arles, France: Actes Sud/Sinbad, 2008.

Firro, Kais. *Inventing Lebanon: Nation and State Under the Mandate*. London: I.B. Taurus, 2003.

———. "Ethnicizing the Shi'is in Mandatory Lebanon." *Middle Eastern Studies* 42, no. 5 (2006): 741–759.

Foley, Michael, and Bob Edwards. "The Paradox of Civil Society." *Journal of Democracy* 7, no. 3 (July 1996): 38–52.

Fox, Jonathan. "The Difficult Transition from Clientelism to Citizenship: Lesson from Mexico." *World Politics* 46, no. 2 (1994): 151–184.

Friedman, Elizabeth, and Kathryn Hochstetler. "Assessing the 'Third Transition' in Latin American Democratization: Civil Society in Brazil and Argentina." *Comparative Politics* 35, no. 1 (2002): 21–42.

Gates, Carolyn. *The Historic Role of Political Economy in the Development of Modern Lebanon*. Oxford: Center for Lebanese Studies, 10 September 1989.

———. *The Merchant Republic of Lebanon: The Rise of an Open Economy*. London: The Center for Lebanese Studies and I.B. Taurus, 1998.

George, Alexander, and Andrew Bennett. *Case Studies and Theory Development in the Social Sciences*. Cambridge, MA: MIT Press, 2005.

Gilsenan, Michael. "A Modern Feudality? Land and Labour in North Lebanon, 1858–1950." In *Land Tenure and Social Transformation in the Middle East*, edited by Tarif Khalidi, 449–464. Beirut: American University of Beirut Press, 1984.

Goetz, Anne Marie. *The Politics of Integrating Gender to State Development Processes: Trends, Opportunities and Constraints in Bangladesh, Chile, Jamaica, Mali, Morocco, and Uganda*. UNRISD, 1995. http://www.unrisd.org/80256B3C005BCCF9/(httpPublications)/8856EC9F7738F32A80256B67005B6AD5?OpenDocument.

Goria, Wade. *Sovereignty and Leadership in Lebanon, 1943–1976*. London: Ithaca, 1985.

Gough, Ian, and Geof Wood. "Introduction." In *Insecurity and Welfare Regimes in Asia, Africa, and Latin America: Social Policy in Developing Countries*, edited by Ian Gough and Geof Wood, 1–12. Cambridge: Cambridge University Press, 2004.

Gould, Roger. "Uses of Network Tools in Comparative Historical Research." In *Comparative Historical Analysis in the Social Sciences*, edited by James Mahoney and Dietrich Rueschemeyer, 241–269. Cambridge: Cambridge University Press, 2003.

Grab, Gerald. Review of *Insanity, Institutions, and Society, 1980–1914: A Social History of Madness in Comparative Perspective. Medicine History* 44, no. 3 (July 2000): 416–417.

Haddad, Fanar. *Sectarianism in Iraq: Antagonistic Visions of Unity*. London: Hurst and Company, 2011.

Haddad, Gregoire. "Comprehensive Secularism: The Intellectual and Political Dimensions." *Tayyar al-Mujtamàa al-Madani*, 6 April 1999.

Hamdan, Kamal. "La Classe moyenne dans la guerre du Liban." In *Le Liban aujourd'hiu*, edited by Fadia Kiwan, 193–203. Paris: CNRS Editions, 1994.

Hamzeh, Nizar. "Clientelism, Lebanon: Roots and Trends." *Middle East Studies* 37 (2001): 167–178.

Handan, Fuad. "The Ecological Crisis in Lebanon." In *Lebanon's Second Republic: Prospects for the Twenty-first Century*, edited by Kail Ellis, 175–187. Gainesville: University of Florida Press, 2002.

Hanf, Theodor. "Homo Oeconomicus-Homo Communitaris: Crosscutting Loyalties in a Deeply Divided Society." In *Ethnicity, Pluralism, and the State in the Middle East*, edited by Milton Esman and Itamar Rabinovich, 172–188. Ithaca: Cornell University Press, 1988.

———. *Co-Existence in Wartime Lebanon: Decline of a State, Rise of a Nation*. Oxford: Center for Lebanese Studies, 1993.

Hanssen, Jens. *Fin de siècle Beirut: The Making of an Ottoman Provincial Capital*. Oxford: Oxford University Press, 2005.

Harb, Mona, and Lara Deeb. "Les autres practiques de la Resistance: tourisme politique et loisirs pieux." In *Le Hezbollah: etat des lieux*, edited by Sabrina Mervin, 227–246. Arles, France: Actes Sud/Sindbad, 2008.

Harb, Mona. "Towards a Regionally Balanced Development Program." In *Linking Economic Growth and Social Development in Lebanon*, 117–133. Beirut: UNDP, 2000.

Harik, Judith. *The Public and Social Services of the Lebanese Militias*. Vol. 14, *Papers on Lebanon*. Oxford: Centre for Lebanese Studies 1994.

———. *Hezbollah: The Changing Face of Terrorism*. London: I.B. Taurus, 2004.

Harris, William. *Faces of Lebanon: Sects, Wars, and Global Extensions*. Princeton: Markus Weiner Publishers, 1997.

Harriss-White, Barbara. "Disability." In *Encyclopedia of International Development*, 156–159. London: Routledge, 2005.

Hatoum, Leila. "Disabled Declare Their Candidacy for Elections: Seats in Parliament Are the Only Way to Secure Rights." *Daily Star*, 15 May 2005.

Hawthorn, Geoffrey. "The Promise of 'Civil Society' in the South." In *Civil Society: History and Possibilities*, edited by Sudipta Kaviraj and Sunil Khilnani, 269–286. Cambridge: Cambridge University Press, 2001.

Helmke, Gretchen, and Steven Levitsky. "Informal Institutions and Comparative Politics: A Research Agenda." *Perspectives on Politics* 2, no. 4 (December 2004): 725–740.

Hillenkamp, Bernard. "From the Margins to the Centre? Kurds and Shi'a in a Changing Zokak el-Blat in West Beirut." In Orient-Institute, *History, Space and Social Conflict in Beirut: The Quarter of Zokak el-Blat,* 213–246. Beirut: Orient Institute, 2005.

Hinnebusch, Raymond. "Pax Syriana? The Origins, Causes and Consequences of Syria's Role in Lebanon." *Mediterranean Politics* 3, no. 1 (Summer 1998): 137–160.

Hirst, David. *Beware of Small States: Lebanon, Battleground of the Middle East.* New York: Nation Books, 2010.

Horowitz, Donald. *Ethnic Groups in Conflict.* Berkeley: University of California Press, 1985.

Hottinger, Arnold. "*Zuama* in Historical Perspective." In *Politics in Lebanon,* edited by Leonard Binder, 85–105. New York: Wiley, 1965.

Hourani, Albert. "Lebanon: The Development of a Political Society." In *The Emergence of the Modern Middle East,* 124–141. London: Macmillan Press Ltd./St. Antony's College, 1981.

Hudson, Michael. The *Precarious Republic: Political Modernization in Lebanon.* Boulder: Westview Press, 1968.

Ingels, Christophe. "L'administration Libanias au sortir du conflit civil." PhD diss., Political Science, L'universite Aix-Marseille III, 1998–1999.

International Crisis Group. *Lebanon: Managing the Gathering Storm,* Middle East Report #48, December 2005. http://www.crisisgroup.org/~media/Files/Middle%20East%20North%20Africa/Iraq%20Syria%20Lebanon/Lebanon/Lebanon%20Managing%20the%20Gathering%20Storm.pdf.

Iskandar, Mawwan. *Rafiq Hariri and the Fate of Lebanon.* London: Saqi, 2006.

Ismail, Ghena. "Women-Headed Households in Lebanon." *al-Raida* XIV, no. 76 (Winter 1997).

Ismail, Ghena, "Life Stories—Sylvana Lakkis: NGO Activist." *al-Raida* XVI, no. 83–84 (Fall/Winter 1998–1999): 70–72.

Jabour, Ghada. "Le prix des dons." Master's thesis, L'Ecole de Formation Sociale, University of St. Joseph, 2002.

Jad, Islah. "The NGOization of the Arab Women's Movement." *al-Raida* XX, no. 100 (Winter 2003): 44–47.

Jawad, Rana. "Human Ethics and Welfare Particularism: An Exploration of the Social Welfare Regime of Lebanon." *Ethics and Social Welfare* 1, no. 2 (July 2007): 123–146.

———. "Religion and Social Welfare in the Lebanon: Treating the Causes or Symptoms of Poverty?" *Journal of Social Policy* 38, no. 1 (2008): 141–156.

Jenkins, Rob. "Mistaking 'Governance' for Politics: Foreign Aid, Democracy and the Construction of Civil Society." In *Civil Society: History and Possibilities,* edited by Sudipta Kaviraj and Sunil Khilnani, 250–268. London: Cambridge University Press, 2001.

Johnson, Michael. *Class and Client in Beirut: The Sunni Muslim Community and the Lebanese State, 1840–1985.* London: Ithaca Press, 1986.

———. "Managing Political Change in Lebanon: Challenges and Prospects." In *Breaking the Cycle: Civil Wars in Lebanon,* edited by Youssef Choueiri, 137–166. London: Stacey International, 2007.

Joseph, Suad. "Elite Strategies for State-Building: Women, Family, Religion, and State in Iraq and Lebanon." In *Women, Islam, and the State*, edited by Deniz Kandiyoti, 176–201. Philadelphia: Temple University Press, 1991.

———. "Problematizing Gender and Relational Rights: Experiences from Lebanon." *Social Politics* 1, no. 3 (January 1994): 271–285.

———. "Gender and Family in the Arab World." In *Arab Women: Between Defiance and Restraint*, edited by Suha Sabbagh, 194–202. New York: Olive Branch Press, 1996.

———. "Women Between Nation and State in Lebanon." In *Between Women and Nation: Nationalism, Transnational Feminisms, and the State*, edited by Caren Kaplan, Norma Alarcon, and Minoo Moallem, 162–181. Durham: Duke University Press, 1999.

———. "Civic Myths, Citizenship, and Gender in Lebanon." In *Gender and Citizenship in the Middle East*, edited by Suad Joseph, 107–136. New York: Syracuse University Press, 2000.

———. "Gendering Citizenship in the Middle East." In *Gender and Citizenship in the Middle East*, edited by Suad Joseph, 3–32. New York: Syracuse University Press, 2000.

Kabakian-Khasholian, Tamar, Afamia Kaddour, Jocelyn DeJong, Rawan Shahayoob, and Anwar Nassar. "The Policy Environment Encouraging C-section in Lebanon." *Health Policy and Planning* 83, no. 1 (2007): 37–49.

Kabbara, Nawaf. "Daring for Peace." *New Internationalist*, no. 233 (July 1992). www.newint.org/issue233/liberation.htm.

———. "Lebanon." In *Affirmative Action in the Employment of Ethnic Minorities and Persons with Disabilities*, edited by Jane Hodges-Aeberherd and Carl Roskin, 45–51. Geneva: ILO Office–ILO, 1997.

———. "Abstract." *Echoes of the Disabled*, 47 (December 2003).

———. "Abstract." *Echoes of the Disabled*, 54–55 (December 2005).

Kabeer, Naila. "IDS Working Paper 191, Re-Visioning the Social: Towards a Citizen-Centered Social Policy for Developing Countries," January 2004. http://www.ids.ac.uk/files/Wp191.pdf.

Kandiyotti, Denis. "Bargaining with Patriarchy." *Gender and Society* 2, no. 3 (September 1988): 274–290.

Karam, Karam. *Revendiquer, Mobiliser, Participer: Les associations civils dans l'apres guerre*, Docteur de L'Universite Paul Cezanne—Aix Marseille en Science Politique, 30 October 2004.

———. *Le Mouvement Civil au Liban: revendications, protestations et mobilizations associatives dans l'apres guerre*. Paris: KARTHALA Editions, 2006.

———. "Resistances civiles?" In *Liban, une guerre de trente-trois jours,* edited by Frank Mermier and Elizabeth Picard, 51–57. Paris: La decouverte, 2007.

———. "An Analysis of Political Change in Lebanon in the Light of Recent Mobilization Cycles." In *The Arab State and Neo-Liberal Globalization: The Restructuring of State Power in the Middle East*, edited by Laure Guazzone and Danielle Pioppi, 47–72. London: Ithaca, 2009.

Kassir, Samir. "A Polity in an Uncertain Regional Development." In *Lebanon in Limbo*, edited by T. Hanf and N. Salam, 87–106. Baden-Baden: Nomos Verlagsgesellschaft, 2003.

Keck, Margaret, and Kathryn Sikkink. *Activists Beyond Borders: Advocacy Politics in International Politics*. Ithaca: Cornell University Press, 1998.

Khalaf, Samir. *Lebanon's Predicament*. New York: Columbia University Press, 1987.

———. "Family Associations." In *Lebanon's Predicament*, 161–184. New York: Columbia University Press, 1987.

———. "Peasants, Commoners, and Clerics: Resistance and Rebellion, 1820–1860." In *Civil and Uncivil Violence in Lebanon: A History of the Internationalization of Communal Conflict*, 62–102. New York: Columbia University Press, 2002.

Khayat, Rita, and Oona Campbell, "Hospital Practices in Maternity Wards in Lebanon." *Health Policy and Planning* 15, no. 3 (2000): 270–278.

Khilnani, Sunil. "The Development of Civil Society." In *Civil Society: History and Possibilities*, edited by Sudipta Kaviraj and Sunil Khilnani, 11–32. Cambridge: Cambridge University Press, 2001.

Kilani, Hala. "Greenpeace Lashes Out at Local Activist." *The Daily Star*, 15 April 1999.

Kingston, Paul. "Patrons, Clients and Civil Society: Environmental Politics in Postwar Lebanon." *Arab Studies Quarterly* 23, no. 1 (Winter 2001): 55–72.

———. "Sectarianism, Paternalism, and Patriarchy: Reflections on Culture and Politics in Lebanon," Review Article in *MIT E-Journal of Middle East Studies*. http://web.mit.edu/cis/www/mitejmes (October 2002).

———. "Promoting Civil Society Advocacy in the Middle East at Home and Abroad: NGOs, CIDA, and the Middle East Working Group, 1991–2001." In *Canada and the Middle East: In Theory and Practice*, edited by Paul Heinbecker and Bessma Momani, 117–144. Ontario: Wilfred Laurier Press, 2007.

———. "Donors, Patrons, and Civil Society: The Global-Local Dynamics of Environmental Politics in Postwar Lebanon." In *Global Environmental Challenges: Perspectives from the South*, edited by Jordi Diez and O. P. Dwivedi, 139–154. Peterborough: Broadview Press, 2008.

Kingston, Paul, and Marie Joelle Zahar. "Rebuilding *A House of Many Mansions*: The Rise and Fall of Militia Cantons in Lebanon." In *States within States: Incipient Political Entities in the Post-Cold War Era*, edited by Paul Kingston and Ian Spears, 81–98. New York: Palgrave MacMillan, 2004.

Knight, Jack, and Henry Farrell. "Trust, Institutions, and Institutional Change: Industrial Districts and the Social Capital Hypothesis." *Politics and Society* 31, no. 4 (December 2003): 537–566.

Knight, Jack. *Institutions and Social Conflict*. New York: Cambridge University Press, 1992.

Knoke, David. *Political Networks: A Structural Perspective*. Cambridge: Cambridge University Press, 1990.

Kochuyt, Theiry. "La prise de conscience de la pauvrete en Occident—avec en marge le cas particulier du Liban," Draft paper, 2001.

———. "La misere au Liban: une population appauvrie, peu d'Etat et plusiers solidarities souterraines." *Revue Tiers Monde* XLV, no. 179 (Juillet–Sept. 2004): 515–537.

Kohli, Atul. *State-Directed Development: Political Power and Industrialization in the Global Periphery.* New York: Cambridge University Press, 2004.

Lakkis, Sylvana. "Mobilizing Women with Physical Disabilities: The Lebanese Sitting Handicapped Association." In *Gender and Disability: Women's Experiences in the Middle East,* edited by Lina Abou-Habib, 28–35. Oxford: Oxfam, 1997.

Lakkis, Sylvana (LPHU), and Eddie Thomas (Oxfam-UK). "Disability and Livelihoods in Lebanon." Paper presented to conference at the University of Manchester, UK, on "Staying Poor: Chronic Poverty and Development Policy," 9 April 2003.

LaTeef, Nelda. *Women of Lebanon: Interviews with Champions for Peace.* London: McFarland and Company, 1997.

Le Thomas, Catherine. "Formation et socialization: un projet de (contre)-societe." In *Le Hezbollah: etat des lieux,* edited by Sabrina Mervin, 147–172. Arles, France: Actes Sud/Sinbad, 2008.

———. "Les scouts al-Mahdi: un 'generation resistante.'" In *Le Hezbollah: etat des lieux,* edited by Sabrina Mervin, 173–180. Arles, France: Actes Sud/ Sinbad, 2008.

Lebanese Council of Disabled People (LCDP). "Disability Report in Lebanon: Where Do We Stand Regarding the Application of Law 220/2000 and Admitting the Rights of the Disabled People in Lebanon?" *al-Raida* XXII, no. 108 (Winter 2005): 21–27.

Lebanese Environmental Forum (LEF). "Think Green, Act Green: The Lebanese Environmental Forum." *Cedar Wings* 66 (December/January 2001–2002): 22–26.

Lee, Hayeon. "With Dignity and Independence." *Now Lebanon,* 24 May 2009.

Leenders, Reinoud. "Public Means to Private Ends: State Building and Power in Post-War Lebanon." In *Politics from Above, Politics from Below: The Middle East in the Age of Economic Reform,* edited by Eberhard Kienle, 304–335. London: Saqi Books, 2003.

———. "Nobody Having Too Much to Answer for: Laissez-Faire Networks and Postwar Reconstruction in Lebanon." In *Networks of Privilege in the Middle East,* edited by Steven Heydemann, 169–200. New York: Palgrave, 2004.

———. "Lebanon's Political Economy: After Syria, an Economic Taif?" *MIT-International Electronic Journal of Middle East Studies* (2006): 1–18.

Levy, David, and Peter Newell. "Business Strategy and International Environmental Governance: Towards a Neo-Gramscien Synthesis." *Global Environmental Politics* 2, no. 4 (November 2002): 84–101.

Lijphart, Arend. "Consociational Democracy." *World Politics* 21 (January 1969): 207–225.

———. *Democracy in Plural Societies: A Comparative Exploration*. New Haven: Yale University Press, 1977.

Long, Taylor. "A Nation for Everyone." *Now Lebanon*, 14 October 2009.

Lord, Janet. "NGO Participation in Human Rights Law and Process: Latest Developments in the Effort to Develop an International Treaty on the Rights of People with Disabilities." *Journal of International and Comparative Law* 10, no. 2 (Spring 2004): 311–318.

———. "It Takes a Treaty: Elbowing into the Mainstream Human Rights Movement." Paper delivered to the International Studies Association, Montreal, March 2004.

———. "Disability Rights and the Human Rights Mainstream: Reluctant Gate-Crashers?" In *The International Struggle for New Human Rights*, edited by Clifford Bob, 83–92. Philadelphia: University of Pennsylvania Press, 2009.

Lucas, Ana Maria. "Politics and Property." *Now Lebanon*, 5 November 2010.

Mahoney, James, and Kathleen Thelen. "A Theory of Gradual Institutional Change." In *Explaining Institutional Change: Ambiguity, Agency, and Power*, edited by James Mahoney and Kathleen Thelen, 1–73. Cambridge: Cambridge University Press, 2010.

Mahoney, James. *Legacies of Liberalism: Path Dependence and Political Regimes in Central America*. Baltimore: Johns Hopkins Press, 2001.

Maila, Joseph. "The Ta'if Accord: An Evaluation." In *Peace for Lebanon? From War to Reconstruction*, edited by Deirdre Collings, 31–44. Boulder: Lynne Rienner Publishers, 1994.

Majed, Rayan. "L'engagement politique des etudiants dans l'intifada de l'independence: Etat d'ame ou formation d'un movement estudiantin autonome?" Memoire de Diplome d'Etudes Approfondies en Science Politique, Universite St. Joseph, October 2007.

Makdisi, Karim. "Trapped Between Sovereignty and Globalization: Implementing International Environmental and Natural Resource Treaties in Developing Countries—The Case of Lebanon." PhD diss., Fletcher School of Law and Diplomacy, Tufts University, April 2001.

———. "Implementing Environmental Treaties in Developing Countries: Using Flows to Explain How Lebanon Dealt with Trade in Hazardous Waste." Paper presented at the International Studies Association Annual Meeting 2006, San Diego, 23 March 2006.

Makdisi, Ussama. *The Culture of Sectarianism: Community, History, and Violence in Nineteenth-Century Ottoman Lebanon*. Los Angeles: University of California Press, 2000.

———. "Moving Beyond Orientalist Fantasy, Sectarian Polemic, and Nationalist Denial." *International Journal of Middle East Studies* 40, no. 4 (2008): 559–560.

Makhoul, J., and L. J. Harrison. "Intercessory *Wasta* and Village Development in Lebanon." *Arab Studies Quarterly* 26, no. 3 (2004): 25–41.

Mansour, Marwan George. *Implications of International Policies on National Legislation: A Case Study of Law 220 for the Rights of the Disabled in Lebanon.* Master's thesis, American University of Beirut, 2001.

McGarry, John, and Brendan O'Leary. "Iraq's Constitution of 2005: Liberal Consociation as Political Prescription." *International Journal of Constitutional Law* 5, no. 4 (2007): 670–698.

Melling, Joseph, and Bill Forsythe (eds.). *Insanity, Institutions, and Society, 1980–1914: A Social History of Madness in Comparative Perspective.* Studies in the Social History of Medicine. London and New York: Routledge, 1999.

Migdal, Joel. "The State in Society: An Approach to Struggles for Domination." In *State Power and Social forces: Domination and Transformation in the Third World*, edited by Joel Migdal, Atul Kohli, and Vivien Shue, 7–36. Cambridge: Cambridge University Press, 1994.

———. *State in Society: Studying How States and Societies Transform and Constitute One Another.* Cambridge: Cambridge University Press, 2001.

Mills, Arthur. *Private Enterprise in Lebanon.* Beirut: American University of Beirut/Center for Public Sector Projects and Studies, 1959.

Najem, Tom Pierre. *Lebanon's Renaissance: The Political Economy of Reconstruction.* Reading: Ithaca Press, 2000.

Nasr, Maya Abou. "Jobs Harder to Find for Disabled." *The Daily Star*, 5 August 2004.

Nasr, Salim. "Backdrop to Civil War: The Crisis of Lebanese Capitalism." *MERIP* 73 (1978): 3–13.

———. "New Social Realities and Post-War Lebanon: Issues for Reconstruction." In *Recovering Beirut*, edited by Philip S. Khoury and Samir Khalaf, 63–80. Leiden: Brill, 1993.

———. "The New Social Map." In *Lebanon in Limbo*, edited by T. Hanf and N. Salam, 143–158. Baden-Baden: Nomos Verlagsgesellschaft, 2003.

Norton, Augustus Richard. *AMAL and the Shi'a: Struggle for the Soul of Lebanon.* Austin: University of Texas Press, 1987.

———, ed. *Civil Society in the Middle East*, vols. I and II. Leiden: Konynklijke Brill NV, 1994 and 1996.

Ofiesh, Sami. "Lebanon's Second Republic: Secular Talk, Sectarian Application." *Arab Studies Quarterly* (Winter 1999): 97–116.

*Orient le Jour.* "Au Liban, on peut construire n'importe ou et n'importe quoi," 11 March 2003.

*Orient Le Jour.* "Journee de solidarite pour le protection de la plage de Ramlet al-Baida," 23 September 2003.

Osman, Zeina. "Disabled Still Waiting for Law to Be Passed to Improve Conditions." *The Daily Star*, 6 February 1998.

Osseiran, Lamia. "The Lebanese Council of Women: Mission and Expectations," Masters of Arts in International Affairs, Lebanese American University, June 2006.

Owen, Roger. "The Political Economy of Grand Liban, 1920–1970." In *Essays on the Crisis in Lebanon*, edited by Roger Owen, 23–32. London: Ithaca Press, 1976.

———. "The Economic History of Lebanon, 1943–1974: Its Salient Features." In *Towards a Viable Lebanon*, edited by Halim Barakat, 27–41.Washington, DC: Center for Contemporary Arab Studies, Georgetown University, 1988.

Patran, Tabitha. *The Struggle Over Lebanon*. New York: Monthly Review Press, 1987.

Pearce, Jenny. "Civil Society, the Market, and Democracy in Latin America." In *Civil Society and Democratization*, edited by Peter Burnell and Peter Calvert, 90–116. London: Frank Cass, 2004.

Peleikis, Anja. *Lebanese in Motion: Gender and the Making of a Translocal Village*. London: Transaction Publishers, 2003.

Peteet, Julie. "Imagining the 'New Middle East.'" *International Journal of Middle East Studies* 40, no. 4 (2008): 550–552.

Picard, Elizabeth. "La crise de institutions." In *L'Avenir du Liban Dans le Context Regional et International*, edited by Paul Balta and Georges Corm, 27–38. Paris: Les Editions Ouvriers et Etudes et Documantation International, 1990.

———. *Lebanon—A Shattered Country: Myths and Realities of Wars in Lebanon*. Teaneck, NJ: Holmes and Meier, 1996.

———. "The Dynamics of the Lebanese Christians: From the Paradigm of the 'ammiyyat to the Paradigm of Hwayyek." In *Christian Communities in the Arab Middle East: The Challenge of the Future*, edited by Andrea Pacini, 200–221. Oxford: Oxford University Press, 1998.

———. "The Political Economy of Civil War in Lebanon." In *War, Institutions, and Social Change in the Middle East*, edited by Steven Hydeman, 292–324. Berkeley: University of California Press, 2000.

———. "Beyrouth: la gestion nationale d'enjeux locauz." In *Municipalites et Pouvoirs Locaux au Liban*, edited by Agnes Favier, 295–318. CERMOC: Beirut, no. 24, 2001.

———. "Trafficking, Rents, and Diaspora in the Lebanese War." In *Rethinking the Economics of War: The Intersection of Need, Creed, and Greed*, edited by Cynthia Arnson and I. William Zartman, 23–51. Johns Hopkins University Press: Baltimore, 2005.

Pierson, Paul. *Politics in Time: History, Institutions, and Social Analysis*. Princeton: Princeton University Press, 2004.

Polity-Sharara, Yolla. "Women and Politics in Lebanon." *Khamsin: Journal of Revolutionary Socialists in the Middle East* 6 (1978): 6–15.

Raef, Imad ed-Din. "The Continuing Demands Campaign for the Disabled in Lebanon." *Waw Magazine*, no. 14 (2007): 18–23.

Raymond, Candice. "Samidoun, trente-jours de mobilization civile a Beyroute." In *Liban, une guerre de trente-trois jours*, edited by Frank Mermier and Elizabeth Picard, 58–65. Paris: La decouverte, 2007.

Rhodes, R., and D. Marsh. *Policy Networks in British Government*. Oxford: Oxford University Press, 1992.

Richani, Nazih. "The Druze of Mount Lebanon: Class Formation in a Civil War." *MERIP* 162 (January–February 1990): 26–30.

———. *Dilemmas of Democracy and Political Parties in Sectarian Societies: The Case of the Progressive Socialist Party of Lebanon 1949–1996.* New York: St. Martin's Press, 1998.

Rogan, Eugene. "Madness and Marginality: The Advent of the Psychiatric Asylum in Egypt and Lebanon." In *Outside In: On the Margins of the Modern Middle East,* edited by Eugene Rogan, 104–125. London: I.B. Taurus, 2001.

Rougier, Bernard. *Everyday Jihad: The Rise of Militant Islam among Palestinians in Lebanon.* Cambridge: Cambridge University Press, 2007.

Rueschemeyer, Dietrich, Evelyne Huber Stephens, and John D. Stephens. *Capitalist Development and Democracy.* Chicago: University of Chicago Press, 1992.

Russell, Marta, and Ravi Malhotra. "Capitalism and Disability." In *A World of Contradictions: Socialist Register,* edited by Leo Panitch and Colin Leys, 211–228. Halifax, NS: Fernwood Press, 2002.

Rustum Shehadeh, Lamia. "Women in the Public Sphere." In *Women and War in Lebanon,* edited by Lamia Shehadeh, 45–72. Gainesville: University of Florida Press, 1999.

Saadeh, Sofia. *The Quest for Citizenship in Post Taef Lebanon.* Beirut: Sade Publishers, 2007.

Safa, Oussama. "Getting to Arab Democracy: Lebanon Springs Forward." *Journal of Democracy* 17, no. 1 (January 2006): 22–37.

Salam, Nawaf. "Reforming the Electoral System: A Comparative Perspective." In *Options for Lebanon,* edited by Nawaf Salam, 1–22. London: I.B. Taurus, 2004.

Salibi, Kamal. "Lebanon Under Fuad Chahab, 1958–1964." *Middle East Studies* 2, no. 3 (1966): 211–226.

Salloukh, Bassel. "The Limits of Electoral Engineering in Divided Societies: Elections in Postwar Lebanon." *Canadian Journal of Political Science* 39, no. 3 (September 2006): 635–655.

Salti, Nisreen, Jad Chaaban, and Firas Raad. "Health Equity in Lebanon: A Microeconomic Analysis." *International Journal of Equity in Health* 9, no. 11 (2010): 11.

Sayigh, Yusif. *Entrepreneurs of Lebanon: The Role of the Business Leader in a Developing Economy.* Cambridge: Harvard University Press, 1962.

Scheffler, Thomas. "Religious Communalism and Democratization: The Development of Electoral Law in Lebanon." *Orient* 44, no. 1 (2003): 15–37.

Seddon, David, and Raymond Lang. "Mainstreaming Disability Issues into Development Studies—In Theory and Practice," Paper presented at the 14th annual meeting of the Disability Studies Association, Winnipeg, June 2001.

Seligman, Adam. *The Idea of Civil Society.* New York: The Free Press, 2002.

Seyfert, Karin. Unpublished PhD diss. on NGOs in postwar Lebanon, School of Oriental and African Studies, University of London.

Shaery-Eisenlohr, Roschanack. *Shi'ite Lebanon: Transnational Religion and the Making of National Identities*. New York: Columbia University Press, 2008.

Sharabi, Hisham. *Neopatriarchy: A Theory of Distorted Change*. New York: Oxford University Press, 1988.

Shebaya, Halim. "Intifada 2005: A Look Backwards and a Look Forwards." In *Breaking the Cycle: Civil Wars in Lebanon*, edited by Youssef Choueiri, 255–284. London: Stacey International, 2007.

Shiffman, Jeremy. "Generating Political Priority for Maternal Mortality Reduction in 5 Developing Countries." *American Journal of Public Health* 97, no. 5 (May 2007): 387.

Singerman, Diane. "Civil Society in the Shadow of the Egyptian State: The Role of Informal Networks in the Construction of Public Life." In *The Civil Society Debate in Middle East Studies*, edited by Jim Gelvin, 63–105. Los Angeles: UCLA Near East Center Colloquium Series, 1996.

Skovgaard-Petersen, J. "Religious Heads or Civil Servants? Druze and Sunni Religious Leadership in Post-War Lebanon." *Mediterranean Politics* 1, no. 3 (Winter 1996): 337–352.

———. "The Sunni Religious Scene in Beirut." *Mediterranean Politics* 3, no. 1 (Summer 1998): 69–80.

Slaiby, Ghassan. "Les Actions collectives de resistance civile a la guerre." In *Le Liban aujourd'hiu*, edited by Fadia Kiwan, 119–136. Paris: CNRS Editions, 1994.

Snider, Lewis. "The Lebanese Forces: Their Origins and Role in Lebanese Politics." *Middle East Journal* 38, no. 1 (1984): 1–33.

Stork, Joe. "Gender and Civil Society: An Interview with Suad Joseph." *Middle East Report* 183 (July–August 1993). Reprinted in *Arab Women: Between Defiance and Restraint*, edited by Suha Sabbagh, 203–211. New York: Olive Branch Press, 1996.

Thompson, Elizabeth. *Colonial Citizens: Republican Rights, Paternal Privilege and Gender in French Syria and Lebanon*. New York: Colombia University Press, 2000.

Long, Tony. "A Nation for Everyone." *Now Lebanon*, 14 October 2009.

Torgeson, Douglas. *The Promise of Green Politics*. Raleigh, NC: Duke University Press, 1999.

Traboulsi, Fawwaz. *A History of Modern Lebanon*. London: Pluto Press, 2007.

Turmusani, Majid, A. Vreede, and L. S. Wirz. "Some Ethical Issues in Community-Based Rehabilitation Initiatives in the Developing World." *Disability and Rehabilitation* 24, no. 10 (2002): 558–564.

Turmusani, Majid. *Disabled People and Economic Needs in Developing Countries: The Political Perspective from Jordan*. Burlington, VT: Ashgate, 2003.

Watenpaugh, Keith David. *Being Modern in the Middle East: Revolution, Nationalism, Colonialism, and the Arab Middle Class*. Princeton: Princeton University Press, 2006.

Wehbi, S., and S. Lakkis. "Women with Disabilities in Lebanon: From Marginalization to Resistance." *Affilia: Journal of Women and Social Work* 25, no. 1 (2010): 56–67.

Wehbi, Samantha, and Sylvana Lakkis. "Women with Disabilities in Lebanon: From Marginalization to Resistance" *Affilia: Journal of Women and Social Work* 25, no. 1 (2010): 56–67.

Wehbi, Samantha, and Y. El-Lahib, "The Employment Situation of People with Disabilities in Lebanon: Challenges and Opportunities." *Disability and Society* 22, no. 4 (June 2007): 371–382.

Wehbi, Samantha. "Organizing for Voting Rights of People with Disabilities in Lebanon: Reflections for Activists." *Equal Opportunities International* 26, no. 5 (2007): 449–464.

Weiss, Max. "Institutionalizing Sectarianism: The Lebanese Jafari Court and Shi'a Society under the French Mandate." *Islamic Law and Society* 15 (2008): 371–407.

———. "The Historiography of Sectarianism in Lebanon." *History Compass* 7, no. 1 (2009): 141–154.

———. *In the Shadow of Sectarianism: Law, Shiism, and the Making of Modern Lebanon.* Cambridge: Harvard University Press, 2010.

White, Gordon. "Civil Society, Democratization, and Development: Clearing the Analytical Ground." In *Civil Society and Democratization*, edited by Peter Burnell and Peter Calvert, 6–21. London: Frank Cass, 2004.

Whitehead, Laurence. "Bowling in the Bronx: The Uncivil Interstices between Civil and Political Society." In *Civil Society and Democratization*, edited by Peter Burnell and Peter Calvert, 22–42. London: Frank Cass, 2004.

Wimmen, Heiko. "Rallying Around the Renegade." *Middle East Report Online* (27 August 2007). http://www.merip.org/mero/mero082707.

Wong, Joseph. *Healthy Democracies: Welfare Politics in Taiwan and South Korea.* Ithaca: Cornell University Press, 2004.

Wood, Geof. "Staying Secure, Staying Poor: The 'Faustian Bargain.'" *World Development* 31, no. 3 (March 2003): 455–471.

———. "Informal Security Regimes: The Strength of Relationships." In *Insecurity and Welfare Regimes in Asia, Africa, and Latin America: Social Policy in Developing Countries*, edited by Ian Gough and Geof Wood, 49–87. Cambridge: Cambridge University Press, 2004.

Yehia, Ranwa. "Members of Association for Disabled Resign en Masse." *The Daily Star*, 22 September 1998.

Yoe, Rebecca. "Disability, Poverty, and the New Development Agenda," KaR Programme, September 2005. http://hpod.pmhclients.com/pdf/Developmentagenda.pdf.

Young, Michael. *The Ghosts of Martyrs Square: An Eyewitness Account of Lebanon's Life Struggle.* New York: Simon and Schuster, 2010.

Zaatari, Zeina. "Women Activists of South Lebanon." PhD diss. University of California Davis, 2003.

Zahar, Marie Joelle. "Proteges, Clients, Canon Fodder: Civilians in the Calculus of Militias." *International Peacekeeping* 7, no. 4 (December 2000): 107–128.

Zamir, Meir. *Lebanon's Quest: The Road to Statehood, 1926–1939.* London: I.B. Taurus, 1997.

Ziadeh, Hanna. *Sectarianism and Intercommunal Nation-Building in Lebanon.* London: Hurst and Company, 2006.

Zubaida, Sami. *Islam, the People, and the State.* London: Routledge, 1989.

Zuhur, Sherifa. "Empowering Women or Dislodging Sectarianism? Civil Marriage in Lebanon." *Yale Journal of Law and Feminism* 14 (2002): 177–208.

Zurayk, Rami, and Mona Haidar. "Biodiversity Conservation Priorities: Lebanon." In *Sharing Innovative Experiences: Examples of Successful Conservation and Sustainable Use of Dryland Biodiversity*, Volume 9, 13–20. New York: UNDP, 2004.

Zuwiyya Yamak, Labib. "Party Politics in the Lebanese Party System." In *Politics in Lebanon*, edited by Leonard Binder. New York: Wiley and Sons, 1968.

# Index